Value, Beauty, and Nature

SUNY series in Environmental Philosophy and Ethics

J. Baird Callicott and John van Buren, editors

Value, Beauty, and Nature

The Philosophy of Organism and the
Metaphysical Foundations of Environmental Ethics

BRIAN G. HENNING

Cover: Image of tree roots. Shutterstock

Published by State University of New York Press, Albany

© 2023 State University of New York

For information, contact State University of New York Press, Albany, NY
www.sunypress.edu

Library of Congress Cataloging-in-Publication Data

Name: Henning, Brian G., author.
Title: Value, beauty, and nature : the philosophy of organism and the
    metaphysical foundations of environmental ethics / Brian G. Henning.
Description: Albany : State University of New York Press, [2023] | Series:
    SUNY series in environmental philosophy and ethics | Includes
    bibliographical references and index.
Identifiers: LCCN 2023009068 | ISBN 9781438495576 (hardcover : alk. paper) |
    ISBN 9781438495583 (ebook) | ISBN 9781438495569 (pbk. : alk. paper)
Subjects: LCSH: Philosophy of nature. | Ecology—Religious aspects. |
    Environmental ethics.
Classification: LCC BD581 .H457 2023 | DDC 179/.1—dc23/eng/20230817
LC record available at https://lccn.loc.gov/2023009068

10 9 8 7 6 5 4 3 2 1

Dedicated to Dr. A. Suzie Henning,
without whose support, encouragement, patience, and love
I would not be a philosopher.

Contents

Illustrations

Figure

Tables

Acknowledgments

In that this work advances the view that reality is best understood in terms of interdependence and interrelation, it is appropriate to begin by acknowledging the many vectors that have influenced its becoming. I express my appreciation to the Konrad Lorenz Institute (KLI) in Klosterneuberg, Austria, for a 2017 visiting fellowship during which this book was started and to Gonzaga University for a 2022 sabbatical during which it was finished. I thank my first environmental ethics professor, Daniel A. Dombrowski, in whose class the germ of this book first found fertile soil; and my own environmental ethics students over the last two decades, who helped this work take shape. My deepest gratitude goes to my partner, Dr. A. Suzie Henning, for her love, support, and epic patience.

Earlier versions of several parts of this work first appeared in scholarly journals and collections and are reprinted in revised or partial form here with the permission of their editors. Part of the introduction was originally published as "Unearthing the Process Roots of Environment Ethics: Whitehead, Leopold, and the Land Ethic," *Balkan Journal of Philosophy* 8, no. 1 (2016): 3–12; and "Following Lucretius' Dart" in *Thinking About It*, edited by Sarah Demeuse and Manuela Moscoso (Archive Books, 2014), 89–101. An earlier version of chapter one was published as "Recovering the Adventure of Ideas: In Defense of Metaphysics as Revisable, Systematic, Speculative Philosophy," *Journal of Speculative Philosophy* 29, no. 4 (2015): 437–56. Parts of chapter two appeared as "Process and Morality," in *Handbook of Whiteheadian Process Thought*, Vol. 1, edited by Michel Weber and William Desmond (Ontos Verlag, 2008); and "Sustainability and Other Ecological Mistakes: In Defense of Moral Ideals," in *Beyond Superlatives: Regenerating Whitehead's Philosophy of Experience*, edited by Roland Faber, J. R. Hustwit, and Hollis Phelps (Cambridge Scholars Press, 2014), 76–89.

A minor part of chapter three appeared in "Whitehead in Class: Do the Harvard-Radcliffe Course Notes Change How We Understand Whitehead's Thought?" in *Whitehead at Harvard, 1924–1925*, edited by Brian G. Henning and Joseph Petek (Edinburgh University Press, 2020), 337–56. Portions of chapter four appeared as "Re-Centering Process Thought: Recovering Beauty in A. N. Whitehead's Late Thought" in *Beyond Metaphysics? Explorations in Alfred North Whitehead's Late Thought* (Rodopi, 2010), 201–14; and "Trusting in the 'Efficacy of Beauty': A Kalocentric Approach to Moral Philosophy," *Ethics & the Environment* 14, no. 1 (2009): 101–28. Portions of chapter five appeared as "Animals, Ethics, and Process Thought: Hierarchy without Anthroparchy (A Response to Combs, Donaldson, and Sinclair)," *Process Studies* 42, no. 2 (2013): 221–39; and "Moral Vegetarianism: A Whiteheadian Response to Andrew F. Smith," *Process Studies* 45, no. 2 (2016): 236–49. Parts of chapter six appeared as "Getting Substance to Go All the Way: Norris Clarke's Neo-Thomism and the Process Turn," *The Modern Schoolman* 81 (2004): 215–25; and "Of Termites and Men: On the Ontology of Collective Individuals," in *Beyond Mechanism: Putting Life Back into Biology*, edited by Brian G. Henning and Adam Scarfe (Lexington Books, 2013), 233–48. The first part of chapter seven originally appeared as "Creative Love: Eros and Agape in Whitehead and Peirce," in *Thinking with Whitehead and the American Pragmatists*, edited by Brian G. Henning, William Myers, and Joseph John (Lexington Books, 2015), 149–64. Part of chapter nine originally appeared as "From the Anthropocene to the Ecozoic: Philosophy and Global Climate Change," *Midwest Studies in Philosophy* 40, no. 1 (2016): 284–95.

Introduction

Unearthing the Process Roots of Environmental Ethics

Properly dating the birth of an idea or a movement unavoidably involves a degree of arbitrariness. Ideas are "in the air" decades before they become explicitly thematized in the work of a prescient scholar. And so it is with the field of environmental ethics. One could rightly note that philosophers, mystics, and poets have written on environmental themes for millennia. And it is certainly true that the historical roots of the ecological crisis go very deep indeed. Nevertheless, the birth of environmental ethics is seen as taking place in the last third of the twentieth century. As the Center for Environmental Philosophy's "Very Brief History" puts it, "the inspiration for environmental ethics was the first Earth Day in 1970 when environmentalists started urging philosophers who were involved with environmental groups to do something about environmental ethics."[1] As they go on to note, in the late 1960s small groups of scientists, theologians, and historians had begun discussing the growing ecological crisis, with Rachel Carson's 1962 *Silent Spring* perhaps the greatest catalyst of thought. Much of the framing of early discussions over how to conceive of the ecological crisis were established by historian Lynn White Jr.'s "The Historical Roots of the Ecologic Crisis" in 1967 and ecologist Garrett Hardin's "Tragedy of the Commons" the following year, both in the journal *Science*. Responses and reactions to these essays dominated the discussion in the subsequent years, but philosophers largely "sat on the sidelines."[2] Also important was the republishing of Aldo Leopold's[3] "The Land Ethic." Although the essay had been published in Leopold's *A Sand County Almanac* in 1949, it was not widely read until it was republished in 1970.

1

Philosophers do finally get into the game. The first academic conference explicitly focusing on environmental ethics was organized by William Blackstone at the University of Georgia in 1972. The Norwegian philosopher Arne Naess began the Deep Ecology Movement in 1973 with the publishing of his essay "The Shallow and the Deep, Long-Range Ecology Movement." And Holmes Rolston III is credited with publishing in 1975 the first mainstream journal article explicitly on environmental ethics, "Is There an Ecological Ethic?" in the journal *Ethics*.[4] Finally, Eugene Hargrove gave a name and a voice to the fledging field when he founded the journal *Environmental Ethics* in 1979.[5] (See table I.1.) From here the field grew and expanded to take its current shapes. In many ways, the field is, if not in its infancy, still in its adolescence.

Part of what is missing in this account is the outsized roles that process philosophers—scholars inspired by the thought of Alfred North Whitehead (1861–1947)—played in the birth of environmental ethics. Indeed, it is possible (though, as we will see, perhaps not likely) that Whitehead's work was a chief inspiration for Leopold, whom J. Baird Callicott describes as the "father" and "founding genius" of environmental ethics.[6] However, the role of process philosophers in the inception of environmental ethics is

Table I.1. Key dates in the history of environmental ethics

1949	Publishing of Aldo Leopold's *A Sand County Almanac*
1962	Rachel Carson publishes *Silent Spring*
1967	Lynn White Jr. publishes "The Historical Roots of the Ecologic Crisis" in *Science*
1968	Garrett Hardin publishes "The Tragedy of the Commons" in *Science*
1970	First Earth Day is held and Leopold's *Almanac* becomes widely available in a new issue
1972	William Blackstone organizes the first environmental ethics conference
1973	Arne Naess publishes "The Shallow and the Deep, Long-Range Ecology Movement" in *Inquiry*
1975	Holmes Rolston III publishes "Is There an Ecological Ethic?" in *Ethics*
1979	Eugene Hargrove founds the journal *Environmental Ethics*

Source: Author provided

often forgotten or omitted, and Whitehead's thought is largely unknown by mainstream environmental philosophers. Let's grab a spade and unearth some of these forgotten process roots of environmental ethics.

The first clue regarding the significance of Whitehead is provided by Hargrove, in his 1979 contribution to the inaugural volume of the journal *Environmental Ethics*, "The Historical Foundations of American Environmental Attitudes." Interestingly, he begins by noting, "In large measure, my views are in agreement with many of Whitehead's major themes in *Science and the Modern World*, especially those which deal with a Romantic reaction to science."[7] Hargrove goes on to employ Whitehead to defend the claim that the historical foundations of American environmental attitudes run far deeper than Passmore and others had recognized. He (Hargrove) suggests that some of the roots can be traced back to Whitehead.

> In Whitehead's *Science and the Modern World* there is an even stronger and more spirited environmentalist-style position than [William] James'. Whitehead's aim is to combat science's and philosophy's "assumption of the bare valuelessness of mere matter [which] led to a lack of reverence in the treatment of natural or artistic beauty" and brought about two evils: "one, the ignoration of the true relation of each organism to its environment; and the other, the habit of ignoring the intrinsic worth of the environment which must be allowed its weight in any consideration of final ends." Indisputably, this aim is also an environmentalist aim.[8]

Given its lapse into obscurity in the middle of the twentieth century, it is easy to forget that Whitehead's work at Harvard in the 1920s was met with great excitement and his 1925 *Science and the Modern World* was read widely by the educated public. Here we see Hargrove rightly noting Whitehead's emphasis on both interdependence and intrinsic value—key themes within environmental ethics.

However, Hargrove does not merely point to Whitehead to illustrate the deep historical roots of American environmental attitudes. He also claims that Whitehead's *Science and the Modern World* may have been a key inspiration for Leopold's land ethic.

> Most interesting of all is the similarity of some of Whitehead's comments and those of environmentalist Aldo Leopold. There are long passages in the last chapter of *Science and the Modern World*, for instance, which could easily have served as the source of some

of Leopold's ideas, and which suggest that Leopold's notion of community could be derived from Whitehead's theory of organism without much difficulty. In one place especially Whitehead speaks of "associations of different species which mutually cooperate," and he refers to the forest environment as "the triumph of the organization of mutually dependent species." A few lines further on he adds that, "every organism requires an environment of friends, partly to shield it from violent changes, and partly to supply it with its wants." It is a small step from Whitehead's "environment of friends" to Leopold's "biotic community," one that requires no detours into Oriental philosophy or religion.[9]

As we will consider in chapter four, in addition to noting the similarity between Whitehead's "environment of friends" and Leopold's "biotic community," Hargrove might also have noted the similarity between Leopold's ethical dictum to "preserve the integrity, stability, and beauty of the biotic community"[10] and Whitehead's claims that "morality is always the aim at that union of harmony, intensity, and vividness which involves the perfection of importance for that occasion"[11] and "the real world is good when it is beautiful."[12] Though the concept of environmentalism or environmental ethics would have been foreign to Whitehead, Hargrove is right to note that Whitehead's work anticipates by decades many of the concepts that became central to environmental thought, such as the centrality of constitutive interdependence and interrelation, the recognition of the intrinsic value of reality, the significance of environment, beauty as a moral concept, and the preferencing of the metaphor of organism over mechanism. We will develop and explore each of these themes throughout this volume.

For now, it is enough to note that, if Hargrove is correct that Leopold may have derived his concept of biotic community from Whitehead, and if Callicott is correct that Leopold is environmental ethics' "father," then Whitehead may be seen as an intellectual grandfather of the field of environmental ethics. Yet it is also important to note the tentative nature of Hargrove's claims regarding Leopold and Whitehead. He observes the "similarity" of Leopold's and Whitehead's ideas and suggests that Whitehead's thought "could easily have served as the source" for Leopold's biotic community. Unfortunately, Hargrove does not cite any documentary evidence to support his claims, though he does repeat them in their entirety a decade later in his *Foundations of Environmental Ethics*.[13]

To my knowledge, no one has refuted Hargrove's claims. However, Pete A. Y. Gunter—himself an eminent Whitehead scholar and environmental ethicist—does make the parenthetical comment in a 2000 article that "Leopold was unaware of Whitehead."[14] Unfortunately, there does not seem to be any definitive documentary evidence by which to adjudicate Hargrove's and Gunter's conflicting claims. Leopold's personal library has been dispersed, and a search of the Leopold archives at the University of Wisconsin reveals no reference to Alfred North Whitehead. Further, Curt Meine, Senior Fellow at the Aldo Leopold Foundation, confirms Gunter's assessment, stating that he is "not aware of any documentary evidence that Leopold was aware of Whitehead."[15] This is also the view of the eminent environmental historian Susan Flader, who has written extensively about Aldo Leopold.[16] However, she notes that "just because I can't recall anything doesn't mean Leopold never encountered Whitehead's thought in his reading, but I rather doubt that he would have sought out Whitehead's work."[17]

Overall, there simply is insufficient evidence to make a claim with any high degree of confidence that Leopold was aware of Whitehead's work. Yet the absence of evidence is not evidence of absence. In the end, Hargrove's claims remain in their tentative formulation. It is possible that Whitehead's thought was among the ideas "in the air" that affected Leopold's own thought in ways that are not traceable through documentary evidence. Nevertheless, even if there is no *direct*, traceable, genealogical conceptual dependence from Whitehead to Leopold, it is clear that, in anticipating the central concepts that came to define environmental ethics, Whitehead is nevertheless rightly seen as a founding grandparent of and inspiration for environmental ethics. Thus, Hargrove is right to note that the foundations of environmental ethics should be traced at least as far back as Whitehead's philosophy of organism. This claim is further supported by the role of Whitehead scholars, who actively participated in the originating conversations that gave birth to the field of environmental ethics.

As mentioned earlier, Blackstone organized the first academic philosophy conference on environmental ethics—and two years later published the proceedings as the first anthology on the topic[18]—in 1972 at the University of Georgia. What is often forgotten is that three eminent process philosophers, Charles Hartshorne, John B. Cobb Jr.,[19] and Gunter participated in that first conference. Furthermore, in that same year (1972) Cobb published the now ironically titled book *Is it Too Late? A Theology of Ecology*, which is likely the first monograph written explicitly on environmental ethics.[20]

Moreover, although Rolston is very rightly seen as a father of environmental ethics, his 1975 article in the journal *Ethics* is not the first academic essay on environmental ethics in a mainstream journal. That honor arguably goes to Hartshorne, who published "Beyond Enlightened Self-Interest: A Metaphysics of Ethics" in *Ethics* one year before Rolston, in 1974.

Also often omitted or forgotten in accounts of the history of the origins of environmental ethics is that the first doctoral dissertation on the topic was completed in 1976 at Bryn Mawr College by Susan Armstrong under the direction of the Whitehead and Hegel scholar George R. Kline. Her topic was *The Rights of Nonhuman Beings: A Whiteheadian Study*. Thus, the first dissertation on environmental ethics was Whiteheadian. Finally, it is important to note that in 1979 the first two issues of the journal that gave the field its name, *Environmental Ethics*, included articles by the process philosophers Hartshorne and Cobb.[21] (See Table I.2.) Accordingly, although it is still speculative whether Whitehead *directly* influenced Leopold, by any reasonable measure, Whitehead scholars were key participants in the conversations that shaped the fledgling field of environmental ethics.

Unfortunately, despite this early influence, the significance of Whiteheadian thought gradually fades into obscurity. There are, no doubt, many reasons for this, many of them having more to do with larger trends within philosophy. The story of these shifts and trends is complex and multifaceted and will be pieced together and explored gradually throughout this book. As we will discuss at length in chapter one, part of Whitehead's story from academic rock star to obsolescence tracks the trajectory of twentieth-century metaphysics itself, which was attacked and then abandoned by both Anglo-American and continental philosophers. Beyond this, although leading process philosophers such as Hartshorne and Cobb were no doubt respected contributors to the first conferences, anthologies, and journal issues, their subsequent focus on developing "process theology" led many within mainstream philosophy to view Whitehead's thought with suspicion. This was not helped by many process philosophers' penchant for seemingly insular scholastic debates. Over time, the diminished reputation of and interest in process thought meant that retiring Whitehead scholars at top-tier, doctoral-granting institutions—such as Emory University, Vanderbilt University, University of Chicago, and Yale University—were replaced with philosophers focusing on more fashionable topics; many previously productive academic wells ran dry.

Trends unique to environmental ethics also cut against Whitehead scholarship. For instance, despite significant lines of convergence, deep

Table I.2. The forgotten process roots of environmental ethics

1925	Whitehead's Lowell Lectures are published as *Science and the Modern World*, potentially serving as inspiration for Leopold's land ethic
1949	Publishing of Leopold's *A Sand County Almanac*
1962	Rachel Carson publishes *Silent Spring*
1967	White publishes "The Historical Roots of the Ecologic Crisis" in *Science*
1968	Hardin publishes "The Tragedy of the Commons" in *Science*
1970	First Earth Day is held and Leopold's *Almanac* becomes widely available in a new issue
1972	Cobb publishes the first monograph on environmental ethics
1972	Blackstone organizes the first environmental ethics conference at University of Georgia
	In attendance at the conference are process philosophers Hartshorne, Cobb, and Gunter, all of whom also contributed to the published proceedings of the conference
1973	Naess publishes "The Shallow and the Deep, Long-Range Ecology Movement" in *Inquiry*
1974	Hartshorne publishes what is arguably the first article on environmental ethics, "Beyond Enlightened Self-Interest: A Metaphysics of Ethics" in *Ethics*
1975	Rolston publishes what is often considered the first journal article on environmental ethics, "Is There an Ecological Ethic?" in *Ethics*
1976	Armstrong defends the first dissertation on environmental ethics, "The Rights of Nonhuman Beings: A Whiteheadian Study," at Bryn Mawr College under the direction of Kline, a Whitehead and Hegel scholar
1979	Hargrove founds the journal *Environmental Ethics*
	Hartshorne publishes "The Rights of the Subhuman World" in the first issue and Cobb publishes "Christian Existence in a World of Limits" in the second issue of *Environmental Ethics*

Highlighted portions indicate contributions of process philosophers.
Source: Author provided.

ecologists—perhaps the most metaphysically inclined environmental ethicists—ultimately rejected Whitehead's metaphysics in favor of Spinoza's. At issue for deep ecologists (e.g., George Sessions, Bill Devall, and John Rodman) and some ecofeminists (e.g., Val Plumwood) was the centrality within Whitehead's metaphysics of a hierarchical conception of reality and of value, a topic that will be central to chapter five.[22] Perhaps most puzzling of all is the failure of second-generation Whitehead scholars such as Susan Armstrong to make the case for Whitehead and process thought within the scholarship. Though, as we will discuss in detail in section three of this chapter, Armstrong wrote an early article advocating for the importance of Whitehead as a foundation for environmental ethics, she never published a monograph systematically developing the project.[23] Furthermore, despite being the lead editor of a major textbook on environmental ethics, Armstrong did not include a single essay discussing process thought's significance for environmental ethics.[24] These omissions are in keeping with a confounding trend within Whitehead scholarship. For too long, process scholars have claimed that Whitehead's philosophy *would be* an ideal metaphysical basis for an environmental ethic, but they subsequently failed to develop and defend this claim in a systematic manner. The pattern has been to devote perhaps an article or a chapter in a larger work to the topic, but a systematic philosophical defense of a Whiteheadian environmental ethic has been conspicuous in its absence. My own dissertation and first book, *The Ethics of Creativity*, sought to begin to address this omission.[25]

Let us briefly take stock of what we have concluded so far: (1) elements of Whitehead's philosophy of organism anticipated the development of environmental ethics by half a century; (2) though no definitive documentary evidence is available, Whitehead's thought may have influenced Leopold, whose land ethic is often credited as a chief intellectual source of environmental ethics; and (3) regardless of the actual influence of Whitehead on Leopold, process philosophers were key contributors to the discussions that constituted the field of environmental ethics. It was process philosophers deeply influenced by Whitehead's philosophy of organism who wrote the first dissertation, participated in the first conference, (arguably) published the first article in a major journal, and wrote the first monograph on environmental ethics. On any reasonable measure, Whitehead and the philosophy of organism are rightly celebrated as among the chief intellectual grandparents of environmental ethics. Given this, let us begin to consider what *philosophically*—beyond these historical and genealogical roots—Whitehead's speculative metaphysics has to offer in the development of an adequate environmental ethics. We should begin with an overview of Whitehead's distinctive process ontology.

The Philosophy of Organism

Deeply influenced by developments in late nineteenth and early twentieth-century physics—from Clerk Maxwell's theory of electromagnetism, which was the subject of his doctoral thesis at Trinity College in Cambridge, to relativity theory and early quantum theory—Whitehead defended what might best be called an event ontology. As I will discuss in detail in chapter six, reality is not composed of static, isolated, lifeless, inert substances brought into accidental relations by unflinching laws of nature that necessarily determine the course of reality. As Whitehead put it in his "First Lecture" at Harvard University, September 25, 1924, "Half the difficulties of philosophy result from an exaggerated emphasis on the abstract entity as though it were capable of independent reality."[26] Whitehead realized before most that reality is composed of nothing but constitutively interdependent events—what he variously calls "actual entities" or "actual occasions." Though a stone appears to be an inert substance that passively endures through time, contemporary physics has revealed that stones, and everything else, are nothing but a riot of vibrating atomic activity with complex bonds creating molecular patterns. As Whitehead explained to his students at Harvard:

> Reality is not static: it is a process of becoming. This fluent character of the togetherness of things was already emphasised in Greek philosophy: All things flow, said Heraclitus. Indeed the fact is too obvious to escape notice. But unfortunately things which are too obvious often escape receiving their due emphasis. The result is that there has been a tendency to give an account of reality which omits this essential processional character of the togetherness of things. It is then held that what is processional cannot be real. The fluent togetherness of things is then given a lower place as mere appearance, and we are left with a world in which the appearance which passes is contrasted with the reality in the background, exempt from passage. This train of metaphysical thought has the unfortunate effect of separating philosophy from science. For science is concerned with our experience of the passage of things in their fluent togetherness.

> Whereas, on this metaphysical theory, philosophy is concerned with the ultimately real which lies behind the superficialities which lie within the scope of science.[27]

Ours is an open-ended, processive cosmos, a creative becoming of vibratory vectors of energy defined by mutual dependence and interrelation. Thus, in contrast to modern metaphysics (e.g., Descartes's dualistic metaphysics), Whitehead contends that every moment, every achievement of becoming is itself a unique perspective on the whole of reality; it is a valuation. Accordingly, there is no "valueless, vacuous actuality."[28] As I will discuss in chapters two and three, this commits Whitehead to a truly capacious theory of value. Nothing is a bare fact, devoid of value. To exist, Whitehead contends, is to be a subject relating to and affected by the rest of reality and then thereby to become an object for future occasions in the "creative advance."[29] Indeed, Whitehead calls this the "reformed subjectivist principle," that "apart from the experiences of subjects there is nothing, nothing, nothing, bare nothingness."[30] The full meaning and significance of this breathtaking position will be considered gradually, repeatedly, and in detail throughout the present volume, but let us also explore it briefly here.

Western thought has too often proceeded under the assumption that human subjects are fundamentally different than—an exception to—the rest of reality. "Experience" has been interpreted narrowly to refer to an active cognitive subject surveying a world of passive objects. As Whitehead notes in his 1931 Presidential Address to the American Philosophical Association, "Objects and Subjects," no topic has "suffered more" at the hands of philosophers than the subject-object relation.[31] Though it is unavoidably the seat of our experience, we should reject Descartes's invitation to take the thinking subject as ontologically basic. Whereas Descartes "conceives the thinker as creating the occasional thought," Whitehead's philosophy of organism "inverts the order, and conceives the thought as a constituent operation in the creation of the occasional thinker. The thinker is the final end whereby there is the thought."[32] Consciousness and thought are undeniably important, but they are late-stage, high-grade forms of experience; they are not ontologically basic.[33]

By reducing the subject-object relation to the knower-known relation, philosophers are in danger of committing what Whitehead calls the "fallacy of misplaced concreteness."[34] Too many thinkers proceed under the assumption that their abstract formulations, whether linguistic or mathematical, can, in principle, adequately characterize reality. Though an essential tool for thought,[35] language will always fall short; it can never fully do justice to reality. "Words and phrases must be stretched towards a generality foreign to their ordinary usage; and however such elements of language be stabilized as technicalities, they remain metaphors mutely appealing for an imaginative leap."[36] It is perhaps for this reason that Whitehead often turns to the poets, whose rich use of metaphor may capture a share of the texture of reality omitted by the mathematically precise, but necessarily reductive, accounts of the scientist.[37] With Wordsworth, Whitehead believes that too often "we murder to dissect."[38] Simplification and reduction are useful, but we must not forget that they are necessarily partial formulations—abstractions standing in place of concrete reality. We do great violence to reality when we mistake an abstraction for what is concrete.[39]

Part of the problem with taking the knower-known relationship as fundamental is that it fails to adequately represent the *constitutive* nature of relations. Knowing is always at arm's length, as it were; a subject *has* knowledge of the object. Cognitive relations are external to the subject; they do not affect or constitute what the subject *is*.[40] I can intellectually *understand* what joy is—I can have knowledge of it—but that does not *make* me joyful. Feelings, on the other hand, are internal and constitutive. When I am fearful or angry, it is not a sterile cognitive state. I don't *have* anger or know anger, I *am* angry. It is part of what I am at that moment. It is this sense of internal, constitutive relatedness that Whitehead has in mind in arguing in "Objects and Subjects" that "the basis of experience is emotional."[41] To capture this insight, Whitehead argues that it is not "comprehension" that is the most basic form of relation, but "prehension," from the Latin root "to grasp." Prehension is the most basic form of relation between individuals. To understand this claim, it will be helpful to situate it within the context of Whitehead's complex metaphysics of becoming.[42]

Whitehead envisions a cosmos that is pluralistically populated by individuals referred to as "actual entities" or, equivalently, "actual occasions."[43] Actual occasions, according to Whitehead, "are the final real things of which the world is made. There is no going behind actual entities to find anything more real. They differ among themselves: God is an actual entity, and so is the most trivial puff of existence in far-off empty space."[44] Though not in a crude building-block way, actual occasions are the stuff of which the universe is made. Borrowing a phrase from William James, Whitehead describes actual occasions as "drops" of experience; they come entirely or not at all.[45] Whitehead refers to the becoming of an actual occasion as concrescence (from the Latin *concrescere*, to grow together). In concrescence, the actual occasion brings together or "prehends" past actual occasions or its "actual world." In the "datum" phase of concrescence, the incipient occasion arises out of a sea of intense feeling that surges up from its past. The budding event comes to this sea of "feeling" through a particular perspective of the world, a world as already "settled." The settlement of the world is affected by the limitation of "received decisions" of past actual occasions, which impose themselves on every future occasion. Thus, the first phase concerns the reception of past, achieved occasions as "objects" that serve as the "real potential" for its own aesthetic self-determination.[46] It is from this datum that the occasion will begin its process of self-determination.[47]

The passive reception of the given datum in the first phase is followed by the occasion's active synthesis of this datum in the "process" phase. In this second phase of concrescence, the nascent occasion renders determinate its relationship to each of the elements in its given datum. Specifically, the nascent occasion renders its relationship to each past occasion determinate either by affirming it through what Whitehead calls "positive prehension," thereby making it a part of itself, or by ignoring it through "negative prehension," thereby excluding it from itself. "The 'process,' [therefore,] is the addition of those elements of feeling whereby these indeterminations are dissolved into determinate linkages attaining the actual unity of an individual actual entity."[48] Paradoxically, then, in becoming itself, the entity resolves the question as to what it is to be. This is what Whitehead calls the "principle of process": the determination of that which was indeterminate progressively constitutes *what* the entity is.[49] In a sense, then, the actual occasion creates itself out of its environment by rendering its relations to its actual world determinate. In this limited sense, it is *causa sui*.

When all indetermination has been removed and the process of self-determination is complete, the entity achieves "satisfaction." "It belongs," Whitehead explains, "to the essence of this subject that it pass into objective immortality. Thus its own constitution involves that its own activity in *self*-formation passes into its activity of *other*-formation. It is by reason of the constitution of the present subject that the future will embody the present subject and will re-enact its patterns of activity."[50] In satisfaction, an occasion's subjective immediacy perishes, and it becomes "objectively immortal" in the sense that it becomes a "stubborn fact" that all future occasions must take into account. Accordingly, satisfaction marks the shift from the occasion as "subject" or actuality in attainment, to the occasion as "superject" or attained actuality.[51]

The transition from self-formation to other-formation marks the final stage of concrescence. For, qua satisfied, an entity becomes a "decision" that is then transmitted to succeeding actual occasions. "The final stage, the 'decision,' is how the actual entity, having attained its individual 'satisfaction,' thereby adds a determinate condition to the settlement of the future beyond itself."[52] This is the "principle of relativity": that it is in the nature of every being that it is a potential for becoming. Thus, the circle closes on itself: "the many become one and are increased by one."[53]

According to this philosophy of organism, then, the most basic form of relation is not a subject that *has* knowledge of an object, but a subject that comes to *be* by being affected by others.[54] Following Plato's *Sophist*, Whitehead recognizes that to exist, to be real, is to affect and be affected.[55] The most fundamental relations are constitutive; the object affects, gets inside the subject.[56] As we will explore at greater length in chapter six, this means that the world is not composed of static subjects that *have* relations. Rather, each dynamic subject *is* its relations. An important implication of this view is that it utterly rejects the invidious dualism that bifurcates the world into subjects and objects. Instead, according to this view, "subject and object are relative terms."[57] Every individual is at once a subjective unification of experience *and* an object for others; it is a subject-superject.[58] This is the most basic characterization of actuality. "The oneness of the universe, and the oneness of each element in the universe, repeat themselves to the crack of doom in the creative advance from creature to creature."[59]

Notice that in this view, not only is subjectivity not best understood in cognitive terms, but it is also not limited to human beings. *Every* energetic pulse of reality is in a meaningful sense a subjective center of experience. Subjectivity is not limited to human knowers; it reaches into the deepest depths of reality. "Apart from the experiences of subjects there is nothing, nothing, nothing, bare nothingness."[60] This unique form of pansubjectivism washes away the final vestiges of dualism, irrevocably reshaping the contours of the philosophical landscape.

Given this organic, processive event ontology, human subjects are not an *exception* to the general metaphysical principles at work in the universe, but rather an *exemplification* of the same principles that define every form of existence. A process event ontology unmasks the invidious anthropocentrisms that have for too long infected ethics. The difference between human subjects and nonhuman subjects is ultimately a matter of degree, not kind. There is no bifurcation, no ontological chasm separating human subjects from the rest of reality. Yet, in recognizing the seamless fabric of reality, we need not rush headlong to the embrace of a great ontological leveling, either. The difference between human subjects and nonhuman subjects is a matter of degree, "but it is a difference of degree which makes all the difference."[61] Or, as Whitehead puts it elsewhere, "the Rubicon has been crossed." Though beyond the experience of subjects there is "bare nothingness," not every subject is as complex as every other. In the creative advance, the emergence of complex living beings brings with it the achievement of more intense possibilities for beauty and value, as well as more devastating forms of violence.[62]

Though the window of creativity open to many simple events (e.g., an electron) is narrowly circumscribed by the potentiality left by past events, there is always some (even if negligible) ontological indeterminacy and novelty at even the most basic levels of reality. Though universally affected and limited, nothing is *wholly* determined by what precedes it. As we've seen, the results of this position are as much axiological as they are ontological. To exist, to be actual, is to be a unique achievement of value. "At the base of existence is the sense of 'worth,'" Whitehead tells us. "It is the sense of existence for its own sake, of existence which is its own justification, of existence with its own character."[63] There is no vacuous actuality; each occasion of reality, no matter how simple, fleeting, or seemingly trivial, is a unique, irreplaceable achievement of beauty and value. Given such a conclusion, perhaps it should not be surprising that many Whitehead scholars have long argued that Whitehead's metaphysics would be an ideal foundation for environmental ethics. Let us consider the first person to explicitly make this case.

Whitehead's Metaphysical System as a Foundation for Environmental Ethics

Ten years after defending the first doctoral dissertation on environmental ethics ("The Rights of Nonhuman Beings: A Whiteheadian Study," 1976), Susan Armstrong[64] published in the journal *Environmental Ethics* "Whitehead's Metaphysical System as a Foundation for Environmental Ethics."[65] In this article, Armstrong defends two central claims: (1) environmental ethics would benefit from an adequate metaphysical foundation, and (2) of the candidate metaphysical systems, Whitehead's philosophy of organism is most adequate. Though I differ from Armstrong on several important points, I find her central theses to be essentially right. Indeed, there is a sense in which these two claims are the thesis of the present work. Let's begin with a review of her argument.

Armstrong's approach is to outline and then explain five key "tenets" of Whitehead's thought that are "crucial to a compelling environmental ethic."[66] Given this basis, she then suggests how Whitehead's system avoids many of the difficulties plaguing the alternatives (e.g., utilitarianism, deontology, the land ethic, Spinoza). For Armstrong, the five tenets of Whitehead's thought most relevant to environmental ethics are:

1. Each individual thing is irreplaceably valuable because each thing is a novel, creative contribution to the world.

2. Each thing is inseparably related to all other things.

3. Each thing experiences its own process of self-creation and hence is intrinsically valuable because it is self-significant.

4. The differences between things are due to differences in organization of constituent elements.

5. There is purposiveness in the natural order, a striving toward novelty, harmony, complexity, and intensity of experience.[67]

Given our overview of Whitehead's thought in the previous section, these points should begin to be familiar. Indeed, we've explored how Whitehead's rejection of vacuous actuality leads him to contend that each individual thing is "irreplaceably valuable" as in Armstrong's first tenet. The significance of this position for making progress in the protracted debates over intrinsic value will be discussed at greater length in chapters two and three.

Armstrong's second tenet draws attention to the metaphysical centrality of interrelation in Whitehead's thought. For many environmental ethicists, the focus on interrelation derives from the influence of biology and ecology, which reveal a world in which organisms are parts of complex webs of inter-dependence. This is in direct contrast to modern, Enlightenment worldviews that defined individuality in terms of independence.[68] As Armstrong rightly notes, Whitehead's metaphysics offers a deeper, *metaphysical* basis for this biological emphasis on interrelation: "While many thinkers simply assert that everything is related to everything else, Whitehead's metaphysics offers a reasoned account of the universe in which interrelatedness is crucial. It is crucial because each actual occasion is internally related to all past actual occasions (concreta): the content of each actual occasion is made up of its integration of the contents of past actual occasions. Thus, if the environment is different, the actual occasions are different in their very natures."[69] As we've seen, for Whitehead, it is not merely plants and animals and their environments that are interrelated. According to what he calls the "principle of relativity," internal relatedness (i.e., constitutive interdependence) is the most basic feature of reality itself.[70] In an important sense, individuals *are* their relations.[71]

The third tenet is closely related to the first. In keeping with the "reformed subjectivist principle" mentioned previously, Whitehead's philosophy of organism can, with appropriate qualifications, be described as a pansubjectivism or panexperientialism. Without significant qualification, labels such as these are likely to confuse and distort as much as they reveal about Whitehead's position. Readers are encouraged not to put too much weight on them at this point. We will examine these claims in detail throughout, especially in chapter six. To *be* is to be a unique center of "experience," but experience here is used in an entirely noncognitive sense. Part of the claim, as we will gradually come to understand as we become more familiar with Whitehead's distinctive metaphysical project, is that, since nothing in reality is purely passive or wholly determined, every actual entity partly determines its relation to other, past events, and thereby determines what it is. It is in this very basic sense of the cutting off or resolving of indeterminacy that even the most fleeting and trivial puff of existence in far-off space has "experience."

Armstrong points out that the "use of *experience* in this broad sense allows Whitehead to assert that each thing has intrinsic value because it experiences its own existence. Intrinsic value resides only in the experiencing of value."[72] This is key, Armstrong notes, because it provides a metaphysical basis for the repudiation of anthropogenic theories of value, according to which nonhuman entities can have instrumental value as means for us, but never intrinsic value as ends in themselves. As Armstrong explains, "because for Whitehead intrinsic value resides in the fact that all actual occasions enjoy their own self-creation, no *one* quality or property is arbitrarily singled out to provide intrinsic value, such as rationality, self-consciousness, sentience, and so forth. Such arbitrariness, according to Callicott, is the 'nemesis' of naturalistic theories of value."[73] This claim is at the heart of the current project. As we will see in chapters two and three and indeed throughout this volume, *grounding environmental ethics in Whitehead's metaphysics of organism may allow for the resolution of the central and most "recalcitrant problem" for environmental ethics concerning the nature, scope, and meaning of intrinsic value.*

For Armstrong, the fourth tenet of Whitehead's system relevant to environmental ethics concerns the ontology of individuality, a key problem of metaphysics for millennia and the subject of chapter six. Whitehead's philosophy of organism takes to heart an evolutionary worldview according to which differences of kind result from the accumulation of differences of degree. For Whitehead, this is a feature not only of living organisms, but of reality as such. All differences of kind—such as between living and nonliving or mental and physical—are the result of the accumulation of differences of degree. There is no "bifurcation" in the fabric of reality.[74] Thus, as Armstrong notes, "the differences in kind which we observe, such as between living and nonliving, plants and animals, animals and human beings,[75] are all due to differences in organization of the constituent actual occasions of each entity."[76] There are real and even morally significant differences between different kinds of individuals, and we do find the emergence of novel kinds. But neither of these facts implies that there is any absolute gap in the fabric of reality; we reject all ontological bifurcation. Notably, these views are in keeping with significant trends within contemporary metaphysics and philosophy of mind.[77]

Finally, we have Armstrong's fifth tenet: there is "purposiveness in the natural order, a striving toward novelty, harmony, complexity, and intensity of experience, which is part of what we mean by the presence of divinity in the world process and which allows us to make comparative value judgments."[78] This tenet seems to contain two related but distinct aspects, both concerning teleology. The first part concerns the aim of our cosmos toward "novelty, harmony, complexity, and intensity." For Whitehead, though the process of the universe is open, it does have an overall aim. To appropriate a phrase Holmes Rolston uses to describe ecosystems: the universe has a heading, though it has no head.[79] It is teleologically oriented, though in a rather unique way, as we will see in chapter seven on teleology.

The second part of this fifth tenet concerns "comparative value judgments." Differences in the "complexity, intensity, harmony, and novelty" of different individuals yields a hierarchy of value.[80] Every occasion of existence is equal in *having* value, but not every occasion has value *equally*. Roughly speaking, the hierarchy tracks the complexity and intensity of experience. This hierarchy of value becomes a significant point of concern for some otherwise-sympathetic environmental ethicists and is the focus of chapter five. Indeed, the role of hierarchy within Whitehead's system as it relates to ethics is one of three ways in which I disagree with Armstrong's interpretation of Whitehead and its relationship to environmental ethics. In "Foundations," Armstrong contends that moral agents have "a greater obligation toward entities with more significant experience."[81] It is, I contend, this (arguably invidious) use of hierarchy that brings some deep ecologists and ecofeminists to reject Whitehead's work.[82]

Both deep ecologists and ecofeminists should be natural allies of process philosophers, especially given the former's all-too-rare interest in explicitly grounding environmental ethics in a metaphysical system. Both groups of scholars came to the conclusion that Whitehead's thought embraces a hierarchical conception of value that functionally reduces it to a form of anthropocentrism. Unfortunately, their concern is only confirmed in Armstrong's interpretation from "Foundations" that moral agents have "a greater obligation toward entities with more significant experience."[83]

However, as I argue at length in chapter five, there is a better interpretation of the role of Whitehead's axiological hierarchy within a moral philosophy. I agree with Armstrong and Whitehead that there is an ontological and axiological hierarchy. There are real and meaningful differences in the integrated complexity of different beings, and these differences permit important differences in the intensity of experience available to them. The human brain, for instance, is the most complex thing we have so far discovered in the universe. Thus, it is accurate to note not only that there is a hierarchy of value, but also that humans are high on this hierarchy. *However*, the relationship of this metaphysical fact does *not* function morally in the way Armstrong contends.

As I argue in chapter five, it is in the movement between description and prescription that "anthroparchy" hangs. The recognition of the hierarchical structure of reality does not neatly translate to moral significance, though it is relevant to it. The aim of morality is *not* simply to give preference to the beings with the greatest depth of intrinsic value, which would indeed resolve into an invidious form of anthropocentrism as critics contend. Rather, for Whitehead, the aim of morality is the same as every other process: the creation of beauty and value. Thus, though it is the case that human moral agents are capable of more intense value than, say, a bee, birch, or bear, our *moral* obligation in each situation is to affirm the greatest amount of beauty and value that is possible in each situation taken as a whole. A being's "position" in an onto-aesthetic hierarchy is relevant to, but not strictly determinative of its moral significance. At times it will be the case that to achieve the greatest degree of beauty and value possible in a particular situation it will be necessary to sacrifice the interests of beings capable of more intense intrinsic value. Put more directly, just because humans are capable of a higher degree of intrinsic value does not thereby mean that their interests *automatically* outweigh the interests of other beings because *the aim of morality is not the satisfaction of the interests of the most valuable beings involved, but rather the creation of the greatest whole of value and beauty possible in that situation.*

This points to the second significant difference between Armstrong's interpretation and my own. Although Armstrong, like many Whitehead scholars writing in the 1970s and 1980s, does not draw attention to it, Whitehead is unambiguously clear in characterizing the aim of process in aesthetic terms: "the teleology of the universe is directed to the production of beauty."[84] As I explore in chapter four, our processive cosmos is fundamentally kalogenic; it is beauty generating.[85] Beauty is the ultimate aim of every process, including ethics. A Whiteheadian moral philosophy sees the actions of moral agents as that species of process characteristic of large-scale organisms who are complex enough to be conscious and free enough to be responsible. Though healthy adult humans may be the only moral agents of which we are aware—and in this sense morality may have emerged (become possible) with the evolution of human beings—the *aim* of morality is the same as that of all process: the preservation and creation of harmonious and intense beauty and value. Put syllogistically: all process aims at the production of beauty and value, and morality is a species of process; therefore, morality aims at the production of beauty and value.[86]

Building on and extending Armstrong's work, in the present project I demonstrate that, grounded in Whitehead's philosophy of organism, it becomes possible for environmental ethics to make meaningful progress on key debates over intrinsic value (chapters two and three), beauty (chapter four), non-invidious hierarchy (chapter five), the nature of individuality and the relation of subject and objects (chapter six), teleology (chapter seven), and the naturalistic fallacy (chapter seven). I will demonstrate that Whitehead's fallibilistic, naturalistic event ontology allows for the recovery of systematic, speculative metaphysical thought without a revanchist movement toward a necessitarian philosophia perennis (chapter one). Explicitly and intentionally grounding environmental ethics in environmental metaphysics also makes it possible to return to one of environmental philosophy's founding impulses: the development of a more fundamentally non-anthropocentric worldview (chapter nine). In this way, the present project is fundamentally at odds with and will come to terms with the policy turn advocated by many environmental pragmatists (chapter eight). Thus, taken as a whole, the present project attempts to demonstrate that to make philosophical progress on key debates and problems within environmental *ethics*, philosophers should also explicitly engage in environmental *metaphysics*.

Chapter 1

In Defense of Systematic, Speculative Philosophy

Given that it was founded on the premise that the ecological crisis can only be well and truly resolved by developing a new, more adequate *worldview*, it is perhaps surprising that most environmental philosophers completely ignore *metaphysics*. For is it not one's metaphysics—or ultimate conception of the nature and structures of reality—that finally constitutes and justifies a given worldview? It is, for instance, the Cartesian view that humans are the only thinking things in an otherwise clockwork universe that is the ultimate conceptual foundation for the anthropocentric worldview environmental ethics rightly seeks to overcome. Yet, by refusing to take up the task of developing or adopting a more adequate metaphysics, environmental ethics often adopts by default modern metaphysical dualism or materialism. It is this latent metaphysics that, I contend, continues to infect and undermine the central aim of environmental philosophy to develop a more adequate worldview. Indeed, the central premise of the present volume is that environmental ethics will be unable to fully achieve its task of developing a morally adequate, ecological worldview unless and until it properly understands the structure of reality and its relationship to beauty and value.

It would seem that most environmental ethicists—like nearly all contemporary ethicists—have inherited a pronounced allergy to metaphysics that keeps them from engaging with this aspect of their work. Thus, for many, one of the greatest impediments to the present project to ground environmental ethics in an organicist metaphysics is not this or that inadequacy, but the fact that it is metaphysics at all. Environmental ethicists are not so much hostile to metaphysics as completely ambivalent toward it.[1]

My aim in this chapter is twofold. First, it will be useful to better understand why so many philosophers have an inherited antipathy or even hostility to metaphysics. Thus, in the first part I hope to show that, despite its seeming rehabilitation in some quarters (though not in ethics), metaphysics as systematic, speculative philosophy is no less threatened. Second, I will argue that metaphysics as systematic, speculative philosophy is ultimately revisable. That is, metaphysics is not (or should not be) the aim at a closed system of apodictic truths, but rather an open-ended, fallibilistic pursuit of ever-more-adequate accounts of reality. Specifically, building on the work of Charles Sanders Peirce and Alfred North Whitehead, I argue that we should conceive of metaphysics not as the quest for absolute certainty but as "working hypothesis."[2] Thus, the first part is largely historical and critical, and the second part is positive and exploratory. The result is to have established more clearly what is and is not meant by suggesting that environmental ethics ought to be grounded explicitly in a metaphysical framework such as Whitehead's philosophy of organism. To be very direct, what is *not* intended is an atavistic, retrograde return to modern or ancient metaphysics. The approach to metaphysics provided by Peirce and Whitehead avoids the excesses with which (classical) metaphysics is typically associated, and provides a viable path forward for developing what might be called environmental metaphysics.

The Twentieth-Century Nadir of Metaphysics

Some years ago I had the pleasure of editing with a colleague a volume about the Metaphysical Society of America (MSA).[3] Our goal was to tell the history of the MSA and its role in American philosophy through a selection of its presidential addresses. I was particularly drawn to early addresses, such as the one delivered by William Ernest Hocking in 1958. In the opening of his address Hocking begins by praising the members of the MSA for, as he put it, "being metaphysicians with conscious intent." He continued, "For it is the metaphysician who most completely fulfills the ideal of Living Dangerously. It is he who most fully renounces the security of current certitudes in the search for authentic certitude. It is he who chooses—let me say—to *live out of doors* in complete exposure to what we call Fact."[4] Early presidential addresses such as this are a valuable window into the fight to save metaphysics in the middle of the twentieth century.

Much has changed in the decades since Paul Weiss began the *Review of Metaphysics* (1947) and the Metaphysical Society of America (1950) as responses to an academy grown hostile to metaphysics. Though attacks on metaphysics continue from certain quarters, metaphysics is once again a vibrant area of philosophical investigation. Despite this, I have come to wonder whether in fact metaphysics has lost a bit of its nerve. Where are the great metaphysical system-building projects that dominated previous philosophical epochs? Arguably, Alfred North Whitehead's philosophy of organism is among the twentieth century's only great attempts at metaphysical system-building.

For nearly two and a half millennia, metaphysics has been understood as the attempt to give a systematic account of the necessary and unchanging principles of reality. Although the term *metaphysics* itself was likely unknown to the ancient Greeks,[5] they distinguished the *phusiologoi*, who studied the flux of nature, from the lovers of wisdom, who sought the unchanging *archê*, or the first principles of reality. Similarly, though it was reduced to the status of handmaiden, in the Middle Ages the medieval divines constructed complex metaphysical systems accounting for every element of reality. And despite having been born in opposition to the perceived excesses and failures of the Aristotelianism of the late Middle Ages, modernity did not abandon the metaphysical impulse. Indeed, some might argue that metaphysics reached its zenith in this period.

Take, for instance, Descartes, whose methodical doubt was in service of establishing something, as he put it, "firm and lasting in the sciences."[6] (Here I set aside the claim that Descartes's turn to the subject might be seen as the abandonment, even destruction, of metaphysics by replacing it with epistemology.) Concerned about the march of skepticism and envious of the apparently apodictic proofs of mathematics, Descartes razed all of his beliefs in order to pour a new and unshakable foundation on which to rebuild thought. Setting aside the particulars of his project, my main concern here is to note how Descartes defined the *aim* of metaphysics: the aim of first philosophy is to find a clear and distinct principle, an "Archimedean point,"[7] that will guarantee *absolute certainty*. This is what it means to establish something "firm and lasting in the sciences." Indeed, early scientists defined the aim of their investigations in much the same way. After all, Newton's discoveries were final and permanent "laws," not highly probable inductive generalizations. It will be important to return to this complex relationship between science and metaphysics. For now, my point is merely that, regardless of one's estimation of its success, metaphysics (and science) in the modern period was defined by the quest for absolute certainty, both for those who sought to live up to its high ideal and for those who sought to critique it. It was against this conception of metaphysics as a closed system of necessary and absolutely certain principles that many thinkers of the nineteenth and twentieth centuries protested so strenuously.

Though little unifies the multitude of philosophical tributaries of the twentieth century, a surprisingly common theme is the repudiation of metaphysics. In his 1988 presidential address to the Metaphysical Society of America, Richard Bernstein notes that in the opening decades of the twentieth century, three competing philosophical projects declared war on metaphysics. The first assault on metaphysics started late in the nineteenth century with Auguste Comte and logical positivism. "In one fell swoop," Bernstein writes, positivists "sought to dismiss metaphysics by claiming that metaphysical 'propositions' are pseudo-propositions. They are nonsense; they lack cognitive meaning."[8] In this context I am reminded of a letter from 1936 between Whitehead and his former student Henry S. Leonard in which he is responding to Leonard's book. Whitehead writes:

> Logical Positivism is a topic rarely distant from my thought. Every mathematician and symbolic logician is, in his habit of thought, a logical positivist. Yet to some of the expositions I find myself in violent opposition—especially to the very habit of dismissing questions as unmeaning *i.e.*, unable to be expressed in existing symbolism. Wittgenstein annoys me intensely. He is the complete example of the sayings:
>
> I am Master of the College
>
> What I know not, is not knowledge.
>
> Logical Positivism in this mood—its only mood—will produce a timid, shut in, unenterprising state of mind, engaged in the elaboration of details. I always test these general rules by try-ing to imagine the sterilizing effect of such a state of mind, if prevalent at any time in the last ten thousand years. The fact is that thought in the previous two centuries has been engaged in disengaging itself from the shackles of dogmatic divinity. Thus it unconsciously seeks new fetters, *viz* anything offensive to the

Pope of Rome. But I see no reason to believe that the stretch of Bertrand Russell's mind or of Wittgenstein's mind, or of Carnap's mind, has attained the limits of insight or expression possible in the evolution of intelligent beings. They are bright boys, good representatives of a *stage* of rationalization, but nothing more.[9]

Leaving aside the uncharacteristically harsh tone of Whitehead's comments, it is important to note that what he most objects to, what seems really to have irritated him, is not this or that particular claim, but the "sterilizing effect" of positivism. "Of course most men of science, and many philosophers," Whitehead wrote three years earlier in *Adventures of Ideas*, "use the Positivistic doctrine to avoid the necessity of considering perplexing fundamental questions—in short, to avoid metaphysics—, and then save the importance of science by an implicit recurrence to their metaphysical persuasion that the past does in fact condition the future."[10] *One can choose one's metaphysics, but one cannot choose not to have a metaphysics.* As I will discuss more fully in the second part, the adventures of ideas cannot move forward, metaphysics cannot be progressive, unless it is engaged in explicitly. Lest I get ahead of myself, for now let me simply agree with Bernstein that "whatever judgment we make about the legacy of positivism, it failed in its attempt to rid us of metaphysics. Indeed its own unquestioned metaphysical biases have become evident."[11]

The second "wave" of challenge to metaphysics in the twentieth century crested in the mid-1960s, with the rise of ordinary language analysis. As Bernstein describes it, "the strategy here was not to dismiss metaphysics as nonsense but to bypass it." However, Bernstein continues, "it soon became evident that metaphysical issues could not be avoided. On the contrary, philosophers like Strawson and Sellars argued that analytic techniques could themselves be employed to tackle metaphysical issues."[12] Strawson's book *Individuals*, with its distinction between descriptive and revisionary metaphysics, is a notable illustration of Bernstein's latter point. As Peter Hacker has noted, "Descriptive metaphysics does not differ from conceptual analysis in intent. Like conceptual analysis . . . it is concerned with describing and clarifying the concepts we employ in discourse about ourselves and about the world."[13] In this sense, descriptive metaphysics is simply conceptual analysis "at a very high level of generality."[14] Thus, Hacker continues, "where traditional metaphysicians conceived of themselves as limning the ultimate structure of the world, the descriptive metaphysician will conceive of himself as sketching the basic structure of our conceptual scheme—of the language we use to describe the world and our experience of it."[15] In this sense, from the perspective of speculative philosophy, descriptive metaphysics is not a resurrection of metaphysics but a rejection of it.[16] As Hacker puts it, "Metaphysics thus construed yields no insight into reality, but only into our forms of description of reality. So it is just more grammar, in Wittgenstein's extended sense of the term."[17]

Finally, the third wave of challenge to metaphysics came from deconstructionist postmodernism and is most associated with Heidegger and Derrida.[18] For some, deconstructionist postmodernism is defined by its attempt to overthrow and overcome metaphysics. However, I tend to agree with Bernstein when he argues that "the deconstruction of metaphysics [by Heidegger and Derrida] does not mean abandoning it or completely rejecting it. Rather it means keeping alive what has always been 'central' to this tradition—'the inquisitive energy of the mind' that never stops 'questioning what appears to be obvious and definitive.'"[19]

I will leave it to those more expert in the work of Heidegger and Derrida to debate whether Bernstein is right. At present my concern is merely to highlight how these three diverse, and in many ways opposed, philosophical trends—positivism, ordinary language analysis, and deconstructionist postmodernism—combined early in the twentieth century to create a philosophical environment that was openly hostile to traditional metaphysics.

It was in response to these converging trends that the indefatigable Paul Weiss, a student of Whitehead's, founded in 1947 (by coincidence, the same year of Whitehead's death) the *Review of Metaphysics* and, three years later, the Metaphysical Society of America (MSA). The MSA's second president, John Wild, reflects the mood of the founders of the society in his 1954 presidential address at Harvard:

> In the Western world, this negativistic movement [against metaphysics] has proved to be a far more serious and lasting threat. Failing to take a firm root in Europe, the place of its origin, it moved to England and North America, where the central disciplines of philosophy were found to be less firmly grounded in sound empirical traditions of academic life and thought. Here for many years it has now run its course, and has exerted a powerful destructive effect. In many secular schools and universities, the history of philosophy has been neglected, logic and linguistics have replaced ontology as the focal discipline, and many philosophers moved by the widespread fear and idolatry of "science," have

abandoned the performance of their vital descriptive and synoptic functions. This has had a markedly disintegrating effect on the cultural life of the West at a time of crisis and world upheaval.

But this is, fortunately, not the whole story. Certain thinkers refused to be swept along in the destructive currents and stood firm, especially those, like A. N. Whitehead, who were more intimately acquainted with the restricted sciences and their necessary limitations. Metaphysics, while seriously weakened academically, did not completely die away. One unambiguous indication was the formation of this society five years ago.[20]

Since 1950, the members of the MSA have sought to keep open a clearing in the philosophical wilderness for systematic, speculative philosophy.[21] What is particularly remarkable about the MSA is that, unlike many other philosophical organizations, it is defined primarily by a particular philosophical *attitude*, rather than some particular philosophical *content*.[22] Whether Platonist or Aristotelian, Hegelian or Thomist, Kantian or Whiteheadian, what unites the members of the MSA is their commitment to pursuing the "grand tradition" of metaphysics. As stated baldly in the opening of its constitution, "the purpose of the Metaphysical Society of America is the study of reality."[23] It is this attitude—this willingness to live dangerously out of doors—I wish to explore, recover, and defend.

Yet the observant student of philosophy might nod in recognition of this history lesson but note that much has transpired in the decades since Weiss founded his review and society. As my undergraduate students might say, attacks on metaphysics are so last century. Indeed, some might argue that metaphysics is now among one of the most exciting and growing areas of research in mainstream Anglo-American philosophy. In a certain sense, this is correct. Mainstream philosophy in America is no longer quite so hostile to metaphysics. However, this belies a deeper point. Although in America today metaphysics is considered by many to be a respected and vibrant area of research, it is not clear that systematic, speculative philosophy is any less threatened. Let me try to explain my meaning.

In the introduction to a volume of essays dedicated to the new field called "metametaphysics," David Manley provides a helpful explanation of how many contemporary analytic philosophers conceive of metaphysics: "Metaphysics is concerned with the foundations of reality. It asks questions about the nature of the world, such as: Aside from concrete objects, are there also abstract objects like numbers and properties? Does every event have a cause? What is the nature of possibility and necessity? When do several things make up a single bigger thing? Do the past and future exist? And so on."[24] These topics and more have rightly been a central part of metaphysics for centuries. However, it is worth noting what is missing from this account. Notice that there is no interest here in giving a *systematic* account of the foundations of reality as we find in the work of Aristotle, Aquinas, Kant, Hegel, and Whitehead. Though metaphysics is once again in the embrace of mainstream philosophy, system-building is still out.

A debate such as this over the nature, scope, or aim of metaphysics is part of what is now being called "metametaphysics." According to Manley's introduction, whereas metaphysics is concerned with the foundations of reality, "metametaphysics is concerned with the foundations of metaphysics. It asks: Do the questions of metaphysics really have answers? If so, are these answers substantive or just a matter of how we use words? And what is the best procedure for arriving at them—common sense? Conceptual analysis? Or assessing competing hypotheses with quasi-scientific criteria?"[25] Though the term *metametaphysics* may be new, debates over the nature of metaphysics go back to the origins of Western philosophy. In a sense, the present volume can rightly be seen as being interested in metametaphysics in that part of the topic of study is the nature of metaphysics itself. I am not yet convinced that it is necessary to introduce this neologism, but I do find Manley's subsequent taxonomy of metaphysical positions to be quite revelatory of the current topography of analytic philosophy.

Manley notes that there are still "deflationary" tendencies within contemporary analytic philosophy that are opposed to metaphysics. On one end of Manley's spectrum, the philosophical heirs of "Carnap, Wittgenstein, Austin, Rorty, Ryle and Putnam" continue to defend a *"strong deflationism"*: "[Strong deflationists] dismiss the disputed [metaphysical questions] as entirely misguided, on the grounds that nothing substantive is at issue. Motivated in part by intuitions of shallowness, they argue that the dispute is merely verbal, or that the disputants are not making truth-evaluable claims at all."[26] Notably, Manley contends that "in its new forms, strong deflationism poses as serious a challenge to metaphysics as ever."[27] In the middle of Manley's spectrum are *"mild deflationists,"* who recognize that metaphysical disputes are genuine but who contend that they can "be resolved in a relatively trivial fashion by reflecting on conceptual or semantic facts. Thus, nothing of substance is left for the metaphysician to investigate, and it is in this sense that the view is metaphysically deflationist."[28]

Thus, although it is true that metaphysics is no longer dismissed out of hand, a significant portion of Anglo-American thinkers continue to be hostile to metaphysics. Until recently, these two trends were dominant within contemporary analytic philosophy, as they had been for much of the twentieth century. Though it is still under attack, Manley contends that a "robust realist approach," which he calls simply "*mainstream metaphysics*," is now ascendant:[29] "Most contemporary metaphysicians think of themselves as concerned, not primarily with the representations of language and thoughts, but with the reality that is represented. In the case of ontology, there are deep and non-trivial—but still tractable—questions about numbers, sums, events, and regions of space, as well as about ordinary objects like turkeys and teacups."[30]

Although the sweeping attacks on metaphysics have somewhat subsided, my claim is that metaphysics as systematic, speculative philosophy is no less in danger. That is, it is no longer the *existence* of metaphysics that is under assault but its *essence*. Whereas earlier generations of undertakers sought to bury, overcome, or otherwise bypass metaphysics, many today want instead to replace it with an anemic simulacrum. To be perfectly blunt, I fear metaphysics has lost its philosophical nerve. In the remainder of this chapter, my rather unfashionable goal is to take up once again what Bernstein calls the "utopian impulse" of metaphysics,[31] but one illuminated by the scientific discoveries of the last century. Let us bravely seek to fulfill the ideal of "Living Dangerously." Let us renounce the "security of current certitudes in the search for authentic certitude" and "*live out of doors* in complete exposure to . . . Fact."[32]

Recovering the Adventure of Ideas

Great metaphysicians—whether Aristotle or Kant, Thomas, or Descartes—have always sought to be literate of and adequate to the science of their day. Though I applaud the fact that many contemporary philosophers continue this tradition and recognize the importance of attempting to stay abreast of the latest discoveries in science, I fear that too many simply see themselves as bringing conceptual clarity to the work of scientists, rather than functioning, as Whitehead put it, as a "critic of abstractions"[33] and "to challenge the half-truths constituting the scientific first principles."[34]

As science has pursued its beautiful recursive, self-correcting method of investigation, it has revealed a universe quite different from that pictured by Newton and Descartes. Indeed, I would argue that the moderns were wrong both with respect to their *description* of reality and with respect to their understanding of what can be *achieved* in science. Reality is *not* a *closed* system composed of *inert* bits of matter defined by *absolute*, unflinching laws of nature that can, in principle, be known with *absolute* certainty and represented adequately by mathematics. Rather, it seems that our reality is an *open, evolving, dynamic* system composed of *vibratory energetic events* woven into extraordinarily complex webs of *interdependence* that are inherently indeterminate and, therefore, only asymptotically knowable with statistical and probabilistic certainty.

It turns out, then, that science does not and cannot arrive at absolutely certain truths. Or, as Whitehead provocatively put it, "the Certainties of Science are a delusion."[35] Though supported by centuries of careful observational evidence, there is nothing necessary or absolute about, for instance, Newton's so-called laws. With Whitehead, I would argue that, as he put it, "none of these laws of nature gives the slightest evidence of necessity. They are the modes of procedure which within the scale of our observations do in fact prevail": [36]"Thus, the laws of nature are merely all-pervading patterns of behaviour, of which the shift and discontinuance lie beyond our ken."[37]

The task for the contemporary metaphysician, if they are to live dangerously, is to give a systematic account of such a universe. Yet how can one be adequate to such a universe while not abandoning speculative metaphysics? If the universe is an evolving, emergent process that is not knowable with absolute certainty, then how is the grand tradition of metaphysics possible?[38]

In his 1911 posthumous work *Some Problems of Philosophy*, William James notes that some philosophers object that too often metaphysics is dogmatic: "too many philosophers have aimed at closed systems, established *a priori*, claiming infallibility, and to be accepted or rejected only as totals."[39] However, as James goes on to note, the solution to this problem is not to be found in the rejection of metaphysics in favor of science. No, what James goes on to astutely note is that the dogmatism of metaphysics can be remedied by modeling its *method* on science's self-correcting method of "hypothesis and verification":[40] "Since philosophers are only men thinking about things in the most comprehensive possible way, they can use any method whatsoever. Philosophy must, in any case, complete the sciences, and must incorporate their methods. One cannot see why, if such a policy should appear advisable, philosophy might not end by foreswearing all dogmatism whatever, and become as hypothetical in her manners as the most empirical science of them all."[41] Though he does not mention it here, this is in fact the method developed by Charles Sanders Peirce, whom James rightly credits with founding Pragmatism. As early as the 1860s Peirce was arguing against the dogmatic influences of Cartesian thought, developing in a series of essays over decades a model of philosophy (and of metaphysics) as an open-ended investigation conducted by a "community of inquirers." Metaphysics aims at giving a complete, systematic account of reality, but, like science, it recognizes that such an investigation is fallibilistic, revisable, and open-ended; there is no finality. As Leemon McHenry vividly puts it, "Metaphysical megalomania in the likes of Descartes, Spinoza, Hegel and Bradley is thereby cured by a naturalised approach inspired by the American pragmatists, Peirce, James and Dewey. The quest for certainty is abandoned both in philosophy and science."[42] (It will be important to return to and build on these points when considering environmental pragmatism in chapter eight.)

Peirce's insight is, I contend, one of the most important and under-appreciated discoveries in the last two centuries of metaphysics. According to this model, metaphysics is conceived as an ameliorative and asymptotic form of inquiry that fallibilistically seeks to give ever-more-adequate accounts of reality by testing them against experience. Unfortunately, for a host of reasons, Peirce was never able to provide more than a sketch of such a system. That distinction goes to another mathematician-philosopher, Alfred North Whitehead, who independently developed a very similar model of speculative philosophy.

For Whitehead, speculative philosophy "embodies the method of the 'working hypothesis.' "[43] Thus, just as James had suggested, Whitehead puts the self-correcting, progressive nature of scientific investigation at the heart of metaphysics. In doing so, he fundamentally alters the nature of metaphysical inquiry.[44] Metaphysics is still the attempt to give a *systematic* account of every element of reality, but it finally gives up the pretense that metaphysical principles must be—indeed, that they can be—*necessary* or *absolutely certain*. As Whitehead reminds us, "neither in Science nor in Philosophy, nor in any branch of human achievement do we reach finality."[45] We must become deaf to the siren song of finality and certainty, reminding ourselves always that there are no absolute, final truths to be had in metaphysics—or any other investigation. However, unlike the skeptics who make similar claims, Peirce and Whitehead recognize the progressive nature of metaphysical inquiry. Although metaphysical systems may not be true or false—to be rejected, as James noted, in total—they may certainly be better or worse. This better and worse implies a standard. It is here that Whitehead improves on Peirce.

For Whitehead, metaphysical speculation is to be judged in terms of four criteria, two of which are rational and two of which are empirical. Rationally, our metaphysical systems should aim at being both *logical* and *coherent*. That is, they should avoid contradiction, and each element of the system should be interpretable in terms of the rest. The system should hang together. Avoiding contradiction or being logical is a minimal bar, easily crossed by most theories. However, coherence is a rational ideal toward which systems asymptotically aspire but which few, if any, achieve fully.

However, for Whitehead, speculative philosophy must not be content with constructing self-consistent thought-castles in the sky; we must, as Hocking put it, live in "complete exposure to . . . Fact." Thus, Whitehead also proposes two empirical criteria: speculative metaphysical systems must be not only logical and coherent but also *applicable* and *adequate* to every element of experience. Again, the former empirical condition, *applicability*, is a minimal condition. Our metaphysical theories must be applicable to at least some element of experience. For instance, it is in terms of applicability that, Whitehead argues, Descartes's system fails. The notion of a disembodied cogito is simply inapplicable to our experience.[46] However, the most important and interesting criterion for speculative philosophy is that it must also aim at being *adequate* to every element of reality. It is this insistence on adequacy, again a maximal ideal only asymptotically approached, that fundamentally alters the metaphysical project; for in order to determine whether a metaphysical system is adequate, it must be pragmatically tested. As Whitehead puts it, "Whatever is found in 'practice' must lie within the scope of metaphysical description. When description fails to include 'practice,' the metaphysics is inadequate and requires revision. There can be no appeal to practice to supplement metaphysics, so long as we remain contented with our metaphysical doctrines. Metaphysics is nothing but the description of the generalities which apply to all the details of practice."[47] Metaphysics can only be conceived as "working hypothesis," it can only be progressive, if it is possible for hypotheses to be wrong, to be contradicted. Our abstract formulations must continually be tested for their adequacy to our full experience of reality.

Importantly, then, although metaphysics *aims* at a completely adequate account of reality, Whitehead does not believe any metaphysical system "can hope entirely to satisfy these pragmatic tests." Thus, he continues, "at the best such a system will remain only an approximation to the general truths which are sought."[48] It is in this sense that metaphysics is to be understood as "working hypothesis." Metaphysical categories are not to be taken as "dogmatic statements of the obvious," but rather as, in Whitehead's words, "tentative formulations of the ultimate generalities."[49]

To help explain his view of speculative philosophy, Whitehead provides a useful analogy: he likens this model of speculative philosophy to the flight of an airplane. Our metaphysical investigation "starts from the ground of particular observation" and then "makes a flight in the thin air of imaginative generalization" and system-building. However, and this is key, it must once again land "for renewed observation rendered acute by rational interpretation."[50] It is this recursive nature of speculative philosophy that brings about the amicable marriage of the rationalist and empiricist elements of metaphysics. We start from our own experience and take flight into speculative metaphysical system-building, but we must land again and test the applicability and adequacy of our accounts. Only in this way can metaphysics retain its noble aim but avoid dogmatism. I hasten to note, if only in passing, that if a vicious reductionism is to be avoided, this testing of metaphysical hypotheses must be understood within the context of a very radical empiricism, in the Jamesian sense of the term. Since, for Whitehead, metaphysics is "the endeavor to frame a coherent, logical, necessary system of general ideas in terms of which every element of our experience can be interpreted,"[51] it is vitally important that *every* type of experience be included. We must resist the urge to "explain away" what does not fit with our theory.

One of the things I most admire about Whitehead is that he models this fallibilistic approach to metaphysics in his own life and work. In his magnum opus, *Process and Reality*, Whitehead defends his philosophy of organism as one such attempt at a system. However, unlike so many metaphysicians before him, he does not claim to have arrived at *the* metaphysical system to end all systems. He knows and expects that it will require continuous revision over time: "Philosophy is at once general and concrete, critical and appreciative of direct intuition. It is not—or, at least, should not be—a ferocious debate between irritable professors. It is a survey of possibilities and their comparison with actualities. In philosophy, the fact, the theory, the alternatives, and the ideal, are weighed together. Its gifts are insight and foresight, and a sense of the world of life, in short, that sense of importance which nerves all civilized effort."[52]

Once the pretense at finality is abandoned, metaphysics is free to become a progressive form of inquiry. John Herman Randall relays a humorous anecdote regarding this in his 1967 presidential address to the Metaphysical Society of America: "Metaphysical inquiry thus, like all scientific inquiry, is progressive, never finished; it never reaches final conclusions. I remember once hearing a Teutonic philosopher ask, 'Then metaphysics has no more, and no greater certainty, than physics?' John Dewey, who was present, rose, smiled his inimitable smile, and repeated, 'No greater certainty than physics!' Anyone who finds that a serious objection is obviously not interested in inquiry: he is looking for faith."[53]

The mantra of the metaphysician—as much as the scientist—must be, as Peirce put it, "never block the road to inquiry."[54] Finality and absolute certainty are a sham, but we need not therefore give up on genuine systematic metaphysics. Thus, as Whitehead aptly puts it, "the proper test [of metaphysics] is not that of finality, but of progress,"[55] progress in giving a more logical, coherent, applicable, and adequate account of reality. We seek rational coherence of our metaphysical systems, but these systems must be made to land on the firm ground of experience and demonstrate their applicability and adequacy. It is this, I suggest, that makes it possible to avoid the tendency to dogmatism that has plagued too many efforts at metaphysical system-building. "There is no first principle, which is in itself unknowable, not to be captured by a flash of insight. But, putting aside the difficulties of language, deficiency in imaginative penetration forbids progress in any form other than that of an asymptotic approach to a scheme of principles, only definable in terms of the ideal which they should satisfy. The difficulty has its seat on the empirical side of philosophy."[56] By saying that the difficulty has its seat on the empirical side, Whitehead means to say that reality always necessarily outstrips our ability to adequately characterize it. Though language is the tool of philosophy, he is not enamored of its adequacy in *adequately* capturing the fullness and richness of experience: "Philosophers can never hope finally to formulate these metaphysical first principles. Weakness of insight and deficiencies of language stand in the way inexorably. Words and phrases must be stretched towards a generality foreign to their ordinary usage; and however such elements of language be stabilized as technicalities, they remain metaphors mutely appealing for an imaginative leap."[57] It is for this reason that Whitehead so often recurs to the poets (or neologisms!) who in their evocations capture a share of reality omitted by the scientist's experiments. This brings me to the final implication regarding this revisable model of metaphysics. If it is taken seriously, revisable metaphysics would seem to require a philosophical pluralism. If one is a consistent fallibilist, then one must necessarily recognize that there is no single system, method, or approach.

Personally, I find that Whitehead and Peirce have come closest in living up to the ideals of speculative philosophy. However, I am also convinced that important contributions are made by, among many others, Aristotle,

Kant, and Hegel, as well as Plato and Thomas and many others. However, I hasten to add that the pluralism demanded by a commitment to speculative philosophy is not what Bernstein has aptly called "flabby" or a "pluralism which simply accepts the variety of perspectives, 'vocabularies,' paradigms, language games, etc." Bernstein continues, "[for] such a flabby pluralism fails to take seriously that there are real conflicts and clashes in metaphysical positions which need to be faced."[58] The fallibilist pursuit of metaphysical system-building requires what Bernstein calls "engaged pluralism." As an engaged pluralist, Bernstein writes,

> one accepts the fallibility of all inquiry and even the lack of convergence of metaphysical speculation. One accepts the multiplicity of perspectives and interpretations. One rejects the quest for certainty, the craving for absolutes, and the idea of a totality in which all differences are finally reconciled. But such a pluralism demands an openness to what is different and other, a willingness to risk one's prejudgments, seeking for common ground without any guarantees that it will be found. It demands—and it is a strenuous demand—that one tries to be responsive to the claims of the other. Such an engaged pluralism does not mean giving up the search for truth and objectivity. For metaphysical speculation is always concerned with keeping "the spirit of truth" alive. But the quest for truth and objectivity is not to be confused with the quest for absolutes. Claims to truth and objectivity are always fallible.[59]

Thus, in sum, the many attacks on metaphysics have not led us beyond metaphysics but, rather, back to metaphysics.[60] Like those "utopian diggers" who founded the Metaphysical Society of America,[61] we must have the courage to continue the grand tradition of metaphysical system-building. However, we must also recognize that metaphysics is not the pursuit of final, necessary, or absolute truths. Metaphysical inquiry is as open and dynamic as the reality it seeks to understand. As metaphysicians with "conscious intent," we must have the courage "to *live out of doors* in complete exposure to . . . Fact" and recognize the fallibilism and engaged pluralism inherent within metaphysical speculation. "Rationalism," Whitehead writes in *Process and Reality*, "never shakes off its status of an experimental adventure. The combined influences of mathematics and religion, which have also greatly contributed to the rise of philosophy, have also had the unfortunate effect of yoking it with static dogmatism. Rationalism is an adventure in the clarification of thought, progressive and never final. But it is an adventure in which even partial success has importance."[62]

It should now begin to become apparent that, in contending that environmental ethics would be benefited by being grounded in Whitehead's organicist metaphysics, this is not a retrograde move seeking to harken back to some halcyon days. As McHenry rightly notes, if one were to categorize Whitehead's metametaphysical position, it would be "*revisionary* because it overthrows our ordinary common-sense modes of thought; *naturalistic* because it begins to construct metaphysical principles from the natural sciences—physics and cosmology in particular; and *realistic* because its naturalism demands the scientist's robust sense of a mind-independent reality as a foundation for enquiry into the nature of the physical world."[63] In that Whitehead's organicist, fallibilistic, open-ended, speculative model of metaphysics as working hypothesis recovers the best of the metaphysical tradition by allowing for the attempt at synoptic vision while avoiding the excesses that plagued earlier accounts, it is an ideal foundation for environmental ethics. Whitehead's philosophy of organism is an ideal environmental metaphysics.

Chapter 2

Value

Having unearthed some of the process roots of environmental ethics and situated Whitehead's unique approach within the history of metaphysics, we are now in a position to begin considering a Whiteheadian position on its own terms. If a Whiteheadian ethic were a pigeon, into which hole would we place it? Despite the longstanding consensus among process scholars that Whitehead's philosophy of organism provides an ideal ground for a rich moral philosophy, particularly one encompassing ecological concerns, there is a relative dearth of scholarship on the topic. What is more, among those who engage it, there seems to be no agreement as to how to classify a Whiteheadian ethics, which has at different times been labeled a moral interest theory, a totalizing form of utilitarianism, and a virtue ethic.[1] Some have even suggested that Whitehead's metaphysics is consistent with a deontological approach.[2] As the following passage from Whitehead's final book, *Modes of Thought*, suggests, a Whiteheadian ethics may look quite different than its modern and ancient cousins: "Morality does not indicate what you are to do in mythological abstractions. It does concern the general ideal which should be the justification for any particular objective. The destruction of a man, or of an insect, or of a tree, or of the Parthenon, may be moral or immoral. [. . .] Whether we destroy or whether we preserve, our action is moral if we have thereby safeguarded the importance of experience so far as it depends on that concrete instance in the world's history."[3] It is through passages such as this that we see just how radical and far-reaching Whitehead's thought can be. Whereas for many traditional ethical theories the only relations that are morally significant are interhuman relations, for Whitehead, "the destruction of a man, or of an insect, or of a tree, or of the Parthenon, may be moral or immoral."[4] To understand this initially surprising claim, it will be useful to begin by considering various scholarly attempts to categorize Whitehead's ethics. We will find that, ultimately, any moral philosophy inspired by Whitehead's thought will necessarily be as unique as his event ontology. Given this, we will then consider the contours of a Whiteheadian-inspired ethics on its own terms, by first considering its distinctive theory of value, then the role it gives to moral ideals, and finally its dynamic, open-ended conception of moral philosophy itself.

It should be said at the outset that Whitehead wrote relatively little on the topic of ethics. Indeed, he wrote nothing focused solely and directly on the topic of ethics. What we have is many brief discussions within the corpus of his work. Whitehead was a broadly and deeply educated Cambridge mathematician who became a philosopher interested in speculative metaphysics. He was not focused on or even particularly interested in ethics per se. Given that Whitehead wrote little on the topic, it is probably ill advised to ask what Whitehead's ethics is or is not. There simply isn't enough to go on. Recognizing this, here and throughout references to "Whitehead's ethics" should be taken as shorthand for "a Whiteheadian-inspired ethics." In the end, I am less interested in policing and defending whether Whitehead himself held or would have agreed with the positions defended here than I am in developing and defending what I take to be the most valuable aspects of his work for developing a more logical, coherent, applicable, and adequate metaphysical foundation for environmental ethics. If Whitehead would have disagreed with my conclusions, so much the worse for him.

Categorizing a Whiteheadian Ethic

Whitehead made only occasional references to morality. One of those occasions is found in *Modes of Thought*, where he contends that "morality consists in the control of process so as to maximize importance. It is the aim at greatness of experience in the various dimensions belonging to it. . . . Morality is always the aim at that union of harmony, intensity, and vividness which involves the perfection of importance for that occasion."[5] It is on the interpretation of this definition, which Whitehead himself notes is "difficult to understand," that most of the scholarship on Whitehead's ethics has focused. In particular, it was Paul Arthur Schilpp's 1941 Library of Living Philosophers' essay "Whitehead's Moral Philosophy" that established the context for the interpretation of Whitehead's ethics in the twentieth century, making it an apt point of departure for our own analysis.

The argument that most concerns us at present is Schilpp's claim that Whitehead reduces importance to "interest" and that, therefore, Whitehead's moral philosophy should be classified as a "moral interest theory." Schilpp contends, "unless the essential meaning of Whitehead's notion of 'importance' has been missed, there have appeared no sufficiently adequate reasons for accepting this doctrine of the subordination of morals under 'importance.' "[6] The question, then, is whether Schilpp's characterization of importance is accurate. Does Whitehead make importance equivalent to interest? A closer examination of Whitehead's work reveals that Schilpp has indeed "missed" the essential meaning of Whitehead's notion of importance.

In his first lecture of *Modes of Thought*, which was dedicated to the topic of "importance," Whitehead defines importance in a particularly broad way: "Importance is a generic notion which has been obscured by the overwhelming prominence of a few of its innumerable species. The terms *morality, logic, religion, art*, have each of them been claimed as exhausting the whole meaning of importance. Each of them denotes a subordinate species. But the genus stretches beyond any finite group of species."[7] Insofar as morality, logic, religion, and art are merely a handful of the "innumerable species" of importance, we must take Whitehead's use of the term in a much wider and more fundamental sense than mere "interest." Indeed, Whitehead himself explicitly states that he understood importance to extend beyond interest: "There are two aspects to importance; one based on the unity of the Universe, the other on the individuality of the details. The word *interest* suggests the latter aspect; the word *importance* leans toward the former."[8] Given critics' claims to the contrary, it is ironic that Whitehead intentionally chose the term importance *because* it emphasized the unity of the universe, rather than the interests of individuals. The problem, as Whitehead himself recognizes, is that "the word *importance*, as in common use, has been reduced to suggest a silly little pomposity which is the extreme trivialization of its meaning here. This is a permanent difficulty of philosophic discussion; namely, that words must be stretched beyond their common meanings in the marketplace."[9] Yet, if importance is not limited to interest, then how does Whitehead conceive of it?

A closer analysis of *Modes of Thought* demonstrates that Whitehead makes importance equivalent not to interest, but to value. For instance, as we see in the following passages, Whitehead uses both importance and value to describe what is attained by actuality: "Our enjoyment of actuality is a realization of worth, good or bad. It is a value experience";[10] and "Actuality is the self-enjoyment of importance."[11] Similarly, as the following passages suggest, both importance and value have the same triadic structure of the self, other, whole: "But the sense of importance is not exclusively referent to the experiencing self. It is exactly this vague sense which differentiates itself into the disclosure of the whole, the many, and the self";[12] and "Everything has some value for itself, for others, and for the whole. This characterizes the meaning of actuality."[13] Finally, Whitehead also describes morality in terms of both value and importance: "Morality is the control of process so as to maximize importance";[14] and "Everything has some value for itself, for others, and for the whole. By reason of this character, constituting reality, the conception of morals arises."[15] Thus, value and importance have the same structure and equally characterize morality and actuality. Because of this, I contend that for Whitehead, value and importance are coextensive.[16]

In this way we can begin to understand just how much Whitehead intends to "stretch" the common usage of importance. He conceives of importance as not only the aim of morality, but of every process; that is, of reality itself. "The *generic* aim of process is the attainment of importance, in that species and to that extent which in that instance is possible."[17] This passage gives us a crucial insight into the relationship between Whitehead's systematically developed metaphysics and his nascent moral philosophy. If the general aim of *process* is at the attainment of importance and value, then *morality*, as a particular species of process, must necessarily aim at the attainment of importance and value as well. Morality, then, is but one species of the process of the universe, the whole of which aims at the attainment of importance.

Given that it is not appropriate to define Whitehead's moral philosophy as a moral interest theory, how are we to understand his conception of morality as "the control of process so as to maximize importance"? Since he defines morality as but one instance of the universal drive to maximize importance and value, perhaps Whitehead affirmed some form of totalizing utilitarianism? This is the view put forward by Clare Palmer in her *Environmental Ethics and Process Thinking* (1998).

The heart of Palmer's position lies in her understanding that, for process thinkers such as Whitehead, "the ultimate aim of ethical behaviour is to produce the greatest possible value for the consequent nature of God."[18] If all ethical behavior and all value is only to be understood in terms of how it contributes to God, then morality becomes the maximization of a certain form of experience (value, beauty, importance) for God. Thus, like utilitarianism, one ought to always choose the course of action that maximizes utility/happiness/value for the relevant entity, which, in our processive cosmos, is God. Given this interpretation, Palmer concludes that "value is contributory; God sums the value generated by actual occasions and within Himself; the system must therefore be consequentialist and totalizing."[19] By reducing an individual's value to its possible contribution to God's experience, Palmer argues, Whitehead constructs a totalizing form of utilitarianism and is therefore subject to the same concerns regarding, for instance, justice.

Palmer is certainly correct that any Whiteheadian moral philosophy will have a strong consequentialist element. Our aim as moral agents is to bring about "that union of harmony, intensity, and vividness which involves the perfection of importance for that occasion."[20] Where Palmer's interpretation shoots well wide of its mark, however, is in suggesting that Whitehead's thought leads to a totalizing form of utilitarianism. This position ultimately rests on her mistaken understanding that, for process thought, "what matters is the generation of rich experience for God."[21] The problem is that, while this interpretation of process thought, referred to as "contributionism," plays a prominent role in (some) process theology, it is doubtful Whitehead ever held such a view.[22] Yes, every individual has value for the whole, but, Whitehead insists, an individual's value for the whole cannot be separated from the value it has for itself and for others.

> At the base of existence is the sense of "worth." Now worth essentially presupposes that which is worthy. Here the notion of worth is not to be construed in a purely eulogistic sense. It is the sense of existence for its own sake, of existence which is its own justification, of existence with its own character.[23]
>
> Everything has some value for itself, for others, and for the whole. This characterizes the meaning of actuality. By reason of this character, constituting reality, the conception of morals arises. We have no right to deface the value experience which is the very essence of the universe. Existence, in its own nature, is the upholding of value intensity. Also no unit can separate itself from the others, and from the whole. And yet each unit exists in its own right. It upholds the value intensity for itself, and this involves sharing value intensity with the universe.[24]

Each part of this axiological triad of self, other, and whole *equally* characterizes actuality. "These three divisions are on a level. No one in any sense precedes the other."[25] (In the next chapter we will consider the similarity of Whitehead's triadic theory of value to Holmes Rolston's.) Yet if morality aims at the maximization of importance and value, but value is understood to extend not merely to the self but to others (the past actual occasions in an occasion's actual world) and to the whole (the totality of achieved occasions), then it becomes impossible to interpret Whitehead's moral philosophy as a totalizing form of utilitarianism aimed at maximizing intense experience for God (i.e., contributionism).[26] Morality aims to maximize the value experience not only of the whole or of God, but also of every individual for its own sake and for the sake of its community.

Thus, both Schilpp's interpretation (that Whitehead's philosophy is a moral interest theory) and Palmer's interpretation (that Whitehead's philosophy is a totalizing utilitarianism and, therefore, an unsuitable basis for environmental ethics) rest on faulty interpretations of Whitehead's metaphysics and axiology. Properly understood, Whitehead's philosophy is *not* a moral interest theory, and it does *not* support a totalizing, consequentialist form of utilitarianism.

INTRINSIC VALUE

It is difficult to find a philosophical system that gives a more central role to value than Whitehead's philosophy of organism. To be actual, for Whitehead, is to have value. Every individual—no matter how fleeting or insignificant—has value "for its own sake."[27] However, if it is to be properly understood, this claim must be put within the larger context of Whitehead's organic conception of individuality and its rejection of independent existence (see also chapter six on substance and chapter three on Rolston). In our processive cosmos, every individual begins from and is partially constituted by the achieved values of the past and completes itself by rendering its relationship to each of these past values determinate. Hence, an individual is what it is *because* it is internally and essentially related to other achieved values.[28] This process constitutes the ultimate fact of existence: "the many become one and are increased by one."[29] For Whitehead, therefore, an individual's *self*-value cannot be taken in isolation from the value it contributes to *others* and to the *whole*. The notion that "everything has some value for itself, for others, and for the whole" not only characterizes "the very meaning of actuality," but it is by reason of this fact that "the conception of morality arises."[30]

(This will be very important in chapter three when we relate Whitehead's distinctive, triadic theory of value and to Rolston's environmental ethics.) As suggested by the earlier passage about insects and the Parthenon, in contradistinction to the long-held conception of ethics as being limited to interhuman relationships (or perhaps between sentient animals as with utilitarianism), Whitehead affirms a conception of morality that excludes nothing from its scope. In a universe in which every individual is intrinsically valuable, nothing can be wholly excluded from moral concern. Every action is potentially moral or immoral. Given this triadic conception of value, then, the important question is not *whether* others have intrinsic value, but whether the intrinsic value of oneself, of others, and of the whole is *recognized*, *appreciated*, and *affirmed*. In this way we arrive at a sense of how broadly Whitehead conceives of the scope of ethics. As Whitehead conceives of it, the ideal of morality is to maximize or perfect the importance and value experience for the self, for others, and for the whole.

The novel nature of Whitehead's triadic axiology becomes apparent by relating it to John O'Neill's taxonomy of intrinsic value, according to which there are three different conceptions of intrinsic value: (1) noninstrumental value, (2) nonrelational value, or (3) objective value; each is delineated with a corresponding subscript. Into which of these categories does Whitehead's conception of value fall?

O'Neill defines intrinsic value$_1$ as "a synonym for non-instrumental value. An object has instrumental value insofar as it is a means to some other end. An object has intrinsic value if it is an end in itself. Intrinsic goods are goods that other goods are good for the sake of."[31] On the one hand, we might say Whitehead embraces intrinsic value$_1$. Every achievement of reality is indeed an end in itself and thereby has value for itself. Yet, we must recall that, according to his relational event ontology, to be an "individual" is to be in *constitutive* interdependence with every other event in the cosmos. (See chapter six for a more complete discussion of Whitehead's distinct conception of individuality and its significance for environmental ethics.) Thus, for Whitehead, to have value for oneself necessarily means becoming a value for subsequent occasions; to be an end is at once to be a means. To become is to have value for oneself, which entails becoming a value for others and for the whole. Thus, for Whitehead, *nothing* has noninstrumental value or intrinsic value$_1$.

What about intrinsic value$_2$, according to which "intrinsic value is used to refer to the value an object has solely in virtue of its 'intrinsic properties' "?[32] As O'Neill explains, intrinsic value$_2$ is based on G. E. Moore's view that "intrinsic properties" are those a thing possesses in total isolation from other beings or "solely on their non-relational properties."[33] It should be clear that, according to the environmental metaphysics being defended, there are no purely nonrelational properties. "There is no such mode of existence; every entity is only to be understood in terms of the way in which it is interwoven with the rest of the Universe."[34] If Whitehead is right about the fundamentally interrelational structure of reality, *nothing* has intrinsic value$_2$. (See chapter seven for an extended discussion of the relationship, both biographical and philosophical, between Whitehead and Moore.)

That leaves us with intrinsic value$_3$ which, O'Neill explains, "is used as a synonym for 'objective value' i.e., value that an object possesses independently of the valuations of valuers."[35] While O'Neill goes on to elaborate several subvarieties of this third notion of intrinsic value based on different senses of "independent," these nuances will not be required to dispatch with this third variety. As with intrinsic value$_2$, intrinsic value$_3$ finds no home within an organicist environmental metaphysics. As we will see in chapter three when we consider the protracted debate over value between Callicott and Rolston, if we join Whitehead in rejecting the metaphysical bifurcation of subject and object and affirm that every achievement of reality is at once a subject and an object—or, in Whitehead's technical terms, a subject-super-ject—we see that every entity is a subject (valuer) with value for itself that becomes an object (value) for others. As Whitehead puts it, "Everything has some value for itself, for others, and for the whole. This characterizes the meaning of actuality."[36] It would seem that, grounded in a relational, organicist metaphysics of value as defended here, we have something truly distinctive: intrinsic value$_4$.

This affirmation of the centrality of intrinsic value puts the current volume squarely at odds with environmental pragmatists[37] who have been calling on environmental philosophers to, as Anthony Weston puts it, "abandon the old preoccupation with intrinsic value entirely."[38] In chapter eight I will consider in detail environmental pragmatism and its relationship to the present volume. Here I consider the environmental pragmatists' rejection of intrinsic value. Katie McShane provides a helpful threefold categorization of environmental pragmatists' attacks on intrinsic value:

1. Morito and Weston: "the notion that things can possess intrinsic value independently of relations they have to other things suggest a peculiarly atomistic picture of the world."[39]

2. Norton: "believing in intrinsic value would commit us to a metaphysically elaborate (and therefore dubious) picture of the world."[40]

3. Light and Norton: "intrinsic value claims . . . seem to be unnecessary."[41]

Let's consider each of these three positions in turn.

The first attack on intrinsic value, defended by Morito and Weston, seems to derive once again from the influence of G. E. Moore, whose naturalistic fallacy I consider at length in chapter seven. Moore defended the view that one can discern whether something has intrinsic value by considering "what things are such that, if they existed *by themselves*, in total isolation, we should yet judge their existence to be good."[42] Morito and Weston are right to worry that a Moorean view of intrinsic value is built on latent metaphysical assumptions and that the "isolation method" implies an atomistic conception of reality that is at odds with the relational worldview revealed by physics, chemistry, biology, and ecology.

However, this first attack on intrinsic value bears no relationship to the present organicist environmental metaphysics as it is premised on a relational worldview that explicitly rejects the idea of "independent existence" and affirms a fully and totally relational model of intrinsic value such that to be is to have value for oneself, for others, and for the whole. Thus, I am in complete agreement with McShane:

> Once we give up the idea that believing in intrinsic value means holding some sort of hyper-atomistic picture of the world on which the only thing that matters for purposes of ethics is what each individual thing is like in its own right, there is less reason to be disturbed by the claim that our deeply interconnected world contains things that deserve to be intrinsically valued. Nothing in our world exists in isolation and there is no reason that we should want to think of things just as isolated individuals for the purposes of ethics.[43]

There is no reason to attach ontological independence to the concept of intrinsic value as the Moorean tradition suggests.

On its face, it would seem that Bryan Norton's attack on intrinsic value strikes at the heart of the present project, for it is most certainly the case that the present volume can rightly be seen as a "metaphysically elaborate" defense of intrinsic value. However, Norton is not just rejecting the value of metaphysics for environmental ethics, though he is surely doing that as well, but more specifically the view that intrinsic value can exist "prior to human conceptualization, prior to any worldview."[44] As McShane explains:

> The main target of this criticism seems to be the views of Holmes Rolston, III, who claims that for nature to be intrinsically valuable it has to be the case that the property of value, which is a natural property just as *being made of carbon* is a natural property, exists in the world independently of the existence of any conscious minds. On Rolston's view, the world had value in it before we came along, and it will have value in it long after we are gone.[45]

This is a serious concern not only for Rolston, but also for the present volume. A complete answer to Norton's challenge requires the analyses in chapters three (where I consider Rolston's axiology) and seven (where I address Moore and the naturalistic fallacy). For now, it will be sufficient to mention that one of the benefits of grounding environmental ethics in general and one's theory of value in particular in an organicist metaphysics such as that defended by Whitehead is that one has the means by which to overcome the substance-property metaphysics and subject-predicate logic it spawned. By recognizing that reality is ultimately a dynamic, ongoing process of achievement, ceaselessly moving from subjective determination to objective determination, it is possible to avoid entirely the idea that there are substances with "natural properties." If intrinsic properties refer to properties that are distinct from human or other perceivers, then of course there are a great many such properties. However, if "intrinsic property" means properties that are completely independent, then the philosophy of organism disputes that any such category of reality exists. There is no independence of existence![46]

Again, we find that this second critique of intrinsic value is itself predicated on a latent and mistaken metaphysics. That value is merely an anthropogenic projection onto an otherwise valueless material world is itself only defensible based on a Humean materialism in which all moorings between ontology and axiology have been cast off. However, once one recognizes that the modern conception of vacuous actuality—of matter that is inert, passive, valueless stuff—we can also recognize that to come into existence is to be an achievement of beauty and value. Thus, of course there are values independent of any mind. Of course Rolston is right that there are values present prior to the arrival (evolution) of humans and after their departure (extinction). To be is to be an achievement of value. Norton's worry is a fictional concern spawned by a misguided metaphysics.

The third type of critique, which McShane locates in the work of both Light and Norton, is not so much that the concept of intrinsic value is false as unnecessary and unproductive. It is unnecessary because "the general public is not likely to be moved by claims about so-called intrinsic value in nature" and unproductive because "insisting on intrinsic value claims will make specialists in other fields (e.g., economics) uninterested in what environmental ethicists have to say, since one of the grounding assumptions of these fields is that all value is value-to-humans."[47] For a complete response to these concerns, readers are encouraged to jump to chapter eight on environmental pragmatism. Here it will be sufficient to note that this third type of critique, even if true, does not show that the concept of "intrinsic value" is false, but that it is practically unuseful or unproductive. That is, it would seem that Light's and Norton's concern is that the concept of intrinsic value is not instrumentally valuable. This is an odd standard to use indeed. But it need not detain us as we are concerned with an adequate understanding of the nature of value and its relationship to the structure of reality. We find that ethics itself takes on a different character when situated within a relational event ontology.

Morality in the Making

According to the dominant theories of morality—such as contract theory, utilitarianism, or deontology, which were born out of modern metaphysical projects—the aim of moral philosophy is to construct abstract moral theories capable of determining what one ought to do in any given moral conflict. Although testing the adequacy of proposed moral theories is itself a laudatory goal, from the fallibilist's viewpoint, it is problematic that the motivation behind this procedure often rests on the presupposition that moral inquiry leads to—or is, in principle, capable of—absolute certainty. However, as we discussed more fully in chapter one on metaphysics, pragmatist[48] and process philosophers rightly reject this notion of inquiry, acknowledging that, because absolute certainty is an unrealizable ideal, fallibility is inescapable. Thus, given a Whiteheadian organicist environmental metaphysics, we should no longer understand the task of moral philosophy to be the construction of absolute and unchanging moral laws. The limitations of moral philosophy imposed by the fallibility of human inquiry must finally be recognized—no longer should one expect moral theories to be capable of abstractly prescribing what ought or ought not to be done prior to a particular concrete situation. Unlike elementary mathematics, for example, every moral problem does not have a single indisputable answer existing prior to its solution that we need only divine and then codify in a moral law. Morality, like life, is inherently "messy." Yet without qualification, the rejection of moral codes is likely to be misunderstood as entailing a gross relativism wherein each culture or individual defines what is right. However, upon closer examination, we find that what is needed is not the wholesale rejection of moral laws, but a dramatic revision in how we conceive of their nature and function. In a sense, we should conceive of moral laws as being analogous to physical laws.

Initially, this comparison between moral and physical laws may seem to imply the opposite of my intention. Indeed, for many, science is often understood to epitomize the pursuit of absolutely certain truths. The problem with this interpretation is that it embodies an inaccurate understanding of the nature of scientific theories. Of course, there is little doubt that many scientific theories do possess a great many truths. What is being denied is not that one account may be truer—more explanatorily adequate—than another, but that any of these "truths" are of the sort that could be called "final." The comparison between the laws of morality and the laws of nature is meant to highlight the fact that moral inquiry is a form of inquiry in general and that all forms of inquiry are inherently fallible. Accordingly, the "laws" of science are not infallible formulations immune to development or revision; they are exceedingly probable formulations of observed regularities. Thus, although scientists may still use the language of "laws," few continue to perceive them as absolute formulations as, for example, Newton did.[49] If the last century's scientific discoveries have taught us anything, it should be that the "truths" of science are limited. (Again, see chapter one on metaphysics as fallible.)

Similarly, as Whitehead notes, by carrying us beyond "our own direct immediate insights," abstract moral codes are "useful, and indeed essential, for civilization. But we only weaken their influence by exaggerating their status."[50] Thus, Whitehead does not reject moral codes per se. What he rejects is the notion that one could achieve a timeless expression of moral obligation. Pushed beyond the environment for which it was designed, a moral code becomes nothing more than a "vacuous statement of abstract irrelevancies."[51] Thus, just as physical laws are those "forms of activity which happen to prevail within the vast epoch of activity which we dimly discern,"[52] moral codes are those patterns of behavior that are likely to promote the "evolution" of a given environment toward its "proper perfection."[53] Moral and physical laws are not, therefore, timeless expressions of absolute verities.[54] Just as new experiments may force the revision and reinterpretation of physical laws, the emergence of new forms of social order will inevitably require the revision and refinement of our moral laws.

Just as there is no final or absolute certainty in physics that would allow one to make perfect predictions about future physical events, there is no final truth in ethics that would allow one to dogmatically determine in advance the good in any particular situation.[55] Like the scientist who must wait and revise their conclusions based on the discovery of new evidence, if we are to lead the moral life, we also must continually and resolutely revise our conclusions in light of the goods we can presently see, and resist the temptation to codify these conclusions in absolute moral laws. Just as we have moved beyond the notion that nature's "laws" give us infallible access to natural processes, we must abandon dogmatic views of morality. And just as new experiments may force the revision and reinterpretation of physical laws, the emergence of new forms of social order will inevitably require the revision and refinement of our moral laws. The point, of course, is that science is no more capable of *absolute truths* than any other field of investigation, if by absolute truths we mean something that is final and indubitable. The fact of the matter is that, as Hume showed long ago, scientific "truths" are not absolutely certain; they are more or less probable outcomes based on empirical observation.[56] Thus, as Whitehead once noted, the *true* foe of morality is not change, but "stagnation."[57]

Following Whitehead and his American pragmatist cousins, then, scientists and policymakers need to recognize the inherently provisional and fallible nature of their conclusions. (See chapter eight on environmental pragmatism for more on this important point.) Once we recognize that there are no scientific "facts" in the sense of absolutely certain or final truths, we will recognize that we have no choice but to act on tentative formulations and provisional conclusions. We have no choice, and have never had any choice, but to act on the best state of our understanding, with all of the doubt, risk, and messiness this involves. This is not to say that every truth is as established as every other, nor is it an acceptance of gross relativism. Rather, what I am suggesting is that a Whiteheadian approach to our social and ecological challenges will begin by abandoning this epistemological chimera called "absolute certainty" and embrace fully our unavoidable fallibility. More study will always be needed, but that does not justify the abdication of our responsibility to act today on the best state of our understanding.

Yet in our effort to avoid dogmatism, Whitehead recognizes that we must be equally wary of embracing the opposite extreme and reject all moral codes for some form of pure relativism or crass subjectivism. Novel and intense experiences are only achievable within a sufficiently stable environment. Law and order, for instance, are critical to the functioning of complex human communities. The problem, however, is that too often the conservative becomes obstructionist, particularly in debates over morality. Whitehead has a colorful way of putting this point: "It is true that the defence of morals is the battle-cry which best rallies stupidity against change. Perhaps countless ages ago respectable amœbæ refused to migrate from ocean to dry land—refusing in defence of morals."[58] In attempting to defend absolute, unchanging moral laws, the "pure conservative is fighting against the essence of the universe."[59] To be adequate, therefore, *morality must at once be conservative and adventurous.* Morality requires that we intrepidly revise our moral laws in light of new forms of order, while simultaneously preventing relapse to "lower levels." This is what Whitehead calls the "paradox concerning morals."[60] Ultimately, then, the problem with the idea of absolute moral codes is that they presuppose a static conception of reality. If reality were static, then it would, in principle, be possible to formulate a moral code that described how one always ought to act. However, in light of our dynamic and processive cosmos, such a static formulation is unavailable.

This brings us to a second point: final truths (whether in religion, morality, or science) are unattainable not only due to the finitude and fallibility of human inquirers, but also because we live in what the theologian John F. Haught calls an "unfinished universe."[61] The notion that one could achieve anything like a final or absolute formulation in any field of study presupposes that one's object is static. Thankfully, we do not live in such a universe. Over the last century scientists have consistently discovered that the universe is not a plenum of lifeless, valueless facts mechanistically determined by absolute laws. Rather, we live in a processive cosmos that is a dynamic field of *events* organized in complex webs of interdependence.

Given that every individual in our universe, no matter how small or seemingly insignificant, has some degree of value, the scope of our direct moral concern[62] can exclude nothing. Thus, in rather sharp contrast to the invidious forms of anthropocentrism that characterize much of Western moral thought, our scope of direct moral concern cannot be limited to humans, to sentient beings, or even to all living beings. Morality is not anthropocentric, but neither is it sentiocentric or biocentric. In affirming the value of *every* individual, we must begin to recognize that *every* relation is potentially a moral relation. "The destruction of a man, or of an insect, or of a tree, or of the Parthenon, may be moral or immoral. . . . Whether we destroy or whether we preserve, our action is moral if we have thereby safeguarded the importance [or value] of experience so far as it depends on that concrete instance in the world's history."[63] Morality is not merely about how we ought to act toward and among other human beings, other sentient beings, or even other living beings. Rather, morality is fundamentally about how we (moral agents) comport ourselves in the world, how we relate to and interact with every form of existence.

To summarize my position thus far, in recognizing the fallibility of human knowers and the dynamic nature of the known, a Whiteheadian organicist approach insists that ethics steadfastly recognize the limits of moral inquiry, carefully navigating between the rocks of dogmatic absolutism and the whirlpool of gross relativism. The recognition of nature's dynamism furthermore requires that philosophers finally abandon the artificial bifurcations (dualisms) and unjustified reductions (physicalism and materialism) that distort and destroy the interdependent relationships constituting reality. The world revealed by the last century of scientific investigation can no longer support a mechanistic model that describes the natural world in terms of vacuous facts determined by absolute laws. In its place, I here defend the adoption of an organic model that conceives of reality as vibrant, open, and processive. On this model, individuals are conceived of as ongoing events situated in vast webs of interdependence, each achieving value for themselves, for others, and for the whole of reality.

Moral Ideals

If Whitehead's moral philosophy is neither a moral interest theory nor a totalizing utilitarianism, and if it does not affirm any of the three classic forms of intrinsic value, how are we to classify it? As I have argued previously, we will fail to understand Whitehead's possible contributions to ethics if we insist on trying to force it into ethical pigeonholes constructed by metaphysical projects Whitehead's philosophy of organism was explicitly designed to overcome.[64] Any genuinely Whiteheadian ethic will ultimately be as novel as the metaphysics on which it is based. First, given the equivalence of actuality and value, the scope of morality may exclude nothing.

Any action may be moral or immoral. "Whether we destroy or whether we preserve, our action is moral if we have thereby safeguarded the importance of experience so far as it depends on that concrete instance in the world's history."[65] Second, within an organicist environmental metaphysics, the primary task of environmental ethics (indeed all ethics) is not the divination of moral laws but the development and revision of moral *ideals* that seek to lure, rather than coerce. That is, morality concerns itself not with codifying certain behaviors, but with the formulation of moral ideals. "In ethical ideals we find the supreme example of consciously formulated ideas acting as a driving force effecting transitions from social state to social state. Such ideas are at once gadflies irritating, and beacons luring, the victims among whom they dwell."[66] Thus, perhaps the most important function of moral philosophy is in formulating, testing, and revising our moral ideals. This is perhaps one of the chief functions of ethics: to formulate, pursue, and continually revise moral ideals that guide or lure action toward ever-greater forms of beauty and value.

The respected Dewey scholar John Lachs argues that such an approach, grounding our moral frameworks in unachievable moral ideals, is not only philosophically misguided—it is psychologically damaging.

> The perverse desire to heap infinite obligations on finite individuals guarantees moral failure. Similarly, demanding perfection of our experiences and relationships is a certain way of making life miserable. We do much better if we heed the counsels of finitude and refuse to seek what cannot be obtained. This involves both judgment and resolve: we must be able to decide what is good enough and willing to embrace it as sufficient for our purposes, that is, adequate to satisfy our desires. The romantic quest for the perfect destroys human relationships and converts what could be happy lives into the misery of endless seeking and striving.[67]

Instead of pursuing an unachievable ideal, pursuing a perfection that will never come, Lachs argues that we need to learn to be satisfied with what is "good enough."

> As affirmation of our finitude, it [what is good enough] negates our Faustian tendency to want to have and do everything. It rejects the relevance of the ideal of perfection and strikes at the root of our compulsion to pursue unreachable ideals. It liberates

us to the enjoyment of the possible without eliminating standards or moral effort. It enables us to still our will by achieving what we can and celebrating what we do.[68]

Lachs is clear to note that his position does not require that we settle "for the dregs or live a compromise accepting shoddy goods."[69] Rather, he argues, those who allow themselves to be satisfied by what is "good enough . . . enjoy what is fine and permit themselves to feel fulfilled, refusing to search for some elusive ideal."[70]

Let us attempt to formalize a version of the argument behind Lachs's attack on moral idealism by looking at the defense of being "realistic." Moral theory P is either realistic or idealistic but never both.

1. P is realistic if its ends are achievable.

2. P is idealistic if its ends cannot be fully achieved.

3. Only moral theories that commend us toward an achievable end ought to be subscribed to.

4. Therefore, one ought not to adopt P if it is idealistic.[71]

Lachs's arguments notwithstanding, the problem with this argument is not with the third premise. Indeed, I grant that true ideals are *not* fully achievable. Rather, I suggest that the problem is with the fourth premise, that only fully achievable ends are realistic, are worth pursuing. It will be easiest to illustrate my point by considering a couple of examples.

To pull out the key points of contrast, let us consider Adolf Hitler's (and some contemporary white nationalists') ideal of creating a "perfect" race of blue-eyed, blonde-haired people. It seems to misunderstand the moral situation to say that the problem with Hitler's program is that he was being "too idealistic," that he could never fully achieve his aim, and that, therefore, he should have been more "realistic." The problem is not that his aim is "too idealistic." The problem is that it is a terrible, terrible ideal. To see this more clearly, let's take a rather different example.

In his powerful 1963 speech on the steps of the Lincoln Memorial, Martin Luther King Jr. came to collect on the "promissory note" drafted in the Declaration of Independence.[72] He passionately described his vision for a world in which people of all races and creeds lived together in mutual respect and harmony. This "dream" is clearly and even explicitly idealistic.

And, as an ideal, it is *not* fully achievable. We are not, nor will we ever be, in a world of perfect equality. However, it seems to misunderstand the moral situation to say that, because King's ideal of equality is not fully achievable, we should not pursue it, that we should be "realistic." Or, to use Lachs's formulation, would the proper response be to point out that King's ideal of equality is a "perverse desire to heap infinite obligations on finite individuals"? In pursuing this unattainable ideal of perfect equality, isn't King "guarantee[ing] moral failure" and "making life miserable"? Surely this misunderstands the moral situation. Indeed, I would suggest that this reveals a flawed understanding of the role and nature of moral ideals.

Ideals are not meaningful because they are *achievable*. They are meaningful because they *define* success and failure, better and worse. Without moral ideals, making comparative moral judgments becomes arbitrary. Our ideals are the standards by which we judge the success of our actions. Although we can never *fully* achieve an ideal, we can get closer to or farther away from achieving them. To borrow a geometrical example, moral ideals are like asymptotes: just as an asymptote can infinitely approach, but never reach, a limit, our actions can get closer to or farther away from an ideal. The Emancipation Proclamation (1863), Women's Suffrage (1913), and the Civil Rights Act (1964) each brought the United States a step closer to achieving the ideal of equality. Voter-suppression measures and gerrymandering each move us farther away.

Just as one cannot avoid having a metaphysics, one simply cannot do away with moral ideals. One can choose not to explore or understand the conception of the good that is the basis of one's actions, but one's actions always occur within the context of an understanding of what is good. This is the root of the problem with Lachs's view that we ought to stop beating ourselves about the head and shoulders and instead be satisfied with what is "good enough." The problem is that "good enough" only makes sense relative to what is *good*. Like the environmental pragmatists, in abandoning the project of defining and defending moral ideals, Lachs has lost any basis from which to criticize any given course of action.[73] Despite his claim that we are "rightly horrified" by "destructive processes" like ethnic cleansing, Lachs has removed any basis from which to justify his horror.[74] There is something disingenuous, indeed something dangerous, in refusing to declare and scrutinize one's values and ideals. One can no more avoid axiology than one can avoid metaphysics. One is free to choose one's worldview, but one is not free not to have one. The real question, then, is not whether one *has* moral ideals, but whether one is willing to articulate and defend them. It is here, I believe, that a Whiteheadian approach can be of some assistance.

Rather than jettisoning moral ideals as being the source of infinite dissatisfaction and moral self-flagellation, we might instead recognize that part of the reason we are never satisfied with what is "good enough" is that we may be pursuing the wrong ideals. For instance, if our understanding of happiness is defined by the pursuit of physical pleasure or the acquisition of wealth, then Lachs is quite right that we will never feel satisfied and we set ourselves up for misery and failure. The more pleasure and wealth we have, the more we seem to want. Enough, as Lachs notes, is never good enough. The Dalai Lama puts this point well when he notes that trying to achieve happiness through our senses is like drinking saltwater to sate our thirst: the more we partake, the more our desire and thirst grows.[75] We should indeed learn to be satisfied with what is good enough, instead of aspiring to always have more.

However, contrary to Lachs's conclusion, the problem in this case is not that we are pursuing an ideal that is unachievable, that is unable to be satisfied. Rather, the problem is that material wealth acquisition is a poor ideal. As the Dalai Lama goes on to argue, the situation looks quite different if we pursue a different moral ideal. He suggests the moral ideal of *nying je chenmo* or unconditional love and compassion for all beings.[76] "Of course," the Dalai Lama admits, "even as an ideal, the notion of developing unconditional compassion is daunting. Most people, including myself, must struggle even to reach the point where putting others' interest on a par with our own becomes easy. We should not allow this to put us off, however."[77] As the Dalai Lama argues, unlike the aim at wealth or pleasure, the more we are compassionate or the more we give of ourselves, the more fulfilled, the more satisfied we become. Thus, although as an ideal unconditional love and compassion for all things can never be fully achieved, the closer we get to this ideal the more deeply satisfied we become.

It turns out, then, that this debate over being "realistic" or "idealistic" is a false dilemma. In this way, I submit, the only way to "be realistic," to bring about desirable states in the world, is to concretely pursue the realization of our moral ideals. Or, as the Dalai Lama puts it, "Ideals are the engine of progress. To ignore this and say merely that we need to be 'realistic' in politics is severely mistaken."[78] The only *realistic* actions are those in service of worthwhile *ideals*. The question, then, is not whether we *have* ideals, but whether we have the courage to *declare, scrutinize,* and *pursue* our ideals. Thus, I submit that the real questions one ought to be asking oneself are:

1. First, what are my moral ideals?

2. Second, are they worth pursuing?

3. Third, if they are worth pursuing, what do they require of me here and now?[79]

Note that, despite its teleological function, this understanding of moral ideals is quite different than an Aristotelian telos. As we discuss more fully in chapter seven, unlike Aristotelian teloi, moral ideals are not fixed; they are dynamic and evolving. For instance, when the Declaration of Independence was first penned, its beautiful statement that "all men are created equal" only applied to white, landholding men. However, over time the understanding (content) and application of this ideal has rightly been reinterpreted to include children, women, and people of every ethnic heritage. The ideal itself is an end-in-view, a "developmental telos," an evolving subjective aim.[80] Our actions are constantly in pursuit of the ideals that define success and progress, but our ongoing pursuit of our ideals modifies and shapes their content over time.

Thus, with Whitehead, I would argue that the real threat is not moral ideals, but their ossification into static moral codes. Whitehead argues that moral codes are "useful, and indeed essential, for civilization[81]" in that they can "promote the evolution of that environment towards its proper perfection."[82] The problem, he notes, is that we often "exaggerate their status" by treating them as fixed laws.[83] Our difficult dual aim, then, is simultaneously to conserve achieved forms of order while seeking higher forms. "*Morals consists in the aim at the ideal,* and at its lowest it concerns the prevention of relapse to lower levels."[84] This delicate balance between conservation and adventure is what Whitehead calls the "paradox concerning morals."[85] We must intrepidly and continually define and redefine our moral ideals, if we are to avoid the "deadly foe" of "stagnation"[86] and the sweet "anesthetic" death of "tameness."[87] However, these changes must be made " 'hand in hand, with wand'ring steps and slow.' "[88]

In this sense, Lachs and the environmental pragmatists (see chapter eight) are right that ethics is *not* about the pursuit of a perfect moral code that could once and for all define our moral obligations. As William James put it, "there is no such thing possible as an ethical philosophy dogmatically made up in advance."[89] However, Lachs (and the environmental pragmatists) is wrong in assuming that this requires that we abandon moral ideals. As Whitehead puts it, "Morality does not indicate what you are to do in mythological abstractions. It does concern the *general ideal* which should be the justification for any particular objective."[90] Ideals are the "supreme example of consciously formulated ideas acting as a driving force effecting transitions from social state to social state. Such ideas are at once gadflies irritating, and beacons luring, the victims among whom they dwell."[91]

This dual function of moral ideals as both beacons luring and gadflies irritating is beautifully illustrated by the opening lines of King's speech. "Five score years ago, a great American, in whose symbolic shadow we stand today, signed the Emancipation Proclamation. This momentous decree came as a great *beacon light* of hope to millions of Negro slaves who had been seared in the flames of withering injustice. It came as a joyous daybreak to end the long night of their captivity."[92] The moral ideal of equality is a "beacon light" luring us to that beloved community. However, the ideal of equality is not only a beacon luring, but it is also a gadfly irritating and chastising us for our failure to live up to its high standard. King continues:

> But one hundred years later, the Negro still is not free. One hundred years later, the life of the Negro is still sadly crippled by the manacles of segregation and the chains of discrimination. One hundred years later, the Negro lives on a lonely island of poverty in the midst of a vast ocean of material prosperity. One hundred years later, the Negro is still languished in the corners of American society and finds himself an exile in his own land. And so we've come here today to dramatize a shameful condition.[93]

As gadflies irritating, moral ideals are the indispensable driving force behind all progress. They can help create what in his "Letter from Birmingham Jail" King calls "creative tension."[94] As Whitehead notes in *Adventures of Ideas*, although "itself destructive and evil," discord can create "the positive feeling of a quick shift of aim from the tameness of outworn perfection to some other ideal with its freshness still upon it. Thus the value of Discord is a tribute to the merits of Imperfection."[95] Our ideals define our direction, they define success and failure, and they "nerve all civilized effort."[96]

In this way, Whitehead's approach to ethics and its defense of moral idealism is well aligned with the founding aim since at least Lynn White Jr.'s 1967 "Historical Roots of the Ecologic Crisis." The attempt to develop and defend a more adequate worldview is, in a sense, very idealistic in that it is attempting fallibly to develop and defend a more adequate worldview defining what we are, how we are related to what is, and how we ought to relate to it. For a Whiteheadian, morality, like every process, aims at the attainment of value. In this sense we have found that—contrary to the contemporary ethical offspring of modern metaphysical projects—the aim and nature of ethics grows out of and is continuous with the aim and nature of the creative advance of the universe. Ethics is but one species of process, the whole of which aims at the attainment of value and importance.

Chapter 3

Whitehead, Callicott, and Rolston

In 1978 Kenneth Goodpaster expressed what would become a central concern of environmental ethics: defining the scope of "moral considerability."[1] To put this in the interrogative, environmental ethics seeks to answer the question: What must an individual be like in order to be deserving of direct moral consideration (i.e., for its own sake) and, therefore, direct moral duties? It was the attempt to answer this question that brought many in environmental ethics to focus on what J. Baird Callicott has called the "most critical and most recalcitrant theoretical problem of environmental ethics, the problem of intrinsic value in nature."[2]

Of course, such a value discourse is not new to Western philosophy. In the work of Immanuel Kant, for instance, we find an axiological system in which only those beings with value for their own sake (that are ends in themselves) deserve moral direct consideration (respect); they are owed direct duties. Beings that lack intrinsic value have merely instrumental value (what he calls "price"); they are merely a means, not also ends in themselves.[3] In keeping with modern, dualist metaphysics, Kant contends that only fully rational beings are autonomous agents who set ends for themselves. Thus, for Kant, only rational beings have dignity and deserve respect. All other beings—whether tiger, toad, tulip, or toaster—have *merely* instrumental value (price); they are "things" and are owed, at best, indirect duties.[4] Against the current of much of the history of Western moral theory, many environmental ethicists went about defending broader conceptions of intrinsic value that included variously all sentient beings (sentiocentrism), all living beings (biocentrism), or all living beings and their environments (ecocentrism). The unifying theme between these diverse positions was the rejection of anthropocentrism (and ratiocentrism, in the case of Kant) or the view that all meaning and value derives from something's relationship to human beings.

This chapter is divided into two unequal parts. In the first part, my goal is to demonstrate that philosophers will have better luck in making progress on environmental ethics' "central and most recalcitrant problem" by explicitly grounding it in Whitehead's organicist metaphysics, the philosophy of organism. Specifically, I consider the significance of Whitehead's thought in the context of the extended debate between J. Baird Callicott and Holmes Rolston over intrinsic value—whether it is merely subjective or also sometimes objective. Building on this, the second part focuses more narrowly on relating Whitehead's and Rolston's respective projects. What we will find is surprisingly deep lines of convergence and mutual support. In this second part I begin by examining Rolston's efforts to define the differences between organisms and machines and the role that teleology plays in this contrast. Given that Whitehead's project is an extended effort to overcome the modern, mechanistic view of nature in favor of a philosophy of organism, I suggest that Whitehead's project provides a metaphysical basis for Rolston's claims. Indeed, I contend that Rolston can't recover teleology, secure objective value, and embrace contemporary science without something like Whitehead's system. A chief impediment for Rolston in adopting a Whiteheadian position seems to be his (Rolston's) insistence that nonliving beings are simply "inert." That is, Rolston retains something of a modern, Cartesian account of matter. As Callicott has argued and as we discussed in chapter one, this view of matter has long been disproven by advances in physics. Whitehead's unique philosophy of organism provides just the sort of position Rolston needs to retain important metaphysical distinctions between different types of entities without introducing ontological bifurcations.

Building on this discussion of organisms, machines, and teleology, we will then consider delightful symmetries between Whitehead's and Rolston's accounts of the relationship between organisms and their environment. Both, it turns out, embrace an organism-in-environment model; Whitehead simply extends it beyond biological organisms to chemical, atomic, and subatomic levels, arguing that every individual is only what it is because of its environment.

Though Rolston is consistent in his avoidance of explicitly discussing, much less defending, the metaphysical assumptions on which his ethical commitments are based, at times these commitments do become apparent. A chief example of this is Rolston's claim that there is value wherever there is "positive creativity." Despite the importance of this claim for Rolston's ethics, it seems largely to remain an assertion, perhaps grounded on a deep intuition with some indirect support from his reading of the evidences of science. As I have argued, although one can avoid defending one's assumptions about the basic structure and nature of reality (metaphysics), one cannot avoid having such assumptions. To actually defend this critically important claim, which ultimately grounds his axiology, Rolston needs to provide an account of what this "creativity" is and how it comes about. I will show that here, again, Whitehead's philosophy of organism is a great aid to Rolston. For Whitehead, "creativity" is the "category of the ultimate." Indeed, much of Whitehead's life work can be seen as an attempt to provide an open-ended, fallibilistic metaphysics that accounts for the "creative advance" of the universe.

Finally, in the last section of the second part, I will return to the discussion of Rolston's theory of value. Focusing more directly on a comparison of Whitehead's and Rolston's respective theories of value, we find another surprising symmetry, with both adopting a triadic theory of value. Though there are important differences between their respective positions, we find that, as with the organism-in-environment concept, their respective axiologies are stronger if taken together than they are apart. Rolston would benefit from a metaphysical account that anchors value in the achievements of actuality itself, and Whitehead would benefit from Rolston's account of systemic value, which is likely an improvement on Whitehead's notion of the "value of the whole."

Environmental Ethics' Recalcitrant Problem

To begin to make good on our central thesis—that environmental ethics needs an adequate, metaphysical basis and that Whitehead's philosophy of organism is the most adequate candidate for such a task—let us begin with the "value wars" between two of the most important figures in environmental ethics: J. Baird Callicott and Holmes Rolston III. To start, let's consider the axiology of each in turn so that we might then evaluate how a grounding in an organicist process metaphysics would affect their positions.

In his early work (pre-1985), Callicott explicitly endorsed an anthropogenic, subjectivist axiology according to which all value is "projected" onto a natural world that "excites" the value.[5] Thus, for Callicott, "intrinsic value ultimately depends upon human valuers."[6] Intrinsic value is not "in the world" objectively; it is the subjective projection of values onto an otherwise valueless universe. Though he rejects axiological subjectivism, Rolston does give an apt characterization of the subjectivist position: "According to the reigning [subjectivist] paradigm, there is no value without an experiencing valuer, no percepts without a perceiver, no deeds without a doer, no targets without an aimer. Valuing is *felt* preferring; value is the product of this process."[7] Callicott defended a form of this subjectivist axiology by grounding it in a neo-Humean/Darwinian moral sentiments view. According to such a view, there are no intrinsic values "out there." As Hume put in his *Treatise*:

> An action, or sentiment, or character is virtuous or vicious; why? because its view causes a pleasure or uneasiness of a particular kind. In giving a reason, therefore, for the pleasure of uneasiness we sufficiently explain the vice or virtue. To have the sense of virtue, is nothing but to *feel* a satisfaction of a particular kind from the contemplation of a character. The very *feeling* constitutes our praise or admiration. We go no farther; nor do we enquire into the cause of the satisfaction. We do not infer a character to be virtuous, because it pleases: but in feeling that it pleases after such a particular manner, we in effect feel that it is virtuous. The case is the same in our judgments concerning all kinds of beauty, and tastes, and sensations.[8]

According to this view, presuming, as much of Western philosophy does, that human beings are the only subjects, there is no value independent of human valuing. All value is anthropogenic. (We will return to this key point from Hume in our discussion of the naturalistic fallacy in chapter seven.)

Though, as we will discuss, Callicott's views change considerably over his career, Rolston's position has not appreciably changed. From his first essay on environmental ethics in 1975, Rolston has steadfastly sought to defend the view that, while human subjects undoubtedly do project a great many values onto the world (e.g., sentimental value, economic value, cultural value, educational value), in addition to being value creators we are also value discoverers.[9] Note that Rolston is *not* denying the subjectivist's claim that subjects project value onto their world; this is undeniable. For the objectivist, it is not an either/or problem where nature either has value subjectively or objectively. The question, Rolston insists, is whether the subjectivist's account is the whole of the story, whether value is *merely* subjective, or whether in addition to projecting value onto the world subjects *also* (sometimes) discover value that is objectively in the world. "We might first think that the phrase 'experienced value' is a tautology and the phrase 'unexperienced value' a contradiction in terms, somewhat like the phrases 'experienced thought' and 'unexperienced thought.' But the existence of unexperienced value . . . is not a contradiction in terms unless one builds into the meaning of value that it must be experienced. We must not beg the question of objectivity in value."[10] For Rolston, not all value requires a "beholder"; some value "requires only a holder."[11] The world is able to be valued because it is valu-able, and this is so before an experiencing subject arrives and will be true after they leave. In a nod of his own to Leopold, Rolston contends: "We start out valuing nature like land appraisers figuring out what it is worth to us, only to discover that we are part and parcel of this nature we appraise. The earthen landscape has upraised this landscape appraiser. We do not simply bestow value on nature; nature also conveys value to us."[12] Though in the end he admits that the "resolute subjectivist" cannot be defeated because theirs is a "retreat to definition,"[13] Rolston remains utterly committed to defending the existence of objective value independent of subjects as the fundamental basis of an adequate environmental ethic.

At times Rolston's target seems to be anthropocentrism rather than subjectivism per se. It is important to disentangle these claims before moving on. Subjectivism and anthropocentrism, though often conflated, are in fact distinct positions that are only contingently coincident depending on one's more basic metaphysical commitments. Further, we might briefly distinguish several different forms of anthropocentrism. In particular, it is important to distinguish between phenomenological (or experiential) anthropocentrism and axiological anthropocentrism. The former, phenomenological, position has to do with our experience of ourselves in the world. That we invariably perceive the world from the vantage of our own human experience is unavoidable. There is no "position from nowhere." This form of anthropocentrism, which is merely a description of how we experience our world, is not typically the target of scholars who seek to critique anthropocentrism as the root of the ecological crisis. It is axiological anthropocentrism—the view that nothing has meaning or value apart from its relationship to humans, that all value is ultimately anthropogenic—that is seen as the root of the problem. According to axiological anthropocentrism, prior to and outside of the experience of human beings, value does not exist. It is a human projection onto an oth-erwise valueless universe. It is this anthropogenic view of value——not our human-centered experience of the world—that, since at least Lynn White Jr.'s 1967 essay, is seen as the root of the ecological crisis.

Eileen Crist has recently helped crystalize this central point by noting that what I refer to as axiological anthropocentrism is also ultimately a form of "human supremacy" or "the collective, lived belief system that humans are superior to all the other life forms and entitled to use them and their places of livelihood."[14] As Crist notes, this is not a merely rhetorical claim: "Flagging the interchangeability of 'human supremacy' and 'anthropocentrism' is not simply a semantic clarification, but intended to highlight a substantive point reiterated through this work: anthropocentrism does not in the least serve human interests—anymore than white supremacy has ever served the ostensible interests of the putative Caucasian race. All forms of supremacy entrench violence as a way of life, which, beyond the obvious grave harms it inflicts on the denigrated, profoundly disgraces the perpetrators themselves."[15] Later it will be important to consider in more detail Crist's claim and its relationship to what she calls the Anthropocene discourse (see chapter nine). But, for purposes of our discussion of Rolston's position, my point here is to note the difference between (1) axiological anthropocentrism and (2) axiological subjectivism.

Whereas *axiological anthropocentrism* maintains an anthropogenic theory of value according to which all value is created by human valuers and, therefore, all meaning and intrinsic value is limited to humans, *subjectivism* is the view that only subjects of experience are able to value something and therefore only subjects have intrinsic value. It is the having of felt experiences that gives a being value for the subjectivist. Note that there is a sense in which the pure subjectivist does not believe in intrinsic value in that value is just a subjective feeling and does not "attach" to anything in the world. Hume's position, quoted above, is an instance of this, as is Callicott's early position. For them, value is always a projection, so it is always extrinsic to the being in question. At best, for a consistent subjectivist, it would be the experiences or feelings themselves that are of intrinsic value, not what generates them. That I subjectively value spending time in the shade of my large maple trees does not mean they have *intrinsic* value. It is my subjective experience that has value, not what generates them.

Anthropocentrism and subjectivism may coincide, but only if one maintains the view that the only subjects are human beings (Anthropos). Kant's moral philosophy is an instance of this view, since he seems to be of the mistaken view that only human beings are (rational) subjects. However, if one has a broader metaphysical conception of subjectivity, it is possible to have a non-anthropocentric subjectivist account of value. The work of Tom Regan is an apt example of this in that he demonstrates that many nonhuman beings are "subjects of a life" deserving of respect. Thus, Regan's defense of animal rights is subjectivist but not axiologically anthropocentric.[16]

The distinction between axiological anthropocentrism and subjectivism is important in understanding Rolston's position because at times his aim to reject anthropocentrism is muddled with the rejection of subjectivism per se, as though the former required the latter. A key benefit of grounding Rolston's environmental ethics in Whitehead's organic metaphysics is that it makes it possible to achieve Rolston's goal of giving environmental ethics a non-anthropocentric, axiological basis without having to demonstrate that there is value apart from subjects.

Before explaining and defending this important point, it is helpful to understand the shift in Callicott's thinking with his 1985 essay "Intrinsic Value, Quantum Theory, and Environmental Ethics." In this essay, Callicott admits that his previous subjectivist position was mistaken, not because Rolston's objectivist position is correct, but because he (Callicott) came to realize that the very distinction between a knowing subject and an objective world is the product of a bankrupt Cartesian legacy that infects Hume as much as any other modern philosopher.

> One of the cornerstones constituting the metaphysical foundations of classical modern science is the firm distinction, first clearly drawn by Descartes, between object and subject, between the *res extensa* and the *res cogitans*. The famous distinction of Hume between fact and value and Hume's development of a subjectivist axiology may be historically interpreted as an application or extension to ethics of Descartes' more general metaphysical and epistemic distinction. Logically interpreted, the object-subject dichotomy is a more general conceptual distinction to which the fact-value dichotomy is ancillary. Axiological subjectivism, indeed, may be clearly formulated only if the objective and subjective realms, the *res extensa* and the *res cogitans*, are clearly distinguished. How could it be meaningful to claim that values are not objective, that they are, rather, projected affections, feelings, or sentiments ultimately originating in valuing subjects, if subjects and objects are not clearly separate and distinct?[17]

Callicott has his finger here on points that are central to the current volume. Rather than spilling ever-more ink defending a subjectivist position against Rolston's objectivist view, Callicott realizes that the distinction itself must be abandoned. Callicott explains that he arrived at this conclusion as the result of his coming to terms with developments in physics, specifically quantum theory.

> A fully consistent contemporary environmental ethic thus requires a theory of noninstrumental value of nature which is neither subjectivist nor objectivist. It requires a wholly new axiology which does not rest, either explicitly or implicitly, upon Descartes' obsolete bifurcation. Perhaps quantum theory may serve as a constructive paradigm for a value theory for an ecologically informed environmental ethic, as well as an occasion for the deconstruction of the classical Cartesian metaphysical paradigm and its Humean axiological interpretation. To put this thought in the interrogative, if quantum theory negates the object-subject, fact-value dichotomies, what more positively might it imply for the ontology of natural values?[18]

Thus, Callicott contends that Rolston's objective theory is mistaken not because all value depends upon a human subject, but because the very distinction between subject and object is fundamentally flawed.

> While Rolston's defense of objectivity for natural values, ably utilizing the conceptual resources of the sciences of the "middle-level" world, is a philosophical tour de force and is very rewarding to read, the bottom line appears to me to be that as long as the metaphysical dichotomy of classical modern normal science between subject and object remains an unchallenged background assumption, the axiological dichotomy of modern normal ethics between value and fact will remain intractable.[19]

Callicott's new (post-1985) position bears striking similarities with Whitehead's philosophy of organism. A significant goal of the current volume is to demonstrate that Whitehead's environmental metaphysics provides just such a "wholly new axiology which does not rest . . . upon Descartes' obsolete bifurcation." Indeed, I contend that Callicott's goal cannot be achieved unless it is grounded not merely in an adequate understanding of physics, but ultimately also in an adequate metaphysics. As Armstrong points out in "Foundations,"

From a Whiteheadian perspective, Callicott's [quantum theory] approach is somewhat roundabout. First, since Whitehead's metaphysical theory is consonant with quantum theory, quantum requirements being "reflections into physical science" of individual actual entities, the characteristics of such a quantum theory are fully worked out in his [Whitehead's] system, including the overbelief that organic and microphysical nature manifest the same structure. This unity is evidenced by Whitehead's (rather breathtaking) statement that "the energetic activity considered in physics is the emotional intensity entertained in life." Indeed, Callicott's definition of the self as nature focused in a "knot" of the web of life is Whitehead's actual occasion by another name.[20]

Actually, we might put Armstrong's point more forcefully. It is not just that Callicott's use of quantum theory is "roundabout." Though Callicott is explicit in denying the adequacy of the "classical Cartesian metaphysical paradigm," he replaces it not with a more adequate *metaphysical* framework but with an incomplete *physical* theory.[21] Though the experimental results of quantum theory must undoubtedly be recognized and adequately accounted for, quantum theory does not a metaphysics make.[22] Callicott's project of moving environmental ethics beyond the subject-object dualism of modern metaphysics can really only be achieved by actually being grounded in an adequate account of the basic structure of reality—in a *metaphysics*, not just a physics: one which recognizes that every occasion of reality is at once a subject and an object that occurs within a complex environmental web of independence. This is, as we will increasingly come to appreciate, at the core of Whitehead's philosophy of organism. Thus, with Armstrong, I contend that Callicott's project would benefit greatly from being grounded explicitly in a metaphysics such as the philosophy of organism. But what about Rolston?

Rolston published in 1988 his magnum opus, *Environmental Ethics: Duties to and Values in the Natural World*, forcefully making the case for the objective value of nature as the only adequate basis for an environmental ethic. Much more will be said about Rolston's work and its possible connections to Whitehead's metaphysics in the next part of this chapter. In the present section, rather than addressing Rolston's axiology directly, let us approach his system obliquely by pointing out that there is something of a disconnect in the axiological standoff between Rolston and Callicott. In a sense, Callicott is more right than he realizes. Rolston's claims about objective value are not mistaken because ultimately quantum theory muddies the distinction between subjects and objects, but because, *metaphysically*, every being is both a subject and an object. As explained in the introduction of this volume, to exist is to be a subjective center of experience that then becomes an object for subsequent events. In this way, *an environmental ethic grounded in a Whiteheadian philosophy of organism creates the conditions necessary for resolving the seemingly intractable value wars between Callicott and Rolston.*

First, Callicott's post-1985 view is right that the subject-object, fact-value distinctions are the faulty result of modern thought's presumption of a Cartesian split between thinking things and extended things. Whitehead's metaphysics is the twentieth century's most ambitious attempt to systematically explore the implications of rejecting this split or "bifurcation" and to provide an adequate alternative. Thus, Callicott's own position is strengthened by being grounded in a philosophy of organism according to which every quantum of reality is at once a subject and an object. Interestingly, by grounding Callicott's *post*-1985 quantum theory position in Whitehead's organic process metaphysics, it becomes possible also to affirm his *pre*-1985 position that only subjects of experience have value, in that it is the case that every quantum of existence is *also* a subject of experience with intrinsic value. Thus, as Whitehead himself noted, the "reformed subjectivist principle" simply extends Hume's view more consistently than he himself does."[23] "The subjectivist principle is that the whole universe consists of elements disclosed in the analysis of the experiences of subjects. Process is the becoming of experience. It follows that the philosophy of organism entirely accepts the subjectivist bias of modern philosophy. It also accepts Hume's doctrine that nothing is to be received into the philosophical scheme which is not discoverable as an element in objective experience. This is the ontological principle."[24] Whitehead embraces the "turn to the subject" of modern philosophy, but he follows through with it more fully. This is his reformed subjectivist principle that nothing exists except subjects of experience. But this is not the whole story, for to be a *subject* is also to become an *object* for others.

Callicott is quite right that physics has revealed a world in which subjects and objects are not separate. There are no mere objects, no vacuous actuality. Every achievement of reality is at once a subject and an object. Indeed, Whitehead was so committed to overcoming the subject-object dualism that he adopted the neologism "superject" to refer to the role that subjects play in the world after their subjective self-determination (what he calls "concrescence" or becoming concrete) has been resolved and they become an achievement to be accounted for by subsequent events. In

Whitehead's terms, we should say that every achievement of reality is not either a subject or an object but at once a "subject-superject." As Whitehead puts it in *Process and Reality*,

> It is fundamental to the metaphysical doctrine of the philosophy of organism, that the notion of an actual entity as the unchanging subject of change is completely abandoned. An actual entity is at once the subject experiencing and the superject of its experiences. It is subject-superject, and neither half of this description can for a moment be lost sight of. The term "subject" will be mostly employed when the actual entity is considered in respect to its own real internal constitution. But "subject" is always to be construed as an abbreviation of "subject-superject."[25]

Whitehead provides a robust, systematic, speculative metaphysics that rejects the "bifurcation of nature"[26] and recognizes that to exist is to be both a subject and an object. Another way to put this would be to say that the philosophy of organism provides a metaphysical foundation for environmental ethics that does not require *overcoming* the subject-object split because it begins with an account that fundamentally rejects any bifurcation in the first place. You need not unite that which has never been sundered. Grounding environmental philosophy in an organicist process metaphysics—rather than a (typically) latent modern, Cartesian metaphysics—has a decisive (positive) effect on the subsequent environmental axiology and ethics that follows.[27]

Grounded in Whitehead's process anti-dualist metaphysics, the seemingly intractable axiological conflicts within environmental ethics generally and between Rolston and Callicott (both pre- and post-1985 versions) begin to dissolve. From an organicist perspective, Callicott (pre-1985) is right that value is the creation of the felt experiences of subjects (because there is nothing but the experience of subjects), and Callicott (post-1985) is right that the distinction between subjects and objects is misguided; to be is to be a subject for oneself and to become an object for others. Grounded in a philosophy of organism, both claims are correct. Every being is at once a subject and an object, a subject-superject representing a unique achievement of value.

But Rolston is also right. Value is not merely the subjective projection of human moral agents; value is not primarily, much less exclusively, anthropogenic. It turns out that, contrary to his claim, Rolston was right when he said that "we might first think that the phrase 'experience value' is a tautology and the phrase 'unexperienced value' a contradiction in terms," in that to exist is to be a subject of experience. According to the reformed subjectivist principle, there is nothing apart from the experience of subjects. Yet, by overcoming the subject-object split and recognizing that every form of existence is at once a subject and an object, it is also true to say that every occasion of reality has objective intrinsic value. Rolston's core axiological insight that moral agents discover a world replete with real achievements of value that exist before moral agents arrive and after they leave is *more* safely secured within a Whiteheadian metaphysical framework. All living beings and the systems that produce them have intrinsic value and deserve respect. Value is *not merely* anthropogenic. We human subjects discover ourselves swimming in a sea of value. However, Rolston need not buy into the artificial and damaging bifurcation of subject and object in order to defend this core axiological commitment. Grounded in Whitehead's philosophy of organism, Rolston can achieve his core objective of defending objective value without having to buy into a bankrupt metaphysical worldview.

In this way, we begin to reveal the benefit of grounding environmental ethics in Whitehead's process metaphysics. Grounding environmental ethics in Whitehead's organicist metaphysics of process has the potential to make genuine progress on the "central and most recalcitrant problem for environmental ethics": the nature and locus of intrinsic value. But this is only a down payment, as it were. There are many and deeper lines of convergence between Whitehead's and Rolston's projects.

ROLSTON: VALUES IN AND DUTIES TO THE NATURAL WORLD

Organisms, Machines, Teleology

For half a century, Holmes Rolston III has been a leading figure within environmental ethics. He is often seen as writing the first essay in environmental ethics, and his 1988 *Environmental Ethics: Duties to and Values in the Natural World* continues to be a mainstay in many environmental ethics courses, including my own.[28] In his effort to defend the objective value of living organisms, Rolston finds it important to define the differences between machines and organisms, as only the latter have objective intrinsic value. Rolston rightly notes that organisms (such as a deer or a delphinium) have needs and internal purposes, whereas machines (such as a car) do not.

> A car has no nature of its own; it does not exist by nature. An automobile is a means to human good; spontaneous nature could

not conceivably have produced an automobile. Or, to make the point by playing with language, nature's "automobiles"—its things with genuinely "autonomous motion"—are living organisms. Cars have no self-generating or self-defending tendencies; they are called automobiles only by historical accident, because they are horseless carriages. When a human steps out of a car, she takes all the purposes, needs, programs, interests of the car away with her, all of which she gave to the car in the first place.

But none of this is true when a human walks away from a deer or a delphinium. The car does not "need" spark plugs except as a locution for, "I need plugs for my car." The car is not an automobile except insofar as it needs no horses to draw it. It must have a driver. Nor is the computer automatic; its program was written for it by a person, even if it is a program with elements of learning in it. Machines have an end only mediately as the extrasomatic products of human systems. But the tree has a *telos* before the logger arrives, and the logger destroys it. It is *auto-telic*; it has a law (Greek: *nomos*) on its own (= *autonomous*). It is on autopilot.[29]

Rolston is right to note that (at this time) machines do not struggle to live.[30] They do not have needs of their own. There is no seat of subjectivity, no center of experience. Cars have no needs of their own. Central to defending these claims, for Rolston, is the recovery of that which was long banished in the rise of modern science (and modern metaphysics), namely teleology. A tree, he contends, has a telos, an end, prior to the arrival of the logger, and the logger can help or harm the achievement of that telos.[31] "A machine is a good kind only because it is a good-of-my-kind; an organism can have a good-of-its-kind and be a good kind intrinsically, as well as be dialectically a short-range-bad-fitting-into-a-larger-good kind in an ecosystem. Machines are by us and for us; organisms live on their own. No machine is wild, but it is significantly the wilderness of life that we treasure." Resting the distinction between machines and organisms on the existence of a telos is crucial for Rolston's position because it establishes the "objective" basis of the "needs" of the organism, such as the tree. Just as with Aristotle, it is the telos of an organism that defines what it is and, crucially, defines the good for it. (See chapter seven for an extended discussion of teleology.)

In this way, Rolston joins the likes of Paul Taylor and Gary Varner in recovering a version of teleology as a basis for justifying the intrinsic value of nonhuman nature. Unfortunately, he also joins them in not providing a metaphysical justification for such a position. Rolston understands contemporary biology and ecology well. It is clear he is not embracing a retrograde, nonscientific recovery of teleology. But then what *is* he proposing? How is it possible to retain all that has been learned in the last three centuries of scientific discovery in physics, chemistry, biology, and ecology, but also affirm teleology? Rolston does not provide a direct answer, but at times he seems interested in defending a rather straightforwardly Aristotelian position. "An organism is a spontaneous cybernetic system, self-maintaining with a control center, sustaining and reproducing itself on the basis of information about how to make a way through the world. Organisms employ physical and chemical causes, but, distinctive to life, there is *information* superintending the causes. This information is a modern equivalent of what Aristotle called formal and final causes; it gives the organism a *telos*, an end, though not always a felt or conscious end."[32] But how exactly does this fairly straightforward recovery of Aristotelian notions of formal and final causality sit peacefully alongside contemporary evolutionary biology and quantum physics? I would suggest that it does not. Rolston is right to recover teleology and anchor his axiology in it, but doing so does not require returning to ancient systems that are no longer adequate to what we know of the world. As Rolston likes to note, our ethics should affirm ecology, not deny it.[33] Extending this, we might say that our metaphysics should affirm contemporary science, not deny it. I contend that Rolston's recovery of teleology, which is key to his account of objective value, needs to be secured on an adequate metaphysical basis, and that Whitehead's naturalistic, organicist metaphysics is a far better foundation than the alternatives in that it provides an account of a "developmental teleology" that is consistent with contemporary scientific accounts of reality, including evolutionary biology.

In addition to what might be called local or individual teleology of a single organism, it is worth briefly noting that Rolston also seems to adopt what I will later refer to as cosmic teleology.[34] We see hints of this in his 1988 *Environmental Ethics*, where he defends the strong anthropic principle.[35] Perhaps the most developed defense is in Rolston's 2010 *Three Big Bangs*,[36] where he defends the view that there is a cosmic teleological orientation moving the universe from nothing to something (the first big bang), from matter-energy to life (the second big bang), and from life to mind (the third big bang). The problem with these claims is that, once again, he fails to provide a metaphysics that would explain and justify these views. Indeed, too often it seems that he retains a reductionistic model of physical reality that ultimately makes the cosmological evolution he vividly traces unintel-ligible. That teleological oriented, intrinsically valuable forms of order (life) would emerge from wholly lifeless, inert, valueless, passive matter-energy is metaphysically unintelligible. Calling it "emergence" is simply to give a name to the problem, not an answer.[37] However, grounded in Whitehead's organicist environmental metaphysics, Rolston's consistent defense of a cosmic teleology becomes quite intelligible. As discussed in greater length in chapter seven of this volume on developmental teleology, the view that reality has no head, but does have a heading toward diversification, support, and richness, is quite similar to Charles Sanders Peirce's and Whitehead's notions of developmental teleology in which there is a cosmic orientation.

Crucially, however, if Rolston were to embrace a Whiteheadian posi-tion, it would require him to abandon his dualistic and bifurcated view that sees an absolute split between living organisms, which have intrinsic value, and nonliving entities, which do not. Although Rolston seems interested in beginning to overcome the harmful legacy of Cartesian metaphysics through the recovery of a teleologically secured conception of intrinsic value, he extends this only to the biological realm without really disturbing the more fundamental claim that the constituents of reality are just, in his words, "inert physical nature."[38]

Rolston rightly recognizes that organisms objectively have mind-independent needs that can be helped and harmed and that this is the basis for a robust conception of intrinsic value. Situated within an organicist metaphysics that takes this to be true not only of biological organisms but also, in varying degrees and ways, *every* form and level of reality—by taking organism as the primary metaphor for conceiving of reality per se—it is possible to take Rolston's position and extend it to every level of reality. Thus, rather than making the emergence of life a surd via a miraculous, unintelligible, and incoherent "second big bang"—wherein teleological activity begins to take place out of wholly "inert" and valueless matter—grounded in Whitehead's philosophy of organism, we see that *nothing* is wholly inert. There is a teleological dimension to every real level of reality and activity—there are no great breaks, no big bangs, and no inexplicable jumps. Reality is a continuous organic process that becomes more or less complex. As we will discuss more fully in chapter six, the differences between different types of individuals have to do with the degrees of order and internal complexity that make more or less unity of functioning possible. It does not mean that an "inert rock"[39] is alive. A rock, qua rock, is in fact not an ontological individual. At the macroscopic level at which we experience it, it is more of an aggregate than a proper ontological individual. The highest level of ontological individuality, unity, identity, and wholeness for a rock is at the molecular level that makes the unique quartz or granite or sandstone formations and patterns. These patterns are not alive in the proper biological sense, but neither is it "inert" as Rolston suggests. There is nothing but booming, buzzing confusion at the molecular, atomic, and subatomic levels. The molecules of quartz and granite are patterns perpetuated, degraded, and maintained moment to moment on the frothing, foaming subatomic reality that is nothing but energetic exchange.

Thus, contrary to the caricatures that often plague it, an organicist metaphysics does *not* claim that a rock is no different than a biological organism. Whitehead would largely agree with Rolston's claim that "an organism, unlike an inert rock, claims the environment as source and sink, from which to abstract energy and materials and into which to excrete them. It 'takes advantage' of its environment."[40] However, to maintain this important metaphysical distinction, we need not embrace the additional, unjustified metaphysical distinction wherein this notion of "inertness" has us slip back into a Cartesian view of matter as "inert," passive stuff. We must not affirm in our ethics what we deny in our science and metaphysics.

Though he generally avoids metaphysics, in passing Rolston does consider the "panpsychist" position that "an elementary or attenuated feeling characterizes even plants and microbes." However, he dismisses such a position out of hand as "lacking clear evidence."[41] As we will find throughout the present volume, that an elementary or attenuated "feeling" characterizes not only plants and microbes but *everything* including basic physical constituents of reality is indeed Whitehead's position. However, the term "panpsychism" is inapt for several reasons.

First, because Western philosophers so often are functioning, consciously or unconsciously, within a Cartesian or Kantian dualistic metaphysical framework that separates mind and matter, the notion of "panpsychism" is often misunderstood as the view that every "little thing" has a "mind." However, this is *not* what is being defended here. Those who—like Whitehead, but also Peirce, William James, John Dewey, and Henri Bergson—reject the bifurcation of nature do not pick one side of the dualism between mind and matter and use it to characterize the whole. For the philosophy of organism, idealism is just as mistaken as materialism. An anti-dualist metaphysics also tends to be anti-reductionistic and maintain that all of reality has mind-like and matter-like aspects, but that there is no bifurcation and no reduction.

This points to a second, related confusion over the concept of "panpsychism." Too often philosophers take "mind" to refer to the cognitive activity of high-grade, complex animals with a brain and think panpsychists apply such a notion to protons, electrons, and rocks. Such a view is of course absurd. Cognition is an exceptional and extraordinary evolutionary achievement that is *not* characteristic of every level of reality. What *is* characteristic of every level of reality is an indeterminacy of response to the conditions of the past. The present "feels" the past in that it is internally, constitutively affected and partly determined by the past. But each present moment is not wholly determined by the past; there is an indeterminacy, novelty, creativity of response, though often it is very narrowly constrained in the case of chemical, atomic, and subatomic events. Nevertheless, this novel reaction is a root notion of subjectivity; this is what undergirds Whitehead's reformed subjectivist principle.[42] Thus, it is not wholly inappropriate to see Whitehead's philosophy of organism as a form of pansubjectivism rather than panpsychism. However, even this is potentially misleading for, again, it seems to encourage the mistaken assumption that between subjects and objects one has picked a side and used it as a brush to paint the whole of reality. The truth of the matter is far more complex. Whitehead is committed to a reformed subjectivist principle, but this is one in which to be is to be at once a subject-superject or a subject of experience that becomes an object for subsequent subjects; the many become one and are increased by one "until the crack of doom."[43]

Let us not lose the metaphysical forest for the metaphysical trees. Our point here is that Rolston's rejection of panpsychism is not only hasty and poorly defended but also ultimately at odds with his own defenses of individual and cosmic teleology and the emergence of life and mind that this teleology has led to. Rolston's defense of a distinction between machines and organism via a recovery of teleology (on which his defense of intrinsic value depends) is more secure if grounded in an organicist environmental metaphysics that fundamentally rejects the concept of "inert physical nature" (what Whitehead calls "vacuous actuality"). That is, Rolston's core project of defending duties to and values in nature is better achieved if situated within the philosophy of organism.

Organism-in-Environment

In the previous section we considered how a Whiteheadian philosophy of organism could help ground Rolston's defense of the intrinsic value of individual organisms. Those familiar with Rolston's work know he would be quick to note that it is a mistake to focus only on the intrinsic value of individual organisms (whether defined narrowly as with Rolston or broadly as with Whitehead) and ignore their wider ecosystemic context. Rolston provides many poetic and powerful accounts of the relationship between an organism and its environment. We will find that this is another point on which he and Whitehead are in substantial agreement. Indeed, we will find that, taken together, Whitehead's and Rolston's positions help address respective weaknesses and omissions. To help gain entrance to this discussion, let us begin with Rolston's views on the nature and value of ecosystems.

Contrary to nominalists who might claim that ecosystems do not really exist as a real form of order in the world, that they are just an aggregate of organisms within a geographical area to which a name has been applied (e.g., Yellowstone National Park), Rolston defends a realist account of ecosystems.

> Ecosystems are selective systems, as surely as organisms are selective systems. The system selects over the longer ranges for individuality, for diversity, for adapted fitness, for quantity and quality of life. Organisms defend only their own selves or kinds, but the system spins a bigger story. Organisms defend their continuing survival; ecosystems promote new arrivals. Species increase their kinds, but ecosystems increase kinds, and increase the integration of kinds. The system is a kind of field with characteristics as vital for life as any property contained within particular organisms. The ecosystem is the depth source of individual and species alike.[44]

Again, I am struck by the deep similarities between Rolston's and Whitehead's positions. Although ecology was in its infancy when Whitehead was writing in the 1920s and 1930s and it is somewhat anachronistic to talk about his views of ecosystems, it is clear that Whitehead's metaphysics is uniquely suited to provide support for Rolston's position here. In chapter six we will have an opportunity to discuss at length Whitehead's ontology of individuality. For now, it will be sufficient to look more narrowly at how Whitehead conceives of the role of "environment" in his organicist metaphysics and then relate it to Rolston.

One of the many things revealed by the publishing of Whitehead's Harvard Lectures in the Critical Edition of Whitehead is the influence of his Harvard colleagues.[45] For instance, in the first volume of the Lectures we learn that the Harvard biochemist Lawrence J. Henderson (1878–1942) had a profound influence on Whitehead's understanding of the role of "environment." As Winthrop Pickard Bell and William Ernest Hocking record in their lecture notes of Whitehead's class for December 11, 1924, just a few months into his first semester at Harvard, Whitehead explains that he was "put on to" the central role of the environment by reading two of Henderson's books, *The Fitness of the Environment* (1913) and *The Order of Nature* (1917).[46] It is helpful and interesting to know specifically that Henderson was an inspiration for Whitehead's thought, but of course he goes far beyond Henderson's work in the use to which he puts it. Whitehead takes Henderson's eco-biological concept from evolutionary biology and then applies it to his own problems in physics. Consider this lengthy passage captured in Bell's notes:[47]

> Each organism to some extent creates its own environment—Previous life of organism has stamped itself somehow on whole present environment. How to account for <u>enormous</u> stability of Electrons etc. and for evolution of things in this order of Nature? . . . By survival of fittest. You go back to where within order of Nature you had fitful stretches . . . of emergent enduring entities. An Environment i.e., created by a Society of entities producing an Environment favourable to existence of them all. Environment has evolved as an Environment which secures selection of definite types. Whole theory of Evolution considered largely from other point of view—as if Environment given and Organism had to adapt <u>itself to</u> this . . . think of Brazilian Forest.—No individual tree could have grown without its environment. <u>They produced</u> an <u>environment favorable to each other</u>. That's really the Key! Those animals die out which passively fit themselves to environment. The great lizards e.g., [It's the restless ones that survive]. Physical Science gives us an environment not unlike outside view of great <u>Societies</u>. Electrons, Protons etc.—two or three kinds—large numbers—There builds up higher organisms from these. Here you have cases of Emergent Entities which fit environment to each other. Electrons, Protons, etc. is just as much social being as rest of us are.[48]

In passages like this, one gets a window into how Whitehead extrapolates from the biological account of macroscopic organisms and their environment to the physical account of electrons, something he'd considered since at least his dissertation on James Clerk Maxwell's theory of electromagnetism.[49] The field of activity in which an electron takes place is its "environment."

Whitehead's reference to "survival of the fittest" relates to a second philosophical figure who was not previously known to be an influence on Whitehead's thought. Both Bell[50] and Louise Heath[51] record Whitehead as saying that he realized the importance of cooperation upon reading the Russian philosopher Peter (Prince) Kropotkin's (1842–1921) *Mutual Aid* (1902). Heath captures Whitehead putting it this way: "Social side of evolution is important to keep in mind—natural selection as ruthless competition has been very much run, Other aspect put by Prince Kropotkin—called 'Mutual Aid'—evolution impresses idea of mutual aid quite as much as competition. ∨Philosophic∨ Basis of 'mutual aid' is that it is creation of environment."[52] Whitehead's references to Henderson and Kropotkin put into a new light some of the claims delivered a year later in his famous Lowell Lectures (published as *Science and the Modern World*). In particular, I have in mind his discussion of the same "Brazilian Forest," which is not merely a violent evolutionary scene red in tooth and claw, but *also* an example of species that "mutually assist each other in preserving the conditions for survival."[53] Mutual aid is one of the means by which stable environments are created. Or, as he puts it, "every organism requires an environment of friends, partly to shield it from violent changes, and partly to supply it with its wants."[54]

Notice, then, that it is central to Whitehead's philosophy of organism that entities are not "in" an environment as a bee is in a jar. The claim he is making is that the relationship between entities and their environment is constitutive such that what an organism is, is inseparable from its wider environment. The relationships from the physical to the chemical, biological, and ecological constitute what each "individual" is. Individuals are not defined in terms of their in-dependence but by their inter-dependence and inter-relation, so much so that in his class (though never in his published work) he calls this the "principle of the necessity of the environment."[55] This is quite similar to Rolston's own account of the relationship between organisms and their environment.

Take, for instance, Rolston's description of an ecosystem as a kind of vital "field" of activity that has its own unique teleological "heading" toward increasing diversification and speciation: "An ecosystem generates a spontaneous order that envelops and produces the richness, beauty, integrity and dynamic stability of the component parts. Though these organized interdependencies are loose in comparison with the tight connections within an organism, all these metabolisms are as vitally linked as are liver and heart. The equilibrating ecosystem is not merely push-pull forces. It is an equilibrating of values."[56] Rolston has his finger on the key point that individuality is not an all-or-nothing proposition. To exist as a real form of togetherness—of unity, identity, wholeness—is a matter of degree. The tighter the relationship between the parts, the more central the order and activity; the looser the relationship, the looser the central order. But it is not all or nothing.

> An ecosystem is a spontaneously-organizing system of interrelated parts, simultaneously persisting and evolving through changes over decades and centuries. An ecosystem is a vital and dynamic collection of organisms, each with its capabilities and limits, each species selected over evolutionary history to do rather well in the niche it inhabits, an adapted fit, and with some capacities for adapting to changes in its altering environment. In these ecosystem qualities emerge that are corporate or holistic (such as trophic pyramids or tendencies to succession), not the qualities of any individual parts (such as metabolism and death). The result is the richness of biodiversity over the geological millennia.[57]

Interestingly, Rolston's attempt to define the reality of ecosystems as spontaneous systems with their own form of "downward causation" is the principle Whitehead uses in order to describe all forms of macroscopic order. For Whitehead, an organism is just as much a system of systems as an ecosystem is. The difference is primarily, as Rolston himself hints, a matter of the degree of internal coordination. If there is a "weak organic holism," then we have an ecosystem. If there is a "stronger organic holism," then we have something like a pine tree. The strongest, most unified forms of organic holism we call animals. As noted above, rocks are not systems, qua rocks. The highest level of systemic order there is at the molecular level.

> Philosophers, sometimes encouraged by biologists, may think ecosystems are just epiphenomenal aggregations. This is a confusion. Any level is real if there is significant downward causation. Thus the atom is real because that pattern shapes the behaviour of electrons; the cell because that pattern shapes the behaviour of amino acids; the organism because that pattern co-ordinates the behavior of hearts and lungs; the community because the niche shapes the morphology and behavior of the foxes within it. Being real requires an organization that shapes the existence and the behaviour of members or parts.[58]

This is the basis of Rolston's distinctive form of holism.

> There is weak organic holism—communitarian holism—not strong organismic holism, though the "weakness" (if we must use that term) is a strength in the system. The looseness abets community; too much tightness would abort it. The looseness is not simplicity but is itself a form of environmental complexity that generates organismic complexity.[59]

Rolston beautifully and compellingly explains that elephants are not just in a savannah nor a wolf just in a forest. What it is to be a wolf is to be a wolf-in-forest. To be that type of organism is to be within that environment, but again not in the same way that I am within the supermarket. No, the relationship of wolf to forest is like that between my heart and my body. To be a heart is to play a particular role within the larger body of which it is a part. To be a heart is to be a heart-in-body. Notice the similarity of this to the old Aristotelian idea that a soul (*psuchê*) is not just *in* the body but is rather a soul-body composite. An individual is, for Aristotle, not one thing (a soul) inside another (a body), as with Plato. Rather, an individual is one unified thing: an ensouled body. But again, as with Rolston's recovery of a form of teleology that is consistent with contemporary science, it is possible to conceive of a wolf-in-forest in a way that does not require embracing a substance metaphysics wherein ecosystems are substances in the world. (For more on this, see the discussion of substance metaphysics in chapter six.) Both Whitehead and Rolston seem to agree that to be is to be part of a "vital field" of activity with varying degrees of interdependence and interconnection. The main difference is whether this is true of only biological organisms and their ecosystems (as with Rolston) or also of every form of actuality (as with Whitehead).

Notice that in the previous passage Rolston makes the *metaphysical* claim that something is "real" if it expresses "downward causation." This is, of course, a straightforward metaphysical claim. What he lacks is an account (a metaphysics) that would justify such a claim. This is another instance where grounding Rolston's account in Whitehead's environmental metaphysics can be helpful to him. For Whitehead, anything is real (as Plato noted in the *Sophist*) insofar as it affects and can be affected.[60] Thus, it is not merely "downward causation" (or the ability to affect) but also the ability to be affected (upward causation?) that makes something "real." Once again, we find that claims by Rolston that are largely asserted become more secure when placed within Whitehead's environmental metaphysics of process.

Though the risk of equivocation is real, we might even note Rolston's rather frequent use of the concept of "process" when attempting to describe and defend the value of ecosystems. "If we are concerned about what is value-able, able to sustain value on our landscapes, why not say that it is the productivity of such ecosystems? The products are valuable, able to be valued by the humans who come late in the process; but why not say that the process is what is really valuable, that is, able to produce these values in biodiversity. It would be foolish to value golden eggs and disvalue the goose that lays them."[61] Of course, within Whitehead's metaphysics there is "nothing but" process. That is, even the "products" of an evolutionary cosmology are themselves processes. There are no static products. Indeed, all there is, according to both Whitehead and Rolston, is "creativity": "to praise the individuals (as the creative actors) and to disparage the system (as mere stochastic, inert stage) is to misunderstand the context of creativity."[62]

Creativity

This joint embrace of creativity points to perhaps the most unexpected—and, for me, exciting—result of situating Rolston's project within a Whiteheadian philosophy of organism. Rolston has consistently, but somewhat mysteriously, connected value and creativity, claiming "there is value wherever there is positive creativity."[63] Exactly what "positive" adds here is not explicitly defined. If by "positive" one means creativity that is supportive of the universal heading toward richness and diversity, toward beauty, then I am in complete agreement with Rolston. Indeed, my first book, *The Ethics of Creativity*, took that as its starting assumption. Creativity is, according to Whitehead, the "category of the ultimate"; it is the most basic feature of reality, captured by the koan, that it is the process whereby "the many become one and are increased by one."[64] As I argue in chapter two, grounded within the philosophy of organism, the goal of ethics is for moral agents to comport themselves in such a way as to align their own creativity with the creativity of the universe. Intriguingly, Rolston seems to be defending a similar position.

> Humans are not so much lighting up value in a merely potentially valuable world, as they are psychologically joining ongoing natural history in which there is value wherever there is positive creativity. While such creativity can be present in subjects with their interests and preferences, it can also be present objectively in living organisms with their lives defended, and in species that defend an identity over time, and in systems that are self-organizing

and that project storied achievements. The valuing subject in an otherwise valueless world is an insufficient premise for the experienced conclusions of those who value natural history.[65]

What is lacking here is a metaphysical account that would ground and justify this view of creativity. And that is exactly what an organicist environmental metaphysics can provide. So grounded, we realize that human moral agents are not merely seeking psychologically to join the "ongoing natural history" of life on our planet, but also the creative urge of reality itself. And this creativity is present not only in conscious human subjects, organisms, species, and ecosystems, but in the very fabric of reality itself. To be is to be a creative achievement of beauty and value. Only in this way can we overcome the "insufficient premise" of a "valuing subject in an otherwise valueless world." Rolston is right that "we can, we ought to, respect such creativity." And he is right that "if we see nature only instrumentally, we are inclined to manipulate it, our providing ground, our provisions. If we see these evolutionary and cybernetic *processes* and the resulting products . . . more deeply as having intrinsic value, we are inclined to respect it, and we may pass over unawares to reverence for life. If we come to systematically venerate the productive processes the *Ground* that provides for life, we have passed into the domain of the religious."[66] This is perhaps the closest Rolston will come to seeking to justify his claims regarding the basis of intrinsic value in positive creativity. However, this intuition of the divine is not—as it seems to be for Whitehead—motivation or opportunity to attempt, however partially or haltingly, to provide an account or an explanation.

To be sure, I am confident that Rolston's reference to the divine here is sincere and heartfelt. Nevertheless, Rolston's reference to the divine functions philosophically here more as a deus ex machina, standing in place of an argument rather than as the start of one. Instead, we can, if we have the courage, engage in metaphysics and try, however partially and fallibly, to provide a coherent and adequate account of reality that makes sense of the creative aesthetic orientation of reality.

To summarize our discussion so far, we have found three deep lines of convergence: (1) between Whitehead's philosophy of organism and Rolston's defenses of teleology, (2) in their shared commitment to the concept of organism-in-environment, and (3) their joint embrace of creativity as an ultimate basis for value and the orientation of actuality. The last (creativity) brings us back to the most important concept for Rolston's work: the notion of value.

Value

Rolston begins his 1988 *Environmental Ethics* by considering and defending the basis for ascribing or recognizing intrinsic value in nature. In consecutive chapters he looks first at intrinsic value of nonhuman animals, then organisms such as plants, then species, and finally ecosystems. In each instance, he considers each as a kind of individual and asks whether and to what extent each of those types of individuals, taken by themselves, have intrinsic value. Rolston's overarching goal is to defend the view that every organism has value objectively, prior to and independent of human valuers who may or may not be able or willing to recognize that intrinsic value. Rolston's goal is to secure the intrinsic value as real and independent of any human valuer is better achieved within Whitehead's philosophy of organism. However, intrinsic value is only one leg of Rolston's three-legged value stool: intrinsic, instrumental, systemic.

This triadic theory of value is one of the most distinctive features of Rolston's environmental ethics. He arrives at this position in his effort to properly understand and respect not only the "products" of nature, the individual organisms, but also the "process" that generates these kinds. We should, Rolston suggests, value not only the golden eggs of evolution (i.e., organisms), but also the goose that lays them (i.e., speciating process). Rolston rightly notes that within an ecological worldview, there is something deeply problematic about only considering the value of individuals.

> In an ecological view, however, an overemphasis on intrinsic value, the value of an individual "for what it is in itself" can become problematic. Ecology places individuals in a holistic web, and their intrinsic value is not to be decoupled from the biotic, communal system. Value cannot be too internal and elementary, as though it were located only from the skin-in; this forgets relatedness and externality, the skin-out biology, the locations in which such value is set. Intrinsic value is a part in a whole, not to be fragmented by valuing it in isolation. Everything is good in a role, in a whole; value is a systemic interweaving instrumental and intrinsic value.[67]

Nature's fecundity, according to Rolston, is not reducible to either intrinsic or instrumental value. We are in need, he contends, of a distinct form of value that is related to, but distinct from the other two.

We are no longer confronting instrumental value, as though the system were of value instrumentally as a fountain of life. Nor is the question one of intrinsic value, as though the system defended some unified form of life for itself. We have reached something for which we need a third term: *systemic value*. This cardinal value, like the history, is not all encapsulated in individuals; it too is smeared out into the system. The value in this system is not just the sum of the part-values. No part values increase of kinds, but the system promotes such increase. Systemic value is the productive process; its products are intrinsic values woven into instrumental relationships. Systemic value is what we will call . . . *projective nature*.[68]

This irreducible third kind of value is seemingly unique within environmental ethics. I know of no other environmental ethic that affirms Rolston's position. (For instance, deep ecologists affirm the value of ecosystems and species, but they contend that they have intrinsic or inherent value, not some new kind of value distinct from the others.)

As discussed in chapter two on value, a half century before Rolston, Whitehead also developed a triadic theory of value. I contend that Whitehead's and Rolston's positions are not only compatible but also mutually supportive. Let us start with Whitehead, who, in his 1938 *Modes of Thought*, contends that "everything has some value for itself, for others, and for the whole." This triad not only "characterizes the meaning of actuality," but it is the reason that "the conception of morals arises."[69] Further, each of these three forms of value are "on a level. No one in any sense precedes the other."[70] Exactly fifty years later, in 1988, Rolston writes in *Environmental Ethics*, "Values are intrinsic, instrumental, and systemic, and all three are interwoven, no one with priority over the others in significance, although systemic value is foundational. Each locus of intrinsic value gets folded into instrumental value by the system, and vice versa. There are no intrinsic values, nor instrumental ones either, without the encompassing systemic creativity."[71] Indeed, in his defense of systemic value, Rolston affirms a position strikingly similar to Whitehead's philosophy of organism:

Relations between entities are just as real as the entities themselves. In their interrelations things become and remain what they are. The system is an integrated manifold in which form and being, process and reality, individual and environment, fact and value are inseparably joined. Intrinsic and instrumental values shuttle back and forth, parts-in-wholes and wholes-in-parts, local details of value embedded in global structures, gems in their settings, and their setting-situation a maternal matrix. To change the figure, intrinsic values are particles that are also waves, instrumental values are waves that are also particles, as one shifts valuing perspective or coagulates events this way or that.[72]

Rolston, to my knowledge, never references or cites Whitehead's work. Nevertheless, the similarity between the position above and Whitehead's is breathtaking. Not only does Rolston explicitly use the phrase "process and reality"—which of course is Whitehead's Gifford Lectures published under that title in 1929—here we find Rolston affirming an organicist worldview in which relations "are just as real as the entities themselves" and that it is through these "interrelations" that "things become and remain what they are." This is tantalizingly close to a Whiteheadian relational event ontology. To make the jump, Rolston would only have to transition from an implicit substance metaphysics where relations are properties of entities to an organicist process metaphysics wherein entities are their relations.

Indeed, this is essentially Rolston's position in an earlier 1982 essay, where he argues that "everything is what it is in relation to other things. This kind of relativity does not cause alienation and anthropocentrism; it rather cures it."[73] One would be hard-pressed to find anything here with which Whitehead might disagree. Indeed, one could be forgiven for having thought that Rolston was here quoting Whitehead's "principle of relativity" that "every item of the universe, including all the other actual entities, is a constituent in the constitution of any one actual entity."[74] For the philosophy of organism, every event, in becoming fully determinate, is an achievement of beauty and value and, in this way, has value for itself. Yet, to be a subject is also to become an object for subsequent occasions, to have value for others. But this is not the whole story, for to be a subject-superject or a subject-object that has both intrinsic and instrumental value is also to have value "for the whole." Nothing has "value on its own." Indeed, in that, within an organicist process metaphysics, to be an "individual" is to be in constitutive interdependence and interrelation with—to varying degrees of relevance and irrelevance—everything in the universe, then the very nature of "individuality" essentially entails interrelation with the wider systems of which each individual is a part. Self-value is inseparable from value to others and to the whole. Thus, Whitehead's triadic theory of value—according to which every event has value for itself, for others, and the whole—is grounded in a compelling, systematic, speculative metaphysics that provides an account of the connection between the structure of reality and value.

Whitehead's and Rolston's triadic axiologies are stronger together than apart. For its part, Whitehead's triadic theory of value would benefit from Rolston's somewhat more developed account of systemic value as the value of the projective process of nature/reality. This is consistent with Whitehead's own account and helps ensure that it is not allowed to slip into a misguided axiological "contributionism" or "totalizing utilitarianism" (see chapter two on value). Likewise, by providing a metaphysics that connects intrinsic, instrumental, and systemic value not just to life on Earth but to the nature of reality itself, Whitehead can be of use to Rolston. This is also true of their respective defenses of axiological hierarchy.

Both Whitehead and Rolston affirm, in contrast to many ecofeminists and deep ecologists, a hierarchical view of value wherein the depth of value corresponds to the integrated complexity of the individual. As Rolston notes, if we bracket considerations of instrumental and systemic value and consider only intrinsic value, we have something like the following "intuitive scale" wherein intrinsic value is "highest in humans, descending across animal life in rough proportion to phylogenetic or neural complexity, lower in plant life, and least in microbes."[75] However, we ought never tear intrinsic value out of the whole of which it is a part. This misrepresents both what the individual is, in that the individual is only what it is insofar as it is a part (organism) of a large whole (environment), but also because intrinsic value ought never be taken apart from instrumental and systemic value. We ought not worry, as some deep ecologists and ecofeminists do, that this leads to an invidious hierarchy in which humans trump all else, as with Aristotle's "chain of being."

> True, the highest value attained in the system is lofty individuality with its subjectivity, present in vertebrates, mammals, primates, and preeminently in persons. This is where the most significant of evolutionary arrows tends. But such products are not the sole loci of value, concentrate value though they do. Even the most valuable of the parts is of less value than the whole. The objective, systemic process is an overriding value, not because it is indifferent to individuals but because the process is both prior to and productive of individuality.[76]

A consideration of the role of hierarchy from a Whiteheadian perspective is the topic of chapter four. Here it is sufficient to note that Rolston's axiological hierarchy is more firmly grounded by being lodged not only in a scale of phylogenetic complexity provided by biology, but also within a cosmological hierarchy that encompasses every form of order from the subatomic to the human, the galactic, and beyond.

Finally, keeping these similarities between Whitehead's and Rolston's axiologies in mind, let us push further and explore the *metaphysical* basis of Rolston's theory of value. Though Rolston consistently avoids engaging explicitly in metaphysics, he does seem to recognize that a chief impediment to his ability to affirm objective intrinsic value is the longstanding (metaphysical) distinction between primary and secondary qualities. He is well aware that many who reject the objective reality of intrinsic value suggest that only primary qualities such as extension and mass are primary qualities that objectively exist, whereas values are more like colors. That is, they are secondary qualities that do not inhere in objects themselves but are literally only "in the eye of the beholder." Rolston recognizes that such a position is in conflict with his defense of objective value, but he seems hesitant to engage with the debate over primary and secondary qualities directly, perhaps because it would lead him too far into metaphysical waters he wants to avoid.

> A simpler, less anthropically based, more biocentric theory holds that some values, instrumental and intrinsic, are objectively there, discovered not generated by the valuer. Trees may not be coloured without a perceiver, but they exist *per se*; and only if their existence is dynamically defended. That is not an analogue of colour at all. Trees do not appear to be green, and perhaps we do not want to call the electromagnetic waves actually their "greenness." Trees also photosynthesise with or without humans watching them.[77]

Here we see Rolston come very close to engaging in metaphysics, but characteristically he veers away. My suggestion is that Rolston will really only be able to defend his axiology adequately if he rejects the dubious metaphysical distinction between primary and secondary qualities. Whitehead gives him just the way of doing that.

Whitehead's philosophy of organism fundamentally rejects the doctrine of primary and secondary qualities as a misguided byproduct of a misguided dualistic substance metaphysics.[78] Reality is not composed of "containers" or substances with properties, some of which are real (primary qualities) and others that are not real but are merely projected onto them by conscious minds or subjects who perceive them (secondary qualities). According to such a position, the greenness of the oak's leaves and the brownness of its bark are *merely* wavelengths of light reflecting off the surfaces and striking my retina. The color is not "in" the object but in me, as the perceiver. Similarly, value is not real; it is not "in" objects as primary qualities, but it is a subjective projection onto a valueless world. Actually, for many philosophers, even this position overstates the reality of values. Values are not even like colors (they are not even secondary qualities), which at least have some physical relation to their objects (primary qualities). For some, values are better seen as tertiary qualities. This is the position developed by Samuel Alexander in his *Space, Time, Deity* (1920).

Alexander develops an interesting account that contends that value—along with truth, goodness, and beauty—are "tertiary qualities."[79] Let's briefly consider his position as it will be useful for understanding Rolston's position and how it can be aided by being grounded in Whitehead's environmental metaphysics.

> Consider the proposition that the rose is red. The rose is real, its redness is real, and the redness belongs really to the rose. The elements of the proposition and the fact that they belong to each other are altogether independent of me. This rose would be red whether known to me or another and before there were eyes to see it. But the proposition is *true* only if there is human *appreciation* of it. Similarly the colour of the rose belongs to it irrespective of any human spectator; but it is not beautiful except for a contemplating mind.[80]

Notice here the "lamp light" function of the human perceiver who "lights" up that which is there. Value, truth, goodness, and beauty exist only in being appreciated by the human perceiver.

> Strictly speaking, it is not this totality of knower and known, of subject and object, which is true or good or beautiful. The tertiary qualities are not objective like the secondary ones, nor peculiar to mind and thus subjective like consciousness, nor are

they like the primary qualities common to both subjects and objects. They are subject-object determinations.[81]

    [. . .]

    Values then or tertiary qualities of things involve relation to the collective mind, and what is true, good, or beautiful is not true or good or beautiful except as so combined with the collective mind.[82]

Notice that the distinctions between primary, secondary, and tertiary qualities are entirely predicated on a strong, ontological distinction between subjects and objects.[83] If Whitehead is right to reject both substance metaphysics and the bifurcation of nature (the bifurcation of object and subject), and I believe he is, then there is no reason to spin complex accounts of primary, secondary, and tertiary qualities. As we have learned throughout this volume thus far, according to the philosophy of organism, every achievement of reality, every ontological event is a subject-object that has value for itself, for others, and for the whole. For Whitehead, "the red glow of the sunset should be as much part of nature as the molecules and electric waves by which men of science would explain the phenomenon."[84] There is no vacuous, valueless actuality; no lifeless, naked bits of matter with primary qualities anthropogenically clothed with secondary and tertiary qualities.

What does all of this amount to for understanding Rolston's account of value? First, I contend that Rolston should embrace fully his intuition that value is *not* like the view of color as a secondary quality found only in the mind of the perceiver. But, to make good on his claim, Rolston needs another account that would explain how not only color, smell, touch, but also value and beauty, really exist. And this he does not sufficiently do because he stops short of engaging in the metaphysical theorizing that would make this possible. He seems at times to gesture in this direction, but he always stops short of diving headlong.

In an age of naturalism, philosophers seem as yet unable to naturalize values. They are naturalizing ethics and metaphysics. But philosophers are slow to naturalize axiology. If they do, they try to demonstrate the biological roots of human values. Joining evolutionary psychologists, they show that our values root in our biological needs—for food, shelter, security, resources, self-defense, offspring, stability and status in our societies. Beyond that, philosophers are reluctant to naturalize values in any deeper sense. They cannot disconnect nature from humans so that anything else in nature can have any intrinsic value on its own. Nature comes to have value only when humans take it up into their experience. Humans en-act value.[85]

Rolston's goal of securing the reality of value is far better achieved by adopting a Whiteheadian naturalistic metaphysics and its rejection of the bifurcation of nature as the most viable route to developing a naturalistic axiology. Without a metaphysical defense of the connection of value to the nature of reality and without explaining how one overcomes the metaphysical bifurcation of subject and object, Rolston will forever fall short of his goal of justifying duties to and values in nature. Embracing an organicist metaphysics of process allows him to justify many of his core claims, including teleology, objective intrinsic value, organism-in-environment, and the triadic structure of value. Rolston is right.

Ontologically, we should begin with an account of being and becoming in the world out there, and, at or near the end of this account, move inside to the mind "in here" and how it knows what is out there. Epistemologically, we do have to start within and move out, with *constructed* percepts and constructs. We may find sometimes that objects and processes in the world are conceptually *clarified* as much as conceptually *contaminated* by our linguistic conceptions. Our percepts and concepts *constitute* our knowledge; and, equally, our knowing (to use still another c-word) is *constrained* by our objects and events out there.[86]

Chapter 4

Beauty

For many environmental philosophers, Aldo Leopold's famous land ethic dictum has been a key source of inspiration: "a thing is right when it tends to preserve the integrity, stability, and beauty of the biotic community; it is wrong when it tends otherwise."[1] What if this reference to beauty were taken neither metaphorically nor subjectively? What if we interpreted Leopold's famous injunction literally to mean that the world is only good when it is beautiful? As it turns out, this is precisely what Alfred North Whitehead claims in *The Adventures of Ideas* (1933). A primary goal of this chapter is to explore how Whitehead's organicist metaphysics and its distinctive embrace of aesthetics can provide yet another helpful foundation for environmental ethics and its efforts to properly respect and protect the beauty of other than human nature.

Before examining Whitehead's account of beauty, in the first part I consider Leopold's land ethic and examine and respond to the generally hostile reception of Leopold on the part of Whitehead scholars. Given this, in the second part I explore the role and definition of beauty within Whitehead's philosophy of organism and how it might come to inform the basis for environmental ethics.

The Process Reception and Rejection of Leopold

Leopold opens his essay "The Land Ethic" by noting that over the millennia, the scope of human beings' moral concern has gradually expanded. He likens this to a sort of ethical evolution. Whereas once some humans were treated as mere property and were therefore outside the scope of direct moral concern, now we must recognize that ethical consideration extends to all humans. Leopold contends that the next stage of ethical evolution must commence, shrinking once again the sphere of those beings treated as mere property and limited only by what is expedient. "There is as yet no ethic dealing with man's relation to the land and to the animals and plants which grow upon it. Land, like Odysseus' slave-girls, is still property. The land-relation is still strictly economic, entailing privileges but not obligations. The extension of ethics to this third element in human environment is, if I read the evidence correctly, an evolutionary possibility and an ecological necessity."[2] As in past stages of ethical evolution, the key is in expanding one's concept of community. Though human, Odysseus's slaves were not part of the moral community. They were mere property, to be disposed of as one chooses. For Leopold, a chief impediment to further expanding the moral community beyond the human sphere is an attenuated and inaccurate conception of land. Too often, humans conceive of land as the real-estate developer does, perhaps imagining an empty (often previously forested) lot with a "For Sale" sign on a stake. Unused land (what John Locke calls literally "waste land"[3]) is there to be developed, to be made productive, valuable. Leopold notes that this view of land as mere property suffers from the same problems as the slaveholder who sees his human slaves as mere property.

Biology and ecology have revealed that land is not an inert plot: "land . . . is not merely soil; it is a fountain of energy flowing through a circuit of soils, plants, and animals."[4] This is a truly capacious sense of land. The land, for Leopold, includes the soil, yes, but also the animals that roam on it, the plants that grow out of it, the waters that flow over it, and the air circulating above it. "The land" is the process by which energy moves through complex ecological systems of relationship and dependence. For Leopold, "land" is the prolific fountain of life.

Just as human slavery was abolished by recognizing that all people are rightly part of the moral community, Leopold contends that the next stage in ethical evolution must again extend the moral community, but this time to include all of nature or what he calls the "biotic community." (Recall that it is this concept that, Hargrove wonders, may have been derived from Whitehead.[5]) "The land ethic simply enlarges the boundaries of the community to include soils, waters, plants, and animals, or collectively: the land."[6] In a sense, Leopold is inviting his reader to come to terms with what we have known for a century and a half, but have failed to appropriate into our ethics: humans are not separate from the land, but are a part and product of it. "In short, a land ethic changes the role of *Homo sapiens* from conqueror of the land-community to plain member and citizen of it. It implies respect for his fellow-members, and also respect of the community as such."[7] As Lynn White Jr. put it in 1967, "Despite Darwin, we are *not*, in our hearts, part of the natural process. We are superior to nature, contemptuous of it, willing to use it for our slightest whim."[8] Though most intellectually affirm that humans are a part of and intimately dependent on the biotic community, our ethical systems fail to recognize this fact. Leopold invites us to embrace the next stage of ethical evolution.

It is important to note that Leopold is not arguing that we and other animals cannot or should not use the land. Rather, Leopold is calling for a biology-affirming ethic. As Whitehead noted in *Process and Reality*, "Life is robbery. . . . [But] the robber requires justification."[9] To live is to take from and give to others. The biotic community is a vibrant exchange of energy. The goal of a land ethic is neither to preserve nature *for* humans nor *from* humans, but to recognize that "decent land use" is not merely a matter of economic expedience but also a matter of ethical concern. "The 'key-log' which must be moved to release the evolutionary process for an ethic is simply this: quit thinking about decent land-use as solely an economic problem. Examine each question in terms of what is ethically and esthetically right, as well as what is economically expedient."[10] Leopold is making use here of a forestry metaphor. Loggers for centuries have cut down trees and floated them downstream to a mill. If too many are put into the river, a logjam can result. The key-log is the log that, if removed, would clear the logjam, allowing the stream to flow once again. Leopold believes the shallow anthropocentrism of economic expediency has jammed the evolutionary stream of ethics. We can remove this "key-log" if we "quit thinking about decent land-use as solely an economic problem" and "examine each question in terms of what is ethically and esthetically right, as well as what is economically expedient."[11] This will allow the evolution of a land ethic, in which "a thing is right when it tends to preserve the integrity, stability, and beauty of the biotic community. It is wrong when it tends otherwise."[12] This relatively enigmatic dictum is the central tenant of the land ethic.

Given the affinities between Leopold and Whitehead, one would think process philosophers would see in the land ethic an important resource for developing an adequate environmental ethic. Although there are notable exceptions, such as Jay McDaniel (1988) and Pete Gunter (2000), the reception of Leopold's land ethic among Whitehead scholars has been largely critical, starting with Susan Armstrong (1986), Daniel Dombrowski (1988), and, more recently, Rem Edwards (2014). Armstrong best captures the concerns:

> Despite its attractiveness . . . the land ethic suffers from three main difficulties: (1) the emphasis on the interdependence of the biotic community deprives individuals any value except insofar as they contribute to the system, giving rise to Regan's charge of "environmental fascism." Here Whitehead's balanced approach is superior. (2) No value is accorded to rationality, moral agency, self-consciousness, religious insight, or artistic creativity except insofar as they might contribute to the community. This is a seriously counterintuitive result, since while such activities do often so contribute, we commonly value them as ends in themselves. (3) No criteria are offered by which the community itself can be assessed, unless we simply appeal to short or long-term human interest.[13]

There are good reasons for these worries, which are shared by both Dombrowski and Edwards.[14] As it has often been defended by its chief proponent (J. Baird Callicott), Leopold's land ethic has been understood to be strongly holistic. The concern, Armstrong notes, is that just as twentieth-century fascism sanctioned the sacrifice of individuals for the good of the state, ecological holism justifies the sacrifice of individuals for the good of the ecosystem, the biotic community. Further, the concern, shared by Dombrowski and Edwards, is that the holism of the land ethic does not allow for a value hierarchy in which sentience or consciousness are able to be recognized for their greater degree of intrinsic value.

I do not dispute that an ecological holism is open to the concerns raised by Armstrong, Dombrowski, or Edwards. What I question is whether this strong ecological holism is a necessary aspect of a land ethic. My claim is that it is not. There are several important things to remember. First, Leopold was neither philosopher nor ethicist. His brief essay is more suggestive than systematic. Much like the work of Albert Schweitzer, the value of Leopold's land ethic is in its fecundity and evocativeness, not in its systematicity or analytic adequacy.

Given this context, let us return to Armstrong's three claims above. First, the land ethic's emphasis on the interdependence of the biotic community does *not* deprive individuals of value any more than Whitehead's emphasis on interdependence does. Whether a vicious ecological holism emerges will depend on one's more basic axiological and metaphysical commitments. What has intrinsic value and why? Is all value equal or does it differ by degrees? What is the metaphysical relationship between the one and the many, the individual and the community, and how does this affect the value of each? The answers to these questions will also determine the outcome of Armstrong's second concern: that the land ethic accords no value to rationality, moral agency, or self-consciousness. Whether this is the case depends again on whether one embraces a flat axiology (as in some versions of deep ecology) or an axiological hierarchy (as in, for instance, Rolston). As I argue in chapter five on hierarchy, Whitehead's thought provides an ideal context in which to pursue the compatibility of holism with an axiological hierarchy. Finally, the third concern, that the land ethic provides no criteria by which the community can be assessed, is a complaint regarding the incompleteness of Leopold's statement of the land ethic. It does not refer to an inherent weakness of the system. In a sense, the process critics of Leopold's land ethic are claiming that Leopold's land ethic is totalizing in its holism. However, as we have seen, Leopold provides no axiology. If his land ethic were grounded in an axiology such as Whitehead's, which affirms the intrinsic value of the self, the other, and the whole, then the concerns of a totalizing holism subside, as do the concerns regarding ecofascism. Thus, I encourage Whitehead scholars to reconsider Leopold's land ethic. Yes, the concerns regarding ecofascism are real, but they are not a necessary feature of a land ethic, especially if grounded in Whitehead's organicist environmental metaphysics that recognizes the universal aim at the creation of beauty.

Reality as Kalogenic

Throughout many of his post-London works (1924–1947), we find Whitehead repeat two central claims: first, that the aim of the universe is at the production of beauty, and second, that morality is an "aspect" of aesthetics. For instance, as early as his 1926 Lowell Lectures, *Religion in the Making*, we find Whitehead claim that "all order is . . . aesthetic order, and the moral order is merely certain aspects of aesthetic order."[15] Though a discussion of beauty is notably absent from *Process and Reality* (1929), in *Adventures of Ideas* (1933) Whitehead expands on his earlier claims, arguing that "the teleology of the Universe is directed to the production of Beauty. Thus any system of things which in any wide sense is beautiful is to that extent justified in its existence."[16] He continues, "the real world is good, when it is beautiful."[17] These claims are once again repeated in his last monograph, *Modes of Thought* (1938), where he argues: "The final actuality has the unity of power. The essence of power is the drive towards aesthetic worth for its own sake. There is no other fact. It constitutes the drive of the universe."[18] At first encounter, many are likely to chafe at such claims. Does Whitehead really mean to argue that all forms of order are aesthetic? Why would he give such a prominent role to beauty? Furthermore, does he really intend to reduce ethics to aesthetics? How are we to interpret these claims?

Though notable in its absence from Clare Palmer's negative assessment of process thought, Whitehead's characterizations of beauty are not overlooked by Paul Arthur Schilpp, who, in the Library of Living Philosophers he edited and dedicated to Whitehead, does not hesitate to accuse Whitehead of a vicious aestheticism.[19] While both ethics and aesthetics involve value judgments and value experience, Schilpp argues, this structural similarity is an insufficient justification for reducing the one (ethics) to the other (aesthetics). There are, Schilpp insists, "sufficient differences, both of kind and in number, between the two types of value judgment and value experience to warrant a rather precise method of differing analysis, procedure, and conclusion for the two areas."[20] Because Schilpp conceives of these substantial differences between ethics and aesthetics, he sees the subsumption of ethics under aesthetics as a "disastrous reduction." "After all," Schilpp argues, "morality is not beauty, though the moral life—like a lot of other things—may be beautiful; but it is not the fact that it is beautiful which makes it moral."[21]

If correct, Schilpp's criticism would seriously undermine the viability and appeal of a Whiteheadian-inspired environmental ethic. Thus, to avoid the charge of aestheticism, perhaps we should join Lynne Belaief, who argues in *Toward a Whiteheadian Ethics* (1984) that "the apparent identity of ethical concepts with the basic aesthetic analysis is only apparent, Whitehead [is] being *intentionally metaphorical* when using the language of aesthetics to apply to ethical phenomena, except in the justifiable case when he is discussing the generic origin of moral experience."[22] Initially, Belaief's position seems appealing, for if we interpret Whitehead's statements as being merely metaphorical, the danger of aestheticism subsides. Yet, as a closer analysis reveals, Belaief's position comes at a high price.

The problem with Belaief's solution is that Whitehead's claim that the good is an aspect of the beautiful follows directly from his more basic commitment to the view that *every* process aims at the achievement of beauty.[23] Every process represents some finite achievement of beauty (and value). Thus, if, following Belaief, we argue that Whitehead is merely being metaphorical, then we commit ourselves to the untenable position that morality has an aim and structure different from that of the rest of the creative advance.[24] For in making morality into an inexplicable anomaly, we risk rupturing the coherence of Whitehead's system. We are forced, therefore, to take seriously Whitehead's claims regarding the foundational relationship between aesthetics and ethics. Yet, in doing so have we not granted that he is guilty of a vicious aestheticism as Schilpp contends? How are we to maintain the coherence of Whitehead's system while avoiding the potentially serious charge of aestheticism?

The problem, I contend, is not with Whitehead's alleged aestheticism, but in critics' attenuated conception of beauty. This problem also plagues Aldo Leopold's land ethic dictum. Just as we found in chapters two and three that Whitehead's organicist environmental metaphysics makes it possible to overcome previously intractable debates over intrinsic value, we might also find that the philosophy of organism makes it possible to defend a metaphysical conception of beauty that secures the third leg of Leopold's dictum from the clutches of a simplistic subjectivism that would claim that "beauty is merely in the eye of the beholder."

Indeed, we find that Whitehead's conception of beauty is far more rich and complex than the common usage of the term.[25] Just as "creativity" is the incessant process whereby "the many become one and are increased by one,"[26] Whitehead defines "beauty" as the achievement of a "miraculous balance" wherein "the whole displays its component parts, each with its own value enhanced; and the parts lead up to a whole, which is beyond themselves, and yet not destructive of themselves."[27] For Whitehead, every process aims at the achievement of beauty in the sense that it aims at achieving an ideal balance between *harmony*, which concerns the greatest possible variety of detail with effective contrast, and *intensity*, which concerns the comparative magnitude or depth of the contrasts achieved. In this sense, there is no strictly unbeautiful experience. Actuality is—to use a phrase coined by Frederick Ferré—inherently kalogenic or beauty-generating.[28] Moreover, in defining it in this way, we also come to understand better the relationship between beauty, importance, and value (see chapter two for a discussion of the relationship between importance and value). In that, for Whitehead, each of these three terms is at various times taken to be the aim of both process and morality, beauty, importance, and value are coextensive. Every individual represents a finite achievement of beauty, importance, and value for itself, for others, and for the whole.

Whitehead's most extensive discussion of beauty is found in *Adventures of Ideas*, where he defines beauty as "the mutual adaptation of the several factors in an occasion of experience."[29] He explains this adaptation in terms of a twofold aim. The first aim, what he calls the "minor form" of beauty, is at the "absence of mutual inhibition" so that the elements brought together "do not inhibit each other." Thus, the minor form of beauty involves a harmony of experience in that there is "the absence of painful clash." The major form of beauty then builds on this harmony and "adds to it . . . new contrasts of objective content."[30] Thus, in the major form of beauty, there is not only a lack of mutual inhibition or harmony, but also the introduction of new contrasts that deepen the *intensity* of the experience achieved such that its elements are not only mutually compatible but mutually enhancing.[31] It is contrast that gives depth and richness to the "clutch at vivid immediacy" that is life.[32] This is the very essence of the creative advance wherein, as Whitehead puts it, "the parts contribute to the massive feeling of the whole, and the whole contributes to the intensity of feeling of the parts."[33]

As Whitehead defines beauty as the dual aim at harmony and intensity, the subjective aim of every occasion is at the achievement of the most harmonious and intense experience possible. Harmony—what Whitehead calls the minor form of beauty—is understood as the "absence of mutual inhibition among the various prehensions" that constitute an experience.[34] The aim at harmony, then, is at maximally inclusive unity in diversity. If the inclusion is too great, there is a "painful clash,"[35] and experience risks degenerating into chaos. On the other hand, if the inclusion is too limited, the deficiency of diversity results in a "tame" monotony.

Yet, Whitehead insightfully notes, the absence of mutual inhibition is not sufficient to achieve deeply beautiful experience. Beauty requires not only the absence of conflict (harmony), but also the realization of new contrasts (intensity). It is through the realization of patterned contrasts that "new conformal intensities of feelings" are achieved.[36] It is in the aim at intensity where the depth and richness of experience is purchased. "Thus the parts contribute to the massive feeling of the whole, and the whole contributes to the intensity of feeling of the parts."[37] Each occasion of experience aims at the achievement of beauty, then, in the sense that it seeks to bring the elements within its actual world together in a way that avoids the painful clash of conflicting ends (harmony) and furthermore seeks to relate these elements together in such a way as they not only avoid the conflict of mutual inhibition, but also deepen the intensity of experience felt through the introduction of new contrasts.

Working in a similar vein, Charles Hartshorne describes beauty as a "golden mean" between two pairs of extremes.[38] In this way, it is helpful to conceive of beauty as analogous to a bipolar version of Aristotle's concept of virtue. Whereas, for instance, courage is understood as the mean between a single pair of extremes—that is, rashness and cowardliness—beauty is here defined as the mean between, on the one hand, unity and diversity, and, on the other hand, simplicity and complexity. When diversity is too great and unity is lost, experience becomes chaotic, yet when unity is too great and diversity is lost, experience becomes dull and monotonous. Similarly, an otherwise harmonious experience that is too simple is trivial, while one that is too complex may be so utterly profound that it cannot be grasped.[39] The universal aim at beauty, therefore, is the aim at the ideal balance between a *harmony* of the details and the *intensity* of the contrast between these elements.

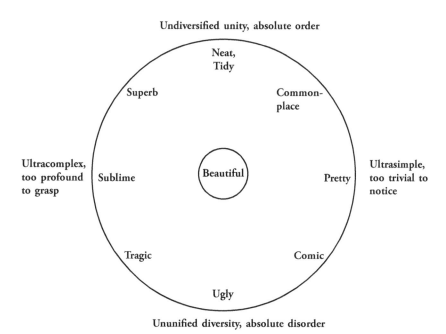

Figure 4.1. The Hartshorne-Dessoir-Davis Aesthetic Circle. According to Hartshorne, this diagram was created by himself; Max Dessoir, whom Hartshorne describes as a German writer on aesthetics; and Kay Davis, whom Hartshorne describes as an artist and a former student of his from Emory University. *Source:* Charles Hartshorne, "The Kinds and Levels of Aesthetic Value," in *The Zero Fallacy and Other Essays in Neoclassical Philosophy*, ed. Mohammad Valady (Chicago: Open Court, 1997), 203–14; and Charles Hartshorne, "The Aesthetic Matrix of Value," in *Creative Synthesis and Philosophic Method* (LaSalle: Open Court, 1970), 302–22.

Hartshorne developed a graphical depiction (see figure 4.1[40]) to help illustrate this point. The vertical dimension connects to classical conceptions of beauty, which conceive it as maximal unity in diversity or harmony. The horizonal dimension is a more distinctive addition on the part of Whitehead and Hartshorne, who conceive of it as maximum effective contrast between simplicity and complexity. This effective contrast allows not only for harmony (vertical dimension) but also for intensity (horizontal dimension). Beauty, then, is this two-dimensional mean between pairs of extremes.

Note that, strictly speaking, there is no truly unbeautiful experience. There is literally nothing (no-thing) outside of the circle. The zero of beauty is in fact the zero of actuality.[41] In achieving *some* degree of harmony and intensity, every individual is, taken by itself, beautiful. However, taken in its larger environment, an individual may indeed be ugly. "Evil, triumphant in its enjoyment, is so far good in itself; but beyond itself it is evil in its character of a destructive agent among things greater than itself. In the summation of the more complete fact it has secured a descent towards nothingness, in contrast to the creativeness of what can without qualification be termed good. Evil is positive and destructive."[42]

AESTHETIC REALISM

Jazz music is a helpful illustration of Whitehead's complex conception of beauty.[43] As the composer Edward Green insightfully notes, jazz is not only an art "of entertainment," "of self-expression," and "of group solidarity," though it is all of these.[44] Jazz is also "a philosophic art, impelled—just as certainly as 'verbally discursive' philosophy—by the desire to tell the truth about reality. . . . The subject matter of jazz is nothing smaller than the world itself. This world is immediate, gutsy, vernacular, and colorful. But it is also abstract—a drama of eternal philosophic opposites."[45] In a great jazz composition, each instrument adds its sonic shape to a harmonic whole that is at once beyond itself, yet not destructive of itself. There is a unity-in-diversity brought into a patterned contrast.

Take, for instance, the work of Duke Ellington, as we find it in *The Mooche* (1928), *Ko-Ko* (1940), or *Far East Suite* (1966). As Green notes, in each of these compositions "Duke Ellington's motivic techniques depend on the simultaneity of opposites: of unity and diversity; of sameness and difference; of something remaining firmly itself while also being utterly flexible."[46] He continues, "Motivic composition depends on ability to perceive these opposites—unity and diversity, change and sameness—together. Ellington was a master of the art."[47] Green does not limit his claims to jazz. Relying on the American poet and critic Eli Siegel, Green argues that "there is no fundamental difference between the structure of reality and the structure of beauty."[48] This is the central tenet of "Aesthetic Realism," which Siegel claims to have founded in 1941. "In Aesthetic Realism, beauty is the putting together of things that can be thought of as opposites. All beauty is a making one of opposites, and the making one of opposites is what we are going after in ourselves."[49] Using examples from music, dance, literature, and even architecture, Siegel argues that all beauty is the making one of opposites, of unity and diversity, permanence and change, simplicity and complexity. "Music, changing in time, insists more and more as it goes on, on the stability, justification, permanence of what it began with. Harmony is that which imposes on the differing and transitory that which will make them coherent and permanent. The pleasure from music can be put in this exclamation: 'As those notes go on, and change, how something I looked for is being heard by me!' Rhythm is any instance of change and sameness seen at once."[50] Yet for Siegel these traditional aesthetic modes are not to be seen as exceptional; reality itself is to be seen as exemplifying this aesthetic unification of opposites. "One of the permanent, ontological situations of reality," Green writes, "is the oneness of change and sameness. Reality is changing all the time, and yet remains coherent. It is not, after all, a verbal accident that we call it a 'universe' and not a 'multiverse.' Art reflects this truth. As Aesthetic Realism sees it, all successful music is oneness of change and stability; diversity and unity; coherence and surprise. Art embodies philosophic honesty."[51] As the creative unification of opposites, art reflects a truth that describes the structure of reality. In this way, Siegel and Green's Aesthetic Realism is in deep sympathy with Whitehead's own claims that aesthetic intensity of experience is the universal aim of all process.

Note that, on both views (i.e., both Whitehead's and Siegel/Green's), as a unique achievement of harmony and intensity, every occasion of experience is, to some degree, beautiful. The zero of beauty, as Charles Hartshorne noted, is the zero of actuality. In determining itself, every occasion necessarily achieves some degree of beauty and is, to that degree, justified in its existence. Yet, it is still very much the case that an occasion of experience can fall short of the maximally unified diversity and balanced complexity open to it. It is, in this sense, ugly.

Whitehead fully recognizes that ugliness is all too real in our finite world. Again, Siegel defends a very similar view, arguing that "ugliness has to do with the fragmentation, fractionality, brokenness, vicissitude, subtraction, division, addition, multiplication, alteration *within* beauty as a whole, or one."[52] The ugliness of violence involves the destruction of achieved forms of beauty in the realization of new forms. As Whitehead readily notes, the great novelty and the intense beauty achieved by living occasions is only possible through such violence. For this reason, although tragic, violence is preferable to the sweet, anesthetic death of experience in which an occasion embraces lower forms of beauty when higher forms are possible. This embrace of "tameness" is far more destructive in the long run for it cuts against the very "essence of the universe" in its pursuit of ever-higher forms of beauty. As the aim of the creative advance of the universe, beauty is the central category of Whitehead's system.

A renewed focus on the aesthetic character of process also provides greater depth to our understanding of Whitehead's ever-enigmatic notion of "creativity." Rather than understanding Whitehead's "Category of the Ultimate" as a sort of koan on which you are meant to meditate, we should understand the content of this central category in more explicitly aesthetic terms. Taken in the context of his discussion of beauty, the claim that "the many become one, and are increased by one" takes on greater depth.[53] The many contribute to a new whole whereby the intensity of each part is greater, yet this increase in intensity does not require the loss of individuality.

Indeed, there is good reason to believe it was reflection on the beauty of great art that increasingly defined Whitehead's understanding of creativity. According to his account in *Modes of Thought* (1938), every occasion represents the achievement of a composition whereby there is "one whole, arising from the interplay of many details."[54] Like great art, the aesthetic synthesis of concrescence achieves a "miraculous balance" between the parts and the whole in which "the whole displays its component parts, each with its own value enhanced; and the parts lead up to a whole, which is beyond themselves, and yet not destructive of themselves."[55] Importance, meaning, and value are achieved not in sacrificing the many parts for a more meaningful whole, but from "the vivid grasp of the interdependence of the one and the many." We trivialize experience "if either side of this antithesis, [the one or the many,] sinks into the background."[56]

PEACE

A kalocentric or beauty-centered approach to our social and ecological challenges seeks to reorient our conception of ourselves and our place in the world so that we begin to understand that there are richer, more meaningful forms of beauty than the anemic simulacra we so often are force-fed. Whitehead calls this expanded consciousness "peace." Peace, he writes in *Adventures of Ideas*, is the "Harmony of Harmonies which calms destructive turbulence and completes civilization" and makes it possible to move beyond "the soul's preoccupation with itself."[57] He continues, "peace carries with it a surpassing of personality." To commit oneself to peace, to this surpassing of personality, is "primarily a trust in the efficacy of Beauty."[58]

This is not a sort of absentminded trust, nor is it a blind faith. "Peace," for Whitehead, is not the mere absence of discord; it is a positive feeling that "crowns the 'life and motion' of the soul."[59] To trust in the efficacy of beauty is to choose in each action to affirm more beauty, to fight against the slow relapse into tameness and anesthesia, and to fight against the violence that destroys the forms of beauty we have inherited. To put one's trust in the "efficacy of beauty" does not mean that we close our eyes to the ills of the world and hope for the best. Rather, to put one's trust in the efficacy of beauty is to strive always and everywhere to realize as much beauty as possible. To trust in the efficacy of beauty is to value deeply and thoroughly the intensely beautiful world around us. In the end, to place one's trust in the efficacy of beauty is to commit oneself to becoming an agent of beauty.

Yet in trusting the efficacy of beauty we must not forget the tragic nature of existence. In many respects, tragedy is both unavoidable and necessary in the achievement of higher forms of beauty. Indeed, life itself necessarily involves violence. In its bid to sustain itself, each living organism robs from others in order to create and sustain itself. "Life is robbery."[60] Like every living organism, human beings destroy other organisms in order to sustain themselves. The problem, as William James vividly puts it, is that "the actually possible world is vastly narrower than all that is demanded; and there is always a *pinch* between the ideal and the actual which can only be got through by leaving part of the ideal behind."[61] Yet this is not the end of the story. Although "life is robbery," as Whitehead continues, "it is at this point that with life morals become acute. The robber requires justification."[62] The question for morality, then, is whether and when this violence, this robbery, is justified.

Given this metaphysically rich understanding of beauty, it becomes possible to affirm that ethics is a species of aesthetics, but in a nonreductive sense. For to do so is simply to understand that morality is a process that is continuous with the creative advance of the universe as a whole. Indeed, given that the aim of the universe itself is at the attainment of beauty, importance, and value, as a particular form of process, morality *must* be a species of aesthetics. It is in this sense that we should understand Whitehead's claim that "the real world is good when it is beautiful."[63] Insofar as *every* process aims at the achievement of beauty, the conditions of beauty are the conditions of maximally effective processes in general, and, by extension, of morality. In this way, aesthetics can serve as a bridge from Whitehead's rich metaphysics of creativity to the development of a full-fledged ethics of creativity. It is this insight that guides my own interpretation and use of Whitehead's moral philosophy.[64]

Environmental philosophers have for half a century debated whether ethics is anthropocentric, biocentric, or ecocentric. Yet even the most capacious of these theories typically have difficulty thinking beyond our own planet and its distinct evolutionary history. As humans consider "colonizing" other planets, mining asteroids, and interacting with extraterrestrial life, it is urgent that we develop an adequate extraterrestrial ethic, a cosmocentric ethic. Just as Europeans' latent metaphysics and ethics defined what was morally defensible in their colonization of this planet, our species' latent metaphysics and ethics define whether certain actions require moral justification. We take our ethics—and our metaphysics—with us as we move into and beyond the solar system.

Grounded in Whitehead's philosophy of organism, it is possible to conceive of a cosmocentric ethic whose ultimate duty is beauty. Reality is fundamentally kalogenic; each drop of actuality is a unique achievement of beauty and value. "The teleology of the Universe," Whitehead tells us in *Adventures of Ideas*, "is directed to the production of Beauty."

By recognizing that to become is to be an achievement of beauty and value—that is, by recognizing the kalogenic nature of reality—Leopold's centering of beauty in his land ethic dictum takes on added depth and meaning. But, whereas Leopold contends that something is right insofar as it tends to preserve the "integrity, stability, and beauty of the biotic community," a Whiteheadian approach might contend that something is right insofar as it affirms the greatest *harmony, intensity, and beauty* which in each situation is possible. Situated within a kalocentric organicist environmental metaphysics, we can appreciate the literal sense in which an action is only good insofar as it preserves the beauty of the biotic community. In this way, environmental ethics can overcome anthropocentrism not just by becoming biocentric or even ecocentric—by recognizing the universal, cosmic aim at beauty, environmental ethics becomes kalocentric.

Chapter 5

Hierarchy

Given the many promising elements of the philosophy of organism, why is Whitehead's work so routinely ignored by mainstream philosophy and by environmental philosophers in particular? We could, of course, point to the difficulty of Whitehead's texts, but given the comparative popularity of philosophers such as Heidegger, Hegel, and Wittgenstein, who are not known for the ease or accessibility of their work, this alone could not explain the trend. Surely "it's too hard" is not an acceptable reason for ignoring a philosophical project? Noting this, others might explain the neglect by suggesting that Whitehead's work had the misfortune of being born out of season; after all, metaphysical speculation has long been out of fashion. As we discussed in chapter one, this is certainly a significant part of the story.

While this line of reasoning might account for the *general* neglect of Whitehead's work among philosophers, there would seem to be a more subtle reason why the philosophy of organism is frequently passed over by potentially sympathetic *environmental* philosophers. The hesitation on the part of many stems not from Whitehead's emphasis on interrelatedness or his characterization of individuals as nested societies of societies, nor does it stem from his affirmation of the intrinsic beauty and value of every individual. For some, the problem is not that Whitehead affirms the equality of every individual in *having* value, but rather his recognition that not every individual has value *equally*. It is this claim—that there are grades or degrees of beauty and value among the types of individuals of the world—that gives some environmental philosophers pause, and for good reason. For too long, the so-called great chain-of-being has not only justified the violent destruction of nature, but also the brutal subjugation of women and

Indigenous peoples. Because of the truly devastating results of this thinking, some philosophers view with great suspicion any philosophy that embraces a hierarchical conception of reality and value.

In this chapter, the goal is to examine the senses in which a Whiteheadian organicist metaphysics does and does not retain hierarchy. I begin by considering critiques from deep ecologists and ecofeminists that a process metaphysics ultimately slides back into an invidious anthropocentrism. Then I transition to examine directly how Whitehead's philosophy of organism makes it possible to retain an axiological and ontological hierarchy without it resulting in an invidious anthropocentrism. It is my contention that if we properly understand the kalocentric nature of the creative advance, then we will see what most process philosophers have failed to recognize: *an individual's onto-aesthetic status—its value and beauty—is not strictly determinative of its moral significance.* I conclude by considering the role of hierarchy in the ethics of eating.

Deep Ecology, Ecofeminism, and Hierarchy

Ecofeminists and deep ecologists would typically be natural allies of a Whiteheadian organicist metaphysics. Yet, for these otherwise sympathetic philosophers, the philosophy of organism's insistence on what appears to be a traditional hierarchy of value is too much like the old hierarchies that have for centuries been used to justify great violence and destruction. Indeed, pointing to this hierarchy of value, some have accused process philosophers of not having fully abandoned their anthropocentrism, noting that even if everything has value, as the most complex form of life known, humans are still likely to be at the top of that hierarchy. The ecofeminist Val Plumwood is representative of those who wonder whether, in retaining a hierarchy, Whitehead scholars have truly abandoned their anthropocentrism: "The criterion of experience builds in an anthropocentric hierarchy, since it conceives the world of nature as similar to but of lesser degree than the human mind, rather than as simply different. Such a position seems to offer little prospect of a real challenge to the thesis that the natural world is inferior to the human sphere, depending as it does on the extension in a weakened form of properties which are exemplified most fully by the human mind."[1] Although process scholars claim to have abandoned anthropocentrism, Plumwood considers, their axiological hierarchy seems to suggest otherwise.

The refusal to repudiate hierarchical thinking has also been the chief point of contention between process scholars and deep ecologists who otherwise maintain a fundamentally similar view of reality as an interdependent system of intrinsically valuable individuals. Deep ecologists, such as John Rodman, George Sessions, and Bill Devall, claim that by insisting on a complex hierarchy of value, a Whiteheadian moral philosophy is simply a thinly veiled anthropocentrism that will always put humans on top. " 'Subhumans' may now be accorded rights," John Rodman writes of process philosophy, "but we should not be surprised if their interests are normally overridden by the weightier interests of humans, for the choice of the quality to define the extended base class of those entitled to moral consideration has weighted the scales in that way."[2] Process philosophy claims to move beyond anthropocentrism, but it ultimately fails because it continues to embrace a conception of values that puts humans at its peak. As Devall and Sessions put it, "this attempt to apply Whiteheadian panpsychism, while positing various degrees of intrinsic value to the rest of Nature, nonetheless merely reinforces existing Western anthropocentrism, and thus fails to meet the deep ecology norm of 'ecological egalitarianism in principle.' "[3] Deep ecologists such as Devall and Sessions insist that the only way to fully repudiate anthropocentrism is to embrace the "intuition of ecological egalitarianism," whereby every individual not only has value, but has value equally.

Responses to these criticisms have not been lacking. For his part, John Cobb has noted consistently—and correctly, in my judgment—that it is a misinterpretation to suggest, as Plumwood does, that process thought is anthropocentric in the sense that it judges the value of an individual by its similarity to humans. The depth of beauty and value achievable by an individual is a function of the complexity of its own internal integration—*not* its similarity to humans, as Plumwood contends. Humans are "more valuable" because of their greater degree of complex integration, which affords them the potential for richer forms of experience. It is this richer experience, this more inclusive, harmonious, and intense experience, that makes human experience ontologically more valuable than simpler organisms. The hierarchy of value is *not* constructed in terms of how *similar* an individual is to us.[4] While Cobb's response does address Plumwood's misinterpretation, the disagreement with deep ecology seems to run deeper. The problem for deep ecologists has to do not only with the relative location of humans within the axiological hierarchy but also with the use to which this recognition is put.

The process philosopher David Ray Griffin takes a rather creative approach to the longstanding impasse between process philosophy and deep ecology. He suggests that the intuition of "biocentric equality" that some deep ecologists are after is in fact something process scholars can embrace alongside a hierarchical conception of value in which not all individuals have equal value. Griffin executes this impressive conceptual contortionism by distinguishing between "intrinsic value," which varies based on individual's complexity, and "inherent value," which is an individual's total value, taking its intrinsic and extrinsic value together.[5] Griffin notes that, given the inverse relationship between an individual's intrinsic value and extrinsic value, those individuals who have less intrinsic value because of their diminished complexity end up having greater extrinsic value within their ecological niche.[6] Thus, taking the individual's total intrinsic and extrinsic value together, Griffin suggests, each individual's "total inherent value" is roughly equal.[7]

Cobb's and Griffin's solutions are insightful and fully consistent with process thought. Cobb is right that it is a misunderstanding to claim that process thought is anthropocentric. Judgments of value are accurate only insofar as they accurately describe the actual depth of value achievable by an individual, not their perceived similarity to humans. He is also right to point out that deep ecologists do in practice, if not in their philosophy, make complex comparative judgments of value and that it would be irresponsible to do otherwise. Griffin's work is also very helpful in pointing out that we must include both an individual's intrinsic value and their extrinsic value in understanding their overall worth.[8] Despite its unpopularity among some deep ecologists and ecofeminists, process scholars steadfastly recognize that in fact different entities are capable of differing degrees of experience and value. Not all individuals are equal in the intensity of experience open to them.

Despite these very valiant efforts, with which I am in significant agreement, I remain convinced that both Cobb's and Griffin's interpretations of process thought fail to properly account for the *moral significance* of these complex judgments of value. There is a reason why their accounts have failed to persuade others. The problem, I contend, is that they continue to fall short of fully addressing critics' core disagreement with process thought. What seems to bother Plumwood, Sessions, Devall, Rodman, and others is not merely the *recognition* that the intensity of experience across individuals varies greatly, but the *use* to which this realization is put. The concern, it would seem, is that recognition of this hierarchy, which puts humans at the top of the scale, inevitably reinforces and repeats the old patriarchal and anthropocentric hierarchies. Although things have value independently of humans, since they have less value, the scales are still going to be tilted in our favor. In a sense, the objection is not metaphysical; it is moral.

It is my contention that, only if we properly understand the kalocentric nature of the creative advance can one properly see what most process philosophers have failed to recognize: *an individual's onto-aesthetic status is not strictly determinative of its moral significance.* I contend that by fully embracing beauty as the teleological aim of every form of process, one can rightly affirm the varying degrees of beauty and value achievable by individuals but refuse to succumb to the logic of domination and to allow this neatly to determine an individual's moral significance.

Hierarchy and the Chain of Being

Hierarchical views of nature have for centuries been used to justify the enslaving of peoples perceived as inferior, the often violent and coercive "reeducation" of Indigenous peoples, the patriarchal subjugation of women, the cruel use of nonhuman animals for often trivial purposes, and the wanton destruction of the natural world. I join those who condemn the oppressive nature of these forms of hierarchical thinking. Yet, I fear that, in their effort to right past wrongs, too many thinkers are in danger of throwing the axiological baby out with the ontological bathwater. That is, in rejecting hierarchy in favor of a flat ontology, one may unintentionally do comparatively more violence. As I will examine in more detail in the third part of this chapter with the help of the ecofeminist Karen Warren, though the aim at a great ontological leveling may be laudable, I fear that in embracing the opposite extreme and rejecting *all* hierarchical thinking, some may be in danger of doing violence to the many real and even morally significant differences between individuals. I am, in this way, in substantive agreement with Rolston: "It is permissible and even morally required to treat unequals with discrimination. One should treat *equals equally* and *unequals equitably.*"[9]

My claim in this section is that Whitehead's philosophy of organism provides a model for how to appreciate the many grades and types of beings in the world, while avoiding an invidious normative hierarchy that inevitably places everything at the whims of human beings. That is, I will argue that it is possible to defend hierarchy without "anthroparchy," or the view that simply because humans are capable of achieving more intense forms of beauty and value, they therefore are justified in dominating and using other beings with comparatively less value. "Anthroparchy" is a neologism playing on the concept of "patriarchy." If patriarchy is the attempt to explain and justify the dominance of men over women—that superiority justifies subordination—then "anthroparchy" is the attempt to explain and justify the dominance of humans over nature. To provide context, let us begin with a brief analysis of Aristotle's "great chain of being" and then contrast it with Whitehead's environmental metaphysics. Given this context, using the subtle and perceptive work of the ecofeminist Karen J. Warren, I present a model for how to recognize a "descriptive hierarchy" while rejecting a simplistic "prescriptive hierarchy."

To situate our discussion historically, let us begin with Aristotle's great chain of being, easily the most influential hierarchical conception of reality in the history of Western thought. Carefully studying the characteristic activities of organisms, Aristotle concluded that *phusis* (nature) is hierarchically organized into different types of substances according to the immanent presence of different kinds of animating *psuchê* (soul) that constitute the telos of each kind. The lowest rung on the ladder of being is the "vegetative" *psuchê*, which makes possible the basic functions of growth, reproduction, and nourishment. The "sensitive" *psuchê* of animals is hierarchically "above" plants in that it includes not only these basic vegetative capacities, but also the ability to move itself and to sense its environment. Finally, the highest rung on the ladder of being is occupied by the rational *psuchê* of humans, which includes all of the lower powers of plants and animals, but also reason with which to understand the eternal *arché* (first principles) of the cosmos.

For Aristotle, the formal and the final causes coincide in organisms; the "good" for each substance is defined by what it is. For instance, the good of an oak tree (e.g., water, light, and soil) is defined by its objective nature, its immanent *psuchê* or form. However, the good of each substance is *also* defined by its place in the larger order of nature such that the "lower" are "for" the "higher." Thus, in addition to immanent aims such as growth, nourishment, and reproduction, an oak tree's telos is also to be "for the sake of" animals such as birds and squirrels. Positioned at the top of the chain of being, then, part of the good for, the purpose of all plants and animals is to be "for the sake of" humans. Aristotle puts it this way in his *Politics*: "[A]fter the birth of animals, plants exist for their sake, and that the other animals exist for the sake of man. Now if nature makes nothing incomplete, and nothing in vain, the inference must be that she has made all animals for the sake of man."[10]

It is important to note that this hierarchy held not only *between* species but also *within* species. "And so," Aristotle continues, "from one point of view, the art of war is a natural art of acquisition, . . . an art which we ought to practice . . . against men who, though intended by nature to be governed, will not submit; for war of such a kind is naturally just."[11] Not only do plants exist for animals and animals for humans, but "inferior peoples," particularly the Germanic tribes in the north, exist for the sake of the "superior" Greeks. Therefore, inferior people ought to submit to the Greeks because, being superior, the Greeks are "by nature" intended to govern the inferior. Should the inferior peoples refuse to recognize this, a war to subjugate them is "naturally just."

In other instances, Aristotle's hierarchical thinking led him to conclude that some people are "natural slaves," who by nature are "living tools" to be used by "freemen."[12] Further, Aristotle explicitly argued that women were inferior to men and, indeed, were incomplete or deformed men.[13] Throughout the intervening centuries, time and again morally reprehensible practices were justified by appeals to the "natural order." The understandable response on the part of many has been to abandon all forms of hierarchical thinking. However, I wonder at this use of an argumentational broadsword when a scalpel might do as well. My claim is that Whitehead's philosophy of organism provides a viable model for recognizing reality's ontological and axiological hierarchical structure while avoiding the invidious moral implications traditionally associated with such a position. Let us turn to his position now.

Whitehead's philosophy of organism contends that there is a single genus of actuality, but that there are a multitude of different kinds and types of "things" in our processive cosmos and that these kinds and types can and should be seen in hierarchical relationships.[14] Thus, although there is but one genus of actuality, making his metaphysics a form of naturalism, Whitehead does *not* embrace a "flat" ontology. As we will explore in greater detail in chapter six, there are many and important differences between actual occasions, nexus, and societies. Some occasions achieve a very trivial depth of experience, while others are capable of intense beauty and value. Whitehead explains that these differences between actual occasions "enable a classification to be made whereby these occasions are gathered into various types."[15]

What Whitehead is rejecting is the dualisms and bifurcations that seek to cleave nature at its supposed joints, such as living/nonliving, mind/body, subject/object, rational/nonrational. However, in strongly rejecting these dualistic ontologies, he does not run to the opposite extreme. There are no "gaps" in the fabric of reality, but neither is reality an undifferentiated plenum. I have always admired Whitehead for seeking to walk this tightrope, rejecting bifurcation while recognizing difference.

To be more precise, there are two levels according to which one might evaluate the value and beauty of a given occasion: (1) relative to its own subjective aim or telos, or (2) relative to other achievements of beauty. Regarding the former, each occasion is capable of a certain magnitude of beauty and value; its subjective aim has a certain depth of achievement possible. In *Adventures of Ideas*, he describes this as the "Platonic Eros" according to which there is for each occasion the "urge toward the realization of [its] ideal perfection."[16] As each occasion progressively eliminates the indeterminacy in its subjective aim, it is determining what it is. Each occasion is thus responsible for what it is.[17]

It is in this context that I understand Whitehead's claim in *Religion in the Making* ([1926] 1996) that it is evil that a man has been degraded to the "level of a hog": "A hog is not an evil beast, but when a man is degraded to the level of a hog, with the accompanying atrophy of finer elements, he is no more evil than a hog. The evil of the final degradation lies in the comparison of what is with what might have been. During the process of degradation the comparison is an evil for the man himself, and at its final stage it remains an evil for others."[18] Previously I have defended the Augustinian elements in this account of evil as a "lack" of the amount of good possible in the subjective aim of an individual.[19] Here I would simply note that, according to Whitehead, we are right to judge an individual relative to its own standard; that is, relative to what it could and perhaps should have become. We hold it accountable for what it is. However, in another sense, seen implicitly here in the claim that the hog is at a lower level than the human person, it is also possible to make comparative judgments of beauty and value across individuals. Thus, in addition to judging an individual relative to its own standard, we might also make comparative judgments regarding the differences in the depth of beauty achieved by different individuals. As Whitehead puts it, "various occasions are thus comparable in respect to their relative depths of actuality. Occasions differ in importance of actuality."[20] Whitehead uses this sort of language throughout his writings.[21] Indeed, I would suggest that it is entirely uncontroversial to claim that Whitehead's speculative philosophy is essentially and necessarily composed of hierarchical conclusions at multiple levels.

The most detailed discussion of hierarchy is found in *Modes of Thought* in which he notes that there is "every gradation of transition between animals and men."[22]

> In animals we can see emotional feeling, dominantly derived
> from bodily functions, and yet tinged with purposes, hopes, and
> expression derived from conceptual functioning. In mankind, the

dominant dependence on bodily functioning seems still there. And yet the life a human being receives its worth, its importance, from the way in which unrealized ideals shape its purposes and tinge its actions. The distinction between men and animals is in one sense only a difference in degree. But the extent of the degree makes all the difference. The Rubicon has been crossed.[23]

I have long been concerned to understand, explain, and defend this claim that, ultimately, all difference is a matter of degree. However, what I have come to realize is that the degree-kind dichotomy is misleading. Whitehead's claim is not that there are no differences of kind, only differences of degree. Rather, Whitehead is defending the more sophisticated claim that all differences of kind are *products* of differences of degree.

To understand this claim regarding differences, imagine the colors red, orange, and yellow on a color-wheel spectrum. It is uncontroversial to note that red, orange, and yellow are each a different *kind* of color. Yet, the differences between these distinct colors are ultimately a result of differences of *degree*. Minute changes in the intensity of the color red gradually shift from red-orange to orange-red, to orange and then from orange to orange-yellow to yellow-orange, and finally to yellow. Notice that between these colors it is impossible to select one particular point and say, "here, this is clearly only red and not orange," or "this is clearly only orange and not yellow." Rather, there is orange-yellow and then yellow-orange and so on. There is no clear break, cut, or gap. Yet, this does not deny the fact that red, orange, and yellow are distinctly different colors. When differences of degree accumulate sufficiently, they result in differences of kind.[24]

In the same way, the dominant account of evolutionary theory teaches us that each species is a product of gradual accumulations of minute changes over millions of years, changes that result in distinct species of animals, such as chimps and humans. Chimpanzees (Pan troglodytes) are clearly one "kind" of animal and human beings (Homo sapiens) another, but the differences between us are ultimately only a matter of degree (they are in the same family, Hominidae). "But," as Whitehead puts it, "it is a difference of degree which makes all the difference."[25] In the end, there are very real and sometimes morally important differences of kind, but these differences of kind are the result of, are products of, differences of degree. Whitehead's system is hierarchical. The question left for us to answer is whether it is the bad, old kind of hierarchy or whether it can be saved. To help us better understand the relationship between hierarchy and oppression, I rely on the subtle and perceptive work of the ecofeminist Karen J. Warren.

Value Hierarchy Thinking and the Logic of Domination

Warren (2000) is concerned to understand what makes a particular worldview or "conceptual framework" oppressive.[26] "An oppressive conceptual framework is one that functions to explain, maintain, and 'justify' relationships of unjustified domination and subordination."[27] She outlines five "common features" of an oppressive conceptual framework. First, she notes, similar to Plumwood, that an oppressive conceptual framework involves "*value-hierarchical thinking*, that is 'Up-Down' thinking, which attributes greater value to that which is higher or Up, than to that which is lower, or Down."[28] For instance, value-hierarchical thinking may "put men Up and women Down, whites Up and people of color Down, culture Up and nature Down, minds Up and bodies Down." Thus, value-hierarchical thinking is the basic claim that some things—experiences, individuals, actions—"have more value than" others.[29]

Second, Warren argues that an oppressive conceptual framework encourages "oppositional value dualisms" such as male/female, white/Black, rational/emotional, such that it is better to be male, white, or rational, than female, Black, or emotional.[30] Process philosophers, who have long fought against the invidious nature of oppositional dualisms that falsely bifurcate reality, are likely to find common cause with Warren.

The third characteristic of oppressive conceptual frameworks is their conception of power as "power-over," usually power of Ups over Downs. Though, as we will discuss, some instances of power-over power are justified and, therefore, not oppressive, "when power-over power serves to reinforce the power of Ups as Ups in ways that keep Downs unjustifiably subordinated (which not all cases of power-over do), such conceptions and practices of power are unjustified."[31]

The fourth characteristic of an oppressive conceptual framework, Warren explains, is that it "creates, maintains, or perpetuates a conception of *privilege* as belonging to Ups and not to Downs."[32] These privileges are unjustified and foster oppression when they function to systematically advantage Ups over Downs.[33]

The fifth and most important characteristic of an oppressive conceptual framework is that it "sanctions the *logic of domination*."[34] Warren perceptively notes that it is the logic of domination that ultimately distinguishes justified from unjustified forms of power, privilege, and subordination, for it is a logic of domination that claims that superiority or being "higher" on a value-hierarchy *justifies* domination and subordination of those that are "lower."[35]

Warren goes on to make a crucial distinction: value-hierarchical thinking is not *inherently* problematic. Value-hierarchical thinking only becomes oppressive when combined with the logic of domination, which "assumes that superiority justifies subordination. A logic of domination is offered as the moral stamp of approval for subordination, since, if accepted, it provides a justification for keeping Downs down."[36] This critically important conclusion is too often omitted by value theorists. The mere claim that X has greater value than Y is logically distinct from the claim that X is justified in using or dominating Y. Thus, contrary to what many feminists, ecofeminists, and deep ecologists claim, Warren rightly notes that there may be "nothing inherently problematic about hierarchical thinking (even value-hierarchical thinking), value dualisms, and conceptions and relations of power and privilege, which advantage the Ups, *in contexts other than oppression*."[37]

> Hierarchical thinking is important for classifying data, comparing information, and organizing material. Taxonomies (e.g., plan taxonomies) and biological nomenclature seem to require some form of hierarchical thinking. Even value-hierarchical thinking may be quite acceptable in some contexts (e.g., in assessing the qualities of contestants or in rank-ordering participants in a contest). Responsible parents may exercise legitimate power and privilege (as Ups) over their infants (as Downs), be assigned higher prestige or value than their infants for some purposes (e.g., as logical reasoners), and yet not thereby be involved in any type of oppressive parent-child relationship.[38]
>
> A logic of domination assumes that superiority justifies subordination. A logic of domination is offered as the moral stamp of approval for subordination, since, if accepted, it provides a justification for keeping Downs down. Typically this justification takes the form that the Up has some characteristic . . . that the Down lacks and by virtue of which the subordination of the Down by the Up is justified.[39]

It is easy to miss the subtlety of Warren's claim here. She is *not* claiming that value-hierarchy thinking simpliciter is morally objectionable. Rather, it is the combination of value-hierarchical thinking with the logic of domination that makes the domination unjustified and creates an oppressive conceptual framework. This is clearly seen in Aristotle's own use of the chain of being.

In *describing*—albeit simplistically and not entirely accurately—the ontological structure of nature in terms of increasingly complex forms of being, Aristotle has done nothing inherently morally objectionable. It is when he makes the further *prescriptive*, normative claim that "the lower are for the higher" that he has adopted the "logic of domination."[40] The illicit jump is from an ontologically *descriptive* hierarchy to an axiologically normative *prescriptive* hierarchy. Just because something is "higher" (an "Up") does not automatically entail that it is right to subordinate and dominate the "lower" (the "Down"). In fact, it could mean the opposite; the "higher" could have responsibility for, not domination over, the "lower." This is what my students sometimes call the "Uncle Ben/Aunt May principle": with great power comes great responsibility.[41] Warren's very careful analysis helps to reveal that the mere fact of being "higher" or even being "more valuable" than another does not yet tell us whether its aims should be given preference over others. That question can only be answered by more basic ethical commitments.

Thus, Warren notes, in contexts other than oppression—that is, in contexts outside the logic of domination—there may be nothing inherently wrong with value-hierarchical thinking, and relations of power and privilege that "advantage the Ups."[42] The fact is that hierarchical thinking is crucial to understanding and categorizing our world. For instance, although we have moved beyond Aristotle's simplistic ontology, contemporary science still reveals a cosmos that is structured hierarchically, from biology's plant and animal taxonomies to the more basic physical structures—the cellular is dependent upon the molecular, the molecular upon the atomic, and the atomic upon the subatomic, but not vice versa. I fear that one who seeks to claim that reality is ontologically flat does more explaining away than actual explaining.[43]

Furthermore, even beyond these "objective" hierarchical structures of reality, as Warren notes, value-hierarchy thinking is quite necessary in everyday life, such as in ranking the winners of a race or evaluating the quality of student work.[44] There are, Warren reminds us, legitimate uses of power and privilege. The mere exercise of power over another is not necessarily evidence of oppression. For instance, Warren explains, "responsible parents may exercise legitimate power and privilege (as Ups) over their infants (as Downs), be assigned higher prestige or value than their infants for some purposes (e.g., as logical reasoners), and yet not thereby be involved in any type of oppressive parent-child relationship."[45] Warren continues:

> If one describes healthy, morally permissible relationships (say between parents and infants) as relationships of domination, then *justified* domination occurs only where the logic of domination

is in place. That is, the logic of domination falsely justifies the power and privilege of Ups over Downs in a way that keeps intact *unjustified* domination-subordination relationships. Child abuse is a case of *unjustified* domination; a parent exercising her power and privilege by forcibly removing a child's hand from a hot burning stove is not. So, if one claims that domination can be either justified or unjustified, then it is cases of unjustified domination that are of interest to ecofeminist philosophy.[46]

Thus, Warren has helped us to establish that, outside of the logic of domination, there are justified and even morally important uses of value-hierarchical thinking. Given this, the question is not *whether* a Whiteheadian view embraces value-hierarchical thinking or domination simpliciter, but whether a Whiteheadian view sanctions *unjustified* domination.

Hierarchy without Anthroparchy

I am now in a position to consider the main questions of this chapter: Is Whitehead's hierarchical axiology and metaphysics non-invidious? Is it possible to have hierarchy without anthroparchy? I am now able to answer both questions in the affirmative, thanks to a key feature of Whiteheadian environmental metaphysics, which affirms and embraces a *descriptive* hierarchy while rejecting the typical *prescriptive* role for this hierarchy. In this way, in line with Warren's position, a Whiteheadian event ontology recognizes the validity of some value-hierarchy thinking while rejecting the logic of domination. As I interpret and build on Whitehead's system, the aim of morality is not that the "more valuable" are simply to be given preference over the "less valuable." As he notes in *Modes of Thought*, although the hermit thrush and the nightingale can "produce sound of the utmost beauty, . . . they are not civilized beings. They lack ideas of adequate generality respecting their own actions and the world around them. Without doubt the higher animals entertain notions, hopes, and fears. And yet they lack civilization by reason of the deficient generality of their mental functionings. Their love, their devotion, their beauty of performance, rightly claim our love and our tenderness in return. Civilization is more than all these; and in moral worth it can be less than all these."[47] There are several noteworthy points here.

First, the hermit thrush and the nightingale are intrinsically beautiful beings who "rightly claim our love and our tenderness." They are, in this sense, individuals deserving of our direct moral concern. Yet, in that the thrush and the nightingale are unable to entertain notions of "adequate generality," we must also recognize that the beauty they are capable of achieving is not as rich as that of a healthy adult human being. In achieving a relatively simple form of unity in diversity, the nightingale's song is a good example of the achievement of a "pretty" form of beauty. Although we rightly appreciate its elegant simplicity, the nightingale's song is trivial in comparison to the profound beauty of a concerto by Mozart. In our efforts to overcome the errors of the past, we must not fail to recognize that there are real differences in the richness of experiences achievable by different types of individuals. Indeed, the hasty rush to an axiological egalitarianism is potentially more destructive than the use of an invidious anthropocentric hierarchy. This is where the final line of the previous passage is important. Despite the greater complexity and beauty achievable by human civilization, in terms of *moral worth*, human civilization may "rank lower" than the hermit thrush and the nightingale.[48] The nightingale's onto-aesthetic status, the depth of beauty and value achievable by it, does not neatly constitute its moral significance. If morality is not about the simple affirmation of the interests of "higher" individuals, what does determine an individual's moral significance? Although as "civilized beings" humans are able to achieve heights of beauty unknown to the thrush and the nightingale, the aim of morality is at the attainment of the greatest harmony and intensity (beauty) possible in each "concrete instance of the world's history."[49]

In *Environmental Ethics*, Rolston makes a similar point:

> "Biocentric" is not the right word, but then "anthropocentric" is not either. The system does not center indiscriminately on life, with one life being equal to another; and the system does not center functionally on humans, who in the ecological sense have little role in the system. Microbes are more important than humans instrumentally. All value does not "center" on humans, though some of it does. Everything of value that happens is not "for" humans; nonhumans defend their own values, and humans need to recognize these values outside themselves. Nevertheless, humans are of the utmost value in the sense that they are the ecosystem's most sophisticated product. They have the highest per capita intrinsic value of any life form supported by the system. The system is *bio-systemic* and *anthropo-apical*.[50]

To put this in Warren's terms, although humans are Ups in that they are higher on a value hierarchy, being an Up does not justify the unjustified subordination of the Downs. Thus, it is possible to recognize the ontologically and axiologically hierarchical structure of reality, but not permit this to systematically justify the privilege and power-over those that are higher on this hierarchy by those that are lower. That is, a Whiteheadian environmental metaphysics would reject the logic of domination. The aim of every process, including morality, is at the maximization of the value and beauty achievable in each concrete instance of the world's history. It is *not* the case that the "lower is for the higher."

An individual's onto-aesthetic status, the depth of beauty and value it is capable of, is an important and morally relevant factor in determining what one ought to do, but ultimately achieving the most harmonious and intense whole, bringing about the most beauty possible, may very well require responsibilities on the part of the "higher" individuals, not privileges.

Hierarchical thinking is invidious when an individual's degree of value *determines* its moral significance, as in the argument: Individual A is less valuable than individual B. Therefore, A may be sacrificed in instances of conflict with B. The problem with this argument, I contend, is not in the premises, but in the conclusion. I argue that while the depth of beauty and value achieved by an individual (its "onto-aesthetic status") is *relevant* in determining its moral significance, an individual's onto-aesthetic status does not strictly *constitute* its moral significance. According to the position I am defending, one's obligation is not simply to give preference to "higher-order" individuals, but to maximize the beauty achievable in a given situation. This is what in my previous work I refer to as the "obligation of peace," or the obligation to avoid destroying another individual, unless not doing so threatens the achievement of the greatest degree of harmony and intensity which in that situation is possible.[51] Accordingly, depending on the situation, it is not only possible but likely that meeting this obligation will require sacrifice on the part of "more valuable" individuals. For the most beautiful whole achievable is often not in keeping with the perceived needs of, for instance, humans. In this way, as discussed in chapter four, by insisting that our moral obligation is to affirm the greatest possible universe of beauty, value, and importance that in each situation we can see, the ethics of creativity is neither anthropocentric nor biocentric; it is kalocentric.

It is, I contend, the central role of beauty, the kalocentric focus of an organicist environmental metaphysics, that makes it possible to recognize that there are real differences in the complexity of individuals, yet not make the mistake of taking these differences as purely normative. That is, by adopting a truly kalocentric approach, it is possible to appropriately recognize differences in degrees of beauty and value without succumbing to the seductive logic that an individual's onto-aesthetic status strictly determines its moral worth. Taking the kalocentric focus of process seriously, we see that an individual's moral significance is ultimately determined not merely by its potential depth of beauty, but on whether the satisfaction of its demands adds to or detracts from the achievement of the most beautiful whole possible in each particular situation. In this way, the fundamental duty within a kalocentric ethic is *always to act in such a way as to bring about the greatest possible universe of beauty and value that in each situation is possible.*[52]

In a kalocentric ethic, the ultimate justification for any action must be whether its affirmation would lead to the most harmonious and intense whole achievable in that situation, whether it affirms the most beauty possible. Or, as Whitehead puts it in *Modes of Thought*, "morality is always the aim at that union of harmony, intensity, and vividness which involves the perfection of importance for that occasion."[53] Individually, this means that every moral agent ought to strive to achieve the most intense form of beauty that is available to it. When ends become mutually incompatible and there is discord, moral agents ought always and everywhere to affirm the most harmonious and intense whole they can see. Whether this means sacrificing or satisfying the interests of one individual over another depends not on its position in a value hierarchy, but on what would achieve the most beauty in that situation. In this way, an individual's onto-aesthetic status—the depth of beauty and value it is capable of achieving—is relevant to but not strictly determinative of its moral significance. The aim of moral action—like that of every form of process—is at the production and promotion of the most harmonious and intense experience possible.

On this view, morality is not about simply affirming the needs of "higher" individuals. When there are true instances of moral conflict and we are forced to choose between different sets of individuals, our obligation is *not* simply to sacrifice the interests of the "lower" for the sake of the "higher," as it was with traditional approaches. Rather, our action is moral only if we affirm the most harmony and intensity (beauty) in the situation *taken as a whole*. That is, in each situation we must strive to be as inclusive of the interests of others without allowing experience to devolve into chaos (harmony) and in choosing between different courses and competing claims we ought always to aim at the whole that is richer and more complex (intensity). We ought always to avoid, therefore, the destruction or maiming of any individual, unless *not* doing so threatens the achievement of the greatest harmony and intensity that in each situation is possible.[54] It may be instructive to conclude by briefly applying this position to Whitehead's example of the nightingale.

Before we can determine the *moral* significance of the nightingale vis-à-vis humans, we must first seek to learn as much as we can about the beauty and value affected by and achievable through our actions.[55] In a sense, then, the first step in any moral decision-making process is education. We must work to achieve a width of understanding and experience to cut against our tendency toward those narrow sympathies that lead to violent destruction and anesthetic tameness. Let us begin, then, by trying to learn more about nightingales.

The nightingale (*luscinia megarhynchos*) is a migratory insectivorous bird that nests in forest and brush areas of Europe and southwest Asia and winters in southern Africa. Its distinctive song has inspired poets and authors for centuries.[56] Although it is not currently threatened with extinction, like other migratory bird populations, nightingale populations are on the decline.[57] While the reasons for the decline of each species is complex, migratory bird populations worldwide are generally on the decline because of (1) the fragmentation and loss of habitat and (2) global climate change.[58] Indeed, these two closely related trends are conspiring to bring about one of the greatest losses of biodiversity since the last mass extinction 65 million years ago that saw the demise of the dinosaurs, ending the Mezozoic and ushering in the Cenozoic. Migratory birds such as the nightingale are particularly sensitive to these changes. It would seem, then, that the activities of human civilization are in conflict with the flourishing of the nightingale. What guidance would a kalocentric approach such as the ethics of creativity provide?

If our aim is to achieve the most beauty possible, our goal is to achieve the most harmonious and intense whole possible in this situation. Understood as maximal diversity in unity, the moral aim at harmony has a bias toward inclusivity. To aim at harmony requires that we be as inclusive as possible of the demands made upon us without allowing experience to degenerate into chaos. The burden of proof, therefore, is not on those who would seek to conserve achieved forms of beauty and value, but on those who would destroy them. Too often, this step in moral decision-making is cut short. The general balkanization of public discourse leads many prematurely to assume that the demands made upon us are mutually exclusive, that we are in a zero-sum game. Although there are certainly very real instances of mutually exclusive demands—as I have already noted, for instance, animal life necessarily requires robbery and violence—in many instances the conflict is only apparent. There is a general failure of moral imagination needed to envision ways of living and acting that avoid unnecessarily destroying achieved forms of beauty.

Yet beauty requires not only harmony or the absence of "painful clash," but also intensity. We ought not only to aim at that course of action that will avoid mutual inhibition, but also at that course that will achieve the most intense form of beauty possible. Intensely beautiful experience is purchased through complex interrelations and patterns of experience that introduce new contrasts that deepen and magnify experience. We ought, therefore, to embrace those forms of living that are qualitatively richer, that foster more complex combinations and more intense contrasts. What would this mean in the context of the conflict between human civilization and the nightingale?

Although the depth of beauty and value achievable by both human beings and nightingales is relevant to our moral decision-making, our aim is not merely to preference the interests of the "higher" individual. Ultimately, our moral obligation is to act in such a way as to bring about the greatest possible universe of beauty and value that in this situation is possible. The conflict in this situation is between the relatively trivial forms of beauty that many humans seek, which are contributing to the loss and fragmentation of habitat and to global climate change, and the vital needs of migratory bird species such as nightingales. Though it will likely require a dramatic revision of our consumeristic lifestyle, even a relatively large human population could thrive alongside a species such as the nightingale. Therefore, while humans have the potential to achieve much more complex and intense forms of beauty than the nightingale, the world would be a less beautiful place if we were to preference human consumption habits over the nightingale's survival and flourishing. Although human civilization has a "higher" onto-aesthetic status, in moral significance many destructive aspects of human civilization rank lower than the nightingale. In the final analysis, then, our obligation to avoid the destruction or maiming of any individual, unless not doing so threatens the achievement of the greatest harmony and intensity possible, requires that we begin to change those practices that undermine the flourishing of these beautiful animals. Perhaps it would be helpful to consider a slightly more poignant example than the nightingale and the thrush. Let us conclude this chapter with a discussion of how a Whiteheadian organicist environmental metaphysics would consider the act of eating other living beings.

Eating Animals and the Robbery of Life

There is a long, if minority, tradition within Whitehead scholarship focusing on moral vegetarianism.[59] For instance, Charles Hartshorne was himself a moral vegetarian, though he did not write about it with any significant frequency or depth. Daniel Dombrowski, the most important and prolific Hartshornean today, has written extensively on vegetarianism.[60] A new generation of process scholars—including perhaps myself, but exemplified best by Brianne Donaldson—have continued and expanded on this tradition, bringing more explicitly Whiteheadian ideas into conversation with wider philosophical circles, including environmental ethics, animal ethics, and critical animal studies.[61]

Of course, this is not the place for anything like a complete cataloging of this ongoing conversation. Let us approach the topic by examining arguments *against* abstaining from eating animal life by considering the provocative work of Andrew F. Smith in *A Critique of the Moral Defense of Vegetarianism*. As someone who has wrestled with the ethics of eating for several decades, I was drawn to this title. I feared that this compact book would be a hackneyed defense of industrial animal agriculture from an industry apologist whose work would be trotted out as proof that there is nothing immoral about our current food practices. Though he does ultimately claim that vegetarianism is "morally indefensible and ontologically illusory," Smith is not a latter-day vegetarian cum meat apologist.[62] Those looking for an ethical defense of eating the meat (flesh) produced by intensive, industrial animal agriculture—which constitutes the vast majority of meat produced in the developed world, especially in the United States—will be sorely disappointed. If you live in a developed country and eat meat at a typical restaurant or buy meat at a typical store, it is difficult to justify it morally.[63] Smith states that "factory farming here is a pharmaceutical and ecological abomination—and an international aberration."[64] However, Smith continues, "once we set aside the obvious problems associated with factory farming, the case for vegetarianism is less cut and dry."[65] That industrial animal agriculture is an immoral and "ecocidal" system that must be abandoned does not tout court imply that vegetarianism is morally obligatory.

Smith suggests that the most common defense of moral vegetarianism is the "sentientist argument." He formalizes it in this way:

1. Sentience is a sufficient condition for having moral standing.

2. Having moral standing entails that one should not be killed and eaten by moral agents.

3. Many animals are sentient, so they have moral standing. It is morally impermissible for moral agents to kill and eat

sentient animals, and there are good reasons to reject eating *any* animals whatsoever.[66]

4. Plants are not sentient, so they do not have moral standing in the relevant sense. It is morally permissible for moral agents to kill and eat them.[67]

A chief problem with this argument, Smith contends, is that recent biological investigations bring into question the fourth premise. The author is right to note that plants' apparent lack of sentience is often taken by many as a given with little or no evidence. "Yet," Smith asks, "what if plants are sentient? What if sentientists mistake our deafness to this fact for plants' dumbness"?[68]

Smith seeks to answer these questions by considering the evidence provided by contemporary "plant neurobiology."[69] Consider these three examples given by Smith:

> tomatoes subject to damage by insects and herbivores produce methyl jasmonate as an alarm signal. Plants in the vicinity detect it and prepare for attack by producing chemicals that ward off their attackers (Farmer and Ryan 1990). They do not do so when subject to mechanically induced wounding, as from high winds. This indicates the capacity for discernment (Paré and Tumlinson 1999). Acacia trees excrete an unpalatable tannin to defend themselves when being eaten by animals. The scent of the tannin is picked up by other acacia trees, which then also excrete it (van Hoven 1991). And when attacked by caterpillars, some plants release chemical signals that attract wasps who attack the caterpillars (Thaler 1999).[70]

Although plants do not have a central nervous system or feel an "ouch" of pain in the same way that animals do,[71] there is nevertheless a meaningful sense in which plants are sentient. Smith points to a significant body of research that suggests that plants "have an information-processing and response system that is homologous to a central nervous system, and they exhibit some key characteristics of beings who suffer. Evidence supports the proposition that they are self-aware[72] and highly attentive to their environments; exhibit intelligence and intentionality; and can remember, nurture, learn, and even teach."[73] Though these claims are still being debated within the scientific literature, the question of plant sentience can no longer be dismissed with the wave of a hand or ridiculed as anthropomorphism.[74] While the ethical offspring of modern metaphysical projects will find it difficult to accommodate the realization that plants are not mere passive objects or stimulus-response machines, proponents of Whitehead's philosophy of organism can and should welcome and embrace the news. Indeed, for the philosophy of organism, this is not news at all, but confirmation. There is no passive, valueless stuff; there is no "vacuous actuality."

Smith considers the sentientist's likely response to evidence that plants are sentient, what he calls the "expansionary sentientist case for vegetarianism." He notes that expansionary sentientists would claim that even if there is evidence that plants are sentient, eating plants instead of animals would still be the lesser evil, both because plants, presumably, suffer less than animals, and because eating grain-fed, factory-farmed animals kills many times more plants than just eating plants alone. Thus, expansionary sentientists would claim, even if plants are sentient, moral vegetarianism is still required.[75]

Smith rightly notes an implication of expansionary sentientism that is often ignored by its advocates: if plants are sentient, they are moral patients deserving of moral consideration for their own sake. Thus, even for expansionary sentientists it matters morally *how* the plants we eat are raised. He states, "this means that not all ways of practicing vegetarianism are equal. Some may cause more harm than others."[76] I have made similar claims elsewhere, suggesting that even if it is clear that eating factory-farmed animals is morally indefensible, it does not follow that a plant-based diet is automatically moral. There are real and morally significant differences between, on the one hand, eating plants grown bioregionally according to organic permaculture and, on the other, monocropped, genetically modified crops (e.g., soy) grown on previously forested land with heavy reliance on petrol-based fertilizers and toxic herbicides and pesticides that are then turned into highly processed meat substitutes requiring constant refrigeration and transportation across long distances.[77] For Smith, "organic farming, preferably done locally and on a small scale, is the best choice if we are to give due consideration to the needs and interests of plants."[78] Thus, vegetarianism "is still preferable to omnivorism, according to expansionary sentientists. But killing and eating plants requires that they be treated with care and respect when cultivated and harvested."[79]

Yet, despite being morally preferable to sentientism, Smith contends, expansionary sentientism is also inadequate because it retains an unwarranted hierarchical view that places animals above plants. Following Daniel

Quinn—likely known to many readers through his book *Ishmael* and a chief inspiration for Smith's project—Smith contends that such a hierarchical view is metaphysically and morally unwarranted: "Our relationship with plants is heterarchical [not hierarchical]. We are moral equals. Presuming otherwise is 'kingdomist' (Quinn 1994, 165) in the same way that positing a morally relevant distinction between humans and other animals is speciesist. Life, shall we say, is life."[80] This is the point at which Smith and I will part ways. Ultimately, Smith contends, the expansionary sentientist defense should give way to a "care-sensitive ecological contextualist" defense of vegetarianism. Unlike the expansionary view, the contextualist defense not only avoids the consumption of animals but also takes care to eat in a way that is cognizant of the broader ecological context in which plants are created for food.

Smith defends his egalitarian view by building on the work of Val Plumwood and her rejection of "ontological veganism" or the "theory that advocates universal abstention from all use of animals as the only real alternative to mastery and the leading means of defending animals against its wrongs."[81] According to such a position, which is often characteristic of animal activists via the writings of Carol Adams, "there is no middle ground. Either one is entirely free from others' use or one is their instrument."[82] Smith contends that a chief problem with ontological veganism is that it fails to recognize that "we are inescapably natural-born killers and natural-born food. Everyone survives on the lives of others and fosters others' lives in death. We are all users and are used in turn, and using and being used need not involve exploitation. To regard this as taboo is simply to deny that which is unavoidable."[83] While the impulse that drives ontological vegans' efforts is laudable, Smith contends, it is ultimately not possible to avoid using and eating sentient beings.

Whitehead might be seen as making a similar claim when he famously notes in *Process and Reality* that "life is robbery."[84] Not only does life necessarily involve a process of eating in which one organism becomes part of another, but equally each life will later become food for another. Indeed, taken in a more basic metaphysical sense, this can be seen as an account of Whitehead's most basic category: the category of creativity. The most basic feature of reality itself is the creative advance whereby each novel subject becomes by positively appropriating or negatively excluding past occasions, only to become an object (superject) for subsequent occasions. The many become one and are increased by one.[85]

Thus, a Whiteheadian will cheer Smith on when he claims that it is not enough to change our food practices; we must upend the "ecocidal axioms" of our culture by adopting a new conceptual framework that recognizes that humans are a part of, not apart from, the community of life. This diagnosis has been a central claim of Whitehead scholars for more than four decades. Indeed, John Cobb made such a claim in the first monograph on environmental ethics, which was written in 1972.[86] Of course, Smith is right that "there is no 'outside nature,' no ontological position of privilege, no ecological separation between humans and other-than human being."[87] It is this inescapable fact, he contends, that makes ontological veganism untenable. There is no moral purity possible. There is no moral system in which we avoid destroying intrinsically valuable beings in order to sustain ourselves. I refer elsewhere to this as the "clean hands fallacy."[88]

Whereas process scholars look to philosophers such as Peirce, Bergson, James, Dewey, and Whitehead for a conceptual framework that refuses artificial dualisms and false bifurcations, Smith turns to the Indigenous animist traditions. Following the work of Graham Harvey, Smith defines an animist as one who recognizes that " 'the world is full of persons, only some of whom are human, and that life is always lived in relationship with others.' "[89] Understanding whether this is in keeping or in tension with an organic metaphysics is made somewhat more difficult, as it often is, by the different use of key terms. It will be important to return to this point shortly. Smith's view of animism brings him to embrace what he calls a "kincentric" and "topocentric" position in which "responsibility for the health and well-being of a place just is responsibility for the health and well-being of the coinhabitants of that place. To be *emplaced* is to be enmeshed in bonds of kinship."[90] The closest analog with which readers may be familiar is Leopold's land ethic. Indeed, Leopold would likely agree with Smith's claim that "the landbase, its health and well-being, is primary."[91] Smith contends that an animist conceptual framework that makes the land primary will be attentive to obtaining food in ways that fosters the "health and well-being of the coinhabitants of our landbase so far as colliding agendas permit."[92] In many ways I am sympathetic to certain kinship models to describe our place within the biotic community. Robin Wall Kimmerer, for instance, has beautifully demonstrated in *Braiding Sweetgrass* the power and promise of merging such an Indigenous kinship animist model with Western scientific practice. In the final chapter I will turn to the work of cultural historian Thomas Berry, who can at times also be seen as embracing a kinship model. Where I find myself in disagreement with Smith is his claim that, within an animist/kinship worldview, the distinction between a vegetarian diet and an omnivore diet no longer has meaning. Indeed, his claim is that vegetarianism is "morally indefensible and ontologically illusory." Both omnivorism and vegetarianism are in fact impossible, Smith contends, because eating is a "transitive relationship."

A transitive property is such that if one element in a sequence relates in a certain way to a second element and the second element relates in the same way to the third, then the first and the third elements relate in the same way as well. As an updated version of the old saying goes, we are *who*[93] we eat. Our food is who our food eats, too. As a result, Smith contends, we are who our food eats in equal measure. As members of the community of life, we and our food are both part of a closed-loop system.[94] As Smith sees it, vegetarians eat plants, and plants eat other plants as well as animals. So, vegetarians eat animals as well as plants. This is so, no matter who constitutes the final strand in the food web that leads to our mouths.[95]

It is not that the distinction between vegetarianism and omnivorism is itself harmful, for Smith, but that the distinction is illusory, the result of a problematic worldview that creates conceptual barriers which keep us from seeing that we are enmeshed in the web of life, part, and product of the whole like any other. He asserts that "the very distinction between vegetarianism and omnivorism derives from a view of ourselves and our place in the world that is rooted in the axioms of our ecocidal culture."[96] It matters greatly, Smith explains, *how* we kill our food, but not *that* we kill. Thus, he concludes, "let us bid farewell to the case for vegetarianism. Let us permit it to vanish. This case has outlived whatever usefulness it once may have had. It no longer works, if it ever did."[97]

Let us consider points of resonance and tension between Smith's thesis and the philosophy of organism, starting first with Smith's topocentric land ethic, a position with which the current project has great affinity.[98] Consider first the evidence for plant sentience. I agree that " 'our perception of plants depends heavily on our philosophical orientation' (Hall 2011, 35)."[99] For those in the thrall of physicalism or reductive naturalism, plants are unlikely to be seen as more than complex stimulus-response biochemical machines. However, for those who embrace an organicist environmental metaphysics, reality is composed of nothing but subjective achievements of beauty and value.[100] To a degree, then, Whitehead scholars will have common cause with Smith. Indeed, as I suggest above, the research regarding the complexity of plant behavior is less a challenge than a confirmation of a nondualistic, nonreductive environmental metaphysics. Thus, far from challenging Smith's claims, I would invite him to join philosophers of organism in recognizing that subjectivity goes "all the way down." That is, it (subjectivity) does not stop with plants. One might even follow Dombrowski in distinguishing between microsentience at the subatomic level (S1) and macroscopic sentience (S2).[101]

Smith would benefit from Whitehead's organic metaphysical architecture, but it is also the case that Whitehead's philosophy of organism would benefit from Smith's research on the complexity of plants. Though an organicist environmental metaphysics may have a richer metaphysical lexicon for explaining and discussing forms of order below the level of plants, the research highlighted by Smith does demonstrate that both Whitehead and Hartshorne (and many of the scholars who followed them) may have been too simplistic in their understanding of plants. Let me briefly explain.

Whitehead repeatedly uses a political metaphor to explain the difference between plants and animals. Lacking a single, "regnant" center of experience, Whitehead describes plants as a "democracy," whereas animals are a "monarchy."[102] Taken as a *metaphor*, this is an instructive distinction. However, at times process scholars have come too close to reifying the distinction; as Jude Jones might put it, our crypto-substantialist tendencies run deep.[103] However, upon consideration, no Whiteheadian could legitimately maintain an absolute *ontological* distinction between plants and animals. Yes, Whitehead rightly notes that nature presents for us "rough divisions"[104]—for instance, between living and nonliving or plant and animal—but ultimately there are no gaps in the fabric of reality. As we will discuss at greater length in chapter six, for Whitehead, "nature suggests for our observation gaps, and then as it were withdraws them upon challenge."[105] Herein is a twin warning: one must avoid ontologizing and reifying distinctions, but one ought also to avoid flattening or papering over them. Are plants more diffusely organized than animals? Yes. But the political metaphor of democracy versus monarchy begins to obscure what it attempts to explain when we conceive of this distinction as more than a matter of degree. This brings me to Smith's discussion of persons.

Scholars embracing a philosophy of organism are likely to agree with Smith when he claims that "characteristics of personhood are not quintessentially human ones that are projected by animists onto other-than-human beings. Rather, we humans share traits and capacities with many other kinds of people."[106] However, Whitehead's organicist metaphysics allows more subtle distinctions than permitted by Smith's animism. For Smith, every plant and animal is a person with *equal* moral worth. For the philosophy of organism, on the other hand, things are a bit more complex than this. Every enduring form of individuality—whether molecule, marigold, mole, or man—is a "society," a particularly intense form of social order or pattern that creates the conditions for its endurance (see chapter six for a complete discussion of this point). All macroscopic order is social, but not all such enduring forms of order are persons. "Persons" are a particular complex form of serially ordered, structured societies. Whitehead puts it this way: a living nexus, though nonsocial in virtue of its "life," may support a thread of personal order along some historical route of its members. Such an enduring entity is a "living person." It is not of the essence of life to be a living person. Indeed, a living person requires that its immediate environment be a living, nonsocial nexus.[107]

In the case of single cells, of vegetation, and of the lower forms of animal life, we have no ground for conjecturing living personality. But in the case of the higher animals, there is a central direction, which suggests in their case that each animal body harbors a living person, or living persons. Our own self-consciousness is direct awareness of ourselves as such persons.[108] According to the organicist environmental metaphysics being defended, it is an empirical question whether a particular macroscopic form of enduring order (i.e., a society of societies) is sufficiently organized to host a "personal society." For Whitehead, plants are living, serially ordered, structured societies. But they are not persons in Whitehead's sense. These finer distinctions are helpful, indeed necessary, if we are adequately to describe and explain not only biological, but also chemical and physical phenomena. Of course, the fact that they are not metaphysical persons does not mean that plants do not deserve respect. In our processive cosmos, nothing can be excluded from the scope of direct moral concern.

One of the most fundamental problems with Smith's position is his ontologically flattening of reality and his embrace of an axiological egalitarianism. Although within an organicist environmental metaphysics there is no absolute bifurcation—whether between human animals and other forms of life or between living and nonliving individuals—there is nevertheless the emergence of real and sometimes morally significant forms of order. Reality is not ontologically or axiologically flat and undifferentiated. There are important degrees in the intensity of existence. As we've found throughout this chapter, properly understood, an organicist environmental metaphysics makes it possible to maintain a hierarchy without anthroparchy. The relationship between an onto-aesthetic hierarchy and ethical decision-making is complex. An individual's degree of beauty and value is relevant to, but not strictly determinative of, its moral significance. Thus, the position being defended is not what Smith and others have called an "extensionist" ethic that is a clandestine anthropocentrism. An individual's beauty and value is not based on its similarity to humans. A subject's beauty and value is recognized, not conferred.

Finally, I would like to comment on Smith's core "transitivity" argument against vegetarianism; namely, that "vegetarians are who plants eat, and plants eat other plants as well as animals. So vegetarians eat animals as well as plants." First, I am concerned that Smith is here equivocating in his use of the term "eat." When moral agents eat, it is a moral act. Moral agents have a choice in what they eat, including choosing not to eat. As Whitehead notes, life is robbery, but the "robber requires justification."[109] Moral patients, on the other hand, do not eat in this sense. Yes, plants appropriate energy, and some of that energy was once an animal. But that is not eating in the same sense as when a human chooses between a pasta primavera and a ribeye steak. Indeed, this also means that many nonhuman animals do not eat in the same sense in which human animals eat. For instance, it is not clear to me that crabs "eat" in the same sense that my teenage daughters do. As moral agents, what my daughters choose to eat (kill and consume) is an ethical act, whereas, since the crab is (presumably) not a moral agent, its eating is not a moral act. This distinction between moral agents' and moral patients' eating is also why humans are not predators in the typical sense of this term. I contend that Smith's equivocation in his use of the term "eat" makes his transitivity argument false; the first instance of "eat" has a meaningfully different sense than the second instance of "eat."[110]

Second, I find that Smith's transitivity argument makes a sort of category error in applying a logico-mathematical concept to a moral problem. Yes, if we are merely talking about abstract quantities, transitivity holds. However, in a world in which subjects are *constituted* by their relationships, transitivity misconstrues the metaphysical situation. If my daughter gives me a coffee mug for my birthday and then I later give that coffee mug to a newly hired colleague, it is not the case that my daughter has gifted the coffee mug to my colleague. The gift-giving between each relata is unique. They are not interchangeable. As a mathematician himself, I take seriously Whitehead's warning that "philosophy has been misled by the example of mathematics."[111] We must not commit the fallacy of misplaced concreteness in confusing abstract categories for the really real subjects and their constitutive internal relationships. This is a second, perhaps equally significant, reason to reject the transitivity argument. Thus, vegetarianism is not "ontologically illusory."

Where does all of this leave us with respect to the ethics of eating? We must rob from others in the maintenance of our life, but we have a moral obligation to affirm the most beauty and value that in each situation is possible. The ultimate answer to this question would require knowing the specific conditions of each moral agent's circumstances. Universal or categorical statements are out of place. Nevertheless, given that it is possible to lead a healthy, flourishing life without eating animals, most people would be morally obligated in general to forgo participating in the system that raises billions of animals in horrific industrial conditions. As I've consistently argued since 2005, for most people, in most circumstances, it is morally unjustifiable to eat animal life.

> Thus, in general—that is, abstracting from the particularities of any given situation—because it is not necessary for human beings to consume animals in order to flourish, the obligation to always act so as to maximize the harmony and intensity of our experience requires us to adopt a plant-based diet. This conclusion follows directly from the obligation of peace, which requires that we avoid the destruction or maiming of any individual, unless not doing so threatens the achievement of the greatest harmony and intensity that in each situation is possible.[112]

However, it matters greatly *how* we treat the plant life from which we rob to sustain ourselves. Within a philosophy of organism that recognizes and seeks to respect the intrinsic value and beauty of all beings, *how* we farm matters as much as *what* we eat.[113]

In the end, the moral framework implied by Whitehead's environmental metaphysics is even more radical than that implied by Smith's neo-animist view. For Whitehead, "the destruction of a man, or of an insect, or of a tree, or of the Parthenon, may be moral or immoral. Whether we destroy or whether we preserve, our action is moral if we have thereby safeguarded the importance of experience so far as it depends on that concrete instance in the world's history."[114] In our kalogenic cosmos, *everything* is a unique achievement of beauty and value. For moral agents, every relationship is a moral relation, whether we destroy or whether we preserve. A unique, kalocentric approach has the potential to bridge many traditional divides within environmental philosophy. Once we recognize more fully the interconnected and interdependent nature of our reality and embrace an organic conception of the world that appreciates the beauty and value of every form of existence without slipping into the excesses of an egalitarianism, we can begin to move beyond the invidious walls that too often separate traditional moral philosophy, environmental ethics, and animal ethics. In a world that is filled with so much ugliness and fear, a kalocentric approach to ethics calls on each of us to fallibly, humbly, and with fear and trembling attempt in each situation to affirm the greatest and most beautiful world possible, knowing always that we cannot in advance know which universe that will be. In the end, human action is like every other form of process in the universe—it is good when it is beautiful. In this way, Whitehead's environmental metaphysics provides a distinctive basis to retain a non-invidious hierarchy that does not result in a vicious anthroparchy.

Chapter 6

Individuals

At first glance, a discussion of substance metaphysics and the ontology of individuals would seem to be quite far afield from the concerns of environmental ethics. However, this impression would be mistaken. Though they are not typically labeled as such, questions regarding the (ontological) definition and nature of beings such as organisms, species, and ecosystems are central to environmental ethics. Take, for instance, Holmes Rolston's *Environmental Ethics*, in which he opens chapters on the value of and duties to organisms, species, and ecosystems respectively with a repudiation of nominalist accounts in favor of a realist position. He notes, for instance, that if ecosystems don't actually exist, if they are *merely* useful geographical designations or linguistic shorthands, then they are not beings to which direct duties can be owed. If they don't exist, they cannot be helped or harmed and are clearly outside the bounds of direct moral considerability. But of course, discussions regarding the definition and nature of various beings are not only a matter of science but also of metaphysics. In this chapter I consider how a Whiteheadian organicist environmental metaphysics and its distinctive ontology provides a better metaphysical foundation for environmental ethics, which depends on the ability to properly recognize the nature of nonhuman forms of being and becoming.

Substance, Event, and Individuality

In her majestic *Braiding Sweetgrass*, Robin Wall Kimmerer presents a compelling vision of how one can merge modern science (in her case botany)

135

and Indigenous forms of knowing (she is an enrolled member of the Citizen Potawatomi Nation). Central to her vision of an Indigenous worldview is the explicit rejection of both Western metaphysical mechanism and dualism in favor of recovering what she calls the "grammar of animacy." Kimmerer notes that, whereas the Western substance metaphysical traditions conceive of reality as composed of static nouns, her Indigenous tradition recognizes that every form of being is a verb.

> A Bay is a noun only if water is *dead*. When *bay* is a noun, it is defined by humans, trapped between its shores and contained by the word. But the verb *wiikwegamaa*—to *be* a bay—releases the water from bondage and lets it live. "To be a bay" holds the wonder that, for this moment, the living water has decided to shelter itself between these shores, conversing with cedar roots and a flock of baby mergansers. Because it could do otherwise—become a stream or an ocean or a waterfall, and there are verbs for that, too. To be a hill, to be a sandy beach, to be a Saturday, all are possible verbs in a world where everything is alive.[1]

Bruno Latour, in his Gifford Lectures *Facing Gaia*, makes a similar claim: "One of the great enigmas of Western history is not that 'there are still people naïve enough to believe in animism,' but that many people still hold the rather naïve belief in a supposedly deanimated 'material world.' And this is the case at which the very moment when scientists are multiplying the agencies in which they—and we—are more and more implicated every day."[2] A century earlier, Whitehead was making very similar claims, pointing out that our subject-predicate logic inherited from Aristotle leads us to think of the world in terms of static substances with accidental qualities.

> All modern philosophy hinges round the difficulty of describing the world in terms of subject and predicate, substance and quality, particular and universal. The result always does violence to that immediate experience which we express in our actions, our hopes, our sympathies, our purposes, and which we enjoy in spite of our lack of phrases for its verbal analysis. We find ourselves in a buzzing world, amid a democracy of fellow creatures; whereas, under some disguise or other, orthodox philosophy can only introduce us to solitary substances, each enjoying an

illusory experience: "O Bottom, thou art changed! what do I see on thee?"[3]

Though they come from very different traditions, Whitehead, Latour, and Kimmerer each recognize that the logic and grammar of our language itself often brings with it latent problematic metaphysical assumptions. We struggle to accurately understand and characterize a world that is alive with activity and process in a language that presents objects as dead containers. Kimmerer notes that learning to think in this way was in fact central to her training as a scientist.

> The questions scientists raised were not "Who are you?" but "What is it?" No one asked plants, "What can you tell us?" The primary question was "How does it work?" The botany I was taught was reductionist, mechanistic, and strictly objective. Plants were reduced to objects; they were not subjects. The way botany was conceived and taught didn't seem to leave much room for a person who thought the way I did. The only way I could make sense of it was to conclude that the things I had always believed about plants must not be true after all.[4]

Whitehead's philosophy of organism can be an important ally in the efforts to overcome latent reductionistic, mechanistic metaphysics and the pernicious bifurcation between subjects and objects. An organicist process metaphysics can be useful in developing a robust metaphysical "grammar of animacy" that recognizes that becoming is more fundamental than being, that process is more basic than product, and that, as the cultural historian Thomas Berry puts it, reality is better understood as being "composed of subjects to be communed with, not as objects to be exploited."[5]

Western thought has too often proceeded under the assumption that human subjects are fundamentally different than—an exception to—the rest of reality. "Experience" has been interpreted narrowly to refer to an active knowing subject surveying a world of passive objects. As Whitehead notes in his 1931 presidential address to the American Philosophical Association, no topic has "suffered more" at the hands of philosophers than the subject-object relation.[6] Though it is unavoidably the seat of our experience, we should reject Descartes's invitation to take the thinking subject as ontologically basic. Whereas Descartes "conceives the thinker as creating the occasional thought,"

Whitehead's philosophy of organism "inverts the order, and conceives the thought as a constituent operation in the creation of the occasional thinker. The thinker is the final end whereby there is the thought."[7] Consciousness and thought are undeniably important, but they are late-stage, high-grade forms of experience; they are not ontologically basic.[8]

"The misconception which has haunted philosophic literature throughout the centuries," Whitehead writes in his very last essay, "is the notion of 'independent existence.' There is no such mode of existence; every entity is only to be understood in terms of the way in which it is interwoven with the rest of the Universe."[9] Perhaps more than any other aspect of his thought, Whitehead's rejection of the notion of "independent existence" or substance has been taken to define his philosophy of organism. Moreover, it is this rejection of enduring substances that has been the source of some of the most significant objections to Whitehead's thought.

Whitehead developed his "philosophy of organism" in opposition to two historical trends: first, the longstanding tradition of substance ontology, particularly as it came to be defined in the modern era by René Descartes, and, second, the early twentieth-century trend toward what Whitehead called "scientific materialism," of which physicalism is the contemporary heir.[10] According to Whitehead's organic view of individuality, there are no discrete individuals (or independent substances) mechanistically determined by absolute laws of nature. Although the mechanistic metaphor has been wildly successful, it ultimately does not do justice to the complex interrelations between individuals. We ought, Whitehead insists, to move beyond the mechanistic metaphor in favor of the metaphor of organism, according to which individuals are constituted by internal relations and nested within ever-expanding environments. "The only way of mitigating mechanism," Whitehead writes in 1925, "is by the discovery that it is not mechanism."[11]

We've already explored in previous chapters how Whitehead embraces an ontology that, in keeping with contemporary physics, rejects the idea that reality is composed of passive, enduring macroscopic objects, the classical substances of much of Western thought. According to the philosophy of organism, reality is composed of nothing but energetic pulses, momentary events that come into and go out of existence moment to moment. Reality is process "all the way down." (See also the discussion of Ross, Ladyman, and Spurrett and their rejection of the metaphysics of "domestication."[12])

Some commentators often indicate sympathy with Whitehead's event ontology but ask: If the world is composed exclusively of microscopic events which neither endure nor have histories,[13] then how can Whitehead account for enduring, macroscopic individuals such as ourselves and other animals and plants? That is, having rejected the notion of unchanging subjects of change, how can Whitehead's account adequately capture the unity and self-identity of macroscopic individuals? The answers to these questions are important in their own right, but particularly for the present project, which seeks to develop and defend an environmental metaphysics as an adequate basis for environmental ethics.

W. Norris Clarke gives voice to these potentially damaging objections. Reviewing aspects of Clarke's work will prove a useful foil in several respects. First, in Clarke's work we find a sophisticated and subtle defense of substance ontology that avoids physicalism and materialism on the one hand and a static account of substance on the other. Whereas a Whiteheadian event ontology can make rather quick work of modern substance ontologies for being far too static, passive, with Clarke we have a robust effort to defend a "dynamic" an account of substance ontology. Second, Clarke explicitly and forcefully gives voice to the objection that Whitehead's system only allows for an attenuated conception of macroscopic individuality. Thus, Clarke's own dynamic interpretation of the classical notion of substance seriously calls into question the very need for Whitehead's "process turn" toward what Clarke sees as a misguided metaphysical atomism.[14] Engaging with Clarke's objection provides a valuable opportunity to respond to the common criticism that Whitehead's system cannot do justice to the unity of macroscopic individuals. Finally, engaging with Clarke's position and objections will bring into stronger relief key aspects of the philosophy of organism's distinctive account of macroscopic individuality and its relationship to the underlying event ontology. Readers who are not particularly concerned with the ontology of individuality and identity may consider skipping to the second section on the ontology of social insects.

In *The One and the Many*, Clarke traces the source of what he sees as Whitehead's misguided metaphysical atomism to his (Whitehead's) repudiation of the doctrine of substance. From Clarke's point of view, what is particularly tragic about this error is that Whitehead's repudiation of substance was itself the result of a flawed understanding of Aristotle's and Thomas Aquinas's notions of substance.[15] Clarke devoted much of his august career to advancing what he calls a "creative retrieval" of St. Thomas that interprets substance dynamically. In contrast to the traditional depiction of substances as independent, unchanging subjects of change, Clarke conceives of every being as inherently active or "self-communicating." According to Clarke, "a non-acting, non-communicating being is for all practical purposes

[. . .] *equivalent* to no being at all. To be *real* is to *make a difference.*"[16] This emphasis on being active and self-communicating also brings Clarke to refute the notion that substances are independent and unrelated. "To have a universe, a community of real existents, its members would have to communicate with each other, be linked together and all communication requires some kind of action."[17] In fact, Clarke goes so far as to state that a completely unrelated, unchanging entity would not only be "totally point-less," but an unchanging entity "could not be the work of a wise creative God. And so we live in a universe where all the real beings that count, that make a difference, are dynamically active ones, that pour over through self-manifesting, self-communicating action to connect up with other real beings, and form a community of interacting existents we call a 'universe.' "[18] Clearly, this is not the notion of "vacuous actuality" Whitehead had in mind when he referred to "independent existence" or "substance."

Therefore, far from joining Whitehead in repudiating substance, Clarke steadfastly affirms the supremacy of substance as "the principle of continuity and self-identity throughout the whole spectrum of accidental change open to a particular being."[19] Clarke is quick to point out, however, that being self-identical is not the same as being unchanging or immutable, as Whitehead, among others, have charged.[20] Clarke reminds his reader that "the authentic meaning of self-identity through change is this: 'In an accidental change, the substance itself changes, but not substantially or essentially, only accidentally.' Thus the subject that changes retains its essential self-identity through the spectrum of accidental change open to it in terms of its natural potencies."[21] For Clarke, then, a substance is some-thing that actively maintains self-identity over time, but this self-identity does not signify something that is static or self-enclosed. On the contrary, Clarke insists, "self-identity is not immutability but the active power of self-maintenance in exchange with others. Thus the best way to maintain psychological self-identity is not by not changing, doing nothing, but by stability of goals, perseveringly pursued."[22] He retorts, "you could not find a more dynamic notion [of substance] than this."[23] In this way, Clarke believes he can at once affirm the traditional concept of substance as well as capture the dynamic, processive nature of reality in systems such as Whitehead's. Accordingly, given his dynamic interpretation of substance, Clarke seems to be arguing not only that Whitehead's complicated account of process is inadequate, but also that it is unnecessary.

Ironically, just as Clarke finds that Whitehead misinterprets Aristo-tle's and St. Thomas's notion of substance, I believe that in participating in misleading aspects of what I refer to as the classical interpretation of Whitehead's metaphysics that, in insisting on a sharp ontological distinction between the past and the present, drains the past of both creativity and value, Clarke misinterprets Whitehead's notion of "society."[24] Thus, before turning to analyze Clarke's "creative retrieval" of the doctrine of substance, let us first examine what I believe are serious flaws in Clarke's interpretation of Whitehead.

In *The One and the Many*, Clarke characterizes Whitehead's system as a metaphysical atomism in which "process itself is made up of many discretely distinct, tiny entities, 'actual occasions' or 'actual entities,' following each other in ordered sequence."[25] Clarke's understanding of Whitehead's account of macroscopic individuals follows directly from this interpretation of process as composed of discrete entities:

> The macroscopic objects we call things—plants, animals, humans, chairs, etc.—are really societies or collections of many actual entities bound together by various relations, causal connections etc., existing at any one time. Down through time there is no actual entity that remains the same, unchanged, but only a series of successive entities that we call one being because the series is closely connected by a chain of "inheritance" of properties one from the other. Thus what we call the human "self," the "I," is really only a succession of selves bound together by a common chain of inheritances.[26]

It is this understanding of Whiteheadian macroscopic objects as "only a series" or "collection" of "discretely distinct" actual entities that brings Clarke to criticize Whitehead's system for not adequately accounting for the experienced unity of macroscopic individuals. Simply stated, Clarke's objection is that a mere succession of entities, no matter how closely connected, could never account for the way we experience ourselves or the way we experience others. As Clarke puts it, a society of "discrete, non-identical selves linked in a temporal and spatial chain is not nearly strong enough to do justice to these powerful experiences of perduring unity and self-identity. [. . .] The unity of a society, founded on external relations, not on the inner unity of the being itself, is again not strong enough to do justice to the evidenced facts."[27] It is primarily this problem—the unity of macroscopic individuals— that makes Clarke unable to embrace process metaphysics. If correct, this objection would be devastating for a system that strives to be adequate to experience. For if Whitehead is indeed affirming that macroscopic individuals are merely a succession of "selves," he would be unable to account for the unity of our own experience and of our experience of others. The question, then, is whether Whitehead's organic model of individuality is able to do justice to the "evidenced facts."

Given that Clarke recognizes that Whitehead's emphasis on interrelatedness is "one of the most fertile of all the Whiteheadian insights into what it means to be in our world,"[28] it is surprising that he characterizes process as being "made up of many *discretely distinct*, tiny entities."[29] Though it is true Whitehead believes that experience comes in "drops" and that, in a sense, actual occasions are the atomic stuff of which the universe is made, it is also important to recognize that this relational atomism is *not* purchased at the expense of the unity of the universe or the reality of macroscopic individuals. The relations obtaining between actual occasions are primarily internal, not external, wherein these internal relations "are constitutive of what the event is in itself."[30] Each actual occasion is, in this sense, its relationship to the universe. Hence, for Whitehead, the concept of individuality (both macroscopic and microscopic) itself requires *essential reference to others*. This emphasis upon interrelation and interdependence is what is meant by referring to Whitehead's model of individuality as "organic." Furthermore, it is in this way that Whitehead sees himself explicitly rejecting Aristotle's dictum, which Clarke affirms, that a substance is never present in another.[31] Indeed, according to Whitehead's principle of relativity, "an actual entity *is* present in other actual entities. In fact, if we allow for degrees of relevance, and for negligible relevance, we must say that every actual entity is present in every other actual entity."[32] Given that every actual occasion is present in every other, actual occasions are anything but "discretely distinct," as Clarke contends. As a matter of fact, given the principle of relativity, they are more nearly the opposite.

Given the constitutive relation between "societies" and "actual occasions," the proper understanding of the latter as organically interrelated has a significant impact on how to conceive of the former. Clarke, incorrectly, I contend, depicts a Whiteheadian "society" as "an *aggregate* of many *distinct* beings held together in an *extrinsic* unity based on *external* relations."[33] Yet, this interpretation of Whitehead's concept of "society" is incorrect on virtually every point. A society is not an "aggregate" of "discrete," "externally related" beings held together in an "extrinsic unity." Rather, a society is a *socially ordered* "nexus" of *internally* related occasions that form an *intrinsic* unity. Societies are *not* mere collections or aggregates of entities to which the same class name applies. Indeed, this is, for Whitehead, central to the difference between a "nexus" and a "society." Whereas a nexus is simply any real fact of togetherness, including extrinsic or aggregative unities such as boulders and mountains, a society is a particular type of nexus that enjoys "social order." That is, a society's constituent occasions share a common, defining characteristic because of the conditions imposed upon them by their *internal* relatedness with previous members of that self-same society. Hence, contrary to aggregate entities, complex, structured societies such as plants and animals are organic entities that, like systematic entities, are characterized by strong internal relations that make possible a regnant unity.

This intimate relationship between a macroscopic whole and its parts brings to light a crucial difference in the role of "interrelation" in Clarke and Whitehead's respective systems. Whereas, for Whitehead, the relations between individuals are *constitutive* of their very identity, for Clarke, although it is essential to the nature of substances that they be related to "some other beings and systems of them," it is merely "accidental to which particular beings and systems [they] are related."[34] In other words, although, according to Clarke, every substance or real being is nested within and depends upon various kinds of order or systems, which others and which systems a substance is or is not related to is purely accidental; that is, it does not affect its essence—it does not affect, much less constitute, what it is. For Whitehead, on the other hand, in a sense, every individual just *is* its relationships to every element in its world. Though some relations may be more central in the constitution of an entity than others, there are no purely accidental, nonconstitutive relationships. Thus, although he may affirm a notion of substance as being in dynamic interrelation with its environment, insofar as these interrelations are only external and accidental to what that substance is, Clarke still adheres to the notion of "independent existence," which, according to Whitehead, is the "misconception which has haunted philosophic literature throughout the centuries."[35]

Hence, I find that Clarke is incorrect in his interpretation both of process as involving discrete entities and of societies as collections of externally related entities. Far from being "discretely distinct," actual occasions are in fact constituted by their internal relations with others. Similarly, rather than being mere "extrinsic unities" composed of "collections" or "aggregates" of "externally related" entities, societies are *intrinsic* unities of socially ordered, actual occasions that, by reason of the conditions imposed upon them by their *internal* relatedness to previous members of the society, share a common characteristic (what has traditionally been called the essential form).[36]

In the opening chapter of their cleverly titled collection *Every Thing Must Go*, Don Ross, James Ladyman, and David Spurrett refer to efforts such as Clarke's as the "metaphysics of domestication." The metaphysics of domestication tries to tame the very odd world revealed by contemporary science by insisting that the "containment metaphor" is still accurate; that is, that the world is made of things (little or otherwise). However, as Ross, Ladyman, and Spurrett note, "causation does not, in general, flow from the insides of containers to their outsides. Indeed, it is no longer helpful to conceive of the world, or particular systems of the world that we study in partial isolation, as 'made of' anything at all."[37] Although we do not here agree with Ross, Ladyman, and Spurrett's defense of scientism, nor their larger metaphysical project, a naturalistic Whiteheadian metaphysics does quite agree with them that every *thing* must go. The world is not "made of" substances, whether macroscopic, as Clarke contends, or microscopic, as suggested by some contemporary physicalists. Whitehead saw more than a century ago that the revolutions within science—from James Clerk Maxwell's theory of electromagnetism (on which Whitehead wrote his doctoral thesis) and Albert Einstein's theories of relativity, to early discoveries in quantum physics—that reality is composed not of things, but of energetic events, pulses of energy, internally related in complex fields of interdependence.

Both of Clarke's misinterpretations of Whitehead's event ontology, I suspect, derive in large part from his (Clarke's) misunderstanding of why Whitehead felt compelled to reject the doctrine of substance. While he is correct that, at least in part, Whitehead developed his philosophy of organism in response to the inadequacies he perceived in substance ontologies, Clarke is mistaken when he further claims that Whitehead's motivation was primarily to "banish any notion of a unitary subject perduring through time."[38] The mistake Clarke and others make is to assume that Whitehead denies that we experience the world in terms of substantial, perduring individuals. Yet, this is clearly incorrect.

Whitehead fully recognizes that it is unavoidable and even important that the human mind think of things in terms of substance and quality.[39] For, he says in *Science and the Modern World*, "without these ways of thinking we could not get our ideas straight for daily use."[40] Things such as tables, dogs, and roses are not fictions, nor do their forms of order derive primarily from the functioning of our minds. Rather, Whitehead's claim is that part of what it is to be the type of high-grade organism that we are is to have the ability to abstract from, as James put it, the "blooming, buzzing confusion" that constantly confronts us.[41] For Whitehead, our experience of the world, indeed the experience of most animals, is the product of a complex physiological process that has as its primary function the attention to a focal foreground purchased at the expense of a massive, neglected background. "There are other elements in our experience, on the fringe of consciousness, and yet massively qualifying our experience. In regard to these other facts, it is our consciousness that flickers, and not the facts themselves. They are always securely there, barely discriminated, and yet inescapable."[42] Consequently, Whitehead claims, if we look closely at the concepts of substance and quality, we will find that they are essentially "elaborate logical constructions of a high degree of abstraction."[43] They are complicated and highly useful abstractions, but they are abstractions nonetheless. Thus, the problem is not the fact *that* we perceive the world in terms of substantial individuals—this is both unavoidable and practically important—but that we fail to *recognize* "that we are presenting ourselves with simplified editions of immediate matters of fact."[44] This inappropriate substitution of the abstract for the concrete is the essence of what Whitehead calls the "fallacy of misplaced concreteness."[45] Ultimately, Whitehead explains, the violation of this fallacy does not result from the mere employment of the word "substance," but from taking, whether consciously or unconsciously, independence rather than interconnection as ontologically ultimate.[46] What Whitehead denies, then, is not the unity of macroscopic individuals, but the notion that these macroscopic, perduring individuals are the most basic ontological units of explanation. Accordingly, I contend that the question at stake is not whether Whitehead seeks to "banish" the idea of perduring individuality, which he does not, but rather *how* perduring individuality is to be explained.

I contend that it is the all-too-common defense of experience in terms of substantial, perduring individuals that is insufficiently explanatory because it arrives at its most basic ontological units—that is, macroscopic, perduring individuals—by means of the way the world appears to us (humans). To put this in Whiteheadian terms, this would be to say that, in taking our perception of the world as delineating the most basic ontological units, substance ontology violates the fallacy of misplaced concreteness. "It is the mistake that has thwarted European metaphysics from the time of the Greeks, namely, to confuse societies with the completely real things which are the actual occasions."[47] Even a dynamic account of substance is ultimately lacking in explanatory force.

If a substance ontology is to truly avoid the conception of substance as a static cabinet of accidental changes, if active self-maintenance is not achieved by "not changing, doing nothing," then it is incumbent upon Clarke to give an *explanation*, not just a description, of how this active self-maintenance takes place.[48] For Whitehead, it is not sufficient simply to say that substance or essential form just is that principle that provides unity and links the accidental attributes of a being. What is needed, I submit, is an *explanation* of *how* the active maintenance of self-identity takes place from moment to moment. Furthermore, I contend that in order to do so, substance ontology must ultimately appeal to some doctrine of internal relations. For if an individual is not essentially the same by *not* changing, but by changing at each moment, by actively responding to changing circumstances in its environment, then at each successive moment, from the time of its creation until its destruction, its self-identity must be continually reaffirmed. Unfortunately, substance accounts are lacking any such account of how this active reassertion of a given character at each successive moment takes place. It is just because self-identity must be continually reasserted and maintained that the fact of the internal relatedness of each moment to the one before it cannot be taken for granted. As a practical demonstration of the greater explanatory power of Whitehead's organic model over Clarke's dynamic substance model, I propose that we briefly examine the ontological status of systems in each.

Having the benefit of the extensive advances in fields such as ecology and biology, Clarke recognizes that he must break with Aristotle and St. Thomas and affirm that a system is "a new mode of unity existing between and binding together individual substances, which is not merely the sum of many different accidental relations but forms a *new unity* with its own properties that is not reducible merely to the sum of all the individual relations, but is a new mode of unity that resides in all the members at once."[49] Quite rightly, Clarke recognizes that "things" such as ecosystems are not simply aggregates of externally related substances. A system is a mode of unity with properties of its own. However, this introduces a problem for Clarke. While systems have properties of their own and therefore are more than a mere aggregate of entities, they have insufficient unity to be considered a substance in their own right. Within his system, it simply is invalid to claim that a system is "partially" or "sort of" a substance; something is either a substance or it is not. Given the constraints of substance ontology, Clarke takes the only option open to him; namely, he argues that a system "belongs to the order of accidents, but it is a unique kind of accident that inheres in many subjects at once—a form of one-in-many—and so deserves a name of its own because of its special properties."[50] Unfortunately, I think

Clarke is appealing to a distinction that, in fact, makes no difference; referring to systems as a type of accident, even a unique type, cannot do justice
to the real form of unity which a system *is*.

Interestingly, Clarke flirts with a model very similar to the one being
defended when he examines systems that so strongly dominate their constituents that "their individuality becomes almost submerged or wiped out, e.g.,
the ants in an ant colony or bees in a beehive are so powerfully governed by
the 'psychic field' of the whole that they surrender themselves instinctively
and totally to the good of the whole, and will die soon if removed from
it, even though they have adequate food, water, etc. The system has almost
totally absorbed them; it so dominates them that they can be almost said
to compose one being, but not quite."[51] What is particularly noteworthy is
that Clarke has his finger on the difference between what Whitehead would
call a structured living society and a personally ordered, structured living
society. For Whitehead, it is the dominance of a single, serially ordered,
continuous society that governs its structured society that characterizes
human experience. Whereas on Clarke's model of substance such a relation
is problematic, for Whitehead it is simply a matter of analyzing the types
of order achieved by a particular nexus of actual occasions. In an organic
metaphysics, macroscopic individuality is a matter of the degree of order. If
the degree of order is particularly high and significant novelty is introduced,
then it is a living society. If it is higher still, it may be a personal society.
The question, then, is not *whether* a particular form of order is or is not a
thing or a *substance*, as it is for Clarke. Though systems, such as ecosystems,
may not have the same degree of intrinsic unity as a plant or animal, for
instance, they are nonetheless real forms of togetherness with properties of
their own. By taking only the macroscopic units which we perceive at our
scale of experience as the ontologically basic units, a substance ontology is
unable to affirm the notion that there are degrees of coordination, each of
which is a real form of togetherness.[52] Thus, I believe it is the substance
tradition that must ultimately make the process turn if it is to truly *explain*,
not merely describe, the fact of dynamic self-identity.

On Whitehead's organic model of individuality, the ontological fabric
of the universe contains no true gaps.[53] Thus, the difference between, for
instance, a wildflower and a boulder is ultimately found not in an appeal to
different ontological kinds, but in the difference in the *degree* of "coordination"
achieved by the occasions of which each is composed.[54] "The organic starting
point is from the analysis of process as the realization of events disposed
in an interlocking community. The event is the unit of things real. The

emergent enduring pattern is the stabilization of the emergent achievement so as to become a fact which retains its identity throughout the process."[55] *All* macroscopic individuality, on this reading, is a matter of order.

As we will discuss in a later section, though a colony of weaver ants or honeybees may not have the same degree of intrinsic unity as a plant or animal, for instance, they are nonetheless real forms of togetherness with properties of their own. In this way, the organic model is better able to *explain* the unity of experience perduring macroscopic individuals possess. A Whiteheadian organic model of individuality not only meets the challenge of providing an adequate account of the experienced unity of macroscopic individuals, but it does so with greater explanatory depth. This is also true of materialist and physicalist metaphysics.

Take, for example, the classical puzzle from the metaphysics of identity concerning the ontological status of Theseus's ship.[56] If over time every piece (all of the matter) of a ship is gradually replaced, such that no part is original, is it still the same ship? This is a difficult problem for modern materialist and contemporary physicalist metaphysics, which would be hard-pressed to defend the view that the ship with all new parts is still the same ship that began the journey. And of course more is at stake than just the identity of constructed artifacts such as Theseus's ship. Given that the cells in my own body are gradually replaced, such that, over my own lifetime, no part of me remains from when I was born, am I still the same person? Indeed, as the physiological biologist J. Scott Turner notes, we can go further and note that "I" am more properly an "us."

> Turning back to look in the mirror, the "I" that seems so unequivocally "me" begins to lose focus as I contemplate that "I" am more of an "us." The assemblage of cells that is my body is populated by ten times as many alien cells—bacteria, yeasts, and fungi—as "my" own cells, and these alien riders carry in them a hundred more genes than the ones I inherited from my parents. Furthermore, "I" would not function as an "I" or even be the same "I" in their absence. What, then, is "I"? Am "I" an organism, or an organism-like system, or something else? At this point, the long-assumed equivalence of organism and individual becomes very strained indeed.[57]

Note that the identity paradox also plagues more traditional Aristotelian and Thomistic substance metaphysics, for such positions typically hold that it is the *matter* that individuates, not the *form*. What about a Whiteheadian event ontology?

Whereas many traditional ontologies (materialist, physicalist, and substance) are stymied by the paradox of Theseus's ship, Whitehead's event ontology has no difficulty. First, recall that, in keeping with contemporary physics, an event ontology rejects that reality is made up of "things" at all. Reality is ultimately comprised of pulses of energy coming into and going out of existence at blistering-fast rates. These are the actual entities or actual occasions of which reality is composed. So, on this view, nothing (and no-thing) endures. The most solid "things," from Mount Rainier to the great pyramids of Giza, are dynamic processes of active maintenance and decay. Even with mountains and pyramids made of stone, what endures is not a static substance or passive physical stuff, but a pattern that is inherited, actively maintained, and gradually changed over time by fleeting momentary events.

Thus, unlike materialist, physicalist, and substance ontologies, the event ontology of a philosophy of organism has no difficulty affirming it is Theseus's ship that begins and ends the journey, for what remains (is repeated moment to moment) is the pattern, the *relationship* between the parts; this pattern endures, even as the "matter" or "stuff" erodes, degrades, or is actively replaced. Again, for an organic event ontology, *all* identity and all microscopic order is a matter of the degree of internal order and the constitutive environment that it creates.

This conclusion brings to light the very important difference between the classical notion of essential form and Whitehead's notion of "defining characteristic." Whereas, according to the substance tradition, the essential form imposes and is the *cause* of the unity and self-identity of a substance by imposing its activity, as it were, from "above," for Whitehead the defining characteristic *arises out* of the mutual immanence of the genetically related nexus of actual occasions that comprise a society. For Clarke and the classical substance traditions, the essential form is "that central unifying force in a material being that binds all its elements together into an intrinsic unity of being and action, not a mere aggregate. It functions as the abiding center of characteristic actions."[58] However, for Whitehead, the defining characteristic of a society is, as Joseph Bracken puts it, "derived moment by moment from the genetic interrelatedness of the actual occasions making up a given society."[59] The defining characteristic provides the environment that makes possible a higher degree of functioning, but it is the actual occasions that actually perpetuate the defining characteristic. In the final analysis, then, I believe that this affords the organic model a decided advantage over sub-stance ontologies.

Whereas for other accounts it is somewhat a mystery *how* a substance's essential form ultimately gives it unity in the present and over time, the organic model has a further level of explanation available to it; namely, the unity of macroscopic individuals arises out of the intense, organic interrela-tion and coordination of actual occasions.[60] In this way, the organic model is better able to *explain* the unity of experience perduring macroscopic individuals possess. Thus, I submit that the most basic difference between an event ontology and a substance ontology is ultimately found in the level of explanation open to each. Whereas substance ontologies typically stop with macroscopic agents, Whitehead's philosophy of organism pushes on to provide an account of how macroscopic agency arises and how it is perpetuated. In this way, Whitehead's organic model not only meets the challenge of providing an adequate account of the experienced unity of macroscopic individuals, but it does so with greater explanatory depth. In the end, then, if he is truly to *explain*, not merely describe, his own notion of substance as dynamic self-identity, I believe the substance tradition must ultimately make the "process turn."[61]

Indeed, in introducing the odd ontological status of social-insect societ-ies, Clarke has unintentionally provided a helpful context for demonstrating how Whitehead's organic model of individuality is able to provide a more adequate metaphysical account of how more complex forms of order (i.e., individuality) arise from simpler physical and chemical constituents. Let us consider more fully the odd ontology of social insects.

The Ontology of Social Insects

It is likely that upon observing the effortless turning and looping ballet of a flock of pigeons or a school of fish you have asked yourself the question, "How do they do it?" As Brian Partridge noted in a *Scientific American* essay from the 1980s:

> [This] question occurs naturally to anyone watching a school of silversides moving slowly over a reef in clear tropical waters. Hundreds of small silver fish glide in unison, more like a sin-gle organism than a collection of individuals. The school idles along on a straight course, then wheels suddenly; not a single

fish is lost from the group. A barracuda darts from behind an outcropping of coral and the members of the school flash outward in an expanding sphere. The flash expansion dissolves the school in a fraction of a second, yet none of the fish collide. Moments later the scattered individuals collect in small groups; ultimately the school re-forms and continues to feed, lacking perhaps a member or two.[62]

Or consider the ostensibly simple act of a honeybee foraging for nectar as Bert Hölldobler and E. O. Wilson describe it in their 2009 collaboration *Superorganism*.

Although simple in appearance, the act is a performance of high virtuosity. The forager was guided to this spot by dances of her nestmates that contained symbolic information about the direction, distance, and quality of the nectar source. To reach her destination, she traveled the bee equivalent of hundreds of human miles at bee-equivalent supersonic speed. She has arrived at an hour when the flowers are most likely to be richly productive. Now she closely inspects the willing blossoms by touch and smell and extracts the nectar with intricate movements of her legs and proboscis. Then she flies home in a straight line. All this she accomplishes with a brain the size of a grain of sand and with little or no prior experience.[63]

Finally, consider the complex forms of social organization achieved by African driver ants.

Viewed from afar, the huge raiding column of a driver ant colony seems like a single living entity. It spreads like the pseudopodium of a giant amoeba across 70 meters or so of ground. . . . As the column emerges, it first resembles an expanding sheet and then metamorphoses into a treelike formation, with the trunk growing from the nest, the crown an advancing front the width of a small house, and numerous branches connecting the two. The swarm is leaderless. . . . These predatory feeder columns are rivers of ants coming and going. The frontal swarm, advancing at 20 meters an hour, engulfs all the ground and low vegetation in its path, gathering and killing all the insects and even snakes and other larger animals unable to escape. After a few hours, the direction of the flow is reversed, and the column drains backward into the nest holes.[64]

How indeed are such coordinated efforts possible? How can each of these simple-brained and seemingly independent individuals achieve such impressive acts of coordination, communication, and collaboration? Witnessing such performances, it is understandable why in the late nineteenth and early twentieth century some researchers believed that the corporate behavior of flocks of birds, schools of fish, and colonies of ants, bees, and termites involved some undiscovered form of telekinesis.

Contemporary research has instead revealed that swarms of birds, fish, and insects are in fact leaderless systems more akin to a single living organism than a mere collection of individuals.[65] The school, flock, and colony, it turns out, has just as much right to the title "individual" as does the solitary fish, bird, bee, ant, or termite.[66] Indeed, the degree of unity achieved by some societies of social insects—such as army ants, weaver ants, termites, and honeybees—is so great that many sociobiologists characterize them as "superorganisms." As one prominent researcher, Thomas Seeley, notes, "A colony of honey bees, for example, functions as an integrated whole and its members cannot survive on their own, yet individual honey bees are physically independent and closely resemble in physiology and morphology the solitary bees from which they evolved. In a colony of honey bees two levels of biological organization—organism and superorganism—coexist with equal prominence."[67]

Coined in 1789 by the geologist James Hutton to refer to Earth in the context of geophysiology, the term "superorganism" was brought to prominent use in sociobiology early in the twentieth century by William Morton Wheeler,[68] who noted the striking similarities between, on the one hand, caste and division of labor in social insect colonies and, on the other hand, the functioning of cells and organs in individual organisms.[69] Individual members of a colony function in much the same way that individual cells do in the human body. For instance, just as particular cells in the body specialize and collectively perform certain functions within the body, particular ants or bees are members of specific "castes" that perform specific tasks, such as reproduction, defense, and food distribution (see Table 6.1). This isomorphism between an individual organism and a superorganism is nicely captured in the following table from Hölldobler and Wilson.[70]

Table 6.1. Comparison of organism and superorganism

Organism	Superorganism
Cells	Colony members
Organs	Castes
Gonads	Reproductive castes
Somatic organs	Worker castes
Immune system	Defensive castes; alarm-defense communication; colony-recognition labels
Circulatory system	Food distribution, including regurgitation between nestmates (trophallaxis), distribution of pheromones, and chemical cues
Sensory organs	Combined sensory apparatus of colony members
Nervous system	Communication and interactions among colony members
Skin, skeleton	Nest
Organogenesis: growth and development of the embryo	Sociogenesis: growth and development of the colony

Source: Hölldobler and Wilson, Figure 5.1.

What is all the more amazing is that this intense coordination of behavior is, in fact, "self-organizing"; there is no leader. By following very simple algorithms or decision rules, colonies collectively achieve feats unthinkable by the individuals of which they are comprised, such as finding the shortest path to food, selecting a suitable nest site, defending the nest from invaders, maintaining a narrow range of optimal nest temperature, allocating workers to different tasks, and distributing food.[71] "Nothing in the brain of a worker ant represents a blueprint of the social order," Hölldobler and Wilson write. "There is no overseer or 'brain caste' who carries such a master plan in his head. Instead, colony life is the product of self-organization. The superorganism exists in the separate programmed responses of the organisms that compose it. The assembly instructions the organisms follow are the developmental algorithms, which create the castes, together with the behavioral algorithms, which are responsible for moment-to-moment behavior of the caste members."[72] They continue, "Thus, a distributed colony intelligence is created greater than the intelligence of any one of the members, sustained by the incessant pooling of information through communication."[73] It is the emergence of a "distributed colony intelligence," or what many researchers call "swarm intelligence," that makes such complex, integrated behavior possible.[74] As a collective individual, they achieve amazing forms of social organization rivaled only by humans.[75]

These findings introduce many interesting and important metaphysical issues. Understanding how millions of insects can coordinate their behavior so closely that they become a single, collective individual introduces fascinating problems regarding individuality, identity, the boundary between living and nonliving, the origin of societies, and perhaps a key to the evolutionary origins of consciousness itself. The philosophical question that seems most immediately pressing is: How are we best to *explain*, not just describe, the emergence and maintenance of these forms of order?

For their part, many scientists continue to use the metaphor of mechanism to describe the order of social insects. For instance, despite the fact that they describe insect societies as "emergent" forms of social order that arise through the collective "decision making" of individual insects, at times Bert Hölldobler and E. O. Wilson describe the colony as "a growth-maximizing machine"[76] composed of "cellular automata"[77] whose operations can adequately be described by the language of physical and computer sciences.[78] Thomas Seeley is even more explicit in his use of the mechanistic model: "In choosing a nest site," he writes, "building a nest, collecting food, regulating the nest temperature, and deterring predators, a honey bee colony containing a queen resembles a smoothly running machine in which each part contributes to the efficient operation of the whole." Indeed, he goes even further, arguing that "it should be very revealing, and at most only slightly misleading, to view a honey bee colony as an integrated biological machine that promotes the success of the colony's genes."[79] Seeley's view is representative of both of the dominant trends within modern biology: molecular biology and neo-Darwinism.

As the biologist Turner perceptively notes, the former (molecular biology) has "relentlessly pursued an understanding of life as a mechanism, as a special case of chemistry, physics, and thermodynamics."[80] The latter (neo-Darwinism) has come to focus exclusively on the transmission of genes, as is perhaps best represented by Richard Dawkins's "extended phenotype." An unintended consequence of these two trends, Turner notes, is the gradual disappearance of the very notion of an organism. For molecular biologists, "the organism itself has become, at best, an unwelcome distraction from the fascinating cellular and molecular business at hand"; for the neo-Darwinist, "the organism has become essentially an illusion, a wraith obscuring the 'real' biology of the genes, bound together in a conspiracy to promote the genetic interests of its members."[81] Much of Anglo-American philosophy is, for its part, largely in keeping with this account. Despite what I take to be its limited explanatory force, some version of mechanistic physicalism is so widely accepted among a certain segment of philosophers that it scarcely requires defense.

However, as Whitehead—along with Charles Sanders Peirce, William James, John Dewey, Henri Bergson, Pierre Teilhard de Chardin, and others—so forcefully argued in response to an earlier generation of physicalists, the mechanistic metaphor cannot adequately do justice to the reality of living, evolving, striving, emoting beings connected in interdependent social relations. Indeed, despite the fact that at times their own language betrays them, Hölldobler and Wilson seem to recognize the inadequacy of the mechanistic model.

> Watched for only a few hours, a colony of social insects might be interpreted as consisting of automata driven with the same uniform set of decision rules. But that is far from the case. Each member of the colony is distinct in some manner or other that affects its behavior. Each has a mind of its own. By mind we do not mean a reflective, self-aware, wide-roaming consciousness of the human kind, but rather a cognitive consciousness built with a relatively complex brain that can store information from all its sensory modalities (taste, smell, touch, sight, and sound) as well as some memory of the events it has experienced during its short life.[82]

Though comparatively simple, an individual insect is not an interchangeable machine part, nor is it "a simple automaton."[83] Even on Hölldobler and Wilson's account, the algorithms upon which individual insects make their decisions are not rigidly deterministic; they are rather "central tendencies"[84] or teleological orientations.

If we are to be adequate to the beauty and dynamism of these complex societies of individuals—if we are to explain, and not just describe, how these patterns of behavior emerge and are perpetuated—we need a more adequate model of the relationships between individuals. We need, as it were, an explanatory framework for describing how social order can emerge from the more basic physical constituents of reality. I argue that Whitehead's philosophy of organism provides a more adequate conceptual system for explaining the ontological status of collective individuals and thereby points beyond the current hegemony of reductive molecular biology.

Taking Whitehead's organic metaphysics of individuality as our context, consider the example of macrotermes colonies or African termites. As Turner notes, opening a mound reveals "a capacious central chimney from which radiates a complex network of passages, connecting ultimately to an array of thin-walled tunnels that lie under the mound's surface like veins on an arm." Beyond the impressiveness of the construction, what is most surprising, Turner notes, is what you do not see; namely, termites. The mound, it turns out, is not built to house the millions of termites that continually maintain it. Rather, they live in a large spherical nest under the mound.[85] To understand the mound's purpose requires that we examine termites' dietary habits.

Termites, Turner explains, are unable to digest the bits of grass, bark, dead wood, and dung that they swallow. Instead, each species of termite cultivates a particular species of fungus that can break down the material into a digestible form. However, this digestive arrangement significantly increases the oxygen requirement of the colony, since the fungus requires five times the oxygen of the termites.[86] According to Turner, "This fungus, together with the bacteria and other soil microorganisms, raises the oxygen requirement to the amount needed by a cow. Indeed, ranchers in northern Namibia think of each termite mound as the equivalent of one livestock unit: each nest's foraging insects eat about the same quantity of grass as would one head of cattle. A cow buried alive would soon die without access to air, and so it is with a termite colony: without ventilation, it would suffocate."[87]

The mound, therefore, is not a residence or even a defensive structure; it is, Turner contends, an external lung. By building the mound up vertically, the natural force of the wind exchanges the air through the network of capillary tunnels.[88] "Thus," Turner concludes, "the regulated environment, maintained by a constructed physiological organ—the mound—furthers the interests of both groups of inhabitants. The termite colony—insects, fungus, mound, and nest—becomes like any other body composed of functionally different parts working in concert and is ultimately capable of reproducing itself. Taken as a whole, the colony is an extended organism."[89] The subterranean nest is like the skin or skeleton of an organism: the fungus serves as its digestive system, the mound is the respiratory system, and various castes serve as the reproductive, sensory, immune, and nervous systems. Though a complete organic unity itself, a single termite is unintelligible apart from the collective organism of which it is a member. Indeed, as Turner himself notes at the end of his article, "understanding the system requires thinking about the mound as not really an object but a process." He continues, "In the case of termite mounds, the termites and fungi certainly qualify as living, but so does the mound, in a sense. After all, it does just what our lungs do for us. The primary difference is in perspective. For a human, what is inside the body is pretty clear, but for the termite colony, 'inside' includes the nest environment."[90]

Despite his critical approach, it is a mistake to infer that Turner is rejecting the modern synthesis. Indeed, he sees his position as complementary with, not contradictory to the gene-centric focus of molecular biology and its "extended phenotype." Turner's claim is not that evolutionary biology is incorrect, but that, by itself, it is inadequate. Whereas evolutionary biologists such as Richard Dawkins see the extended phenotype "as the extension of the action of genes beyond the outermost boundaries of an organism and asks how these extended phenotypes aid in the transmission of genes from one generation to the next,"[91] Turner's work sees the extended organism as the extension of the action of agents beyond the physical boundaries of an organism to include built structures, and asks how these "extended organisms" might make evolution by natural selection possible and may in fact help explain the origins of life itself.

Turner's work with insects has led him to a much broader conclusion. In his 2007 book, *The Tinkerer's Accomplice*, he argues that "organisms are designed not so much because of natural selection of particular genes has made them that way, but because agents of homeostasis build them that way."[92] Indeed, he goes so far as to claim that "nothing about evolution makes sense except in light of the physiology that underpins it."[93] Turner contrasts his position with the dominant, gene-centric model in the following manner:

> Conventionally, Darwinian fitness is *thing*-based, measured in terms of replication of discrete things. In "traditional" Darwinism, for example, the replicate is the offspring, while to a Neo-Darwinist, it is the atom of heredity, the gene. The fitter gene is the one whose bias reaches further into the future. A physiological process can also bias the future, and by this criterion could also qualify as heritable memory. In this instance, the forward reach

in time is embodied in *persistence* of the process: how likely is it that the orderly stream of matter and energy that embodies the process will persist in the face of whatever perturbations are thrown at it? A fit process is therefore a persistent process: if a particular catalytic milieu, or a particular embodied physiology, can more persistently commandeer a stream of energy and matter than can another, the more persistent stream will be the fitter. Homeostasis, therefore, is the rough physiological equivalent of genetic fitness: a more robust homeostasis will ensure a system's persistence over a wider range of perturbations and further into the future than will a less robustly regulated system.[94]

Turner argues that homeostasis, or the ability of an organism to maintain a stable internal environment, is the "second law" of biology, with natural selection being the first. The analogy here is with the laws of motion, and just as the second law of motion is not reducible to or derivable from the first, he claims that homeostasis is a fundamental law of biology not reducible to or derivable from the first.[95]

These scientific frontiers challenge the substance, materialist, and physicalist accounts of individuality. Individuals normally have clearly defined boundaries, a membrane that demarcates where they begin and end. Here we find that, as a single superorganism, the termite colony is extended in space and time without clearly defined boundaries or a skin to define where the environment stops and the superorganism begins. Normally we would say that a single insect crawling on the ground is a proper individual. However, Turner's research shows that a single termite is no more an "individual" than a single cell in a petri-dish solution. This research also muddles the usually sharp distinction between living and nonliving. Here, inorganic soils, living insects, and fungi all constitute a single, collective individual. These built environments shape and determine the individuals that create them, often becoming a sort of external memory that shapes the evolutionary trajectory of the individuals that maintain them.

Recognizing that an entire colony—nest, mound, insect, and fungus—is a single, organic individual undermines the longstanding conception of individuals as discrete beings with "independent existence." As Turner puts it, "If the existence of physiological function is not dependent upon a clear partition of an organism from its environment, then there seems to be little reason to regard the organism as an entity discrete from its environment."[96] Whitehead's philosophy of organism provides a rich metaphysical basis for

Turner's biological account of the "extended organism." Indeed, a holistic, organic model such as that developed by Whitehead provides an avenue for overcoming the reductionism that has come to dominate both science and philosophy throughout the late twentieth and early twenty-first centuries.

It is worth noting, if only briefly, that these findings are not limited to social insects. One of the unexpected fruits of the unprecedented, world-wide scientific investigation of Earth's climate is the conclusion that our planet is not the lifeless rock it is normally taken to be. It is increasingly apparent that the Earth is a single, living system and must be studied as such. Indeed, this surprising conclusion is enshrined in the opening words of the 2001 "Amsterdam Declaration," signed by thousands of scientists at the European Geophysical Union, which states that "the Earth System behaves as a single, self-regulating system comprised of physical, chemical, biological, and human components."[97] Although there is still debate over what is meant by the term "self-regulating," this research is revealing a planet that is, in a meaningful sense, alive.

As with Turner's work on termites, Earth System science is revealing that the reductive and mechanistic tendencies of neo-Darwinism is inadequate to account for the emergence of these forms of planetary-level homeostasis and self-regulation. As Dawkins wrote in *The Extended Phenotype*, planetary-level homeostasis is not explicable via natural selection because it would "have all the notorious difficulties of 'group selection.' "[98] That is, it would be wide open to "cheats." "For instance," Dawkins writes, "if plants are supposed to make oxygen for the good of the biosphere, imagine a mutant plant which saved itself the costs of oxygen manufacture. Obviously it would outrepro-duce its more public-spirited colleagues, and genes for public-spiritedness would soon disappear."[99]

However, as Wilkinson (2004), Lenton (2004), and others have noted, planetary-level feedbacks and homeostatic regulation need only be *consis-tent* with natural selection, not be a *product* of it. For instance, Wilkinson argues that planetary-level self-regulation could be the emergent result of "by-product mutualisms" similar to those found in population ecology.[100]

> In investment mutualisms both organisms provide some service to their partner at some cost to themselves, while in by-product mutualisms a waste product of one organism is used by its partner. Investment mutualisms are open to cheating (one partner could in theory reduce its investment while still taking the benefits). However, many mutualisms are of the by-product type, in which

there are no selective advantages to an organism's withholding its by-product. Indeed, if it were costly to prevent the partner from obtaining the by-product, then the subsequent fitness of a cheat would be lower than if it had cooperated in supplying the by-product. This avoids the criticisms of Dawkins, who, interestingly, used the example of oxygen production by plants, which is a by-product of oxygenic photosynthesis and thus not open to cheating.[101]

Dawkins and other materialist and physicalist philosophers' reductive emphasis on chemistry, physics, and thermodynamics is, arguably, inadequate to fully explain the emergence of these system-level forms of regulation. A mechanistic ontology cannot make sense of the claim that the Earth System functions as "a single self-regulating system." Indeed, my claim is that traditional metaphysical accounts of individuality are unable to make sense of these nontraditional, but nevertheless real, forms of individuality.

I am suggesting that what is needed is a more robust metaphysical model that can make sense of systems of internally related, interdependent individuals that constitute integrated wholes with varying *degrees* of unity and identity. What is needed is a metaphysics that rejects absolute breaks between living and nonliving, and between mental and physical—one that sees reality as a single, continuous whole. What is needed is a model that recognizes the inherently dynamic, processive nature of reality. What is needed is a complex metaphysics that takes as its primary metaphor not enduring substances or inert bits of matter in a vast machine, but the metaphor of internally related organisms woven into systems of varying complexity. Of course, that is exactly what we find in Whitehead's philosophy of organism.

Chapter 7

Teleology and the Naturalistic Fallacy

The birth of modern science was in many ways predicated on the banishment of Aristotelian, scholastic metaphysics, particularly its notions of immaterial forms and teleological final causes. Contrary to ancient and medieval metaphysics, matter does not act in certain regular ways because of an invisible soul or form, but because of impersonal, absolute natural laws. Substances are not best seen as organisms with an internal developmental orientation (telos), but as machines that act according to, as Descartes puts it, the arrangement of their parts.[1] In banishing forms and teleology, several new metaphysics become ascendant: (1) metaphysical materialism (e.g., Hobbes and Hume), according to which reality is nothing but matter controlled absolutely and mechanistically by Newtonian laws of nature; (2) metaphysical dualism (e.g., Descartes and Kant), according to which the immaterial mind is the sole exception to an otherwise mechanistic material universe; or (3) metaphysical idealism (e.g., Berkeley and Hegel), according to which reality is ultimately mind. Focusing on developing experimental habits of patient observation, early scientists found they could learn how the "machinery" of nature works. The result, of course, has been wildly successful. The track record of science is beyond dispute.

For our present project on environmental metaphysics, it is particularly important to note that it is the banishment of teleology that creates and justifies a strong bifurcation between fact and value. For it was the form that defined the telos and it was the telos that defined the "good for" that being, which provided a metaphysical tether between being and value. By cutting that tether, value is set adrift. Matter is meaningless and valueless, "vacuous actuality."[2] Whether the passive bits of reality are organized like this (say, a towering sequoia) or that (say, a pile of logs) does not matter intrinsically. Value and the good are *not* features of reality that can be discovered and understood by understanding the telos or aim of a being, for there are no such things. Matter behaves mechanistically. The universe of value shrinks, for the dualist, to the absolute value of the immaterial mind or, for the materialist, to a subjective projection onto an otherwise meaningless, valueless world.[3] That is, one is left with two different forms of axiological anthropocentrism. According to the former (for dualists), humans alone (or, with Kant, rational beings) have intrinsic value for they alone have a mind in an otherwise clockwork universe. According to the latter (for mechanistic materialists), nothing has *intrinsic* value, for value is merely a subjective projection. Without valuers, there is no value. The dark penumbra of the naturalistic fallacy looms.

This is the background metaphysical context for the protracted debates within environmental ethics over intrinsic value.[4] Indeed, given this, it should come as no surprise that many environmental philosophers seeking to defend the intrinsic value of nonhuman nature have realized that this requires the recovery of some form of teleology (see, e.g., Paul Taylor and Holmes Rolston).[5] But how is this possible if admission through the doors of contemporary science can only be purchased by the repudiation of teleology? And what about the naturalistic fallacy? Generally speaking, even those environmental philosophers who seek to defend some form of teleology explicitly (e.g., Taylor or Rolston) do not provide a *metaphysical* justification for this position. At most, they seek to show how their recovery of teleology does not run afoul of contemporary evolutionary biology and ecology. But what is decidedly lacking is an account of reality that is fully consistent with the world revealed by contemporary science, but which also provides a coherent account of the ways in which *reality* is or is not teleological. That is, what is missing is an adequate environmental metaphysics. This chapter seeks to remedy that omission.

To be sure, we cannot here fully examine or defend the metaphysics of teleology.[6] The more modest but still important goal of this chapter is to frame a discussion of the metaphysics of teleology with the goal of properly recognizing the metaphysical relationship of fact and value. Specifically, in the first section I examine the unique accounts of "developmental teleology" presented by both Charles Sanders Peirce and Alfred North Whitehead. Given this unique model of teleology and the metaphysics on which it is based, we find in the second part that the specter of the naturalistic fallacy need only haunt systems grounded in faulty metaphysics.

Peirce and Whitehead on Teleology

In a series of *Monist* essays published from 1891 to 1893, Peirce critiques the failings of "necessitarianism," developing the contours of a nondualistic metaphysics.[7] For instance, in April of 1892, Peirce published "The Doctrine of Necessity Examined" in which he argued that the Laplacian necessitarianism of late nineteenth-century science made genuine spontaneity and life impossible.[8] Peirce revolts against this "mechanical philosophy" on both epistemological and metaphysical grounds. First, in barricading the "road to inquiry,"[9] necessitarianism commits the gravest of epistemological sins. "To say that there is a universal law, and that it is a hard, ultimate, unintelligible fact, the why and wherefore of which can never be inquired into, at this a sound logic will revolt."[10] Yet, for Peirce, certainty is not fully achievable not only because of the finitude of human knowers, but because of the dynamism of the known. It is impossible, Peirce argues, to account for the "variety and diversity of the universe" unless we recognize "pure spontaneity or life as a character of the universe, acting always and everywhere though restrained within narrow bounds by law, producing infinitesimal departures from law continually, and great ones with infinite infrequency."[11]

Peirce expanded his assault on the mechanist philosophy three months later in "The Law of Mind." Here, Peirce rightly notes that to truly overcome the mechanist model requires the abandonment of an irrational dualism in which mind is an inexplicable island in an ocean of clockwork machines. It is not enough to account for the evolution of living forms if one describes the basic constituents of reality in terms that make the evolution of life itself impossible. A mechanistic account of nature is unable to account for the emergence of living or mental beings. In contrast, Peirce conceives "matter to be mere specialised and partially deadened mind."[12] Thus, continuity and spontaneity, or what he terms "synechism" and "tychism," are two pillars of Peirce's speculative metaphysics. Yet, by themselves, continuity and spontaneity are insufficient to account for our evolutionary cosmos. Though spontaneity or chance is a fundamental character of reality, this chance is, Peirce writes, "to some degree regular."[13] Indeed, as he will go on to argue, it is teleological.

Although the discussion of this third principle is not named and is fully investigated by Peirce for several more months—until the publishing of "Evolutionary Love" in January of 1893—his interest in teleology is already apparent at the end of "The Law of Mind," which concludes with an important discussion of the teleological role of personality.

Peirce begins by noting that personality does not occur at an instant. No manner of close inspection of a time-slice of one's life could discover the role of personality in coordinating one's actions in pursuit of a goal. "It has to be lived in time; nor can any finite time embrace its fullness."[14] Personality, Peirce writes, "implies a teleological harmony in ideas."[15] Our personality is an instance of a teleological orientation that guides and informs our every decision. Yet, as Peirce notes, this is not a traditional, Aristotelian form of teleology in which there is a single, "predeterminate end" toward which the organism runs on rails.[16] Peirce's point is that our personality at once *guides and is guided by* our decisions. Our personality is what helps determine the ends at which we aim, and the actions taken in pursuit of them, but the decisions made and actions taken constitute the person that we are. Thus, personality at once *determines* and is *determined by* the decisions taken.

This is critically important to emphasize as it demarcates a clear difference between Peirce's (and Whitehead's) conception of teleology and the much-maligned ancient and medieval notions. Indeed, I think Peirce has made a momentous discovery. Peirce is defending what I believe is a novel and underappreciated form of teleology. In both determining and being determined by our decisions, our personality is not a "predeterminate end"; it is, Peirce writes, a "developmental teleology."[17] Recall that, for Aristotle, the end or telos of an organism was perfectly determinate and unchanging. While a substance may not necessarily achieve its end, there is one and only one end at which an organism aims. This is in large part due to the fact that, for Aristotle, the final cause corresponds to the formal cause. What an organism *is* defines what it is to *become*. The acorn aims (nonconsciously) at becoming an oak tree, not a dog, nor a salamander, nor a venus flytrap. Although there is a sense of dynamic orientation toward an end for Aristotle, the form that defines an organism's telos is eternal, fixed, and hermetically sealed off from all other ends.[18] Early modern science defined itself in opposition to this teleological view of nature. Though biologists study complex, living organisms that seem to strive, fight, pursue, and desire, biology today is still partly defined by the extent to which it provides nonteleological, mechanistic accounts.[19]

The problem Peirce has with classical Aristotelian teleology is that, in effect, it sets the organism on rails, moving toward one and only one destination. It is not processive or developmental. Since the end is predetermined, there is no true growth or genuine novelty. "Were the ends of a person already explicit, there would be no room for development, for growth, for life; and consequently there would be no personality. The mere carrying out of predetermined purposes is mechanical."[20] If, as Peirce believes, pure spontaneity or life is a character pervading every element of reality, then there must be room for genuine growth.

Of course, Peirce's target is not Aristotle, whose teleology had long since been successfully banished by the likes of Bacon, Hobbes, Descartes, and, later, Hume. Instead, Peirce's comments about "predeterminate ends" are aimed at what we might now call "genetic determinism." Though mechanists such as August Weismann claimed to champion Darwin, Peirce rightly noted that for Weismann and those who have come to follow in his footsteps, "nothing is due to chance, but that all forms are simple mechanical resultants of the heredity from two parents."[21]

It seems that Peirce's brief but important introduction of teleology at the end of "The Law of Mind" may have brought him to conclude that synechism and tychism are not, by themselves, sufficient to account for the development of the universe. He needs to have an account of teleology that avoids making the emergence and development of life, mind, and consciousness (1) a mere accident or (2) a necessary outcome of a preordained end. As I take it, this is the task of his dramatically titled 1893 *Monist* essay "Evolutionary Love."

Peirce opens with a poetic observation: "Philosophy, when just escaping from its golden pupa-skin, mythology, proclaimed the great evolutionary agency of the universe to be Love. Or, since this pirate-lingo, English, is poor in such-like words, let us say Eros, the exuberance-love. Afterwards, Empedocles set up passionate-love and hate as the two coordinate powers of the universe."[22] Peirce at once identifies with and distinguishes himself from this ancient philosophical tradition of locating the reason for the development of the cosmos in love or eros. He agrees that love defines the ultimate teleological impulse of reality, but that the "exuberance-love" of eros—which, at least for Empedocles, is set at odds with strife—is not the form of love that drives the development of reality. Recall that Aristotle claimed it was eros that defined the ultimate final cause of the unmoved mover, for it is able to move others without itself being moved.[23]

Instead of this asymmetrical teleological account of love as eros, Peirce turns to the "ontological gospeller" St. John, who "made the One Supreme Being, by whom all things have been made out of nothing, to be cherishing-love" or agape.[24] Peirce notes that, unlike eros, agape is not the contrary of hate or strife, but it is "a love which embraces hatred as an imperfect stage of it."[25] Thus, Peirce argues, the evolution of the cosmos is driven not by eros (the love of perfection that moves without itself being moved), but by agape (the cherishing love that both moves and is moved by the other).[26] Notice the isomorphism between these accounts of teleology and his discussion of the developmental teleology of personality from "The Law of Mind." Whereas the movement of eros is linear, the movement of agape "is circular, at one and the same impulse projecting creations into independency and drawing them into harmony."[27] Only agape, not eros, makes true novelty, growth, and development possible. "Love, recognising germs of loveliness in the hateful, gradually warms it into life, and makes it lovely."[28]

Thus, in an important sense, Peirce's account of agape deepens and expands his account of developmental teleology and synechism outlined in "The Law of Mind." Specifically, he distinguishes three different forms of cosmological evolution: "anacasm," "tychasm," and "agapasm." Anacastic evolution is evolution by "mechanical necessity"; tychastic evolution is "evolution by chance or fortuitous variation"; and agapastic evolution is "evolution by creative love."[29] Peirce argues that, whereas evolution via chance (tychasm) is "heedless" and evolution via inward necessity (anacasm) is "blind," evolution via love (agapasm) brings about change "by an immediate attraction for the idea itself . . . , by the power of sympathy, that is, by virtue of the continuity of mind."[30] Thus, Peirce explains, agapastic evolution is distinguished from the pure spontaneity of tychasm and the mechanical necessity of anacasm in its "purposive character."[31] The cosmos is evolving not on rails toward a predetermined end nor because of an unintelligible and meaningless randomness, but toward an end that is itself in the process of development. Love is "warming"[32] life into existence, inviting it to become, to flourish, to grow. Though there is the invitation to become more, each organism, in its own decisions relative to this aim, helps constitute the nature of the end. The end and aim of the universe has a bias toward diversity and variety on the one hand and regularity and order on the other, but there is no necessity in this trajectory. There is, as Holmes Rolston puts it, a heading but no head.[33] The decisions made are affected by this loving orientation, but the character (personality) of this loving orientation is itself determined by the decisions. Progress is not guaranteed. The universe is, as Whitehead would later write, an adventure.[34]

Three decades later, Whitehead joins his Classical American Pragmatist cousins in their fight against dualism and mechanistic materialism, developing a speculative philosophy that defends both microscopic (what I will call local, but which has historically often been referred to as "proximate" teleology) and macroscopic (what I will call cosmic or ultimate teleology) teleology. Like Peirce before him, Whitehead is provoked by what he sees as the inadequacies of the mechanistic view of reality defended by scientific materialism, which eliminates all meaning, value, and purpose from reality. In its place he defends a "reformed subjectivism," according to which every element of reality, from the subatomic to the galactic, is a subjective unification of and reaction to the impress of the past. The becoming concrete ("concrescence") of each occasion of reality ("subject-superject") is guided by its "subjective aim."[35] This subjective aim provides a "lure for feeling," setting out a range of "real possibility" achievable by the nascent subject-superject.[36] Importantly, for Whitehead, each moment of reality, each event or actual occasion determines what it is to be in its teleological process of becoming. The subject does not gradually *uncover* a predeterminate end, as with the classical account of the sculptor removing the marble to reveal the form within. Rather, the subject *becomes itself* in its attempt to eliminate the indeterminacy implied in its subjective aim, its telos. The sculptor decides what she is making in the act itself. As Whitehead puts it in *Process and Reality*, "The subject-superject is the purpose of the process originating the feelings. The feelings are inseparable from the end at which they aim; and this end is the feeler. The feelings aim at the feeler, as their final cause. The feelings are what they are in order that their subject may be what it is. It is better to say that the feelings *aim at* their subject, than to say that they *are aimed at* their subject."[37] Thus, similar to but independent of Peirce, Whitehead is defending a "developmental teleology" at every level of existence. The universe is composed of nothing but teleological subject-superjects.

For Whitehead, the local teleology of each actual occasion's subjective aim is set within a broader, cosmic teleological orientation of the universe.[38] Showing that Plato is never far from his mind, in *Adventures of Ideas* Whitehead discusses the "Platonic Eros"[39] that urges the "victory of persuasion over force."[40]

> In his [Plato's] view, the entertainment of ideas is intrinsically associated with an inward ferment, an activity of subjective feeling, which is at once immediate enjoyment, and also an appetition which melts into action. This is Plato's Eros, which he sublimates into the notion of the soul in the enjoyment of its creative function, arising from its entertainment of ideas. The word Eros means 'Love,' and in *The Symposium* Plato gradually elicits his final conception of the urge towards ideal perfection.[41]

Thus, again similar to Peirce before him, Whitehead claims that the teleology of the universe aims at "intensity and variety."[42] Indeed, he defines the "essence of life" as the "teleological introduction of novelty."[43] The role of the Platonic Eros is in providing the ultimate lure toward the creation of intensity and variety; it is the urge toward the ideal perfection for each occasion.[44] "Eros is the urge toward the realization of ideal perfection."[45] Thus, along with Frederick Ferré, I have argued that Whitehead defends a kalogenic metaphysics.[46] The universal aim of the creative advance is the production of beauty. The creative advance does not just aim at novelty; the lure for feeling involved in the subjective aim of each occasion is a lure, an invitation to become a harmonious and intense ordering of experience. Every being is lured toward higher forms of beauty. "The teleology of the Universe is directed to the production of Beauty."[47]

As much as I am committed to Whitehead's account of beauty, I've always found confusing his appeal to the love of eros to account for the universal aim of beauty. Of course, given his fondness for his work, Whitehead's appeal to Plato is entirely unsurprising. Yet, despite this, my concern is that, at its root, eros is the form of love that moves others without itself being moved. This, of course, is why Aristotle described the relationship between the unmoved mover and nature as eros. The perfection of the unmoved mover is the ultimate final cause of nature, but the unmoved mover is impassive, self-thought thought eternal thinking of nothing but itself; it is walled off from and only externally related to the world.[48] Now, I grant that this is Aristotle's conception of divine eros, not Plato's, but it is not clear to me that Plato's account fairs much better. Though I am appreciative of, indeed committed to, Plato's claim that the good and the beautiful are one and that the universe is aimed at the achievement of the good and the beautiful, even in *Symposium* Plato's account of eros seems to me to be an account in which the beauty of others draws them in but is itself unaffected by the relationship. Beauty for Plato is a static, eternal form—not an evolving, open-ended adventure. Thus, my suggestion is that Whitehead's system would benefit from a reciprocal form of love, such as agape.[49] To be true to his relational and open-ended metaphysics, Whitehead would do well to follow Peirce's lead in conceiving of the teleological orientation of the universe in terms of agape, rather than eros. Indeed, there is reason to believe that true creativity and growth is incompatible with eros, that Whitehead needs Peirce's agapastic account of cosmological evolution.[50]

As Carl Hausman argues in "Eros and Agape in Creative Evolution: A Peircean Insight," "There is reason to insist that the kind of love which operates in creativity cannot be adequately described exclusively in terms of eros."[51] Hausman argues that eros impels the movement from incompleteness to completeness through the attraction of the perfection of the other. The subject aims at this completeness because of the lure, the attractive nature of the end that fulfills it. The problem with this account, he notes, is that it does not really permit true creativity, true novelty, and growth because the end sought after is predetermined. As Hausman puts it:

> If eros were the exclusive dynamic principle of a process, that process would not be creative, for it would not allow for a change in the subject as determined by its initial direction. The subject would appropriate what it lacks, but it would have no way of varying its growth against the background of established goals and patterns of development. Novelty in the intelligible structure of the outcome would be absent. The structure of the process, the manner of developing, and the character of the subject would be predetermined according to the conditioning called for in the telos. The process would evolve in accord with a pattern, as an acorn evolves into an oak tree.[52]

Of course, as Hausman goes on to point out, this is not compatible with the open, dynamic, processive account of teleological development that Whitehead so carefully develops. The subjective aim that is a lure for feeling is not like an Aristotelian form; process does not run on rails to a predetermined end. Genuine novelty is possible because the end itself changes in light of the decisions of the subject. As Whitehead himself notes:

> The feelings are inseparable from the end at which they aim; and this end is the feeler. The feelings aim at the feeler, as their final cause. The feelings are what they are in order that their subject may be what it is. It is better to say that the feelings *aim at* their subject, than to say that they *are aimed at* their subject. An actual entity feels as it does feel in order to be the actual entity it is. The creativity is not an external agency with its own ulterior purposes. All actual entities share with God this characteristic of self-causation.[53]

If Whitehead is to maintain a teleologically oriented but truly open developmental process, then agape, not eros, is the form of love that characterizes the universal drive to achieve beauty, for agape is that form of love that affects while itself being affected. Hausman summarizes the key difference between eros and agape well.

> Eros is love that is expressed by what seeks something more perfect, or more fulfilling, than what is possessed by the lover in the absence of union with the beloved. Thus, eros is expressed by what seeks something more perfect, or more fulfilling, than what is possessed by the lover in the absence of union with the beloved. Agape, on the other hand, is love expressed by an agent already fulfilled in its own terms, and it is directed not as a seeking but as a concern for the beloved. Agape is not the power to overcome dependence; it is the power to overflow in interdependence toward an other which is not something to be identified with but which may be dependent and in need of the love that overflows.[54]

Given this interpretation, it seems to me that agape better captures the open-ended, creative adventure of the universe Whitehead sought to characterize. True growth and genuine novelty require the cherishing love of agape, not the sterile perfection of eros. "In creating valuable novelty, a subject is not impelled by a desire to fulfill itself. Instead, it offers itself by permitting its creation to grow in its own terms. Thus, paradoxically, in offering itself, it generates the excellence which, out of agape, it gives to its creature. Creative love must be agapastic."[55]

On the other hand, Peirce's strength in accounting for agapastic cosmic teleology is not matched in his account of individual creative teleology. In a sense, Whitehead's weakness (cosmic teleology) is Peirce's strength, and Peirce's weakness (local teleology) is Whitehead's strength. Peirce does not really give an adequate account of individual creativity. Although he speaks thoughtfully about the developmental teleology involved with personality, he does not give a metaphysical account of the teleological development of subjects in general. The reason for this likely has to do with his fundamental commitment to "synechism," or metaphysical continuity. Although Peirce and Whitehead were both mathematicians who were concerned with overcoming mechanism and dualism, they took alternative metaphysical paths in their attempts to provide an alternative, with Peirce embracing the pure continuity of synechism and Whitehead embracing a relational atomism. In a sense, each philosopher's project can be seen as a different response to

Zeno's paradox. Or, to put it differently, both Peirce and Whitehead were concerned with how the past really affects the present.

For Peirce, the past cannot merely be "vicariously" in the present. Rather, the past must be present by "direct perception." "That is, it cannot be wholly past; it can only be going, infinitesimally past, less past than any assignable past date. We are thus brought to the conclusion that the present is connected with the past by a series of real, infinitesimal steps."[56] For Peirce, then, there is no need to explain how the smallest bit of reality is achieved, because there is no smallest bit. The doctrine of synechism is that reality is "infinitesimally" continuous.

Though equally concerned with accounting for how the past "gets inside" and affects the present, Whitehead rejects Peirce's notion of infinitesimals. Whitehead would concur with James, who in *Some Problems of Philosophy* writes, "Your acquaintance with reality grows literally by buds or drops of perception. Intellectually and on reflection you can divide these into components, but as immediately given, they come totally or not at all."[57] Whitehead embraced this model via his "reformed subjectivism" in which reality is composed of irreducible "drops" of experience that are internally related to past subjective achievements. "There is a becoming of continuity, but not continuity of becoming."[58]

I wade into these murky and turbulent metaphysical waters with significant trepidation. My own background in mathematics is inadequate to feel confident in my appreciation of these two competing solutions to Zeno's paradox and the problem of the one and the many. However, wade I must. I feel a bit like James: "Being almost blind mathematically and logically, I feel considerable shyness in differing from such superior minds, yet what can one do but follow one's own dim light?"[59] Although I am deeply sympathetic with Peirce's emphasis on continuity and his embrace of a panpsychism in which matter "is not completely dead, but is merely mind hide-bound with habits,"[60] I ultimately find that Peirce is unable to account for the pure continuity of experience at which he aims. Indeed, to go one step further, I would argue that Peirce's doctrine of synechism is only possible with an account of internal relatedness such as that developed by Whitehead.

I am not convinced that Peirce's synechism explains the real presence of the past in the present. If, as Peirce noted in "The Law of Mind," the past is not "wholly past," then it must in some real sense be in the present. That the beads on the string, to use Bergson's phrase, are infinitesimally past merely infinitely repeats, but does not truly solve, the problem of how one moment comes to be in the next. In this respect, an infinitesimally near past is no different than a more distant past. Both fail to explain how the past "gets inside" the present. Thus, without an account of internal relatedness, Peirce cannot in fact achieve the genuine continuity at which he aims. For this reason, I ultimately find that Peirce would greatly benefit from Whitehead's relational atomism. (See chapter six of this volume on individuals.) In particular, what is needed, I contend, is an account of "individual" teleological achievement that grounds novelty and spontaneity in the "decisions" of subjective centers of experience.

Thus, although Whitehead gives a very useful and detailed account of the teleological growth and development of every actual occasion, his account of cosmic evolution via eros seems somewhat in tension with his otherwise relational account and would benefit from an agapastic account. On the other hand, while Peirce gives a rich and interesting account of cosmic evolution via the cherishing love of agape, he lacks a developed account of individual teleological development such that each occasion is internally and constitutively related to the past. Thus, Whitehead's system would benefit from Peirce's account of agape, and Peirce's system would benefit from Whitehead's account of concrescence.

To summarize this first section, one of the great neglected achievements of the process-pragmatist tradition is its conception of developmental teleology. In a way, both Peirce's and Whitehead's metaphysics may be seen as giving accounts of metaphysical or cosmological evolution. They take the lessons from Darwin and ask: If there are organisms that strive in this way, what must the universe be like? This brings both of them to embrace a form of teleology, but, chastened by three hundred years of modern science, this is not your philosophical grandparent's teleology.

Philosophers, especially those looking to reintroduce teleology into environmental ethics, will find allies in Peirce and Whitehead, who each developed an important, novel form of teleology that is distinct from, and avoids many of the problems ascribed to, the static teleology of philosophers like Aristotle. Peirce and Whitehead develop a unique *developmental teleology* that recognizes goal-directed activity, but within an open-ended, dynamic, and processive universe—a universe that is evolving toward a future that is not predetermined. The universe and the individuals populating it have a heading, but not a particular destination. Like a Star Trek captain, the universe's mission is to boldly go into the creative advance, but where this will take us is not fully determined.

In providing a naturalist metaphysical account of reality that rejects dualism and materialism and its notion of vacuous actuality, it finally becomes possible to overcome the false bifurcation of fact and value that plagues so much of environmental ethics. As we will see in the next section, by grounding ethics in an adequate environmental metaphysics, we need no longer be afraid of the naturalistic fallacy. By mending the tether between the structure of reality and value, we can recognize that, sometimes, understanding what something *is*—what its aims and purposes and goals are—does tell us how we *ought* to relate to it.

Moore, Whitehead, and the Naturalistic Fallacy

The shadow of Moore's naturalistic fallacy has long loomed over environmental ethics and its attempts to construct a more adequate worldview that recognizes the intrinsic value and beauty of nature. Many philosophers within environmental ethics, concerned about such an accusation, seek to show how their project does not run afoul of this fallacy. Fewer philosophers discuss whether what Moore describes is rightly seen as a fallacy at all. In this section I will argue that Moore's defense of the naturalistic fallacy is predicated on an implicit and undefended view of reality (metaphysics) that is itself mistaken. Just as a *solution* to the mind-body problem is only needed if one first *creates* the problem by adopting a dualistic metaphysics, one will find that the naturalistic fallacy only has bite if one accepts as given a Humean materialist metaphysics and the resulting bifurcation of fact and value. If instead one adopts, as I do here, Whitehead's fallibilistic, open-ended, speculative metaphysics that conceives of reality as composed *not* of static material substances with properties or parts that can be considered in isolation, but of inherently temporal events whose very becoming represents a unique, teleological achievement of beauty and value, then the naturalistic fallacy evaporates. We will find that we need not bring together—fact and value; is and ought; metaphysics and ethics—that which was never apart. But let's return to the beginning of this story, as it were, starting with the relationship between G. E. Moore and Whitehead.

It is interesting to note at the outset the considerable biographical intersections between Alfred North Whitehead and George Edward Moore, both of whom can rightly be seen as key figures in the history of analytic philosophy.[61] The two philosophers were of roughly the same age, with Whitehead born in 1861, a mere twelve years earlier than Moore. These twelve years separated their respective admissions to Trinity College in Cambridge in 1880 and 1892, respectively. Both were elected as Fellows of Trinity (Whitehead in 1884 and Moore in 1898). Though at Trinity Whitehead taught mathematics and Moore philosophy and one would (co)author *Principia Mathematica* and the other *Principia Ethica*, they crossed paths regularly via their memberships in both the Cambridge Apostles and the Aristotelian Society. In these venues they would likely have directly engaged with each other's ideas at regular intervals. That they were good colleagues and indeed on friendly terms is confirmed by the survival of nearly a dozen personal, handwritten letters from Whitehead to Moore over the span of nearly twenty years, from 1917 to 1936.[62] Finally, it is somewhat tragic to note that, despite their considerable importance to early twentieth-century philosophy, the work of both philosophers fell into relative obscurity as the century progressed. It is interesting to keep these many points of connection between these two figures in mind as we proceed to bring their respective philosophical projects into conversation in this chapter.

Given these biographical connections, if I were more adventurous and a better writer, it would have been enjoyable to present this section in the form of an actual dialogue between the two philosophers. Alas, what follows is a straightforward presentation, first an exposition of Moore's *Principia* and his defense of the naturalistic fallacy, and then a critical response to Moore from the perspective of Whitehead's philosophy of organism.

Moore and the Naturalistic Fallacy

Moore's 1903 *Principia Ethica* starts with the claim that—as "the general enquiry into what is good"[63]—the first question of ethics is, "What is good?"[64] The problem with this question, Moore contends, is that "good" cannot in fact be defined. He likens "good" to the color yellow, noting that both are utterly simple notions and, therefore, cannot be defined.[65] "It [i.e., 'good'] is one of those innumerable objects of thought which are themselves incapable of definition, because they are the ultimate terms by reference to which whatever *is* capable of definition must be defined."[66] We describe other things in terms of good (or yellow), but not the reverse. The sunflower is yellow, but yellow is not like anything. As a simple concept lacking parts, it cannot be defined. "Good," he contends, is equally indefinable.

Despite the fact that "good" cannot be defined, a chief goal of ethics is to determine the "unique property of things" such that they are good.[67] Whatever "good" is, it is not a property that "we can take up in our hands, or separate from it even by the most delicate scientific instruments, and transfer to something else. It is not, in fact, like most of the predicates which we ascribe to things, a *part* of the thing to which we ascribe it."[68] Much of Moore's *Principia* focuses on demonstrating the inadequacy of the two dominant attempts to provide an account of what makes something good: one he calls "naturalistic ethics" and the other "metaphysical ethics." Let us take each in order.

Notably for environmental ethicists, discussion of "naturalistic ethics" is primarily focused on the attempt to conceive of intrinsic value. Initially it would seem that environmental ethics and its interest in defining the scope of direct moral concern by defining the nature of intrinsic value is in keeping with Moore's understanding of ethics. However, the problem, according to Moore, is that too many philosophers think by naming these "natural properties" they can thereby define what makes something good, that these properties are what define intrinsic value. This, Moore contends, is the root of the "naturalistic fallacy."[69] "To hold that any proposition asserting 'Reality is of this nature' we can infer, or obtain confirmation for, any proposition asserting 'This is good in itself' is to commit the naturalistic fallacy. And that a knowledge of what is real supplies reasons for holding certain things good in themselves is either implied or expressly asserted by all those who define the Supreme Good in metaphysical terms."[70] One cannot legitimately infer from the nature of reality any statement about what is good in itself. To do so is to commit the naturalistic fallacy or the taking of some "natural properties" of things and substituting those for what is "good," what has "intrinsic value." That is, the "naturalistic" method of ethics "consists in substituting for 'good' some one property of a natural object or a collection of natural objects; and in this replacing Ethics by some one of the natural sciences. In general, Psychology has been the science substituted, as by J. S. Mill; or Sociology, as by Professor Clifford, and other modern writers."[71]

It is important to see the senses in which Moore's understanding of "good" and "intrinsic value" are informed by and presuppose a subject-predicate logic and a substance metaphysics (a point to which I will return when considering our Whiteheadian response). For instance, in defending against "naturalistic ethics," Moore notes that, unlike other natural properties of objects, whose "existence . . . is independent of the existence of those objects," the property "good" cannot be "existent *by itself* in time."[72] Moore attempts to demonstrate that the error of substituting some natural property for "good" (i.e., the naturalistic fallacy) is shown by appealing to the idea that what is "good" cannot exist by itself in time.

Can we imagine "good" as existing *by itself* in time, and not merely as a property of some natural object? For myself, I cannot so imagine it, whereas with the greater number of properties of objects—those which I call the natural properties—their existence does seem to me to be independent of the existence of those objects. They are, in fact, rather parts of which the object is made up than mere predicates which attach to it. If they were all taken away, no object would be left, not even a bare substance: for they are in themselves substantial and give to the object all the substance that it has. But this is not so with good. If indeed good were a feeling, as some would have us believe, then it would exist in time. But that is why to call it so is to commit the naturalistic fallacy. It will always remain pertinent to ask, whether the feeling itself is good; and if so, then good cannot itself be identical with any feeling.[73]

This is crucial, as it demonstrates that Moore, in keeping with a latent Cartesian metaphysics, sees no essential relationship between time and actuality. This is a point on which he and Whitehead will diverge, as we will see shortly. For now, it is sufficient to note that Moore is presupposing a metaphysics that conceives of reality as composed of "substances" or "objects" with "properties" that attach to them, and that there are some properties that can exist independently of a substance and some that cannot. Unlike other properties, "good" is not a property that can "exist by itself in time." This is why it is a fallacy to substitute some natural property, which is separable and can exist by itself in time, for "good," which cannot exist by itself in time. The very notion of the naturalistic fallacy is based on a substance metaphysics and a subject-predicate logic.

In contrast to naturalistic approaches to ethics, which commit the naturalistic fallacy, "metaphysical ethics" propose some metaphysical theory that explains what makes something "good." First, it is important to note that Moore takes "metaphysical" as the contrary of and indeed "in opposition to" what is "natural."[74] Whereas naturalistic ethics are concerned with the properties of natural objects that exist in time, he conceives of metaphysics as concerned with objects or properties that "do not exist in time"—that is, they are "eternal"—and are therefore not "part of Nature."[75] That is, to put it differently, as Moore conceives of it, metaphysics investigates what is "*not* a part of Nature" or what is, by definition, therefore "supersensible reality."[76] Perhaps the easiest example of "metaphysical objects" are Plato's

Forms, which are both supersensible and eternally outside of time. Plato's attempt in *Republic* to define the good via the divided line simile and the allegory of the cave is an example of metaphysical ethics as Moore defines it.[77]

Moore's assessment of the value of metaphysical ethics is swift and negative. The answer to the question "What bearing can Metaphysics have upon the question, What is good?" is simple: "obviously and absolutely none."[78] Or, if it does have relevance to ethics, "it must be of a purely negative kind."[79] This follows directly from Moore's definition of metaphysics. If metaphysics is, by definition, concerned exclusively with supersensible, eternal reality that is, again, by definition, not able to be affected by our actions, then what possible relevance to ethics could metaphysics have? As we will soon discuss, it would be hard to imagine a view of metaphysics more diametrically opposite of Whitehead's than Moore's. (See chapter one of this volume on Whitehead's distinctive approach to metaphysics.)

Given that both naturalistic and metaphysical ethics fail to help us understand what is good, what has intrinsic value, how are we to make progress in answering the fundamental question of ethics? Moore's answer is reminiscent of Descartes's *Meditations on First Philosophy*. Just as Descartes deployed his so-called methodical doubt in order to discover a firm and immovable "Archimedean point" on which to found all certain knowledge,[80] Moore develops what he calls the "isolation method" for determining what has intrinsic value. As its name suggests, to determine what is good or has intrinsic value, we need only "consider what things are such that, if they existed *by themselves*, in total isolation, we should yet judge their existence to be good."[81] If, in "total isolation," something is still judged good, then it has intrinsic value. Employing this method, Moore contends that only two things have intrinsic value, in that only they are good even if they existed by themselves in total isolation: "the pleasures of human intercourse and the enjoyment of beautiful objects."[82] Moore proposes an interesting thought experiment to illustrate his point:

> We can imagine the case of a single person, enjoying throughout eternity the contemplation of scenery as beautiful, and intercourse with persons as admirable, as can be imagined; while yet the whole of the objects of his cognition are as absolutely unreal. I think we should definitely pronounce the existence of a universe, which consisted solely of such a person, to be *greatly* inferior to the value to one in which the objects, in the existence of which he believes, did really exist just as he believes them to do; and

that it would be thus inferior *not only* because it would lack the goods which consist in the existence of the objects in question, but *also* merely because his belief would be false. That it would be inferior *for this reason alone* follows if we admit, what also appears to me certain, that the case of a person, merely imagining, without believing, the beautiful objects in question, would, *although these objects really existed*, be yet inferior to that of the person who also believed in their existence.[83]

A universe constituted solely of one person who *imagines* enjoying beauty and interacting with other people is "greatly inferior" to one in which one does not only imagine but is in fact enjoying beauty and engaging with other people. Initially, this seems surprisingly similar to Whitehead's claims regarding beauty (see chapter four, this volume). Yet closer examination reveals this is only a passing resemblance. For it is not beautiful *things* in the world that are themselves of intrinsic value but only "certain states of consciousness."[84] It is the *enjoyment* of beautiful objects (and the pleasures of being with other humans) that are of intrinsic value, not the objects themselves. Or it is the *true belief* in the enjoyment of the beautiful objects (and pleasures of being with other people) that is of intrinsic value.

Having rejected naturalistic ethics, for Moore, it is not that some *entities* have intrinsic value. If I understand Moore rightly, not even *humans* have *intrinsic* value. In keeping with the Humean metaphysics that he seems to presuppose, no *thing* has intrinsic value, including humans. (For more on this point, see chapter two of this volume on intrinsic value.) Value is the projected feelings of valuers onto an actually valueless world. As Hume put in his *Treatise*:

> An action, or sentiment, or character is virtuous or vicious; why? because its view causes a pleasure or uneasiness of a particular kind. In giving a reason, therefore, for the pleasure of uneasiness we sufficiently explain the vice or virtue. To have the sense of virtue, is nothing but to *feel* a satisfaction of a particular kind from the contemplation of a character. The very *feeling* constitutes our praise or admiration. We go no farther; nor do we enquire into the cause of the satisfaction. We do not infer a character to be virtuous, because it pleases: but in feeling that it pleases after such a particular manner, we in effect feel that it is virtuous.

The case is the same in our judgments concerning all kinds of beauty, and tastes, and sensations.[85]

There is no connection between the structure of reality (metaphysics) and value or goodness. In keeping with Hume's view, what has intrinsic value, according to Moore, is the *enjoyment* of beauty and the *pleasure* of human intercourse, nothing more. And it is solely for their sake that ethics exists.

> What has *not* been recognized is that it is the ultimate and fundamental truth of Moral Philosophy. That it is only for the sake of these things—in order that as much of them as possible may at some time exist—that any one can be justified in performing any public or private duty; that they are the *raison d'être* of virtue; that it is they—these complex wholes *themselves*, and not any constituent or characteristic of them—that form the rational ultimate end of human action and the sole criterion of social progress: these appear to be truths which have been generally overlooked.[86]

Whitehead, Value, and Naturalistic Metaphysics

In considering Whitehead's position, let us begin in reverse order, starting with Moore's argument against "metaphysical ethics." If "metaphysics" concerns supersensible "objects" that are "outside of time," as Moore contends, then metaphysics does indeed have nothing useful to say about ethics. But, as we've discussed throughout the present volume (see especially chapter one), this is not the only way of conceiving of metaphysics. Indeed, from the perspective of the philosophy of organism, Moore's definition of metaphysics is unrecognizable. For the philosophy of organism, metaphysics is the attempt to develop a logical, coherent, applicable, and adequate account of every element of experience. It is a working hypothesis and open to revision. It has no more claim to *absolute* certainty than physics, which is to say, none at all. And the same is true of ethics (see chapter two, "Morality in the Making," on a fallibilistic account of ethics).

Further, whereas for Moore ethics is either naturalistic (concerned with objects in time) or metaphysical (concerned with objects that are not in time), for Whitehead nothing is "outside of time" because the very act of coming to be is the realization of a quantum of space-time. Indeed, it is not an exaggeration to say that the whole of Whitehead's philosophy is an extended effort to take the problem of time seriously, a conception of time fundamentally informed by advances in relativity and quantum physics. Thus, whereas Moore sees naturalistic and metaphysical accounts as contraries, Whitehead defends a naturalistic metaphysics founded on the "ontological principle"[87] that beyond the events of the universe there is nothing. However, more is at stake here than the meaning of key terms. More important is that Moore's view of ethics is itself predicated on a view of the structure of reality that is mistaken, and it is this mistaken metaphysics that generates and justifies his famous naturalistic fallacy.

Recall the point made in the introduction to this chapter that modernity was born out of the explicit and often vehement rejection of all immaterial forms and the teleology that came with them. Despite the differences between them, Hobbes, Bacon, and Descartes worked hard to banish scholasticism and its Aristotelian hylomorphism wherein all living beings are form-matter composites teleologically developing toward an end. It is not the form or *psuchê* or internal principle of organization and change that organizes a being's matter (i.e., material cause), defines what a being is (i.e., formal cause), and what its characteristic powers and potentials are (i.e., final cause or telos). No. To make progress in natural philosophy (now called science), early modern philosophers tell us that we must recognize that there are no immaterial forms; there are no teloi guiding the maturational patterns and organizations of matter; there are but the unflinching mechanistic laws of nature.

Note two key features of both metaphysical dualism and metaphysical materialism: (1) nature, matter, res extensa is purely passive, vacuous, mechanistic, and valueless, and (2) individuality is defined primarily in terms of independence. The most striking version of the latter is found in Descartes, who defines a substance as "that which requires nothing other than itself in order to exist."[88] These two (metaphysical) claims are the basis for the bifurcation of fact and value and the ultimate justification for the distinction between is and ought. It is on these metaphysical foundations that Moore's fallacy is built. The problem with both of these claims—vacuous actuality and independence of existence—is that, I contend, they are utterly mistaken.

Let's consider the isolation test and the substance metaphysics on which it is based. As we explored in chapter six, contemporary science has revealed that substances so defined do not seem to exist. According to Moore's vaunted isolation method, we are to "consider what things are such that, if they existed *by themselves*, in total isolation, we should yet judge their existence to be good." This method reveals the lingering invidious impact of Cartesian substance metaphysics, with its emphasis on independence. However, even at the start of the twentieth century when Moore was writing, contemporary science had already revealed that nothing can exist in total isolation. As Whitehead reminds us time and again, "The misconception which has haunted philosophic literature throughout the centuries is the notion of 'independent existence.' There is no such mode of existence; every entity is only to be understood in terms of the way in which it is interwoven with the rest of the Universe."[89] Indeed, contemporary physics continues to confirm Whitehead's view. In the end, reality is not composed of "things" at all. The domesticating metaphysics and its "container metaphor" is fundamentally and fatally mistaken. The substance view of reality and the subject-predicate logic on which it is based is a useful but high-level abstraction.[90] "All modern philosophy hinges round the difficulty of describing the world in terms of subject and predicate, substance and quality, particular and universal," Whitehead tells us in *Process and Reality*. "The result always does violence to that immediate experience which we express in our actions, our hopes, our sympathies, our purposes, and which we enjoy in spite of our lack of phrases for its verbal analysis. We find ourselves in a buzzing world, amid a democracy of fellow creatures; whereas, under some disguise or other, orthodox philosophy can only introduce us to solitary substances, each enjoying an illusory experience: 'O Bottom, thou art changed! what do I see on thee?' "[91]

In the end, the naturalistic fallacy is only such—that is, it is only a fallacy—if one adopts the Humean metaphysics on which it is premised. That is, the movement from a statement of how something *is* to how it *ought* to be is only illicit if one presupposes that there is no connection between the good or value and the structure of reality. This premise is secured by having banished teleology. However, if one begins, as I am suggesting environmental ethics should, with a conception of reality that appreciates that reality is not composed of little things or containers; if one understands that reality is ultimately an ongoing dynamic process and that this process involves the internal, constitutive interrelatedness of every event to its past; if one understands that to be is to be in dynamic interrelation and interdependence; if one understands that to become is to be a decision and an achievement of beauty and value for oneself, for others, and for the whole; if one understands that beyond the experience of subjects there is bear nothingness and that to be a subject is to become an object for others; if one understands that the process of becoming involves a developmental teleological aim, then we will see that the naturalistic fallacy is a problem for a metaphysics that no one ought to adopt. The naturalistic fallacy is a problem of modern metaphysics' own making. In the end, the naturalistic fallacy is the misguided product of a misguided metaphysics.[92] Let us finally exorcize the specter by adopting a more adequate metaphysics on which to base environmental ethics.

Chapter 8

Environmental Pragmatism

Much of early environmental ethics was born out of the belief that the ecological crisis can only truly be solved by overcoming a pernicious, dualistic worldview that separates and limits all value to human beings.[1] That is, a central task of much of environmental ethics is, as J. Baird Callicott puts it, "worldview transformation."[2] Central to this approach to environmental ethics is the development of a non-anthropocentric axiology (whether sentiocentric, biocentric, or ecocentric) that could better ground expanded conceptions of moral considerability and moral responsibility. From Val Plumwood's ecofeminism to Holmes Rolston's ecocentrism and from Robin Attfield's biocentric consequentialism to Arne Naess's deep ecology, the first generations of environmental philosophers developed complex and nuanced conceptions regarding the nature, locus, and scope of intrinsic value.

As some tell the story, despite the complexity and sophistication of these worldview transformation projects, there was growing frustration with the perceived irrelevance and ineffectiveness of environmental ethics theories to the creation of good environmental policies. Since the mid-1990s, this sort of frustration with worldview remediation has been given voice in the literature by "environmental pragmatists,"[3] such as Andrew Light and Eric Katz, who are unequivocal in their assessment of the utter failure of environmental ethics. "The intramural debates of environmental philosophers, although interesting, provocative and complex, seem to have no real impact on the deliberations of environmental scientists, activists, and policy-makers. The ideas within environmental ethics are, apparently, inert—like Hume's *Treatise*, they fall deadborn from the press."[4] This is a harsh characterization. A primary aim of this chapter is to evaluate whether this critique is accurate.

This task is made more complex by the fact that environmental pragmatism is not a single position, one theory in competition with others. "Rather than denoting one uniform view in environmental philosophy, environmental pragmatism seems to be best regarded as an umbrella term covering many different approaches to the field, approaches which are, however, taken to have something important in common."[5] As we will see in more detail in the following sections, some of the features they have in common include: (1) a movement away from theory and toward practice (sometimes called the "policy turn"); (2) an acceptance of intergenerational anthropocentrism, the abandonment of debates over intrinsic value, and the general rejection of the premise that axiological anthropocentrism is the root cause of the ecological crisis; and (3) the rejection of the quest for certainty and "moral monism" in favor of a fallibilistic pluralism.

In calling for the abandonment of theoretical discussions of intrinsic value and worldview transformation, environmental pragmatism and its "policy turn" presents a serious challenge to the current project, which calls for a further deepening of the theoretical work of environmental ethics to include its explicit grounding in environmental metaphysics. Thus, in addition to the historical philosophical headwinds blowing against metaphysical system-building, environmental pragmatism presents a second challenge that must be squarely met. Though I am sympathetic with the very real temporal urgency that partly motivates environmental pragmatism and though I share the frustration with the lack of adequate environmental policymaking in response to our many ecological and social crises, I ultimately find that environmental pragmatism is a fundamentally flawed and inadequate environmental philosophy. First, let us begin by considering the key features of environmental pragmatism and the policy turn.

Environmental Pragmatism and the Policy Turn

A central theme among the diverse set of positions that go under the label "environmental pragmatism" is the claim that, by insisting on the development of a single, fully adequate moral theory that properly understands the nature and locus of intrinsic value, environmental ethics has unintentionally contributed to the failure to develop adequate environmental policies.[6] Environmental philosophers' theoretical debates (e.g., over intrinsic value or anthropocentrism) have not just been a waste of time, environmental pragmatists contend, but they are in fact "problematic for the development of environmental policy."[7] Light and Katz argue that if philosophers are going to be relevant in responding to the unprecedented challenges facing humanity, they should finally abandon the never-ending, theory-heavy, intramural debates over intrinsic value and worldview remediation and instead seek to assist in the development of "effective" or "good" policy. Thus, environmental pragmatism seeks to usher in the "policy turn" in environmental ethics. Instead of writing essays to other philosophers spinning ever-more-complex theories, environmental philosophers should be "doing interdisciplinary research and working on projects with public agencies, policy makers, and the private sector."[8] Rather than litigating, for instance, a never-ending debate between the subjectivist theory of value and the objectivist theory of value or between biocentric consequentialism and ecocentric holism, the policy turn is a "third approach, where philosophers begin from specific environmental problematics as defined by those outside of academia, and from the growing sense among policy makers—within public science agencies and other governmental organizations—that society's standard method for addressing environmental problems is inadequate."[9] The measure of success for environmental ethics should be defined not in terms of conceptual or theoretical coherence or adequacy, but based on whether it helps activists, land managers, scientists, and policy-makers develop and implement good environmental policy, where "good" is defined as having "positive implications for humans."[10]

Thus, one way of seeing environmental pragmatism is as a rejection of a founding premise of environmental ethics: that to truly address the "roots of the ecologic crisis," we must reconceive of what we are as a species and how we conceive of our relationship to the rest of life on the planet, that we must develop a more adequate worldview. Despite decades of work by environmental philosophers, environmental pragmatist Bryan Norton claims, "The search for a 'Holy Grail' of unified theory in environmental values has not progressed toward any consensus regarding what inherent value in nature is, what objects have it, or what it means to have such value. Nor have environmental ethicists been able to offer useful practical advice by providing clear management directives regarding difficult and controversial problems in environmental planning and management."[11] For many environmental pragmatists, the root problem is not a pernicious, anthropocentric worldview, but the lack of good policies that make a real difference in addressing our many ecological problems. Environmental ethicists should, they suggest, turn their considerable intellectual talents to this vitally important task—that is, to environmental policy—before it is too late. Indeed, many environmental pragmatists contend that attempts at worldview transformation and theory-making impede, rather than facilitate, much-needed action addressing the ecological crises. To become relevant to policymaking, philosophers should declare a truce in the value wars and give up the "misguided mission" for a more adequate axiological conceptual framework, a more adequate worldview.[12] Instead of this ill-advised push for "moral monism," the environmental pragmatists embrace a philosophical, epistemological, and methodological pluralism. After all, Norton contends, differences in theoretical value commitments (e.g., between anthropocentrism, biocentrism, and ecocentrism) ultimately make no meaningful difference to environmental practice and policy. Whether, for instance, a grey wolf, a great sequoia, or the Amazon rainforest have intrinsic value or merely instrumental value ultimately makes no difference to what would constitute good environmental policies in respect to them. This is what Norton calls the "convergence hypothesis" in that, despite irreconcilable differences in value commitments between, for instance, anthropocentrists and biocentrists, there is a convergence on what constitutes a good environmental policy.[13] For instance, although the anthropocentrist, biocentrist, and ecocentrist each differ on whether the Amazon rainforest has merely instrumental value or also intrinsic value, they would all agree: limit logging now! Thus, Norton explains, "theoretical differences often need not impede progress in developing current policy; if all disputants agree on central management principles, even without agreeing on ultimate values, management can proceed on these principles."[14]

Environmental pragmatists like Norton think, therefore, that the approach of environmental ethics has been misguided from the start. Environmental philosophers should stop seeing themselves "laboring in the tower," developing arcane theories of value that are then thrown down to the environmental policy "streetfighters" below.[15] As Light and Katz put it, if environmental ethics is to overcome its "ineffectual" start and become a "practical discipline," "the fruits of this philosophical enterprise must be directed towards the practical resolution of environmental problems—environmental ethics cannot remain mired in long-running theoretic debates in an attempt to achieve philosophic certainty."[16]

If true, environmental pragmatism's indictments present very serious challenges to theoretical environmental ethics. Indeed, if environmental pragmatists are right, then the present project is wholly misguided and perhaps even harmful in addressing our ecological crises. It would seem that nearly every environmental philosopher, of every sort, agrees that our ecological crises are various and urgent. To the crises of pollution and habitat fragmentation and loss that spurred the first philosophers to take up environmental ethics in the 1970s and 1980s can now be added the threats of global climate change and spiraling species extinction. We are told that if we are to avoid catastrophe, we have precious little time to dramatically modify how we create energy, move our vehicles, and eat our meals.[17] The urgency of these and other ecological and social crises are not in doubt. But what role ought environmental philosophers, *as philosophers*, play in addressing these crises? I contend that environmental pragmatism's answer to this—that environmental philosophers should stop pursing the development of a more adequate worldview and conceptual framework that properly understands the nature of intrinsic value and the duties it generates and instead help policymakers develop good and effective environmental policy—is fundamentally mistaken in at least five different ways. In terms of environmental pragmatism, I contend: (1) that it is mistaken in its understanding of what environmental ethics has achieved; (2) that its convergence hypothesis is likely false, as different values seem to lead to different policies; (3) that it is question-begging in its account of what defines "good" policy; (4) that too often it is anti-philosophical; and (5) that, despite its name, it bears too little resemblance to pragmatism in the classical American philosophical tradition. On this final point, it is worth noting at the outset that there is a meaningful sense in which, although the present project is at odds with "environmental pragmatism" as it has come to be defined by its leading proponents, the philosophy of organism is itself an expression of a strand within classical American pragmatism and could, in this wider sense, be seen as an alternative form of environmental pragmatism, one primarily informed by the work of Peirce and Whitehead, instead of Dewey. Thus, the chapter will ultimately conclude with a defense of the value of theoretical environmental ethics as worldview transformation and that a key part of such work requires environmental metaphysics. Let us consider each of the five points above in turn.

Has Environmental Ethics Been Ineffectual?

Let us begin with the environmental pragmatists' claim that environmental ethics has been ineffectual and was "stillborn" from its inception. To start, assessment of the historical significance and impact of theoretical environmental ethics is premature. Ultimately, whether environmental ethics will be shown to have had an impact (positive or negative) will only be clear in another half century or more; it is notoriously difficult to properly discern historical trends when living among them. This is perhaps especially true regarding the possible impact of philosophical ideas, whose effects are often only discernible with the benefit of considerable hindsight. Nevertheless, let us do our best to step back and briefly consider whether environmental ethics has had a discernable positive (or negative) effect on public consciousness and environmental policy.

It is certainly true that since the 1980s, there has been frustratingly little progress (at least in the United States) in passing significant environmental legislation. But is it true that environmental ethics has had "no real impact on the deliberations of environmental scientists, activists, and policy-makers"?[18] To start, it depends on how one understands "impact." To be seen as having a "real impact" on policy, does one need to be able to draw a neat line between X policymaker reading Y theoretical environmental ethic and then have X explicitly cite Y as justification for passing Z environmental policy?

Callicott takes up this challenge, citing several instances that match this pattern. He notes, for instance, that in the landmark 1972 case of Sierra Club v. Morton, Chief Justice Douglas cites Aldo Leopold's land ethic in defense of his minority opinion.[19] Although the case was ultimately unsuccessful, it does seem to be an instance where X public official read Y environmental ethic and X cited Y as justification for Z environmental policy. Callicott also notes that the following year, in 1973, the United States passed perhaps the most significant and far-reaching environmental law ever passed: the Endangered Species Act. Callicott makes the reasonable claim that a law giving very strong protections to endangered species against the interests of humans is a clear instance of an ecocentric environmental ethic having influenced public policy.[20]

But surely this is much too simplistic an account of how philosophical ideas come to affect the world. As one of my favorite undergraduate professors liked to put it, most ideas published by philosophers "sink to the bottom without a ripple." However, some ideas are so potent that they forever change the course of history. Carl Marx, to take one of dozens of examples, wrote a densely philosophical and theoretical treatise and forever changed the trajectory of the twentieth century. People quite literally fight and die for ideas, some bad (as with white nationalism) and some good (as with the civil rights movement).

If we take a less simplistic view of how ideas sometimes affect change, it is rather easier to see that theoretical environmental ethics likely has already had a discernable and real impact on the deliberations of environmental scientists, activists, and policymakers by helping shift public environmental consciousness. Although much of that consciousness is still what some environmental philosophers might call "shallow ecology"—concerned primarily with limiting pollution and maintaining resources for humans—it is clear that, in most developed nations and across the political and ideological spectrum, the environmental sustainability discourse has moved quickly from the periphery to mainstream.

Thus, if properly situated within the slow historical processes by which public consciousness shifts and the eventual impact of those shifts on policymaking, we see that, far from being ineffectual, it is perhaps remarkable that, in only half a century, one can *already* discern a positive trend in ecological consciousness. Undoubtedly, it is true that this change is not matching the speed and scale of the ecological crisis itself, but that is not the environmental pragmatists' claim nor environmental ethics' fault. As Callicott notes, rightly in my judgment, "Theoretical environmental philosophy has had and is having a profound, albeit indirect, practical effect on environmental policy. It has done so by creating a new discourse that environmental activists and environmental professionals have adopted and put to good use. At the heart of this new discourse is the concept of intrinsic value in nature."[21] Dense and theoretically complex they may be, but the ideas of environmental ethics seem to have sufficient vitality to have begun to insinuate themselves into public consciousness and are therefore rightly seen as impacting the development of environmental policy. It is remarkable, Callicott continues, that in only a generation, "the rethinking of our old religion that White called for is virtually a fait accompli. The stewardship interpretation of the God-'man'-nature relationship set out in Genesis is now semiofficial religious doctrine among 'people of the Book'— Jews, Catholics, Protestants, even Muslims. Such an interpretation and its dissemination would not have come about, or at least it would not have come about so soon, had White's despotic interpretation not provoked it."[22] Thus, there is ample reason to question the initial premise from which environmental pragmatism begins. Environmental philosophers should not be afraid to ask and answer the question, "How effective has environmental philosophy been?" The answer seems clearly to be, "Surprisingly so!" Once again, Callicott is helpful here:

> All environmentalists should be activists, but activism can take a
> variety of forms. The way that environmental philosophers can

be the most effective environmental activists is by doing environmental philosophy. Of course, not everyone can or wants or needs to be an environmental philosopher. Those who are not can undertake direct environmental action in other ways. My point is that environmental philosophers should not feel compelled to stop thinking, talking, and writing about environmental ethics, and go do something about it instead—because talk is cheap and action is dear. In thinking, talking, and writing about environmental ethics, environmental philosophers already have their shoulders to the wheel, helping to reconfigure the prevailing cultural worldview and thus helping to push general practice in the direction of environmental responsibility.[23]

THE CONVERGENCE HYPOTHESIS

Setting aside for the moment the question as to whether environmental ethics has been effective, let us consider environmental pragmatists' more substantive philosophical claims, starting with those related to environmental philosophy's focus on the concept of intrinsic value—specifically, that debates over intrinsic value are, at best, an unnecessary waste of time because theoretical value commitments do not result in different policies. That is, let us next consider Norton's convergence hypothesis.

In a clever 2002 essay, Mikael Stenmark seeks to test directly whether Norton's convergence hypothesis is true: that differences in basic value commitments have no meaningful impact on the choice of environmental policies. Stenmark calls this the "theory-policy" issue. According to the logic of the convergence hypothesis, non-anthropocentric positions—such as biocentrism or ecocentrism, which recognize the intrinsic value of and direct duties to nonhuman beings—ultimately will *not* support different environmental policies than an intergenerational anthropocentrism—which does not recognize the intrinsic value of or direct duties to nonhuman beings. By considering specific environmental policies, Stenmark convincingly shows that convergence may only be apparent: different theoretical value commitments lead to different *goals* of policymaking and justify different *means* in service of those ends.

On the one hand, the *goal* of intergenerational anthropocentric policymaking is "*to ensure that the natural resources are used in an efficient and farsighted way so that the needs of present and future human generations can be satisfied.*"[24] On the other hand, the *goal* of biocentric policymaking would accept not only that goal but also the much more expansive goal *"to ensure that humans in their treatment of nature do not violate the rights of other living things to be left alone and to flourish."*[25] Although, to recur to our earlier example, it seems that both intergenerational anthropocentrists and biocentrists agree to the goal that we should reduce logging in the Amazon, it turns out that this convergence is only apparent. For, as soon as each group proceeds to explain what this goal entails, they diverge rather quickly. Why? Because they don't agree what the *goal* of environmental policy should be with respect to logging in the Amazon. One environmental ethic wants to maintain sustainable harvest consistent with ecosystem function, whereas the other wants to protect the living beings there from being "harvested." One wants to protect the Amazon *for* human use, whereas the other wants to protect the Amazon *from* human use. This is divergence, not convergence, of environmental policy. But, beyond the *goals* of environmental policymaking, what about the *means*? Perhaps despite a lack of convergence on goals, there is nevertheless a convergence on the means environmental policies should adopt in service of those different goals?

Here again Stenmark brings convergence into doubt. He considers several different environmental policies (concerning human population, wild-life preservation, and wildlife management) and examines whether, beyond having different goals, anthropocentrists, biocentrists, and ecocentrists would converge on the same means. In each case, the result is the same: theoretical difference in values commit each group to *different* means in service of *different* ends, with biocentrists and ecocentrists embracing more capacious goals pursued by much more dramatic means—means that anthropocentrists would find unacceptable.

To take an example not considered by Stenmark, let us examine the domain of international climate policy, something with which the environmental pragmatist Andrew Light is deeply familiar.[26] For the intergenerational anthropocentrist, the *goal* of good and effective climate policy might be to stabilize emissions at a level compatible with the United Nations' (UN's) goal of "sustainable development," which—since the 1987 Brundland Commission Report—has been defined as "meeting the needs of the present [humans] without compromising the ability of future generations [of humans] to meet their needs."[27] The *means* to achieve this might be something like the 2015 Paris Climate Agreement, which calls on signatories to limit emissions "well below"[28] 2 degrees Celsius warming above preindustrial levels by midcentury (preferably below 1.5 degrees) because, beyond 2 degrees warming, human civilization and sustainable development become much more difficult, if not impossible. The Paris Agreement is neutral as to the means to achieve its goals. Each signatory voluntarily commits to "nationally determined contributions" and achieves them via whatever means they prefer, including various market-based (e.g., carbon tax or cap-and-trade programs) or regulatory schemes (e.g., corporate average fuel-efficiency standards for vehicles) that would reduce climate emissions. Overall, then, the *goal* of such policies is to *stabilize* emissions well below 2 degrees by midcentury via a green-energy revolution.

How might a deep ecologist, who defends an ecocentric holist perspective, approach international climate policy? For deep ecologists—given that not only present and future humans have intrinsic value and deserve respect but also all living beings and the systems of which they are a part— the *goal* of a good climate policy should be not just to make consumption and development sustainable or to stabilize emissions. They would likely note that many hundreds more species and fragile habitats will be forever lost at 2 degrees warming, as well as the increasingly unlikely 1.5 degrees Celsius. Thus, ecocentrists would likely argue that the goal of climate policy should not be to *stabilize* but to dramatically *reverse* emissions so that *all* life can thrive.[29] But even more than this goal of negative emissions, the ecocentrist's *goal* would be to transform society not just for "sustainable development," which they would likely see as an oxymoron, but toward a model of happiness that is based on voluntary simplicity over mindless consumption and to conceive of forms of human living and thriving as a part of a thriving, integral biotic community.

Thus, in terms of international climate policy, differences in *theoretical* value commitments bring intergenerational anthropocentrists and ecocentrists to hold *different policy goals* pursued via *different means*. Yes, it is true that both anthropocentrists and ecocentrists would agree that we should immediately "take action" to address the climate crisis. But this seeming convergence is only apparent and masks a fundamental divergence. And, at least in the case of climate policy, it is important to note that it will not work to tell the ecocentrist to join the intergenerational anthropocentrist for now and then take up their more expansive goals later. As inhabitants of low-lying island nations rightly point out, Paris's 2 degrees C limit is in fact an agreement that it is okay to allow their nations, their homes, their lands to go out of existence. For, according to current scientific projections for sea-level rise due both to melting land-based ice and thermal expansion, many of these island nations are likely to become uninhabitable with even 1.5 degrees C warming. With submersion and salinization, there is no meaningful "later" for them. Similarly, once a species is extinct, once a glacier is lost, once a biotic community is destroyed—it is gone. Too often, there is no meaningful "later" on human timescales. Thus, asking the ecocentrist to agree to the intergenerational anthropocentrist's goals now is not a temporary decision. Adopting some goals, such as limiting warming to 2 degrees C, means the *permanent* forgoing of many of the ecocentrist's most fundamental goals. Thus, contrary to the environmental pragmatists' claim, what constitutes a "good" climate policy will fundamentally differ for intergenerational anthropocentrists and ecocentrists. Environmental pragmatists who claim that differences in theoretical value commitments do not lead to meaningfully different environmental policies are mistaken. Perhaps, Callicott quips, Norton's thesis should instead be called the " 'divergence hypothesis.' "[30]

Further, as Callicott rightly notes, recognizing the intrinsic value of nonhuman nature has the important practical effect of shifting the "onus of justification" of environmental destruction.

> The mere fact that moral agents must be able to justify their actions in regard to their treatment of entities that are intrinsically valuable means that recognizing the intrinsic value of the nonhuman world has a dramatic effect upon the framework of environmental debate and decision-making. If the nonhuman world is only considered to be instrumentally valuable then people are permitted to use and otherwise interfere with any aspect of it for whatever reasons they wish (i.e., no justification is required). If anyone objects to such interference then, within this framework of reference, the onus is clearly on the person who objects to justify why it is *more useful* to humans to leave that aspect of the nonhuman world alone. If, however, the nonhuman world is considered to be *intrinsically valuable* then the onus shifts to the person who wants to interfere with it to justify why they should be allowed to do so: anyone who wants to interfere with any entity that is intrinsically valuable is morally obligated to be able to offer a *sufficient justification* for their actions. Thus recognizing the intrinsic value of the nonhuman world shifts the *onus of justification* from the person who wants to protect the nonhuman world to the person who wants to interfere with it—and that, in itself, represents a fundamental shift in the terms of environmental debate and decision-making.[31]

Accordingly, environmental philosophers are right to explore and seek to clarify which beings do and do not have intrinsic value and are or are not owed direct moral consideration from moral agents. Their answers will have a *practical* and meaningful effect on the goals and means of any environmental policies that are developed in support of these value commitments. Thus, as we will see in the next section, what Stenmark has revealed in his analysis of the shortcomings of Norton's convergence hypothesis is that formulating good environmental policy unavoidably and necessarily *presupposes* a conception of what is good, of what has value. Indeed, the goals and means of environmental policymaking are ultimately *defined* by one's most basic value commitments.

"Good" Environmental Policy

Environmental pragmatists suggest that the standard of success of environmental ethics should *not* be measured in terms of conceptual or theoretical coherence or adequacy, but whether it helps in the creation of good environmental policy wherein a policy is "good" if it has "positive implications for humans."[32] Of course environmental pragmatists can only go so far in giving a theoretical defense of this position. Indeed, given that it is central to the definition of environmental pragmatism that it rejects and condemns *theoretical* defenses of one's value commitments, environmental pragmatists must ultimately *assert* this new standard for evaluating environmental ethics, and, in so doing, environmental pragmatists *presuppose* a conception of what is good, of what has value. That is, environmental pragmatism is fundamentally question-begging.

There is no non-question-begging way of defining "good policy" without defending a view as to what makes something *good*, what has intrinsic value. To explain and justify what makes a policy *good* (or bad), environmental pragmatists would have to appeal to value commitments that justify any such a claim. However, it is exactly these value commitments that, environmental pragmatists tell us, are irrelevant to good environmental policymaking. We are told that environmental philosophers should not attempt to give theoretical defense of what has intrinsic value, as these debates are contributing to policy paralysis and "moral monism." The problem is that environmental pragmatists have already eliminated any non-question-begging basis that could justify their own claims. As problematic as this is, there is a second concern with environmental pragmatists' account of "good" environmental policy, at least as it is defended by Norton.

According to Norton, environmental pragmatism is of the view that good environmental policy is ultimately to be understood as one that "has positive implications for values associated with the various scales on which humans *are in fact* concerned, and also on the scales on which environmentalists think we *should* be concerned if we accept responsibly for the impacts of our current activities on the life prospects and options—the 'freedom' of future generations."[33] Notice, then, that in one breath, the environmental pragmatist tells environmental philosophers to stop debating about what has intrinsic value, and, in the next breath, claims that, by the way, only humans have value. The environmental pragmatist excoriates environmental philosophers for focusing on arcane debates between anthropocentrism, biocentrism, and ecocentrism because, after all, anthropocentrism is true.[34] This bald-faced question-begging is perplexing. The only way I can see environmental pragmatists defending both intergenerational anthropocentrism *and* their conception of "good" policy would be to provide exactly the sort of theoretical defense of value they say should be abandoned. They've painted themselves into a conceptual corner.[35]

Anti-Philosophical

A fourth, distinct line of response to environmental pragmatism is that, in arguing for the abandonment of theory in favor of a turn to policy, environmental pragmatism is not so much a novel *philosophical* project as an *anti-philosophical* project. Environmental pragmatists' call for philosophers to take the "policy turn" and to stop "writing philosophy essays for other philosophers" and instead start "doing interdisciplinary research and working on projects with public agencies, policy makers, and the private sector"[36] is, in a real sense, a call to stop doing philosophy and to start doing policymaking and community-organizing. Those are very worthwhile and important endeavors. But are they what philosophers, *as philosophers*, should be doing?

Of course, at stake here is the very definition of what constitutes philosophy. Lars Samuelsson contends that, since its inception, a central aspect of philosophy is the attempt to seek conceptual clarity on various "puzzling problems"[37]—indeed, that "seeking clearness about puzzling problems should be one of the minimal (necessary) requirements in a philosophical position." Any intellectual project that does not seek clearness about puzzling problems, "or which recommends that we avoid seeking clarity with regard to puzzling problems, is just not a *philosophical* position."[38] Perhaps it is part of another important branch of inquiry or part of a larger cultural project, but whatever it is, it is not on this account philosophy. In this way, there is a sense in which environmental pragmatism is "not a proper philosophical position at all, on this very understanding of *philosophy*."[39] That is not to say that it is bad or that it should be rejected. It means only that it is not a *philosophical* project.

Seeking greater clarity regarding puzzling problems as to the nature of value and the scope of direct moral concern is among the core jobs of an environmental philosopher, as a philosopher. They might *also* seek to pass good policies within their community, but it is not clear that doing so is an obvious expression of their work as a *philosopher*.

> If we abandon the theoretical questions, and reduce disagreements to an allegedly harmless moral pluralism—as environmental pragmatists want us to do—this "liveliness" may disappear, and environmental ethics may become a philosophically empty shell, interesting only for those who already accept the environmental goals which it would then be its sole purpose to defend. Such a pluralist "ethic" would be pointless for the purpose of moral reasoning, if not question-begging; it could be used to defend almost any goal that its adherents want to defend.[40]

Given Samuelsson's position, environmental pragmatists' claim that nothing practically useful has come out of environmental ethics may not even be a *philosophical* concern.

> It is difficult to see the direct practical relevance of several (most?) questions within, e.g., epistemology, metaphysics, and the philosophy of language. There is no reason why environmental philosophy should constitute a special case here. If epistemologists are allowed to continue pursuing their philosophical investigations without first establishing the practical relevance of these investigations, then, surely environmental philosophers who are interested in the possibility of intrinsic value in nature should be equally allowed to continue pursuing their investigations into this question without first establishing its practical relevance. Philosophy is theoretical by nature.[41]

It is not that our ecological (and social challenges) are not significant and urgent. They are. The question is what role environmental philosophers ought, as *philosophers*, play in addressing these crises. Having worked among environmental philosophers for decades, it is not obvious to me that they are likely to be useful in the endeavor to pass good environmental policy. They have no particular training or expertise in how policy is crafted and passed through democratic or regulatory processes. And even if they do have these skills, it is not clear that, when they are engaging in such activity, they are doing work qua philosopher.[42]

Beyond this, it is fair to ask the environmental pragmatist: Why, in the face of our ecological crises, do philosophers bear special responsibility to stop writing philosophical essays and instead start doing interdisciplinary research and working on projects with public agencies, policymakers, and the private sector? Why shouldn't physicists stop their arcane investigations into the nature of the microscopic functionings of reality and instead make themselves useful to policymakers and climate activists? Given the magnitude and urgency of the ecological crises before us, is environmental pragmatism the call for *every* discipline to stop pursuing its theoretical work and immediately take the "policy turn"? Part of every domain of inquiry involves theoretical work advancing debates concerning fundamental conceptual issues particular to that field. If philosophy is a form of inquiry that is inherently theoretical, environmental pragmatism isn't just one philosophical position among others within environmental philosophy; in calling for the abandonment of theory, environmental pragmatism is anti-philosophical.

Before proceeding further, let us take stock of what we have concluded with respect to environmental pragmatism. First, environmental pragmatism's overly pessimistic assessment of the practical significance and impact of environmental philosophy is historically premature. Indeed, there is some reasonable evidence that environmental philosophy has already had some significant, positive impact on public environmental consciousness and, thereby, on environmental policy. Second, Norton's convergence hypothesis is not clearly true; theoretical differences concerning intrinsic value are fundamental to defining both the goals and the means of environmental policymaking. Third, environmental pragmatism is question-begging in that it *presupposes* that "good" policy is defined as good for humans; and it is contradictory in giving theoretical defenses of intergenerational anthropocentrism while condemning all attempts to give theoretical defenses of value commitments. And fourth, environmental pragmatism and its "policy turn" are ultimately not a call to *improve* environmental philosophy but to *abandon* it. Before concluding, I would like to focus on one final point that is not typically considered in the vigorous and voluminous literature discussing environmental pragmatism: I contend that environmental pragmatism is not a particularly good expression of classical American pragmatism, from which it claims to take its inspiration.

ENVIRONMENTAL PRAGMATISM AND CLASSICAL AMERICAN PRAGMATISM

Environmental pragmatism is seen as genealogically related to—a subspecies of, if you will—American pragmatism. This branch of philosophy, what is sometimes also called classical American philosophy, began in the late nineteenth and early twentieth centuries in the work of not only Charles Sanders Peirce, William James, and John Dewey, but also of philosophers such as Josiah Royce, George Herbert Mead, Alain Locke, and Jane Addams. As the philosophical debates over the connotations and denotations of the labels "analytic" and "continental" reveal, it is no easy thing to define what does or does not fall within a particular philosophical tradition. I will not here attempt to provide such an account for American pragmatism or classical American philosophy.[43] I will, however, suggest that environmental pragmatism—especially as it has been developed by Light, Weston, and Norton—is not the only, the best, or even a good expression of what I take to be core philosophical commitments of the classical American philosophical tradition. This is a strong claim. Allow me to explain.

First, any philosophical tradition that is capacious enough to be inclusive of philosophers as diverse as Peirce, James, Dewey, Lock, Mead, Royce, and Addams—all of whom are rightly seen as defining members of classical American pragmatism—is a big philosophical tent. For the purposes of this discussion, I am referring especially to the philosophers associated with the Society for the Advancement of American Philosophy, of which I am a proud, though of late not especially active, longtime member. One of the largest groups of philosophers working in this space is particularly inspired by and committed to the work of John Dewey. This Deweyan dominance often gives classical American philosophy a fairly pronounced allergy to metaphysics. But this is not because the founding figures of classical American pragmatism are uninterested in metaphysics. Take Peirce—who, all agree, is a key founder of American pragmatism—who was a mathematician and philosopher with deep and explicit metaphysical interests. Indeed, as we found in both chapter one and chapter six of this volume, Peirce was committed to a unique, open, fallibilistic approach to metaphysics, as was James, though he did not live long enough to make good on the interest. My point is *not* to claim that Dewey is not an expression of classical American pragmatism. He most decidedly is, and Light and Norton are right to look to him as an expression of American pragmatism. Rather, my claim is simply that Dewey's philosophy and his keen distrust in and dislike of metaphysical speculation *do not define what American pragmatism is.*

This has important bearing on the discussion of the role of theory in pragmatism. To be direct, I find the environmental pragmatists' antipathy toward philosophical theory-making to be perplexing. As I suggested in the previous section, it too often veers into anti-philosophical terrain. To that I would now add that while environmental pragmatists may want to subsume or even abandon theory for policymaking, such an attitude is not an expression of classical American pragmatism and its views of theoretical philosophy. The relationship between theory and practice, particularly within American pragmatism's unique approach to epistemology, is complex and varies depending on the philosopher one preferences. (And, at least in the case of Peirce, it depends on whether one gives priority to his earlier or later writings, as his own views shift considerably over his career.)

Too often, philosophers from other traditions present American pragmatists as though they are simple relativists who believe that the truth is "whatever works." This is a gross misreading. Classical American pragmatisms' epistemology is far more nuanced than this caricature. Part of the difficulty is that it is not easy to characterize pragmatist epistemology as either a coherence or a correspondence model. It seems often to have elements of both. What is clear is that pragmatism does not hold that "whatever works" is true, but that what is true will in fact make some difference and that this difference will allow for one to make progress toward a truer position. In this way, I would suggest that American pragmatism is committed not to relativism but to fallibilism—a fallibilism grounded in an expansive, anti-reductive empiricism, which James rightly called a "radical empiricism."[44] This fallibilism, grounded in a radical empiricism, is also the basis for their deep engagement with and commitment to pluralism. However, as Richard Bernstein, himself a classical American pragmatist, argues, this is not a "flabby pluralism" that results in relativism, but an "engaged pluralism" fallibilistically and humbly progressing along the road of inquiry (see chapter one for more on Bernstein's discussion of pluralism and its relationship to metaphysics).

In keeping with this thoroughgoing fallibilism and pluralism comes American pragmatism's fundamental rejection of modern philosophy's obsession with finality, apodicticity, and absolute certainty. However, as demonstrated in chapter one and contrary to the claims of environmental pragmatists, rejecting finality and certainty in favor of fallibilism and pluralism does *not* lead to the *abandonment* of metaphysics. Metaphysics— even speculative, systematic metaphysics—that rejects finality, certainty, and apodicticity is possible, as Peirce, James, and Whitehead all explicitly contend.[45] Put in terms used in chapter one, classical American pragmatism adopts a metametaphysical view wherein metaphysics is defined as "working hypothesis" grounded in a radical empiricism and modeled after the recursive model of scientific progress.

Indeed, I would suggest that in addition to a fallibilistic conception of metaphysics, many classical American pragmatists are committed to several important metaphysical claims. As I've argued at greater length in my *Ethics of Creativity*,[46] in the work of Peirce, James, and Dewey, there is a consistent metaphysical commitment to the rejection of mechanism, "necessitarianism," and dualism in favor of a non-dualistic metaphysical worldview.[47] Although it is most pronounced in the work of Peirce, we also see in James (especially *Pluralistic Universe*) and Dewey (especially *Experience and Nature*) a consistent rejection of dualistic metaphysics that would seek to carve reality into mental and material components. As Peirce puts it in his inimitable style, we must fundamentally reject Descartes's "paper doubts" and the dualisms that result from them. For Peirce, matter is "but hide bound mind."[48] In rejecting dualism, they also reject a mechanistic, "necessitarian" form of materialism. In the preface to *Process and Reality*, Whitehead recognizes being "greatly indebted to Bergson, William James, and John Dewey" and goes on to suggest that one of the goals of his project is to "rescue their type of thought from the charge of anti-intellectualism, which rightly or wrongly has been associated with it."[49] The deep affinities between Whitehead and the pragmatists, particularly Peirce and James, is demonstrated in this volume in chapter one on metaphysics and in chapter seven on teleology.[50] Indeed, Whitehead is deeply sympathetic to the pragmatists, writing in 1935: "Harvard is justly proud of the great period of its philosophic department about thirty years ago. Josiah Royce, William James, Santayana, George Herbert Palmer, Münsterberg, constitute a group to be proud of. The group is a group of men individually great. But as a group they are greater still. It is a group of adventure, of speculation, of search for new ideas. To be a philosopher is to make some humble approach to the main characteristic of this group of men."[51]

I would suggest that what most characterizes the American pragmatist tradition is (1) epistemological commitments to the rejection of dogmatism, finality, and absolute certitude, in favor of pluralism, open-endedness, and fallibilism, and (2) metaphysical commitments to rejecting dualism, mechanism, and materialism, in favor of a view of reality as non-dualistic, organic, and developmental. Although environmental pragmatists such as Light, Weston, and Norton have no doubt been inspired by their reading of the classical American philosophers, and they are of course free to use whatever philosophical label they like, there is reason to question whether, philosophically, environmental pragmatism is a robust expression of core philosophical values of American pragmatism. Like Peirce, who out of frustration with William James's simplistic appropriation of the term "pragmatism" once suggested renaming his philosophy to "pragmaticism" because it is a term "ugly enough to be safe from kidnappers,"[52] perhaps "environmental pragmatism" might better be called "environmental practicalism." For, as Callicott quips, "simply being pragmatic does not a Pragmatist make."[53] Pragmatists in the classical American tradition are not against complex and intricate theoretical discussions of the nature and structure of reality for exactly the reason that these positions have practical significance: they matter. Whether reality is a dualistic split between matter and mind, whether reality is wholly deterministic and necessarily determined, whether mind is a feature of reality—these deeply and explicitly theoretical metaphysical questions are central to the work of Peirce, James, and Dewey. They are central to American pragmatism. And they are central to environmental ethics.

Environmental philosophers should not see American pragmatism as anything but an ally in the goal of worldview transformation. Indeed, one way of seeing the present volume is as an alternative form of environmental pragmatism, one that is inspired by the anti-dualist, anti-mechanistic impulse of classical American philosophy infused with Whitehead's philosophy of organism. Grounded in pragmatist epistemology and Whiteheadian metaphysics, environmental ethics is more likely to make progress on the long "road to inquiry." We need not choose between theory and practice. We are looking for theory in practice. And it matters greatly in practice whether one's theory recognizes the intrinsic value and beauty of nonhumans.

Chapter 9

From the Anthropocene to the Ecozoic

A few years ago, I was invited to write an essay on the presidential addresses of the American Philosophical Association (APA) of the 1930s (1931–1940).[1] While grappling with the diverse philosophical themes represented in the thirty-odd addresses, I couldn't help but think also about the dramatic events unfolding during the tumultuous decade. After all, at the beginning of the 1930s the world was sinking into the depths of the Great Depression, with a full quarter of all wage-earners in America unemployed. And by the end of the decade, virulent nationalist movements in Germany, Italy, and Japan had provoked the Second World War. Juxtaposing these crises with the addresses of the presidents of the APA was as revelatory for what was said as what was not.

On the one hand, the presidential addresses delivered at the start of the decade—including by prominent philosophers such as Alfred North Whitehead (1931–1932) and C. I. Lewis (1933–1934)—make not even passing reference to the global economic crisis.[2] Though images of breadlines no doubt featured in their morning papers may have affected them greatly, the state of global capitalism and human suffering apparently did not merit philosophical discussion. The deafening silence regarding the Great Depression stands in contrast to many of the presidential addresses in the closing years of the decade, which often focused on the growing geopolitical threats that resulted in the Second World War.[3] For instance, in his 1937–1938 Western Division presidential address, "History as the Struggle for Social Values," J. A. Leighton boldly argues for the moral responsibility of philosophers to become engaged, as philosophers, in the defense of democracy.

Democracy is emerging in one of the most momentous secular crises in the history of culture. On us teachers falls, I think, a heavy share of the burden of democracy. If the confusion continues, and some rabble-rouser, greedy for power, arises, we may all be either shut up or shot. If philosophers remain content to pursue the owlish habit of reflection only in the soft evening twilight of abstract speculation, they are in for a long and dreadful night. Civilization is poised on a razor edge over an abyss. To say that we Americans have no responsibility and freedom of choice in this hour of decision is a counsel of cowardice and despair. I believe that you and I and all of us are confronted with the challenge to choose whether we shall knuckle down to tyranny controlled by demonic powers or march forward with resolute wills towards the dawn of an earth of worthy and comradely persons—a world set free.[4]

Many of the addresses of the second half of the 1930s similarly reveal that the struggle between democracy and tyranny was as much a war of ideas as of warring armies. And the presidents of the APA were calling on their fellow philosophers to "enlist."[5]

This disparity in the philosophical responses to the twin crises of the 1930s brought me to consider the philosophical addresses of more recent APA presidents in the context of our current ecological crises. Arguably, the greatest existential threat of the twenty-first century is not economic calamity or the march of tyranny—though we see that these remain all-too-real problems—but the accelerating extinction of species and the inexorable rise of the seas fueled by global warming.[6] Anthropogenic global climate change is a challenge the magnitude and nature of which humanity has never confronted.[7] As we lurch toward a hotter planet, in combination with an accelerating and ongoing mass-extinction event, at stake is not a nation or ideology or even economic well-being, but the very fate of our species and millions of other species with which we have evolved. What sort of philosophical responses to *this* crisis do we find in the presidential addresses of the APA?

Given the content of their philosophical addresses, it would seem that the recent presidents of the APA are no more *philosophically* concerned with global climate change or species extinction than Whitehead and Lewis were with the Great Depression. Indeed, if the content of these addresses were one's only source, it would be nearly impossible to know that the Earth is in the midst of multiple not-so-slow-motion ecological crises. Among the fifty-four presidential addresses delivered since 2003, not a single president makes more than a passing reference to global warming or climate change, and there are no references to species extinction.[8] Though of course philosophers are not blind to its significance, it would seem that too few consider climate change or species extinction relevant to their *philosophical* work or their work relevant to climate change. Stephen Gardiner's 2004 observation that "very few moral philosophers have written on climate change"[9] remains stubbornly true.[10]

The dual aim of this final chapter is, first, to add my voice to those calling on more philosophers to take up the important conceptual work of understanding and responding to the species-extinction crisis and anthropogenic global climate change and, second, accept this challenge myself by considering just one of the many roles philosophers might play by critiquing what I take to be the underlying conceptual framework[11] that has precipitated and that perpetuates the ecological crisis. Taking the latter first, I begin by considering what Eileen Crist calls the "Anthropocene discourse," after which I consider an alternative framing offered by the cultural historian Thomas Berry. With Berry, I conclude that the challenges of species extinction and global climate change can only be met by transitioning not to the "Anthropocene Epoch," but to the "Ecozoic Era" in which humans take their place within, not over, the vital community of intrinsically valuable beings. The philosophical work of worldview reconstruction is more important than ever and the philosophy of organism and environmental metaphysics can play a key role in it.

The Anthropocene Discourse

The International Union of Geological Science's (IUGS) Anthropocene Working Group has since 2009 been considering whether, after roughly 12,000 years, the Holocene Epoch of the Quaternary Period has prematurely ended and the Anthropocene Epoch has begun.[12] Were it not for the cumulative impact of human activity, the relatively temperate Holocene that defines the climatic "normal" for our species may have continued for perhaps another 50,000 years.[13] However, the argument goes, the collective impact of human activity has now reached a geological order of magnitude, ushering in a wholly new geological epoch. "Welcome to the Anthropocene," writes the popular magazine *The Economist*:

The Earth is a big thing; if you divided it up evenly among its 7 billion inhabitants, they would get almost 1 trillion tonnes each. To think that the workings of so vast an entity could be lastingly changed by a species that has been scampering across its surface for less than 1% of 1% of its history seems, on the face of it, absurd. But it is not. Humans have become a force of nature reshaping the planet on a geological scale—but at a far-faster-than-geological speed.

A single engineering project, the Syncrude mine in the Athabasca tar sands, involves moving 30 billion tonnes of earth—twice the amount of sediment that flows down all the rivers in the world in a year. That sediment flow itself, meanwhile, is shrinking; almost 50,000 large dams have over the past half-century cut the flow by nearly a fifth. That is one reason why the Earth's deltas, home to hundreds of millions of people, are eroding away faster than they can be replenished.[14]

Following Eileen Crist, I'm interested in considering "the shadowy repercussions of naming an epoch after ourselves."[15] Crist's thesis is that the concept of the "Anthropocene" is not a neutral, scientific description, "but instead a reflection and reinforcement of the anthropocentric actionable worldview that generated 'the Anthropocene'—with all its looming emergencies—in the first place."[16] With Crist, I would contend that global climate change and the ecological crises it is precipitating are the result of an anthropocentric, human-supremacist[17] worldview and narrative that have for millennia sanctioned human dominion over a world denuded of all (intrinsic) value.

Simply clarifying the direct and ultimate causes of life's crisis does not get us any closer to understanding why humanity is doing vanishingly little to address it. On the contrary, barefaced inaction—despite established knowledge of the causes of life's devastation—begs that question. I argue that the answer lies in the reigning worldview of human supremacy (or anthropocentrism) that stands as an intractable obstacle to the historical shift required, because it both normalizes and promotes ongoing human expansion. Human supremacy is the collective, lived belief system that humans are superior to all the other life forms and entitled to use them and their places of livelihood.[18]

In keeping with the founding impulse that launched many of the first efforts at environmental ethics, Crist rightly reminds us that we will be unable to fully and successfully address the ecological crisis unless and until we conceive of a non-anthropocentric, nonhuman supremacist worldview. Throughout the present work I have suggested that an important part of this work of worldview reconstruction is the development of an adequate environmental metaphysics, such as that found in Whitehead's philosophy of organism.

Rather than challenging the narrative of human dominance and control over every aspect of nature, the Anthropocene discourse effectively enshrines it in seemingly neutral, objective language. "The vocabulary that we are 'changing the world'—so matter-of-factly portraying itself as impartial and thereby erasing its own normative tracks even as it speaks—secures its ontological ground by silencing the displaced, killed, and enslaved whose homelands have been assimilated and whose lives have, indeed, but changed forever; erased, even."[19] Part of the effect of the Anthropocene discourse's euphemistic, sanitizing language is to present the threats of extinction and climate change not as the predictable results of an axiologically and metaphysically mistaken worldview, but as an environmental challenge to be "managed" through the application of ever-more-aggressive forms of technology, geoengineering the very climate if necessary.[20] It would seem that much of the popular sustainability movement aims to protect, not challenge, our consumption-based model of happiness; it is an effort to stabilize and sustain the Anthropocene epoch, not overcome it.[21]

As Dale Jamieson rightly notes, a management approach to global ecological crises such as anthropogenic climate change and extinction ultimately fail because it does not properly understand the nature of the problem and, therefore, proposes inadequate solutions. "Science has alerted us to a problem, but the problem also concerns our values. It is about how we ought to live, and how humans should relate to each other and to the rest of nature. These are problems of ethics and politics as well as problems of science."[22] Indeed, global warming is a complex philosophical problem in that it concerns how we conceive of ourselves and our relationship to nature (metaphysics); it concerns the nature of value (axiology); and it concerns humanity's conceptions of progress and the good life (ethics). It is not enough economically to internalize the costs of greenhouse gas–intensive activities (such as burning fossil fuels or eating grain-fed animals) or to create low-carbon forms of energy and transportation, though these changes are certainly needed. Ultimately, "management approaches are doomed to failure . . . [because] the questions they can answer are not the ones that are most important and profound. The problems posed by anthropogenic global climate change are ethical as well as economic and scientific."[23] I would suggest that explaining and defending the importance of this claim is a crucial first step in demonstrating to scientists, economists, and policymakers the importance of philosophy to addressing our ecological crises. As Jamieson insightfully notes, "Economics may be able to tell us how to reach our goals efficiently, but it cannot tell us what our goals should be or even whether we should be concerned to reach them efficiently."[24] Of course, the analysis and scrutiny of the ultimate aims of human existence and human beings' place within the wider cosmos has been a central task of philosophy for millennia. And for nearly half a century, environmental ethicists have sought to expand this conversation to include the nonhuman world as well. Contrary to the claims of environmental pragmatists, this should remain a central task of environmental ethics.

To sum, my concern is that the Anthropocene discourse embraces and codifies a management approach to our ecological problems. To be sure, many who make use of the Anthropocene discourse do so out of a desire to reverse its effects. But by leaving unchallenged and even geologically enshrining human domination over nature, it takes off the table the very changes needed to address the crisis. As Crist puts it, "The very concept of the Anthropocene crystallizes human dominion, corralling the already-pliable-in-that-direction human mind into viewing our master identity as manifestly destined, quasi-natural, and sort of awesome."[25] If we are truly to address the roots of the ecological crises we have created, we must resist the "Promethean self-portrait" provided by the Anthropocene discourse.[26]

THE ECOZOIC ERA

But what, one might reasonably ask, is the implication of rejecting the Anthropocene discourse? First, rejection of the Anthropocene discourse does not entail the rejection of the claim, supported by a considerable body of scientific evidence, that human activity is collectively a geological force shaping the planet. This would now seem all but indisputable. Indeed, following the cultural historian Thomas Berry (1914–2009), I would go even further and suggest that there is reason to wonder whether the collective impact of human activity is bringing about the end not merely of the geological *epoch*, but of the geological *era*.[27] Well before Paul Crutzen's talk of the Anthropocene Epoch, Berry defends the claim that human activity is bringing about not just the end of the Holocene Epoch (which began some 11,700 years ago), or even the end of the Quaternary Period (which began 2.588 million years ago). Rather, Berry contends that we are witnessing, and bringing about, the end of the Cenozoic Era (which began 65.5 million years ago). My aim in introducing Berry's claim is not to enter into a geological debate that is rightly decided by geologists of the International Union of Geological Science (IUGS). In agreeing with Berry I am interested philosophically in recognizing the magnitude of the changes taking place and to provide an alternative path to rejecting the anthropocentric narrative underlying the Anthropocene discourse. In a sense, envisioning what comes after the "terminal Cenozoic Era" was the primary objective of much of Berry's long life. Indeed, as we will see, Berry thinks such envisioning is the "Great Work" of this generation and the next. If this is true, philosophers have a significant role to play in such work.[28]

Berry is convinced that in precipitating the end of the Cenozoic we have arrived at a critical point in the Earth's history. As he puts it, humanity has the choice whether to embrace a "nonviable Technozoic-Industrial era" or set about the work of transitioning to an "Ecozoic-Organic era."[29] The similarity between Berry's understanding of the Technozoic era and the previous discussion of the Anthropocene discourse is notable. The aim of the Technozoic era is to extend human dominion over the Earth and then out into the rest of the solar system and beyond. Though this possibility may seem like science fiction, it is increasingly clear that many within the scientific and corporate communities are actively working to realize this possibility.[30] Just how far down this path we've already proceeded became clear to me when participating in the Blumberg Dialogues on Astrobiology, cohosted by the Library of Congress and NASA.[31] During the course of the Dialogues, it became clear that many within industry and science are actively pursuing a path toward "colonizing" the solar system. The devastating legacy of colonialism on our own planet seemed not to have even occurred to most of the scientists and NASA staff attending the Dialogues. Similarly, the idea that there should be some form of ethical review of efforts to discover and interact with (likely microbial) life on other planets—perhaps analogous to Institutional Review Boards (IRB) or Institutional Animal Care and Use Committees (IACUC)—was met with a mixture of lip service and resistance.

Environmental philosophers have for half a century debated whether ethics is anthropocentric, sentiocentric, biocentric, or ecocentric. Yet even the most capacious of these theories typically have difficulty thinking beyond our own planet and its distinct evolutionary history. As some humans consider "colonizing" other planets, mining asteroids, and possibly interacting with extraterrestrial life, it is urgent that we develop an adequate extraterrestrial ethic. We need to move beyond geocentric ethics, toward cosmocentric ethics, and Whitehead's organicist environmental metaphysics is an ideal basis for doing just that. Just as Europeans' latent metaphysics and ethics defined what was morally defensible in their colonization of this planet, our species' latent metaphysics and ethics define whether certain actions require moral justification. We take our ethics—and our metaphysics—with us as we move into and beyond the solar system.

At present, the dominant anthropocentric, human-supremacist worldview places virtually no moral limits to human use and exploitation of the Earth, our solar system, and beyond. In contrast to this Technozoic trajectory, Berry contends that the Ecozoic era is to be built on a new narrative, a new conceptual framework that invites humans to reconceive of what they are and how they are related to the cosmos. As Berry presents it, the key to transitioning to the Ecozoic era is for humans to shed their arrogant and illusory anthropocentrism and to finally become an integral part of the Earth community and the cosmic community.

> What is needed is a bonding of all the various forms of life on the planet Earth into a single, yet differentiated, community. Even beyond the living forms, there is the urgency to establish a comprehensive community of all the constituents of the planet, both the geological and biological components. Even beyond this, there is the necessity for humans to recognize the unity of the universe itself. There is ultimately only a single community. No community at any level can survive that is not founded in the unity of the universe. Every component of the universe is a subsystem of the universe system.[32]

Humanity must begin to recognize that it is a part of the wider community of beings, not apart from it or lords over it. In a sense, then, the key to bringing about the Ecozoic era is not merely for humans to *include* nonhumans in their moral community, but to recognize more fundamentally that the human community is *a part of* the wider planetary, solar, and cosmic communities.

Many will recognize more than a passing similarity between Berry's position here and Aldo Leopold's land ethic (though as far as I can tell, Berry does not make more than passing references to Leopold and seems to have come to his own views independently of Leopold). In his *Ursprung*

1949 essay "The Land Ethic," Leopold argues that the gradual expansion of the moral community is a sort of ethical evolution.[33] He contends that the key to bringing about the next stage in ethical evolution is for humanity to reenvisage how it conceives of itself and its relationship to nature. "A land ethic changes the role of *Homo sapiens* from conqueror of the land-community to plain member and citizen of it. It implies respect for his fellow-members, and also respect of the community as such."[34] It is, Leopold writes, an "evolutionary possibility and an ecological necessity" that we recognize that we are a part of the wider "biotic community."[35] Or, as Berry puts it:

> We misconceive our role if we consider that our historical mission is to "civilize" or to "domesticate" the planet [or the solar system!], as though wildness is something destructive rather than the ultimate creative modality of any form of earthly being. We are not here to control. We are here to become integral with the larger Earth community. The community itself and each of its members has ultimately a wild component, a creative spontaneity that is its deepest reality, its most profound mystery.[36]

The aim is not to become more benevolent "stewards" of nature. We are not here to manage, control, or fix nature, but to become "integral with the larger Earth community."[37] The notion of "integrity" or becoming "integral" is central to this transition.[38] The call for humans to become "integral" is also echoed by Crist, who notes that "integration calls for embracing our planetary [and cosmic] membership."[39] She continues: "Integration within an organism, an ecosystem, a bioregion, a family, or a community signals a state of being within which gifts of wellness can flow. Being integral, along with the kin quality of possessing integrity, means working harmoniously together, enhancing and complementing one another, supporting mutual flourishing, respecting distinct identities and appropriate boundaries, and experiencing union-in-diversity."[40] Again, the compatibility of this position with Leopold's land ethic is notable. The goal is to overcome the colonizing, conqueror mentality and to embrace an ethic in which an activity is right insofar as it preserves the integrity, stability, and beauty of the biotic community and wrong when it tends otherwise.[41] Thus, the Great Work[42] of this moment in our species' history is to conceive of ways of living that are "mutually enhancing" rather than mutually destructive.[43]

Crucially for the present project, this transition to the Ecozoic era requires a fundamental rejection of the dualistic and reductionistic metaphysics that have for centuries (arguably for millennia) bifurcated humans from the rest of nature and refused to recognize nature's intrinsic value and beauty. Part of this realization is bound up in the recognition that "the universe is composed of subjects to be communed with, not of objects to be exploited."[44] Contrary to the narrative created by, for instance, modern metaphysics, nature is not best understood as a vast machine.[45] With Alfred North Whitehead, I have argued that the metaphor of organism is far more adequate in describing the reality revealed by contemporary science. Indeed, Whitehead's philosophy of organism is among the richest, and most neglected, philosophical projects of the twentieth century. Reacting to the scientific revolutions of evolutionary biology, relativity theory, and quantum mechanics, Whitehead systematically develops a naturalistic metaphysics that fundamentally repudiates the mechanistic account of nature as valueless, vacuous actuality in favor of a nondualistic, nonreductive relational event ontology that conceives of interdependence, value, and beauty as the most pervasive features of reality.[46] Every being is constituted by its relationships to the whole and is a unique achievement of beauty and value for itself, for others, and for the whole. As we have seen, this results in a kalocentric or beauty-centered form of ethics.

Berry rightly contends that the transition to an Ecozoic era requires that humans reconceive of themselves and their relationship to the broader natural world. This is not primarily about inventing a new technology or a novel economic model, though perhaps both are needed. Again, in contrast to the claims of environmental pragmatists, what is required is far more fundamental. "What is demanded of us now is to change attitudes that are so deeply bound into our basic cultural patterns that they seem to us as imperative of the very nature of our being, a dictate of our genetic coding as a species."[47] In a very real sense, then, the Great Work before us is no less than "to reinvent the human—at the species level, with critical reflection, within the community of life-systems, in a time-developmental context, by means of story and shared dream experience."[48] A central part of this philosophical work is the development and defense of an adequate environmental metaphysics.[49]

Notes

Introduction

1. "A Very Brief History of the Origins of Environmental Ethics for the Novice," March 14, 2011, https://www.cep.unt.edu/novice.html.

2. "A Very Brief History."

3. Leopold was an American author, scientist, and conservationist who began his career with the US Forest Service and later became a professor at the University of Wisconsin.

4. "A Very Brief History."

5. The journal was later moved to the University of North Texas, where it currently resides.

6. "Partly because it is so new to Western philosophy (or at least heretofore only scarcely represented) *environmental ethics* has no precisely fixed conventional definition in glossaries of philosophical terminology. Aldo Leopold, however, is universally recognized as the father or founding genius of recent environmental ethics. His 'land ethic' has become a modern classic and may be treated as the standard example, the paradigm case, as it wore, of what an environmental ethic is." See J. Baird Callicott, "Animal Liberation: A Triangular Affair," *Environmental Ethics* 2 (1980): 311.

7. Eugene Hargrove, "The Historical Foundations of American Environmental Attitudes," *Environmental Ethics* 1 (1979): 210. Hargrove continues, "One major difference, however, is that by separating the natural history sciences from the physical sciences—a distinction which Whitehead does not seem to make—I am able to claim that even though the Romantic reaction was most certainly opposed to some aspects of physical science, it was, nonetheless, in tune with the natural history sciences which were strongly value-oriented from the very beginning" (210).

8. Hargrove, "Historical Foundations," 238.

9. Hargrove, "Historical Foundations," 238–39. Hargrove's claims about Leopold have been widely repeated by many Whitehead scholars. Unfortunately, as the analysis to follow shows, Hargrove's claims must be significantly qualified.

10. Aldo Leopold, *A Sand County Almanac; And Sketches Here and There* (Oxford: Oxford University Press, 1949), 224–25.

11. Alfred North Whitehead, *Modes of Thought* (New York: Free Press, 1938), 13–14.

12. Alfred North Whitehead, *Adventures of Ideas* (New York: Free Press, 1933), 268.

13. Eugene Hargrove, *Foundations of Environmental Ethics* (Englewood Cliffs, NJ: Prentice Hall, 1989). On three separate occasions over the span of three years I tried without success to obtain more information from Professor Hargrove on what evidence he has to support the claim he makes here in 1979 and repeats again without modification in his 1989 book *Foundations of Environmental Ethics.* I have not received any reply to my inquiries.

14. Pete A. Y. Gunter, "Whitehead's Contributions to Ecological Thought: Some Unrealized Possibilities," *Interchange* 31 (2000): 217. Gunter explained in personal correspondence that the source of his claim, which is not given in the article, was Leopold's brother, Carl Starker Leopold. However, the brother admitted that he was not sure what Leopold had studied or was acquainted with in college. Unfortunately, Leopold's library was dispersed, and I have not yet been able to locate a single catalog listing its contents. Personal correspondence, March 25, 2015.

15. Curt Meine, email message to author, March 3, 2015.

16. Susan Flader, email message to author, March 16, 2015.

17. Susan Flader, email message to author, March16, 2015.

18. William T. Blackstone, ed., *Philosophy and Environmental Crisis* (Athens, GA: University of Georgia Press, 1974).

19. Charles Hartshorne had already completed his dissertation at Harvard prior to Whitehead's arrival, but he quickly found deep affinity with his processive view of reality. Hartshorne went on to have a long and distinguished career and is, along with John B. Cobb Jr., a chief exponent of what is called "process theology": a major branch of twentieth-century theology, especially within progressive protestant theological circles.

20. The Center for Environmental Philosophy does recognize this. See "A Very Brief History." http://www.cep.unt.edu/novice.html.

21. Charles Hartshorne, "The Rights of the Subhuman World," *Environmental Ethics* 1, no. 1 (1979): 49–60; and John B. Cobb Jr., "Christian Existence in a World of Limits," *Environmental Ethics* 1, no. 2 (1979): 149–58.

22. "Philosophers such as Charles Hartshorne and John Cobb, Jr., have recently argued its relevance as a basis for the New Philosophy of Nature. But many of these theorists, who also happen to be Christian theists, when applying Whiteheadian metaphysics to problems of environmental ethics, argue that, in their estimation, humans have the greatest degree and highest quality of sentience, or consciousness, hence humans have the highest value and the most rights in Nature. In a manner similar to the attempt to 'extend' humanistic ethical theory to the nonhuman, there

is what Rodman points to as a 'pecking order in this moral barnyard.' This attempt to apply Whiteheadian panpsychism, while positing various degrees of intrinsic value to the rest of Nature, nonetheless merely reinforces existing Western anthropocentrism, and thus fails to meet the deep ecology norm of 'ecological egalitarianism in principle.' " See Bill Devall and George Sessions, *Deep Ecology: Living as If Nature Mattered* (Salt Lake City: Gibbs Smith, 1985), 236.

23. Susan Armstrong, "Whitehead's Metaphysical System as a Foundation for Environmental Ethics," *Environmental Ethics* 8, no. 3 (1986): 241–57.

24. Susan Armstrong and Richard G. Botzler, *Environmental Ethics: Divergence and Convergence* 1st ed., 1993, 2nd ed., 1998, 3rd ed. 2003 (New York: McGraw-Hill).

25. Brian G. Henning, *The Ethics of Creativity: Beauty, Morality, and Nature in a Processive Cosmos* (Pittsburgh: University of Pittsburgh Press, 2005).

26. Alfred North Whitehead, "First Lecture," in *Whitehead at Harvard, 1924–1925*, eds. Brian G. Henning and Joseph Petek (Edinburgh: Edinburgh University Press, 2020), 50.

27. Whitehead, "First Lecture," 50–51.

28. Alfred North Whitehead, *The Function of Reason* (Princeton: Princeton University Press, 1929), 30.

29. Whitehead, *Process and Reality*, 228.

30. Whitehead, *Process and Reality*, 167, 29.

31. Alfred North Whitehead, "Objects and Subjects," in *Proceedings and Addresses of the American Philosophical Association* 5 (1931): 130. https://doi.org/10.2307/1483082. Whitehead's address also appeared under the same name as a chapter in his *Adventures of Ideas* (New York: Free Press, 1933).

32. Whitehead, *Process and Reality*, 151.

33. "I contend that the notion of mere knowledge is a high abstraction, and that conscious discrimination itself is a variable factor only present in the more elaborate examples of occasions of experience. The basis of experience is emotional. Stated more generally, the basic fact is the rise of an affective tone originating from things whose relevance is given." See Whitehead, "Objects and Subjects," 130.

34. Whitehead, *Process and Reality*, 151.

35. "Thus in philosophy linguistic discussion is a tool, but should never be a master. Language is imperfect both in its words and in its forms. Thus we discover two main errors to which philosophic method is liable, one is the uncritical trust in the adequacy of language, and the other is the uncritical trust in the strained attitude of introspection as the basis for epistemology." See Whitehead, *Adventures*, 228.

36. Whitehead, *Process and Reality*, 4.

37. See, for instance, "The Romantic Reaction," chapter five of *Science and the Modern World* (75).

38. Whitehead, *Process and Reality*, 224.

39. "There are two main forms of such overstatement. One form is what I have termed, elsewhere, the 'fallacy of misplaced concreteness.' This fallacy consists

in neglecting the degree of abstract involved when an actual entity is considered merely so far as it exemplifies certain categories of thought. There are aspects of actualities which are simply ignored so long as we restrict thought to these categories. Thus the success of a philosophy is to be measured by its comparative avoidance of this fallacy, when thought is restricted within its categories. The other form of overstatement consists in a false estimate of logical procedure in respect to certainty, and in respect to premises. Philosophy has been haunted by the unfortunate notion that its method is dogmatically to indicate premises which are severally clear, distinct, and certain; and to erect upon those premises a deductive system of thought. But the accurate expression of the final generalities is the goal of discussion and not its origin. Philosophy has been misled by the example of mathematics; and even in mathematics the statement of the ultimate logical principles is beset with difficulties, as yet insuperable." See Whitehead, *Process and Reality*, 7–8.

40. Descartes defined individuals in terms of their existential substance, as that which "requires nothing other than itself in order to exist." If something can be separated in thought, it is in fact separable in reality. Aristotle also emphasized the essential independence of individuals in *Categories*, defining a substance as that which is "neither said of nor in another." In contrast to both Aristotle and Descartes, Whitehead is claiming that there is "no independence of existence. There is no such mode of existence; every entity is only to be understood in terms of the way in which it is interwoven with the rest of the Universe." See Alfred North Whitehead, *Essays in Science and Philosophy* (New York: Philosophical Library, 1947), 3.

41. Whitehead, "Objects and Subjects," 130. Indeed, Whitehead goes so far as to suggest that his "philosophy of organism" could be seen as a sort of "critique of pure feeling" in place of Kant's *Critique of Pure Reason* (*Process and Reality*, 113).

42. For a more complete account of Whitehead's metaphysics, see Henning, *The Ethics of Creativity*, especially chapters one and two.

43. According to Whitehead, "the term 'actual occasion' is used synonymously with 'actual entity'; but chiefly when its character of extensiveness has some direct relevance to the discussion, either extensiveness in the form of temporal extensiveness, that is to say 'duration,' or extensiveness in the form of spatial extension, or in the more complete signification of spatio-temporal extensiveness" (*Process and Reality*, 77). In my own use, I privilege "actual occasion" (often abbreviated simply as "occasion") over "actual entity" because "entity" connotes properties such as "static," "enduring," and "independent"—properties Whitehead explicitly rejects—whereas "occasion" emphasizes "temporality," "relation," and "dynamism."

44. Whitehead, *Process and Reality*, 18.

45. See William James, *A Pluralistic Universe*, in *William James' Writings 1902–1910* (New York: Library of America, 1987), 733–34.

46. "The initial situation includes a factor of activity which is the reason for the origination of that occasion of experience. This factor of activity is what I have called 'Creativity.' The initial situation with its creativity can be termed the initial

phase of the new occasion. It can equally well be termed the 'actual world' relative to that occasion. It has a certain unity of its own, expressive of its capacity for providing the objects requisite for a new occasion, and also expressive of its conjoint activity whereby it is essentially the primary phase of a new occasion. It can thus be termed a 'real potentiality.' The 'potentiality' refers to the passive capacity, the term 'real' refers to the creative activity, where the Platonic definition of 'real' in the *Sophist* is referred to" (Whitehead, *Adventures of Ideas*, 179).

47. "Thus the primary stage in the concrescence of an actual entity is the way in which the antecedent universe *enters into* the constitution of the entity in question, so as to constitute the basis of its nascent individuality. If experience be not based upon objective content, there can be no escape from a solipsist subjectivism" (Whitehead, *Process and Reality*, 152, emphasis added).

48. Whitehead, *Process and Reality*, 150.

49. The principle of process is Whitehead's eighth category of explanation: "(ix) That *how* an actual entity *becomes* constitutes *what* that actual entity is; so that the two descriptions of an actual entity are not independent. Its 'being' is constituted by its 'becoming.' This is the 'principle of process'" (Whitehead, *Process and Reality*, 23). See also Whitehead, *Process and Reality*, 150, 222, 255.

50. Whitehead, *Adventures of Ideas*, 193.

51. "There are two species of process, macroscopic process, and microscopic process. The macroscopic process is the transition from attained actuality to actuality in attainment; while microscopic process is the conversion of conditions which are merely real into determinant actuality. The former process is efficient; the latter process is teleological" (Whitehead, *Process and Reality*, 214).

52. Whitehead, *Process and Reality*, 150.

53. Whitehead, *Process and Reality*, 21.

54. To be precise, "others" should be read as other subject-superjects. It is in this context that I understand Whitehead's appeal in his 1931 "Objects and Subjects" to the Quaker notion of "concern": "the occasion as subject has a 'concern' for the object" (131). What Whitehead is after is the "affective tone" that comes with "concern": "It must be distinctly understood that no prehension, even of bare sense, can be divested of its affective tone, that is to say, of its character of a 'concern' in the Quaker sense. Concernedness is of the essence of perception" (135).

55. See Whitehead, "Objects and Subjects," 134. To be more precise, Plato says *eite* (or) rather than *kai* (and) in that being either exerts influence *or* is influenced by others. My thanks to Daniel Dombrowski for reminding me of this important point.

56. "The position here maintained is that the relationships of an event are internal, so far as concerns the event itself; that is to say, that they are constitutive of what the event is in itself" (Whitehead, *Science and the Modern World*, 104).

57. Whitehead, "Objects and Subjects," 131.

58. "This is the doctrine of the emergent unity of the superject. An actual entity is to be conceived both as a subject presiding over its own immediacy of

becoming, and a superject which is the atomic creature exercising its function of objective immortality. It has become a 'being'; and it belongs to the nature of every 'being' that it is a potential for every 'becoming' " (Whitehead, *Process and Reality*, 45). See also Whitehead, *Process and Reality*, 245: "The subject, thus constituted, is the autonomous master of its own concrescence into subject-superject. It passes from a subjective aim in concrescence into a superject with objective immortality. At any state it is subject-superject."

59. Whitehead, *Process and Reality*, 228.

60. Whitehead, *Process and Reality*, 167.

61. Whitehead, *Process and Reality*, 179.

62. "Violence" is, for Whitehead, a technical term referring to the destruction of achievement forms of beauty and value. For more on this as well as the related notion of "anesthesia" see also Henning, *The Ethics of Creativity*, chapter four.

63. Whitehead, *Modes of Thought*, 109.

64. Susan Armstrong published her early work under the name Susan Armstrong-Buck. I will be referring to her by her currently preferred name (Susan Armstrong).

65. Susan Armstrong, "Whitehead's Metaphysical System as a Foundation for Environmental Ethics," *Environmental Ethics* 8 (1986): 241–57.

66. Armstrong, "Whitehead's Metaphysical System," 242.

67. Armstrong, "Whitehead's Metaphysical System," 242.

68. Descartes famously defined a substance as that which requires nothing other than itself in order to exist. See René Descartes, *Principles of Philosophy*, in *The Philosophical Writings of Descartes*, vol. 2, trans. John Cottingham, Robert Stoothoff, and Dugald Murdoch (Cambridge: Cambridge University Press, 1985), 210.

69. Armstrong, "Whitehead's Metaphysical System," 244.

70. Whitehead, *Process and Reality*, 148. See also Whitehead, *Science and the Modern World*, 104: "The position here maintained is that the relationships of an event are internal, so far as concerns the event itself; that is to say, that they are constitutive of what the event is in itself."

71. As Leemon McHenry has demonstrated in his work on Whitehead's event ontology, current advances in physics and cosmology continue to confirm Whitehead's metaphysics; interdependence and interrelation are fundamental aspects of reality at every level. See Leemon B. McHenry, *The Event Universe: The Revisionary Metaphysics of Alfred North Whitehead* (Edinburgh: Edinburgh University Press, 2015).

72. Armstrong, "Whitehead's Metaphysical System," 245.

73. Armstrong, "Whitehead's Metaphysical System," 245.

74. Alfred North Whitehead, *The Concept of Nature* (Cambridge: Cambridge University Press, 1920), 26.

75. A better formulation might have been "human and non-human animals."

76. Armstrong, "Whitehead's Metaphysical System," 246.

77. See, for instance, Thomas Nagel's *Mind and Cosmos*. See also Galen Strawson et al. *Consciousness and Its Place in Nature: Does Physicalism Entail Panpsychism?* (ed. Anthony Freeman), Imprint Academic, 2006.

78. Armstrong, "Whitehead's Metaphysical System," 246.

79. Holmes Rolston III, *Environmental Ethics* (Philadelphia: Temple University Press, 1988), 175.

80. Armstrong, "Whitehead's Metaphysical System," 250.

81. Armstrong, "Whitehead's Metaphysical System," 251.

82. See George Sessions and Bill Devall, *Deep Ecology: Living as if Nature Mattered* (Salt Lake City: Gibbs Smith, 1985), 236; John Rodman "Four Forms of Ecological Consciousness Reconsidered," in *Deep Ecology for the 21st Century: Readings on the Philosophy and Practice of the New Environmentalism*, ed. George Sessions (Boston: Shambhala, 1995), 125; and Val Plumwood, *Feminism and the Mastery of Nature* (London: Routledge, 1993), 130.

83. Armstrong, "Whitehead's Metaphysical System," 251.

84. Whitehead, *Adventures of Ideas*, 265. This quotation continues: "Thus any system of things which in any wide sense is beautiful is to that extent justified in its existence. It may however fail in another sense, by inhibiting more Beauty than it creates. Thus the system, though in a sense beautiful, is on the whole evil in that environment."

85. This term was coined by Frederick Ferré, *Being and Value: Toward a Constructive Postmodern Metaphysics* (Albany: SUNY Press, 1996), 340.

86. A final interpretive point of disagreement between Armstrong's work and my own concerns the value of Leopold's land ethic and its relationship to the philosophy of organism. As I argue in chapter four, contrary to Armstrong, Dombrowski, and others, there are deep and valuable points of connection, both historical and philosophical, between Whitehead's philosophy of organism and Leopold's land ethic.

Chapter 1

1. A notable exception is deep ecologists, who recognize that their project of a deep, long-range ecological movement to develop a fundamentally more adequate worldview can only be successful if grounded in a more adequate metaphysics, which many see in the work of Spinoza.

2. Alfred North Whitehead, *Adventures of Ideas* (New York: Free Press, 1933), 222.

3. Brian G. Henning and David Kovacs, eds., *Being in America: Sixty Years of the Metaphysical Society* (Amsterdam: Rodopi, 2014).

4. William Ernest Hocking, "Fact, Field, and Destiny: Inductive Elements of Metaphysics," *Review of Metaphysics* 11, no. 4 (1958): 525.

5. As Peter van Inwagen and Meghan Sullivan explain, the word *metaphysics* derives from the title of Aristotle's book of the same name, but Aristotle himself did not know the word. It is likely that the name was coined more than a century after Aristotle's death by an editor who gave the book the appellation due to its coming after Aristotle's *Physics*: "The title was probably meant to warn students of Aristotle's philosophy that they should attempt Metaphysics only after they had mastered 'the physical ones,' the books about nature or the natural world—that is to say, about change, for change is the defining feature of the natural world" (Peter van Inwagen and Meghan Sullivan, "Metaphysics," in *Stanford Encyclopedia of Philosophy*, Winter 2014, ed. Edward N. Zalta, http://plato.stanford.edu/archives/win2014/entries/metaphysics/).

6. René Descartes, *Meditations on First Philosophy* (1641), trans. Donald A. Cress (Indianapolis: Hackett, 1993), 13.

7. Descartes, *Meditations*, 17.

8. Richard J. Bernstein, "Metaphysics, Critique, and Utopia," *The Review of Metaphysics* 42, no. 2 (1988): 260.

9. Alfred North Whitehead, "Alfred North Whitehead to Henry S. Leonard," January 10, 1936, Manuscript Division, The Library of Congress.

10. Whitehead, *Adventures of Ideas*, 126.

11. Bernstein, "Metaphysics, Critique, and Utopia," 260.

12. Bernstein, "Metaphysics, Critique, and Utopia," 260.

13. P. M. S. Hacker, "Strawson's Rehabilitation of Metaphysics," in *Strawson and Kant*, ed. Hans-Johann Glock (Oxford: Oxford University Press, 2003), 49.

14. Hacker, "Strawson's Rehabilitation," 53.

15. Hacker, "Strawson's Rehabilitation," 55.

16. "So conceived, descriptive metaphysics *breaks* with the metaphysical tradition, which purported to give us insights into the necessary structure of reality" (Hacker, "Strawson's Rehabilitation," 55).

17. Hacker, "Strawson's Rehabilitation," 59.

18. Hacker, "Strawson's Rehabilitation," 59. The birth of postmodernism is often dated from Jean-François Lyotard's *La Condition Postmoderne*, published in 1979. I follow Bernstein's more expansive use.

19. Bernstein, "Metaphysics, Critique, and Utopia," 267.

20. John Wild, "The New Empiricism and Human Time," *Review of Metaphysics* 7 (1954): 537–38.

21. See Bernstein, "Metaphysics, Critique, and Utopia," 258: "At a time when anti-foundational slogans are being abused to dismiss the entire history of philosophy and metaphysics, caricaturing the entire tradition as if it were exclusively concerned with discovering such an *Urgrund*, we should not forget how much has been opened up by those utopian diggers. Their enduring philosophical significance is in keeping the spirit of truth alive, in not allowing the inquisitive energy of the mind to go to sleep."

22. Ernan McMullin, "Two Faces of Science," *Review of Metaphysics* 27 (June 1974): 655–56: "The aim of the Metaphysical Society was to hold lines open to the diversity of past philosophies that the overly harsh criteria of positivism threatened to reduce to meaninglessness or self-deception. There was room in the new Society for Whig pragmatism and Tory Thomism, for the radical world-view of Marxism as well as the apolitical individualism of the existentialists, for the cautious temper of a Husserl just as much as for the cosmic assurance of a Hegel. A diverse group, to be sure, at loggerheads on most issues, in agreement perhaps only on one: that the reach of rational inquiry was not simply to be measured by the modes of verification of natural science nor by the constructive resources of the *Principia Mathematica*."

23. Or as Edgar Sheffield Brightman put it in his 1936 presidential address to the Eastern Meeting of the American Philosophical Association: "It is conceivable that the current disrepute of philosophy is due in part to philosophers who decline to philosophize. If a thinker fails to build a metaphysic, whether because of intellectual humility, or fear of compromising intellectual honesty by yielding to desire or social pressure, or a conviction that science renders metaphysics superfluous, or any other prompting, nevertheless, pure though his motives be, such a thinker fails to contribute to the clarification of the central problem of philosophy, namely: What is reality?" See "An Empirical Approach to God," in *Presidential Addresses of the American Philosophical Association: 1931–1940*, ed. Richard T. Hull (Tallahassee: RTH, 2012), 411).

24. David Manley, "Introduction: A Guided Tour of Metametaphysics," in *Metametaphysics: New Essays on the Foundations of Ontology*, ed. David J. Chalmers, David Manley, and Ryan Wasserman (Oxford: Oxford University Press, 2009), 1.

25. Manley, "Introduction," 1.

26. Manley, "Introduction," 4.

27. Manley, "Introduction," 4.

28. Manley, "Introduction," 4. At the opposite end of the spectrum from strong deflationists are what Manley calls "*reformers*": "They hold both that there is a genuine dispute at issue, and that the answer is far from trivial. Indeed, pursuing the answer is an appropriate task for metaphysics. But in response to the concerns of deflationists, reformers reject various details of mainstream metaphysics—whether about how to understand the questions of metaphysics, or how to go about answering them" (Manley, "Introduction," 4.).

29. Manley, "Introduction," 4.

30. Manley, "Introduction," 3–4.

31. Bernstein, "Metaphysics, Critique, and Utopia," 257–58.

32. Hocking, "Fact, Field, and Destiny," 525.

33. Alfred North Whitehead, *Science and the Modern World* (New York: Free Press, 1925), 87.

34. Alfred North Whitehead, *Process and Reality* (New York: Free Press, [1929] 1978), 10.

35. Whitehead, *Adventures of Ideas*, 154.

36. Alfred North Whitehead, *Modes of Thought* (New York: Free Press, 1938), 155. Cf. 87: "Life on this planet depends on the order observed throughout the spatio-temporal stellar system, as disclosed in our experience. These special forms of order exhibit no final necessity whatsoever. The laws of nature are forms of activity which happen to prevail within the vast epoch of activity which we dimly discern" (see also 95).

37. Whitehead, *Modes of Thought*, 143. Cf. Whitehead, *Adventures of Ideas*, 41–42: "The laws are the outcome of the character of the behaving things: they are the 'communal customs' of which Clement spoke. What we know of external nature is wholly in terms of how the various occasions in nature contribute to each other's natures. The whole environment participates in the nature of each of its occasions. Thus each occasion takes its initial form from the character of its environment. Also the laws which condition each environment merely express the general character of the occasions composing that environment. This is the doctrine of definition of things in terms of their modes of functioning."

38. It is important to note that Whitehead distinguishes between "cosmology" and "speculative philosophy." Some scholars make much of the fact that Whitehead's *Process and Reality* is published with the subtitle *An Essay in Cosmology*. However, as Christoph Kann argues, Whitehead's use of the term *cosmology* does not map neatly either with Wolff's use or with contemporary physics': "Neither traditional cosmology in Wolff's sense of the word nor cosmology as a modern discipline among the natural sciences can serve as a convenient classification of Whitehead's project of a philosophical cosmology. With regard to the traditional division, his approach is by no means restricted to cosmology as a *metaphysica specialis* but rather overlaps with both the area of the other *metaphysicae speciales* and with *cosmologia generalis*. What is of particular relevance for Whitehead's cosmology, however, is not the complete generality of metaphysics, but rather the present cosmic epoch or stage of reality as exemplifying the most general metaphysical characters" (Christoph Kann, "Renewing Speculation: The Systematic Aim of Whitehead's Philosophic Cosmology," in *Beyond Metaphysics? Explorations in Alfred North Whitehead's Late Works*, ed. Roland Faber, Brian G. Henning, and Clinton Combs [Amsterdam: Rodopi, 2010], 29). I commend the reader to Kann's careful analysis for more on this. Also helpful is Hans Poser, "Whitehead's Cosmology as Revisable Metaphysics," in *Whitehead's Metaphysics of Creativity*, ed. Friedrich Rapp and Reiner Wiehl (Albany: SUNY Press, 1990), 94–114.

39. William James, *Some Problems of Philosophy: A Beginning of an Introduction to Philosophy* (New York: Longmans, Green, 1911), 25.

40. James, *Some Problems of Philosophy*, 25. As William Hamrick pointed out in personal correspondence March 9, 2014, more useful than verification here would be Popper's concept of the logic of scientific discovery as falsification. See Karl Popper, *The Logic of Scientific Discovery* (London: Hutchinson, 1959).

41. James, *Some Problems of Philosophy*, 25–26

42. Leemon B. McHenry, *The Event Universe: The Revisionary Metaphysics of Alfred North Whitehead* (Edinburgh: Edinburgh University Press, 2015), 5.

43. Whitehead, *Adventures of Ideas*, 222.

44. Though Whitehead and Peirce are framing metaphysics as "working hypothesis," it is important to note that they are not thereby reducing metaphysics to science. In *Process and Reality* (p. 3), Whitehead defines cosmology in terms of speculative philosophy, which he defines as "the endeavor to frame a coherent, logical, necessary system of general ideas in terms of which every element of our experience can be interpreted." Thus, as Poser notes, "Such a cosmology is intended to accomplish what in Wolff's view was the task of metaphysics. Its statements are *not* part of the empirical sciences, but are metaphysical" ("Whitehead's Cosmology as Revisable Metaphysics," 94–95).

45. Whitehead, "First Lecture," 54.

46. Descartes, *Meditations*.

47. Whitehead, *Process and Reality*, 13.

48. Whitehead, *Process and Reality*, 13.

49. Whitehead, *Process and Reality*, 8.

50. Whitehead, *Process and Reality*, 5.

51. Whitehead, *Process and Reality*, 3.

52. Whitehead, *Adventures of Ideas*, 98.

53. John Herman Randall Jr., "Metaphysics and Language," *Review of Metaphysics* 20 (June 1967): 600.

54. Charles Sanders Peirce, "The First Rule of Logic," *The Essential Peirce*, Vol. 2, ed. the Peirce Edition Project (Bloomington: Indiana University Press, 1992 [1899]).

55. Whitehead, *Process and Reality*, 14.

56. Whitehead, *Process and Reality*, 4.

57. Whitehead, *Process and Reality*, 4.

58. Bernstein, "Metaphysics, Critique, and Utopia," 270. Bernstein also distinguishes two other forms of pluralism that he rejects: "fortress-like pluralism" and "anarchic pluralism."

59. Bernstein, "Metaphysics, Critique, and Utopia," 271.

60. See Bernstein, "Metaphysics, Critique, and Utopia," 272: "I do not think that metaphysics can solve practical problems of everyday life. But in keeping alive the utopian impulse, metaphysics keeps open the space for critique. Metaphysical questioning requires us to uncover and probe the ideals that are presupposed in critique. When we think through the various attempts to kill metaphysics in our time, they do not lead us beyond metaphysics but back to what has always been central to the metaphysical tradition. The danger today does not come from the utopian impulse of metaphysics but rather from the various attempts to kill off metaphysics. Against those who are deeply suspicious of all forms of utopian thinking,

I want to claim we need more utopian thinking. Metaphysicians have always been stargazers and dreamers. We need to keep open the oppositional space of critique."

61. Bernstein, "Metaphysics, Critique, and Utopia," 258.

62. Whitehead, *Process and Reality*, 9.

63. McHenry, *Event Universe*, viii.

Chapter 2

1. These positions are defended respectively by: Paul A. Schilpp, "Whitehead's Moral Philosophy," in *The Philosophy of Alfred North Whitehead*, ed. Paul Arthur Schilpp, 2nd ed. (LaSalle, IL: Open Court, 1951); Clare Palmer, *Environmental Ethics and Process Thinking* (Oxford: Clarendon Press, 1998); Nicholas F. Gier, "Whitehead, Confucius, and the Aesthetics of Virtue," *Asian Philosophy* 14 (2004): 171–90.

2. See John W. Lango, "Does Whitehead's Metaphysics Contain an Ethics?" *Transactions of the Charles S. Peirce Society* 37 (2001): 515–36.

3. Whitehead, *Modes of Thought*, 14–15.

4. Whitehead, *Modes of Thought*, 14.

5. Whitehead, *Modes of Thought*, 13–14

6. Schilpp, 610.

7. Whitehead, *Modes of Thought*, 11.

8. Whitehead, *Mode of Thought*, 8, Whitehead's emphasis.

9. Whitehead, *Modes of Thought*, 12.

10. Whitehead, *Modes of Thought*, 116.

11. Whitehead, *Modes of Thought*, 117.

12. Whitehead, *Modes, of Thought* 117.

13. Whitehead, *Modes of Thought*, 111.

14. Whitehead, *Modes of Thought*, 13–14.

15. Whitehead, *Modes of Thought*, 111.

16. If there is a difference, it would seem merely to be a matter of emphasis. Whereas the term *value* seems to suggest that which is achieved in process, *importance* seems to emphasize the end toward which process strives.

17. Whitehead, *Modes of Thought*, 12, emphasis added.

18. Palmer, *Environmental Ethics*, 15.

19. Palmer, *Environmental Ethics*, 213.

20. Whitehead, *Modes of Thought*, 14.

21. Whitehead, *Modes of Thought*, 25.

22. It is referred to as contributionism in that all meaning and value is ultimately based on an entity's "contribution" to the divine life. In several articles, scholars have sought to respond to Palmer's criticisms from within the contributionist framework. See the exchange between Palmer, Cobb, and Dombrowski: John B. Cobb Jr., "Palmer on Whitehead: A Critical Evaluation." *Process Studies* 33 (2004):

4–23; Daniel A. Dombrowski, "The Replaceability Argument." *Process Studies* 30 (2001): 22–35; Clare Palmer, "Response to Cobb and Menta," *Process Studies* 33 (2004): 46–70.

23. Whitehead, *Modes of Thought*, 109.

24. Whitehead, *Modes of Thought*, 111.

25. Whitehead, *Modes of Thought*, 116–17.

26. A complete analysis of this claim would require a more thorough analysis of Whitehead's conception of individuality, particularly the relationship between the subject and the superject. See the introduction and chapter six in this volume for more on this important topic. How one resolves this relationship significantly affects how one interprets Whitehead's axiology and moral philosophy. In contrast to the "classical interpretation" of Whitehead's work, which insists on a sharp ontological distinction between the subject and the superject, I defend what I refer to as the "ecstatic interpretation" of Whitehead's metaphysics. See *The Ethics of Creativity*, especially 41–65; and Brian G. Henning, "Saving Whitehead's Universe of Value: An 'Ecstatic' Challenge to the Classical Interpretation," *International Philosophical Quarterly* 45 (2005): 447–66.

27. Whitehead, *Modes of Thought*, 109.

28. Whitehead, *Science and the Modern World*, 194.

29. Whitehead, *Process and Reality*, 29.

30. Whitehead, *Modes of Thought*, 111.

31. John O'Neill, "The Varieties of Intrinsic Value," *The Monist* 75 (1992): 119.

32. O'Neill, "Varieties," 120.

33. O'Neill, "Varieties," 120.

34. Whitehead, "Immortality," 687.

35. Whitehead, "Immortality," 119–20.

36. Whitehead, *Modes of Thought*, 111.

37. See, e.g., Andrew Light, "Contemporary Environmental Ethics: From Metaethics to Public Philosophy," *Metaphilosophy* 33 (2002): 426–49; Bruce Morito, "Intrinsic Value: A Modern Albatross for the Ecological Approach," *Environmental Values* 12 (2003): 317–36; Bryan G. Norton, "Why I Am Not a Nonanthropocentrist: Callicott and the Failure of Monistic Inherentism," *Environmental Ethics* 17 (1995): 341–58; Anthony Weston, "Beyond Intrinsic Value: Pragmatism in Environmental Ethics," in *Environmental Pragmatism*, ed. Andrew Light and Eric Katz (London: Routledge, 1996), 285–306; and Katie McShane, "Why Environmental Ethics Shouldn't Give Up on Intrinsic Value," *Environmental Ethics* 29 (2007): 43–61.

38. Weston, "Beyond Intrinsic Value," 333.

39. McShane, "Why Environmental Ethics," 44.

40. McShane, "Why Environmental Ethics," 45.

41. McShane, "Why Environmental Ethics," 46.

42. G. E. Moore Moore, *Principia Ethica*, ed. Thomas Baldwin, revised ed. (Cambridge: Cambridge University Press, [1903] 1993), 236.

43. McShane, "Why Environmental Ethics," 59.

44. Quoted in McShane, "Why Environmental Ethics," 45.

45. McShane, "Why Environmental Ethics" 45.

46. Alfred North Whitehead, *Essays in Science and Philosophy* (New York: Philosophical Library, 1947), 3.

47. McShane, "Why Environmental Ethics," 45–46.

48. Here and throughout, I draw a distinction between pragmatism as the school of thought inspired by classical American philosophers such as Peirce, James, and Dewey, and environmental pragmatists. The current volume is deeply sympathetic with many aspects of classical American pragmatism, especially the work of Peirce and James, but is in nearly complete disagreement with environmental pragmatism. See chapter eight.

49. For Newton and most early scientists, to discover a law, such as the law of gravity or the laws of motion, is to discover a necessary and unchanging description of the behavior of natural bodies. Subsequent investigation has revealed that, while Newton's laws are very useful approximations when dealing with large bodies, his accounts are inadequate in describing the behavior of things that are extremely small (e.g., subatomic particles) or very fast. For the former one needs quantum mechanics, and for the latter one requires relativity theory. With Whitehead, I hold that "the laws of nature are merely all-pervading patterns of behaviour, of which the shift and discontinuance lie beyond our ken" (Whitehead, *Modes*, 143). "These special forms of order exhibit no final necessity whatsoever. The laws of nature are forms of activity which happen to prevail within the vast epoch of activity which we dimly discern" (87).

50. Whitehead, *Modes of Thought*, 14.

51. Whitehead, *Modes of Thought*, 13.

52. Whitehead, *Modes of Thought*, 87; see also 143 and 155.

53. Whitehead, *Adventures of Ideas*, 292.

54. See, "The notion of the unqualified stability of particular laws of nature and of particular moral codes is a primary illusion which has vitiated much philosophy" (Whitehead, *Modes*, 13).

55. Whitehead, *Adventures of Ideas*, 290

56. See David Hume, *Enquiry Concerning Human Understanding* (Cambridge: Hackett, 1993). See also Whitehead, *Modes*, 13, 87, 143; and Whitehead, *Adventures of Ideas*, 41–42.

57. Whitehead, *Adventures of Ideas*, 269. "For after all, we can aim at nothing except from the standpoint of a well-assimilated system of customs—that is, of *mores*. The fortunate changes are made 'Hand in hand, with wand'ring steps and slow'" (Whitehead, *Adventures of Ideas*, 269). Though Whitehead is primarily concerned with the exaggeration of the status of moral codes of behavior, his criticisms would seem to equally apply to a conception of morality grounded in categorical imperatives. Though I would hesitate to adopt such language, one might say that

for Whitehead all imperatives are ultimately hypothetical. For a more developed discussion of this view and the relationship between a Whiteheadian moral philosophy and deontology, see Lango, "Does Whitehead's Metaphysics?"; and Henning, *Ethics of Creativity*, especially chapters five and seven.

58. Whitehead, *Adventures of Ideas*, 268.

59. Whitehead, *Adventures of Ideas*, 274.

60. Whitehead, *Adventures of Ideas*, 269.

61. John F. Haught, *God After Darwin: A Theology of Evolution*, 2nd ed. (Boulder, CO: Westview Press, 2008).

62. The scope of direct moral concern refers to those individuals (moral patients) whom moral agents ought to, for their own sake, consider in their moral deliberations and whom are owed direct moral duties.

63. Whitehead, *Modes of Thought*, 14–15.

64. See Henning, *Ethics of Creativity*, chapter seven.

65. Whitehead, *Modes, of Thought* 15.

66. Whitehead, *Adventures of Ideas*, 17–18.

67. John Lachs, "Good Enough," *Journal of Speculative Philosophy* (2009): 1.

68. Lachs, "Good Enough," 7.

69. Lachs, "Good Enough," 2.

70. Lachs, "Good Enough," 2.

71. My thanks to David Kovacs for his help with this argument.

72. Martin Luther King Jr., "I Have a Dream" (Lincoln Memorial, Washington DC, August 28, 1963), in *I Have a Dream: Writings and Speeches that Changed the World*, ed. James M. Washington (San Francisco: Harper Collins, 1986), 102.

73. See chapter eight of this volume on environmental pragmatism.

74. Lachs, "Good Enough," 5.

75. Dalai Lama, *Ethics for the New Millennium* (New York: Riverhead, 1999), 52.

76. Dalai Lama, *Ethics for the New Millennium*, 124.

77. Dalai Lama, *Ethics for the New Millennium*, 130.

78. Dalai Lama, *Ethics for the New Millennium*, 197

79. An anonymous reviewer provides a helpful reminder that it is important not to take this discussion of ideals as too individualistic. "Ideals are always embedded in societal processes and for W[hitehead] it is clear that whether an ideal was good or not is mostly as post-hoc evaluation possible, although anticipation plays a role and the responsibility of estimating consequences and implications as well. In any choice there is always a risk, because all the factors cannot be taken into account."

80. I explore this unique form of teleology in the work of Charles Sanders Peirce and Whitehead in chapter seven of this volume.

81. Whitehead, *Modes of Thought*, 14.

82. Alfred North Whitehead, *The Aims of Education and Other Essays* (New York: Free Press, 1929), 292.

83. Whitehead, *Modes of Thought*, 13.

84. Whitehead, *Adventures of Ideas*, 269, emphasis added.

85. Whitehead, *Adventures of Ideas*, 269.

86. Whitehead, *Adventures of Ideas*, 269.

87. Whitehead, *Adventures of Ideas*, 264.

88. Whitehead, *Adventures of Ideas*, 269.

89. William James, "The Moral Philosopher and the Moral Life," in *The Will to Believe and Other Essays in Popular Philosophy* (New York: Dover [1891] 1956), 184.

90. Whitehead, *Modes of Thought*, 14–15, emphasis added.

91. Whitehead, *Adventures of Ideas*, 17–18.

92. King Jr., 102, emphasis added.

93. King Jr., 102.

94. Martin Luther King, "Letter from Birmingham Jail," in *I Have a Dream: Writings and Speeches That Changed the World* (San Francisco: HarperCollins, 1986), 86.

95. Whitehead, *Adventures of Ideas*, 257.

96. Whitehead, *Adventures of Ideas*, 89. There is an unexpected and interesting historical connection between Whitehead and King. King, it turns out, was intimately familiar with Whitehead's work from his graduate studies at Boston University. For more on this, see Brian Henning, "A. N. Whitehead's Influence on Martin Luther King Jr.," Whitehead Research Project, accessed January 7, 2023, http://whitehead-research.org/2022/01/17/a-n-whiteheads-influence-on-martin-luther-king-jr/.

Chapter 3

1. Kenneth Goodpaster. "On Being Morally Considerable," *The Journal of Philosophy* 22 (1978): 308–25.

2. J. Baird Callicott, "Intrinsic Value, Quantum Theory, and Environmental Ethics," *Environmental Ethics* 7, no. 3 (1985): 271.

3. Immanuel Kant, *Groundwork of the Metaphysics of Morals* (New York: Harper Torchbooks, 1964).

4. Kant, *Groundwork*, 4:428.

5. J. Baird Callicott, "Non-Anthropocentric Value Theory and Environmental Ethics," *American Philosophical Quarterly* 21, no. 4 (1984): 305.

6. Rolston, *Environmental Ethics*, 113.

7. Rolston, *Environmental Ethics*, 110. Callicott notes that he is quite careful to avoid equating valuing with preferring, see his, *Beyond the Land Ethic*, 49–51, 358–60.

8. David Hume, *A Treatise of Human Nature* (New York: Penguin, 1969), 523, emphases added. See chapter one of Henning, *Ethics of Creativity*, for a more complete treatment of Hume in particular and modern axiology in general.

9. Holmes Rolston III, "Is There An Environmental Ethic?" *Ethics* 18, no. 2 (1975): 93–109. Hartshorne beat him by one year.

10. Rolston, *Environmental Ethics*, 27.

11. Rolston, *Environmental Ethics*, 222.

12. Rolston, *Environmental Ethics*, 208.

13. See Rolston, *Environmental Ethics*, 215: "Resolute subjectivists cannot, however, be defeated by argument, although they can perhaps be driven toward analyticity. One can always hold on to the claim that value, like a tickle or remorse, must be felt to be there. Its *esse* is *percipi*. Nonsensed value is nonsense. It is impossible by argument to dislodge anyone firmly entrenched in this belief. That theirs is a retreat to definition is difficult to expose, because here they seem to cling so closely to inner experience. They are reporting, on this hand, how values always touch us. They are giving, on that hand, a stipulative definition. That is how they choose to use the world value."

14. Eileen Crist, *Abundant Earth: Toward an Ecological Civilization* (Chicago: University of Chicago Press, 2019), 2–3.

15. Crist, *Abundant Earth*, 45.

16. See Tom Regan, *The Case For Animal Rights* (Berkeley: University of California Press, 1983).

17. J. Baird Callicott, *In Defense of the Land Ethic: Essays in Environmental Philosophy* (Albany: SUNY Press, 1989),165.

18. Callicott, *In Defense of the Land Ethic*, 166.

19. Callicott, *In Defense of the Land Ethic*, 167.

20. Armstrong, "Whitehead's Metaphysical," 246.

21. The modifier "incomplete" here is referencing the fact that quantum theory is not complete. Physics is still in pursuit of a "unified theory" that would make sense of and provide a consistent account of the strange world of the subatomic and the large scale of massive bodies.

22. See McHenry, *Event Universe*.

23. See Whitehead, *Process and Reality*, 160: "In contrast to Hume, the philosophy of organism keeps 'this stone as grey' in the datum for experience in question. It is, in fact, the 'objective datum' of a certain physical feeling, belonging to a derivative type in a late phase of a concrescence. But this doctrine fully accepts Descartes' discovery that subjective experiencing is the primary metaphysical situation which is presented to metaphysics for analysis. This doctrine is the 'reformed subjectivist principle,' mentioned earlier in this chapter. Accordingly, the notion 'this stone as grey' is a derivative abstraction, necessary as an element in the description of the fundamental experiential feeling, but delusive as a metaphysical starting-point. This derivative abstraction is called an 'objectification.'"

24. Whitehead, *Process and Reality*, 166.

25. Whitehead, *Process and Reality*, 29. Whitehead relates this position to Kant's transcendental philosophy in the following manner: "The philosophy of organism is the inversion of Kant's philosophy. *The Critique of Pure Reason* describes the process by which subjective data pass into the appearance of an objective world. The philosophy of organism seeks to describe how objective data pass into subjective

satisfaction, and how order in the objective data provides intensity in the subjective satisfaction. For Kant, the world emerges from the subject; for the philosophy of organism, the subject emerges from the world—a 'superject' rather than a 'subject.' The world 'object' thus means an entity which is a potentiality for being a component in feeling; and the world 'subject' means the entity constituted by the process of feeling, and including this process" (Whitehead, *Process and Reality*, 88).

26. Whitehead, *Concept of Nature*, 26.

27. As I argue in chapter four, Armstrong is wrong to see points of tension between Aldo Leopold's land ethic (a version of which both Callicott and Rolston defend) and Whitehead's system.

28. In the introduction to this volume, I suggest that the first article on environmental ethics may in fact have been published by Charles Hartshorne. Charles Hartshorne, "Beyond Enlightened Self-Interest: A Metaphysics of Ethics," *Ethics* 84 (1974): 210–16.

29. Rolston, *Environmental Ethics*, 105.

30. Rolston, *Environmental Ethics*, 106. It is important to note that neither Rolston nor Whitehead need to defend the stronger metaphysical claim that it is impossible for machines to have their own telos and, therefore, objective intrinsic value. It is theoretically possible that someday a machine will exist that is not just a good of our kind but with aims and needs and purposes of its own, at which time it will have and become a good of its own kind. Indeed, for Whitehead, it is important not to create a metaphysical bifurcation by insisting that machines cannot have intrinsic value or a telos. Rather, what is being defended is the weaker but still important claim that no machines currently in existence have purposes or ends of their own. Thus, no machines currently in existence have intrinsic value.

31. A number of environmental ethicists recover teleology. A notable example is biocentrists such as Paul W. Taylor, *Respect for Nature: A Theory of Environmental Ethics* (Princeton: Princeton University Press, 1986); and Gary Varner, *In Nature's Interests?: Interests, Animal Rights, and Environmental Ethics* (Oxford: Oxford University Press, 1998).

32. Holmes Rolston III, "Caring for Nature: From Fact to Value, From Respect to Reverence," *Zygon* 39, no. 2 (2004): 288. "This information is a modern equivalent of what Aristotle called formal and final causes; it gives the organism a telos, 'end,' a kind of (nonfelt) purpose. Organisms have ends, although not always ends-in-view" (Rolston, *Environmental* Ethics, 98).

33. Rolston, *Environmental Ethics*, 56.

34. See also chapter seven of this volume on teleology.

35. Rolston, *Environmental Ethics*, 195–97. See also Holmes Rolston III, *Three Big Bangs: Matter-Energy, Life, Mind, Book, Whole* (New York: Columbia University Press, 2010), especially, 11, 14–24, 32.

36. Rolston, *Three Big Bangs*.

37. Rolston does seem to embrace a form of emergence theory, though it is not systematically developed. See Rolston, *Three Big Bangs*, 8, 36, 45, 103, 109, 116, 121.

38. Holmes Rolston III. "Perpetual Perishing, Perpetual Renewal," *The Northern Review* 28 (2008): 113.

39. Holmes Rolston III, "Value in Nature and the Nature of Value," in *Philosophy and the Natural Environment*, ed. Robin Attfield and Andrew Belsey (Cambridge: Cambridge University Press, 1994), 17.

40. Rolston, "Value in Nature and the Nature of Value," 17.

41. Rolston, *Environmental Ethics*, 107.

42. See this volume, page 16.

43. Whitehead, *Process and Reality*, 228.

44. Rolston, "Value in Nature and the Nature of Value," 24.

45. See the editors' introduction for more information about the nature of these lecture notes. Alfred North Whitehead, *The Harvard Lectures of Alfred North Whitehead, 1924–1925: Philosophical Presuppositions of Science*, eds. Paul A. Bogaard and Jason Bell (Edinburgh: Edinburgh University Press, 2017).

46. Whitehead, *The Harvard Lectures of Alfred North Whitehead, 1924–1925*, 135. We also know from his course gradebook that in the 1930s Whitehead listed both of these books as assigned reading for his PHIL3b class (e.g., 1936–1937, 299).

47. Because these are the lecture notes of colleagues and students, they are understandably fragmentary by nature. After all, the intended audience for the notes was no one but the notetaker. Also, according to the editorial conventions of the Critical Edition of Whitehead, only items in angular brackets (i.e., "⟨") are added by the editors. All other items, such as double underlining and square brackets, are in the original.

48. Whitehead, *The Harvard Lectures of Alfred North Whitehead, 1924–1925*, 135

49. It is a terrible thing to realize that Whitehead's 1884 dissertation does not seem to have survived.

50. Whitehead, *The Harvard Lectures of Alfred North Whitehead, 1924–1925*, 141.

51. Whitehead, *The Harvard Lectures of Alfred North Whitehead, 1924–1925*, 461.

52. Whitehead, *The Harvard Lectures of Alfred North Whitehead, 1924–1925*, 461.

53. Whitehead, *Science and the Modern World*, 206.

54. Whitehead, *Science and the Modern World*, 207. This is the passage to which Hargrove was referring when he said Whitehead could have been an inspiration for Leopold's "biotic community." See pg XX in the introduction to this volume.

55. Whitehead, *The Harvard Lectures of Alfred North Whitehead, 1924–1925*, 461, 115.

56. Rolston, "Value in Nature and the Nature of Value," 23.

57. Holmes Rolston III, "The Land Ethic at the Turn of the Millennium," *Biodiversity and Conservation* 9 (2000): 1051.

58. Rolston, "Value in Nature and the Nature of Value," 25. See also Rolston, "The Land Ethic," 1049: "Ethicists, sometimes encouraged by biologists, may think ecosystems are just epiphenomenal aggregations. This is a confusion. Any level is real if there is significant downward causation. Thus the atom is real because that pattern shapes the behavior of electrons; the cell because that pattern shapes the behaviour of ammo [*sic*] acids; the organism because that pattern coordinates the behavior of hearts and lungs; the community because the niche shapes the morphology and behavior of the foxes within it. Being real requires an organization that shapes the existence and the behavior of member/parts. A complex system, such as an ecosystem, is one whose properties are not fully explained by an understanding of its components."

59. Rolston, *Environmental Ethics*, 172–73.

60. As Daniel Dombrowski kindly reminds me, in the *Sophist* Plato (unfortunately) says *eite* (or) rather than *kai* (and) in that being either exerts influence *or* is influenced by others, where we here would use "and."

61. Rolston, "The Land Ethic," 1049.

62. Rolston, *Environmental Ethics*, 172.

63. Rolston, *Environmental Ethics*, 199.

64. Whitehead, *Process and Reality*, 21.

65. Rolston, "Value in Nature and the Nature of Value," 29–30.

66. Rolston, "Caring for Nature," 289, emphases added; see also, 300: "If anything at all on Earth is sacred, it must be this enthralling creativity that characterizes our home planet. If anywhere, here is the brooding Spirit of God." See also Rolston, "Value in Nature and the Nature of Value," 28: "The creativity within the natural system we inherit, and the values this generates, are the ground of our being, not just the ground under our feet. Earth could be the ultimate object of duty, short of God, if God exists."

67. Holmes Rolston III, "Ecology: A Primer for Christian Ethics," *Journal of Catholic Social Thought* 4, no. 2 (2007): 307.

68. Rolston, *Environmental Ethics*, 188; see also, 187: "Neither of these traditional terms [intrinsic and instrumental value] is completely satisfactory at the level of the holistic ecosystem. Member components serve the system, as when warblers regulate insect populations; perhaps that is systemic instrumental value. But—if we reconsider this terminology—the decentered system, despite its successions and headings, has no integrated program, nothing it is defending, and to say that an ecosystem makes instrumental use of warblers to regulate insect populations seems

awkward. We might say that the system itself has intrinsic value; it is, after all, the womb of life. Yet again, the 'loose' system, though it has value in itself, does not seem to have any value for itself, as organisms do seem to have. It is not a value owner, though it is a value producer. It is not a value beholder; it is a value holder in the sense that it projects, conserves, elaborates value holders (organisms)."

69. Whitehead, *Modes*, 111.

70. Whitehead, *Modes*, 116–17.

71. Rolston, "Value in Nature and the Nature of Value," 25. See also Rolston, *Environmental Ethics*, 198: "From a short-range, subjective perspective we can say that the value of nature lies in its generation and support of human life and is therefore only instrumental. But from a longer-range, objective perspective systemic nature is valuable intrinsically as a projective system, with humans only one sort of its projects, though perhaps the highest. The system is of value for its capacity to throw forward (pro-ject) all the storied natural history. On that scale humans come late and it seems shortsighted and arrogant to say that the system is only of instrumental value for humans, who alone possess intrinsic value, or who "project" intrinsic value back to nature. Both of these are inappropriate responses. The only fully responsible behavior is to seek an appropriate relationship to the parental environment, which is projecting all this display of value."

72. Rolston, *Environmental Ethics*, 217–18.

73. Holmes Rolston III, "Are Values in Nature Subjective or Objective?" *Environmental Ethics* 4 (1982): 150.

74. Whitehead, *Process and Reality*, 148; see also, 50: "The principle of universal relativity directly traverses Aristotle's dictum, 'A substance is not present in a subject.' On the contrary, according to this principle an actual entity *is* present in other actual entities. In fact if we allow for degrees of relevance, and for negligible relevance, we must say that every actual entity is present in every other actual entity. The philosophy of organism is mainly devoted to the task of making clear the notion of 'being present in another entity.' This phrase is here borrowed from Aristotle: it is not a fortunate phrase, and in subsequent discussion it will be replaced by the term 'objectification.' "

75. Rolston, *Environmental Ethics*, 120–21. Rolston warns, "that is only an intuitive scale; it will need to be corrected by the detailed descriptions of biological science." A more complete account of a hierarchy is in Rolston, *Environmental Ethics*, 223–24.

76. Rolston, *Environmental Ethics*, 191.

77. Rolston, "Value in Nature and the Nature of Value," 19.

78. See also chapter six of this volume on substance and individuals.

79. Samuel Alexander, *Space, Time, and Deity*, vol. 2 (New York: Macmillan, [1920] 1966), 236.

80. Alexander, *Space, Time, and Deity*, 237–38.

81. Alexander, *Space, Time, and Deity*, 238.

82. Alexander, *Space, Time, and Deity*, 240–41. He continues: "By collective mind I do not mean a new mind, which is the mind of a group. There is no sufficient evidence that such a mind exists. It is but a short symbol for that co-operation and conflict of many minds which produces standards of approval or disapproval."

83. Alexander argued that, properly speaking, values cannot be considered as qualities because they inhere neither in the object nor in the subject. Rather, they are *subject-object determinations* of a new character of reality, "which arise through the combination of mind with its object" to form a compound whole (Alexander, *Space, Time, and Deity*, 244.). For an excellent discussion of Whitehead's position and its rejection of primary, secondary, and tertiary qualities, see Barbara Muraca, "Relational Values: A Whiteheadian Alternative for Environmental Philosophy and Global Environmental Justice," *Balkan Journal of Philosophy* VIII, no. 1 (2016): 19–38.

84. Whitehead, *Concept of Nature*, 29.

85. Holmes Rolston III, "F/Actual Knowing: Putting Facts and Values in Place," *Ethics & the Environment* 10, no. 2 (2005): 167.

86. Rolston, "F/Actual Knowing," 150.

Chapter 4

1. Leopold, *A Sand County Almanac*, 224.

2. Leopold, *A Sand County Almanac*, 203.

3. John Locke, *Second Treatise of Government*, edited by C. B. Macpherson (Indianapolis: Hackett, 1980 [1690]), sec. 36.

4. Leopold, *A Sand County Almanac*, 216.

5. See page X.

6. Leopold, *A Sand County Almanac*, 204.

7. Leopold, *A Sand County Almanac*, 204.

8. White, "Historical Roots," 1206, emphasis in original.

9. Whitehead, *Process and Reality*, 105.

10. Leopold, *A Sand County Almanac*, 224.

11. Leopold, *A Sand County Almanac*, 224.

12. Leopold, *A Sand County Almanac*, 224–25.

13. Armstrong, "Whitehead's Metaphysical System," 257–58.

14. The concern, as Dombrowski notes and Edwards repeats, is that "this conception deprives individuals of any value except as they contribute to the biotic community . . . and it grants no additive value to rationality or even to sentiency except as they might contribute to the community" (Daniel A. Dombrowski, *Hartshorne and the Metaphysics of Animal Rights* [Albany: SUNY Press, 1988], 47). Edwards repeats this claim, continuing, "land ethics turns unique, conscious, self-valuing individuals into mere means to the ends of a greater biosphere that

is not a conscious individual and has no ends" (Rem B. Edwards, *An Axiological Process Ethics* [Claremont, CA: Process Century, 2014], 88).

15. Whitehead, *Religion in the Making*, 105.

16. Whitehead, *Adventures of Ideas*, 265.

17. Whitehead, *Adventures of Ideas*, 268.

18. Whitehead, *Modes of Thought*, 119.

19. See chapter two, section 1 on value for a discussion of Schilpp's and Palmer's respective critiques of Whitehead.

20. Schilpp, "Whitehead's Moral Philosophy," 615.

21. Schilpp, "Whitehead's Moral Philosophy," 615.

22. Lynne Belaief, *Toward a Whiteheadian Ethics* (Lanham, MD: University Press of America, 1984), 53, emphasis added. Belaief reiterates this claim in "Whitehead and Private-Interest Theories," *Ethics* 76 (1996): 279.

23. Whitehead, *Adventures of Ideas*, 265; Whitehead, *Modes of Thought*, 119.

24. Donald Sherburne, in *A Whiteheadian Aesthetic* (New Haven: Yale University Press, 1961), was the first to consider Whitehead's work closely on this topic. However, Sherburne's interest is aesthetics defined primarily in terms of the evaluation of fine art, so he has little to contribute to the metaphysical status or significance of beauty within Whitehead's system overall.

25. For more on this, see Henning, *Ethics of Creativity*; and Brian G. Henning, "On the Possibility of a Whiteheadian Aesthetics of Morals," *Process Studies* 31 (2002): 97–114.

26. Whitehead, *Process and Reality*, 21.

27. Whitehead, *Modes of Thought*, 62.

28. Ferré, *Being and Value*, 340.

29. Whitehead, *Adventures of Ideas*, 252.

30. Whitehead, *Adventures of Ideas*, 252.

31. Cf. Whitehead, *Modes of Thought*, 62: "The whole displays its component parts, each with its own value enhanced; and the parts lead up to a whole, which is beyond themselves, and yet not destructive of themselves." For an eloquent and powerful discussion of the importance of intensity and contrast, see Judith Jones, *Intensity: An Essay in Whiteheadian Ontology* (Nashville: Vanderbilt University Press, 1998).

32. Whitehead, *Process and Reality*, 105

33. Whitehead, *Adventures of Ideas*, 252. For a more systematic development of Whitehead's complex conception of beauty and also its relationship to Charles Hartshorne's aesthetics, see Henning, *Ethics of Creativity*, chapter four ("Process as Kalogenic," 99–124).

34. Whitehead, *Adventures of Ideas*, 252.

35. Whitehead, *Adventures of Ideas*, 252.

36. Whitehead, *Adventures of Ideas*, 252.

37. Whitehead, *Adventures of Ideas*, 252.

38. Charles Hartshorne, "The Aesthetics of Birdsong," *The Journal of Aesthetics and Art Criticism* 26 (1968): 311. See also, 311: "On both dimensions, (1) chaos versus monotony, (2) the profound versus the superficial, beauty is the golden mean, balanced between excess of unity and excess of variety, between excess of depth and excess of superficiality." For an excellent treatment of Hartshorne's aesthetics, see Daniel A. Dombrowski, *Divine Beauty: The Aesthetics of Charles Hartshorne* (Nashville: Vanderbilt University Press, 2004).

39. A helpful way of conceiving of this is in terms of Hartshorne's aesthetic circle, a defense of which can be found in chapter four of Henning, *Ethics of Creativity*.

40. According to Hartshorne, this diagram was created by himself; Max Dessoir, whom Hartshorne describes as a German writer on aesthetics; and Kay Davis, whom Hartshorne describes as an artist and former student of his from Emory University. Charles Hartshorne, "The Kinds and Levels of Aesthetic Value," in *The Zero Fallacy and Other Essays in Neoclassical Philosophy*, ed. Mohammad Valady (Chicago: Open Court, 1997), 203–14; and Charles Hartshorne, "The Aesthetic Matrix of Value," in *Creative Synthesis and Philosophic Method* (LaSalle: Open Court, 1970), 302–22.

41. This is what Hartshorne terms the "zero fallacy." "A logical requirement of any value system is that it should clarify the idea of no value, or the value zero. I hold that, as value diminishes, its limit of zero is not in a form of existence without value, but in total nonexistence. The zero of feeling, or of intrinsic value, and of actuality are one and the same" (Hartshorne, "The Rights of the Subhuman World," 54).

42. Whitehead, *Religion in the Making*, 95. See also, 96–97: "It must be noted that the state of degradation to which evil leads, when accomplished, is not in itself evil, except by comparison with what might have been. A hog is not an evil beast, but when a man is degraded to the level of a hog, with the accompanying atrophy of finer elements, he is no more evil than a hog. The evil of the final degradation lies in the comparison of what is with what might have been. During the process of degradation the comparison is an evil for the man himself, and at its final stage it remains an evil for others."

43. I thank Vincent Colapietro for the suggestion to include this discussion of jazz.

44. Edward Green, " 'It Don't Mean a Thing If It Ain't Got That Grundgestalt!'—Ellington a Motivic Perspective," *Jazz Perspectives* 2, no. 2 (2008): 244.

45. Green, " 'It Don't Mean a Thing,' " 244.

46. Green, " 'It Don't Mean a Thing,' " 222.

47. Green, " 'It Don't Mean a Thing,' " 245.

48. Edward Green, "A Note on Two Conceptions of Aesthetic Realism," *British Journal of Aesthetics* 45, no. 4 (2005): 439. Green describes Siegel in the following manner: "After being awarded *The Nation's* esteemed prize for poetry in 1925, Eli Siegel moved from Baltimore to New York and was active in jazz circles. In 1935, he became the first coordinator of jazz and poetry events at the Village Vanguard"

(Green, " 'It Don't Mean a Thing,' " 221n20). The Aesthetic Realism Foundation in New York City is dedicated to the study of Siegel's work (http://www.aesthetic-realism.org/). A short biography of Siegel can be found on their website at http://www.aestheticrealism.org/Siegel-Biography.html.

49. Eli Siegel, *Aesthetic Realism: Three Instances* (New York: The Terrain Gallery & Definition Press, 1961), 6–7.

50. Eli Siegel, "The Aesthetic Center," *Definition* 10 (1962). Siegel describes dance in the following manner: "A coalition and continuity accompanied by details in motion are what one finds in a dance. There is idea in a dance, modern or ancient. The idea is the continuing thing, the same thing—made one, through being its lively self, by the steps, the motions, the attitudes, the gestures, the pauses as detail. A dance, too, shows the oneness and manyness of anything that is real; that is, of anything" (Eli Siegel, "Art & Your Life: The Same Subject," *The Right of Aesthetic Realism to Be Known*, no. 1686 [2007], http://www.aestheticrealism.net/tro/tro1686.html).

51. Green, " 'It Don't Mean a Thing,' " 223.

52. Eli Siegel, "Ugliness & Beauty in Oneness," *The Right of Aesthetic Realism to Be Known*, no. 1691 (May 2, 2007), https://aestheticrealism.net/tro/ugliness-beauty-appreciation/.

53. Whitehead, *Process and Reality*, 21.

54. Whitehead, *Modes of Thought*, 60.

55. Whitehead, *Modes of Thought*, 62.

56. Whitehead, *Modes of Thought*, 60.

57. Whitehead, *Adventures of Ideas*, 285.

58. Whitehead, *Adventures of Ideas*, 285.

59. Whitehead, *Adventures of Ideas*, 285.

60. Whitehead, *Process and Reality*, 105.

61. James, "The Moral Philosopher," 202.

62. Whitehead, *Process and Reality*, 105.

63. Whitehead, *Adventures of Ideas*, 268.

64. In *Ethics of Creativity*, I seek to systematically develop an organic ethical paradigm grounded in Whitehead's rich aesthetico-metaphysics of process by developing the moral implications of a kalocentric conception of reality. Our most basic moral obligation, I argue, is the "obligation of beauty," or the obligation to act in such a way to affirm the greatest possible universe of beauty, value, and importance that we can see (see *Ethics of Creativity*, 146).

Chapter 5

1. Plumwood, *Feminism*, 130.
2. Rodman, "Four Forms," 125.

3. Devall and Sessions, *Deep Ecology*, 236.

4. See John B. Cobb Jr., "Protestant theology and deep ecology," in *Deep Ecology and World Religions*, ed. David Landhis Barnhill and Roger S. Gottlieb (Albany: SUNY Press), 224–25: "We do know that human beings are capable of remarkable scope and depth of experience, and that, accordingly, human experience often has great intrinsic value. Other creatures that are like us in relevant respects, we judge, also have rich experience and thus great intrinsic value. But our judgment is about the probable richness of experience of other animals, not about the similarity of their experience to our own. Because of our limited imagination, this judgment may be distorted by similarities. We may underestimate the richness of a dolphin's experience and overestimate that of a monkey because the latter is more like us. But this would be an error in judgment; it is not built into the basis for judgment." See also, 227–28: "As a Protestant process theologian I reject anthropocentrism in the following ways. 1. God cares for all creatures, not just for human beings, and human beings should follow in that universal care. 2. The value of other creatures is not limited to their value for us. Their value for God, for one another, and for themselves is also important. Human values should sometimes be sacrificed for the sake of others. . . . As a process Protestant theologian, I retain what deep ecologists call anthropocentrism in the following respects. 1. In all probability individual human beings are the greatest embodiments of intrinsic value on the Earth. 2. Human beings have a responsibility for other creatures in a way that is shared by no other species. . . . 3. In order to exercise our responsibility well, we must make judgments of relative value about other creatures."

5. This is similar to the distinction drawn by Tom Regan, but ultimately it is different in that it does not use the same neo-Kantian framework. "Inherent value" is ultimately not defined in the same way, for Griffin. David Ray Griffin, *Whitehead's Radically Different Postmodern Philosophy: An Argument for Its Contemporary Relevance* (Albany: SUNY Press, 2007).

6. This claim is vaguely similar to Holmes Rolston's position in *Environmental Ethics* (1988).

7. Cf. Griffin, *Whitehead's Radically Different*, 83: "The central implication of this terminological discussion is that a rough equality in the inherent value of the various species results from an inverse relation that exists, in general, between intrinsic value and ecological value. . . . [A]ssuming that this inverse correlation generally obtains throughout the ecological pyramid, we can say that *all forms of life have, roughly, the same inherent value.*" See also, 83: "The distinctive point of egalitarian deep ecology is, therefore, compatible with the Whiteheadian emphasis on many different levels of intrinsic value."

8. For more on this important point, see chapter two on Whitehead's triadic theory of value and chapter three for its relationship to Rolston's similar but distinctive triadic axiology.

9. Rolston, *Environmental Ethics*, 65.

10. Aristotle, *The Complete Works of Aristotle* (Princeton: Princeton University Press, 1984); Artistotle, *Politics* 1256b15–25.

11. Aristotle, *Politics* 1256b15–25.

12. Aristotle, *Politics* 1.3–7.

13. For a catalog of these and other Aristotelian claims, see Cynthia Freeland, "Nourishing Speculation: A Feminist Reading of Aristotelian Science," in *Engendering Origins: Critical Feminist Readings in Plato and Aristotle*, ed. Bat-Ami Bar On (Albany: SUNY Press), 145–46.

14. Whitehead, *Process and Reality*, 22.

15. Whitehead, *Process and Reality*, 110

16. Whitehead, *Adventures of Ideas*, 275.

17. Whitehead, *Process and Reality*, 222.

18. Whitehead, *Religion in the Making*, 96–97.

19. Henning, *Ethics of Creativity*, 115.

20. Whitehead, *Religion in the Making*, 103.

21. See, for example, Whitehead, *Process and Reality*, 99, 103, 111–12, 114–15; Whitehead, *Adventures of Ideas*, 205–7; Whitehead, *Modes of Thought*, 7, 24–28, 157–59.

22. Whitehead, *Modes of Thought*, 27.

23. Whitehead, *Modes of Thought*, 27.

24. This example is taken from Brian G. Henning, "From Exception to Exemplification: Understanding the Debate Over Darwin," in *Genesis, Evolution, and the Search for a Reasoned Faith* (Winona, MN: Anselm Academic, 2011), 73–98.

25. Whitehead, *Process and Reality*, 179.

26. Warren, *Ecofeminist Philosophy*, 46. According to Warren, "a conceptual framework is a set of basic beliefs, values, attitudes, and assumptions which shape and reflect how one views oneself and one's world. A conceptual framework functions as a socially constructed lens through which one perceives reality. It is affected and shaped by such factors as sex-gender, race/ethnicity, class, age, affectional orientation, marital status, religion, nationality, colonial influences, and culture" (Karen J. Warren, *Ecofeminist Philosophy: A Western Perspective on What It Is and Why It Matters* [New York: Roman and Littlefield, 2000], 46.

27. Warren, *Ecofeminist Philosophy*, 46.

28. Warren, *Ecofeminist Philosophy*, 46, emphasis in original.

29. Warren, *Ecofeminist Philosophy*, 46.

30. Warren, *Ecofeminist Philosophy*, 46.

31. Warren, *Ecofeminist Philosophy*, 47.

32. Warren, *Ecofeminist Philosophy*, 47.

33. Warren states, "The privileges of driving a car, taking out a home equity loan, living in high-income housing areas, or attending a college of one's choice

should belong to those who qualify. Sometimes small privileges are given to Downs (e.g., to house slaves or middle-class housewives) to keep them from challenging the power and privilege of Ups" (Warren, *Ecofeminist Philosophy*, 47).

34. Warren, *Ecofeminist Philosophy*, 47.

35. Warren, *Ecofeminist Philosophy*, 47.

36. Warren, *Ecofeminist Philosophy*, 47.

37. Warren, *Ecofeminist Philosophy*, 47, emphasis in original.

38. Warren, *Ecofeminist Philosophy*, 47.

39. Warren, *Ecofeminist Philosophy*, 47.

40. Warren distinguishes oppression from domination in the following way: "By contrast, not all domination involves oppression. This is basically because oppression limits choices and options. So it is only beings who can meaningfully be spoken as "having options" who also can meaningfully be said to be oppressed. Since I assume that from a Western philosophical perspective trees, rivers, mountains, communities of flora and fauna, species, and ecosystems are not the sort of things that make choices or have options, I assume that they cannot be oppressed. But they can be dominated" (Warren, *Ecofeminist Philosophy*, 55).

41. This phrase is often attributed to the character of Uncle Ben or the character of Aunt May from the *Spiderman* comics and movie. However, versions of it can be found much earlier. For instance, see "Tammany Is Satisfied," *New York Times*, November 15, 1892, https://www.nytimes.com/1892/11/15/archives/tammany-is-satisfied-mr-gilroy-interviewed-at-neworleans-democratic.html.

42. Warren, *Ecofeminist Philosophy*, 47.

43. As Whitehead says, "philosophy destroys its usefulness when it indulges in brilliant feats of explaining away" (*Process and Reality*, 17).

44. Warren, *Ecofeminist Philosophy*, 47.

45. Warren, *Ecofeminist Philosophy*, 47.

46. Warren, *Ecofeminist Philosophy*, 48, emphases added.

47. Whitehead, *Modes of Thought*, 3–4.

48. Whitehead's choice of the term "civilization" is likely to be seen as problematic by many contemporary scholars aware of the abhorrent uses of the term in justifying the wholesale genocide of Indigenous peoples. At times Whitehead's Victorian upbringing does seem to lead him uncritically to adopt a problematic use of the term. However, a systematic study of the term throughout his corpus also reveals that for him the term did not ultimately or primarily refer to a colonial Western mindset and values, but rather is another word for what Whitehead regularly refers to as "beauty." See chapter four of this volume for more on this important concept for the philosophy of organism.

49. Whitehead, *Modes of Thought*, 14–15.

50. Rolston, *Environmental Ethics*, 73.

51. Henning, *Ethics of Creativity*, 146.

52. This is the "obligation of beauty" in Henning, *Ethics of Creativity*; for a presentation and defense of the five obligations of beauty, see chapter five, especially 146.

53. Whitehead, *Modes of Thought*, 13–14.

54. This is the "obligation of peace" in Henning, *Ethics of Creativity*, 146, 148–49, 153, 158, 160–61.

55. Keeping in mind the claims made in the first section, this analysis is necessarily limited because it is not in the context of a concrete moral situation with a specific history, actors, and possibilities.

56. For a recording of the nightingale's song, visit The Free Sound Project: http://freesound.iua.upf.edu/samplesViewSingle.php?id=17185.

57. According to Hewson et al. (2018), nightingale populations have decreased in the UK by 61 percent in 25 years. Chris M. Hewson et al., "Estimating National Population Sizes: Methodological Challenges and Applications Illustrated in the Common Nightingale, a Declining Songbird in the UK," *Journal of Applied Ecology* 55, no. 4 (2018): 2008–18, https://doi.org/10.1111/1365-2664.13120.

58. See Christine Howard et al., "Disentangling the Relative Roles of Climate and Land Cover Change in Driving the Long-Term Population Trends of European Migratory Birds," *Diversity and Distributions* (2020). https://doi.org/10.1111/ddi.13144.

59. Note that for the purposes of this paper I will follow Andrew Smith in not making a distinction between vegetarianism, in which no animals are consumed, and veganism, in which no animals or their products are consumed. Smith's book could just as well have been called *A Critique of the Moral Defense of Veganism*.

60. See Daniel A. Dombrowski, *The Philosophy of Vegetarianism* (Amherst: University of Massachusetts Press, 1984); and *Hartshorne and the Metaphysics of Animal Rights* (Albany: SUNY Press, 1988). See also Jan Deckers, "Should Whiteheadians Be Vegetarians? A Critical Analysis of the Thoughts of Hartshorne and Dombrowski," *Journal of Animal Ethics* 1, no. 2 (2011): 195–209.

61. See Brianne Donaldson, ed., *Beyond the Bifurcation of Nature: A Common World for Animals and the Environment* (Newcastle, UK: Cambridge Scholars Press, 2015); Brianne Donaldson, *Creaturely Cosmologies: Why Metaphysics Matters for Animal and Planetary Liberation* (Lanham, MD: Lexington, 2015); and Brianne Donaldson and Christopher Carter, *The Future of Meat Without Animals* (Lanham, MD: Rowman & Littlefield, 2016). See also the special issue of the journal *Process Studies* on moral vegetarianism: *Process Studies* 42, no. 2 (2013).

62. Andrew F. Smith, *A Critique of the Moral Defense of Vegetarianism* (New York: Palgrave Macmillan, 2016), 6.

63. As I have argued elsewhere, "considering both the direct and indirect effects, the overconsumption of animal meat is now a (if not the) leading cause of or contributor to both malnourishment and obesity, chronic disease, antibiotic

resistance, and the spread of infectious disease; the livestock sector may now be the single greatest source of freshwater use and pollution, the leading cause of rainforest deforestation, and the driving force behind spiraling species extinction; finally, livestock production is among the largest sectoral sources of greenhouse gas emissions contributing to global climate change"; Henning, "Standing in Livestock's Long Shadow: The Ethics of Eating Meat on a Small Planet," *Ethics and the Environment* 16, no. 2 (Fall 2011): 64.

64. Smith, *Critique*, 5.

65. Smith, *Critique*, 5.

66. I am not sure that the sentientist would add this second sentence. The paradigmatic sentientist position would be Peter Singer's utilitarian view, which would not be able to make any categorical claims such as this. If, because of geography, health, or other considerations it was necessary to consume an animal to survive, then a utilitarian would be hard-pressed to deny it was moral. However, the categorical nature of this claim is more characteristic of what Smith calls, following Plumwood, "ontological veganism."

67. Smith, *Critique*, 12–13.

68. Smith, *Critique*, 12.

69. In collecting these rich bibliographical resources, Smith has done a great service for anyone interested in this interesting biological frontier.

70. Smith, *Critique*, 22.

71. Smith, *Critique*, 19.

72. I must admit that I see ample evidence of awareness, but little for self-awareness.

73. Smith, *Critique*, 28.

74. I tend to agree with Smith and Plumwood that "the charge of anthropomorphism may perhaps prove useful in some cases when humans fail to respect ways in which other-than-human people are indeed different. Usually, however, this charge 'begs the question of non-human minds. That has become its major function now, to bully people out of "thinking differently." It is such a highly abused concept, one often used carelessly and uncritically to allow us to avoid the hard work of scrutinizing and revealing our assumptions, that there is a good case for dropping the term completely' (Plumwood 2013, 452)" (Smith, *Critique*, 55).

75. Smith, *Critique*, 29.

76. Smith, *Critique*, 31.

77. See Brian G. Henning, "Towards 2050: The Projected Costs and Possible Alternatives to Industrial Livestock Production," in *The Future of Meat Without Animals*, ed. Brianne Donaldson and Christopher Carter (Lanham, MD: Rowman & Littlefield, 2016), 7–34. See also Henning, "Standing in Livestock's 'Long Shadow.' "

78. Smith, *Critique*, 34.

79. Smith, *Critique*, 39

80. Smith, *Critique*, 32. Smith cites Quinn's definition of "kingdomism" or humans assigning " 'a greater sacredness to members of their own kingdom (the animal kingdom) than to the plant kingdom' (Quinn 1994, 165)" (Smith, *Critique*, 96).

81. Cited in Smith, *Critique*, 42.

82. Smith, *Critique*, 43.

83. Smith, *Critique*, 44.

84. Whitehead, *Process and Reality*, 105.

85. Whitehead, *Process and Reality*, 21.

86. John B. Cobb Jr., *Is It Too Late? A Theology of Ecology* (Beverly Hills: Bruce and Glencoe, 1972). See the introductory chapter of this volume for a complete discussion of the process roots of environmental ethics.

87. Smith, *Critique*, 46.

88. See Henning, "Toward 2050" and "Standing in Livestock's 'Long Shadow.'"

89. Graham Harvey (2006), quoted in Smith, *Critique*, 53.

90. Smith, *Critique*, 57.

91. Smith, *Critique*, 57.

92. Smith, *Critique*, 63.

93. It is important to note that Smith intentionally says "who" here, not "what," because within an animist framework plants are persons, a who and not a what.

94. Smith, *Critique*, 71–72.

95. Smith, *Critique*, 86.

96. Smith, *Critique*, 97.

97. Smith, *Critique*, 98.

98. See chapter four of this volume. It should be noted that Smith's lack of engagement with the rich literature on the land ethic is disappointing to the point of being irresponsible. J. Baird Callicott has, for instance, written much on the relationship between animal ethics and Leopold's land ethic. This is a serious omission, both because of the importance of this work and because it would be a natural point of entry and comparison for his own project.

99. Smith, *Critique*, 29.

100. Of course, it is always important that a philosophy of organism not conflate actual entities with the enduring forms of order with which one interacts—indeed, which we ourselves are. Whereas fleeting atomic occasions "perpetually perish" and never really are, the patterns they create endure. As discussed in chapter six of this volume, within the philosophy of organism, all macroscopic order is social order derived from the intense, internal relations of generations of actual occasions.

101. See Dombrowski, *Hartshorne and the Metaphysics of Animal Rights*, 43.

102. See Whitehead, *Process and Reality*, 108–9; *Adventures of Ideas*, 205–26; and *Modes of Thought*, 24, 27–28.

103. Jones, *Intensity*, 103.

104. Whitehead, *Modes of Thought*, 157.

105. Whitehead, *Adventures of Ideas*, 206.

106. Smith, *Critique*, 53.

107. Whitehead, *Process and Reality*, 107.

108. Whitehead, *Process and Reality*, 107.

109. Whitehead, *Process and Reality*, 105. In context, Whitehead writes, "thus, all societies require interplay with their environment; and in the case of living societies this interplay takes the form of robbery. The living society may, or may not, be a higher type of organism than the food which it disintegrates. But whether or not it be for the general good, life is robbery. It is at this point that with life morals become acute. The robber requires justification" (Whitehead, *Process and Reality*, 105).

110. My thanks go to my friend and colleague David Kovacs, who helped me think through this argument.

111. Whitehead, *Process and Reality*, 8.

112. Henning, *Ethics of Creativity*, 169–70. I go on to provide several important qualifications to this claim.

113. For my most comprehensive treatment of this topic, see Henning, "Standing."

114. Whitehead, *Modes of Thought*, 14–15.

Chapter 6

1. Robin Wall Kimmerer, *Braiding Sweetgrass: Indigenous Wisdom, Scientific Knowledge, and the Teachings of Plants* (London: Penguin, 2020), 55.

2. Latour, *Facing Gaia*, 70. See also, 67–68: "It takes just a few moments' reflection, however, to notice that the idea of an inert world is itself *an effect of style*, a particular *genre*, a certain way of muting the agencies that we cannot prevent ourselves from proliferating as soon as we begin to describe any situation whatsoever. Speaking in a mechanical voice is still speaking. Only the tone is different, not the link of words. Similarly, the idea of a deanimated world is only a way of linking animations *as if* nothing were happening there. But agency is always there, whatever we may do."

3. Whitehead, *Process and Reality*, 50. See also Whitehead, *Science and the Modern World*, 151: "The technical phrase 'subject-object' is a bad term for the fundamental situation disclosed in experience. It is really reminiscent of the Aristotelian 'subject-predicate.' It already presupposes the metaphysical doctrine of diverse subjects qualified by their private predicates. This is the doctrine of subjects with private worlds of experience. If this be granted, there is no escape from solipsism. The point is that the phrase 'subject-object' indicates a fundamental entity underlying the objects. Thus the 'objects,' as thus conceived, are merely the ghosts of Aristotelian predicates."

4. Kimmerer, *Braiding*, 42.

5. Thomas Berry, *The Great Work: Our Way Into the Future* (New York: Broadway Books, 2000), x–xi. See also Brian Swimme and Thomas Berry, *The Universe Story: From the Primordial Flaring Forth to the Ecozoic Era—A Celebration of the Unfolding of the Cosmos* (New York: HarperOne, 1992), 243; and Thomas Berry, *Evening Thoughts: Reflections on Earth as a Sacred Community* (Berkely, CA: Counterpoint, 2015), 17–18. See chapter nine, this volume, for more on Berry and the present project.

6. Whitehead, "Objects and Subjects," 130.

7. Whitehead, *Process and Reality*, 151.

8. See Whitehead, "Objects and Subjects," 130: "I contend that the notion of mere knowledge is a high abstraction, and that conscious discrimination itself is a variable factor only present in the more elaborate examples of occasions of experience. The basis of experience is emotional. Stated more generally, the basic fact is the rise of an affective tone originating from things whose relevance is given."

9. Whitehead, "Immorality," 687.

10. Though Whitehead called his thought the "philosophy of organism," it is often referred to as "process philosophy" because it conceives of reality in terms of dynamic pulses of energy, rather than static bits of matter.

11. Alfred North Whitehead, *Science and the Modern World*, 76.

12. Internal page reference.

13. See Whitehead, *Adventure of Ideas*, 204: "An actual occasion has no [. . .] history. It never changes. It only becomes and perishes. Its perishing is its assumption of a new metaphysical function in the creative advance of the universe."

14. Clarke also objects to Whitehead's conception of God and its relation to creativity. However, this objection does not concern the present investigation directly. See W. Norris Clarke, "God and the Community of Existents: Whitehead and St. Thomas," *International Philosophical Quarterly* 158 (2000): 266–68.

15. For an extended discussion of this point, see James Felt, "Whitehead's Misconception of 'Substance' in Aristotle," *Process Studies* 14 (1985): 224–36.

16. W. Norris Clarke, *The One and The Many* (Notre Dame, IN: Notre Dame University Press, 2001), 32, emphases in original.

17. Clarke, *The One and The Many*, 32.

18. Clarke, *The One and The Many*, 33.

19. Clarke, *The One and The Many*, 129.

20. See Clarke, "God and Community," 272: "In a word, *self-identity and immutability* are not at all identical or interchangeable concepts. The self-identity of a real being is not a static, immutable 'thing' but more like an abiding force that actively assimilates and integrates all of the less-than-substantial changes which it undergoes: a unity-identity-whole that maintains itself within certain flexible limits; when these are breached, the identity collapses."

21. Clarke, *The One and The Many*, 128.

22. Clarke, *The One and The Many*, 129.

23. Clarke, *The One and The Many*, 129.

24. See Henning, *Ethics of Creativity*, chapters 2–3.

25. Clarke, *The One and The Many*, 102.

26. Clarke, *The One and The Many*, 125.

27. Clarke, "God and Community," 268.

28. Clarke, "God and Community," 276.

29. Clarke, *The One and the Many*, 102, emphasis added.

30. Whitehead, *Science and the Modern World*, 104.

31. Aristotle, *Categories* 2a15: "What is called substance most fully, primarily, and most of all, is what is neither said of any subject nor in any subject."

32. Whitehead, *Process and Reality*, 50.

33. Clarke, "God and Community," 271, emphasis added.

34. Clarke, *The One and The Many*, 136.

35. Whitehead, "Immortality," 687.

36. I explicitly examine the similarity between a society's defining characteristic and the classical notion of essential or substantial form more fully in the following sections.

37. Don Ross, James Ladyman, and David Spurrett, "In Defence of Scientism," in *Every Thing Must Go*, ed. James Ladyman and Don Ross (Oxford: Oxford University Press, 2007), 4.

38. Clarke, "God and Community," 269.

39. Whitehead, *Science and the Modern World*, 52.

40. Whitehead, *Science and the Modern World*, 52.

41. William James, *The Principles of Psychology* (Cambridge, MA: Harvard University Press, 1981 [1890]), 462. As Whitehead puts it, "We find ourselves in a buzzing world, amid a democracy of fellow creatures; whereas, under some guise or other, orthodox philosophy can only introduce us to solitary substances, each enjoying an illusory experience: 'O Bottom, thou art changed! What do I see on thee?'" (Whitehead, *Process and Reality*, 50).

42. Whitehead, *Adventures of Ideas*, 163.

43. Whitehead, *Science and the Modern World*, 52. See also Whitehead, *Process and Reality*, 79: "The simple notion of an enduring substance sustaining persistent qualities, either essentially or accidentally, expresses a useful abstract for many purposes in life. But whenever we try to use it as a fundamental statement of the nature of things, it proves itself mistaken. It arose from a mistake and has never succeeded in any of its applications. But it has had one success: it has entrenched itself in language, in Aristotelian logic, and in metaphysics. For its employment in language and in logic, there is—as stated above—a sound pragmatic defence. But in metaphysics the concept is sheer error." See also Whitehead, *Adventures of Ideas*, 219: "This error [of a vacuous substratum] is the result of high-grade intellectuality. The instinctive interpretations which govern human life and animal life presuppose a contemporary world throbbing with energetic values."

44. Whitehead, *Science and the Modern World*, 52.

45. See Whitehead, *Science and the Modern World*, 51–53, 58.

46. See Whitehead, *Process and Reality*, 79.

47. Whitehead, *Adventures of Ideas*, 204.

48. In the following passage from *Adventures of Ideas*, Whitehead eloquently captures the challenge at stake: "consider our derivation from our immediate past of a quarter of a second ago. We are continuous with it, we are the same as it, prolonging its affective tone, enjoying its data. And yet we are modifying it, deflecting it, changing its purposes, altering its tone, re-conditioning its data with new elements. We reduce this past to a perspective, and yet retain it as the basis of our present moment of realization. We are different from it, and yet we retain our individual identity with it. This is the mystery of personal identity, the mystery of the immanence of the past in the present, the mystery of transience" (163).

49. Clarke, *The One and The Many*, 135, emphasis in original. See also, 136: "*What is a system*? It is a set of relations forming a new unified order, or "togetherness," being-together (*mit-sein* in German), which has its own set of properties as a system and influences its members accordingly."

50. Clarke, *The One and The Many*, 136.

51. Clarke, *The One and The Many*, 136–37.

52. In a passage from his essay "God and the Community of Existents," Clarke gets surprisingly close to the interpretation being advanced. Rather than simply affirming something as having sufficient unity to be a substance or not a substance, Clarke advances the idea that an essential form can have greater or lesser degree of control over its parts. "The ontological unity of living beings is not just a static state, either given univocally or not, but an active achievement, an ongoing act of cohering achieved by the energy and power of the central form. And there seems to be a spectrum of degrees of control of the form over its parts: certain basic ones are firmly under the control of the form; others, for various reasons, show a little more resistance to orders from above [. . .]. The unity of real material beings turns out to be complex, changing in intensity—in a word, messy—and needs a flexible theory of degrees of unity to do justice to it" (272). In the end, however, this does not help him with the question as to the ontological status of systems. For Clarke is considering the degree of control exercised by an essential form, again from above, as it were, rather than the degree of coordination of the parts that brings about a form of a particular type. Thus, even with this model he still is only talking about degrees of control by the substance, rather than allowing for a level of explanation more basic than the macroscopic level of the essential form.

53. Whitehead, *Process and Reality*, 110.

54. See Whitehead, *Adventures of Ideas*, 207: "It seems that, in bodies that are obviously living, a coördination has been achieved that raises into prominence some functionings inherent in the ultimate occasions. For lifeless matter these functionings thwart each other, and average out so as to produce a negligible total effect. In the

case of living bodies the coördination intervenes, and the average effect of these intimate functionings has to be taken into account."

55. Whitehead, *Science and the Modern World*, 152.

56. This paradox can be traced perhaps as far back as Heraclitus and is also touched on by Plato in *Parmenides*. It was also discussed by Plutarch. *Theseus* (23.1), The Internet Classics Archive, accessed April 5, 2022, http://classics.mit. edu/Plutarch/theseus.html.

57. J. Scott Turner, *Purpose and Desire: What Makes Something Alive and Why Modern Darwinism Has Failed to Explain It* (New York: HarperOne, 2017), 189–90. See also, 219–20: "The extended organism idea also seems to dissolve whatever equivalence there might be between organism and individual. 'I' am no longer an autonomous being but a superorganism. 'I' includes the multitude of genetically diverse microbial riders, as well as numerous other adaptive interfaces that extend outward from 'me': the farmers who grow my food, the soil microbes that help the farmers, the government bureaucrats who ensure that the little pieces of paper I give farmers will compensate them fairly for their efforts, the contributions of the vast assemblage of taxpayers who give me the little sheets of money in the first place. In this tangled web of physiological conspiracies, the individual that is 'me' dissolves away into the vast collective 'we.'"

58. Clarke, *The One and The Many*, 102.

59. Joseph A. Bracken, *Society and Spirit: A Trinitarian Cosmology* (London: Associated University Presses, 1991), 111.

60. See Whitehead, *Science and the Modern World*, 152: "The organic starting point is from the analysis of process as the realization of events disposed in an interlocking community. The event is the unit of things real. The emergent enduring pattern is the stabilization of the emergent achievement so as to become a fact which retains its identity throughout the process."

61. Note that it is this notion of an emergent, defining characteristic that is the metaphysical explanation for the developmental teleology discussed in chapter seven of this volume. The relations between the parts create an environment suitable for the emergence of more complex forms of order, which create the conditions for more complex teleological orientations.

62. Brian L. Partridge, "The Structure and Function of Fish Schools," *Scientific American* 246, no. 6 (1982): 114.

63. Bert Hölldobler and E. O. Wilson, *The Superorganism: The Beauty, Elegance, and Strangeness of Insect Societies* (New York: Norton, 2009), 4. As the prominent researcher Thomas Seeley noted, "Within colonies there are various tappings, tuggings, shakings, buzzings, strokings, wagglings, crossing of antennae, and puffings and streakings of chemicals, all of which seem to be communication signals. The result is that within a honey bee colony there exists an astonishingly intricate web of information pathways, the full magnitude of which is still only dimly perceived" (Thomas D. Seeley, "The Honey Bee Colony as a Superorganism," *American Scientist*

77, no. 6 (1989): 550. See also Hölldobler and Wilson, *The Superorganism*, 169: "The essential element in the performance is the waggle run, or straight run; it is the middle piece of the figure-eight dance pattern, and it conveys the direction of the target during the outbound flight. Straight up on the vertical surface represents the direction of the sun the follower will see as she leaves the nest. If the target is on a line 400 to the right of the sun, say, the straight run is made 400 to the right of vertical on the comb." See also, 171: "The waggle dance conveys more information than just the direction of the outbound flight. The duration of the waggle run is correlated with the distance of the food site from the hive: [the] farther away the site, the longer each waggle run takes. Circumstantial evidence suggests that the key element in the signal is the duration of the buzzing sound."

64. Hölldobler and Wilson, *The Superorganism*, xx.

65. As Iain Couzin argues in his 2007 *Nature* essay "Collective Minds," "The organising principles employed by ants provide no evidence for leadership; in fact, they demonstrate that leadership is unnecessary to co-ordinate complex group behaviour. We now know that group behaviour may be co-ordinated by relatively simple interactions among the members of the group, a process termed 'self-organization' " (38).

66. This is not to say that a flock of birds is as integrated as a colony of honeybees. As I will suggest, integration is a matter of degree.

67. Seeley, "The Honey Bee Colony," 546–47.

68. For more on the relationship between Wheeler and Whitehead, see Dennis Sölch, "Wheeler and Whitehead: Process Biology and Process Philosophy in the Early Twentieth Century," *Journal of the History of Ideas* 77, no. 3 (2016): 489–507.

69. See Hölldobler and Wilson, *The Superorganism*, 85. "William Morton Wheeler, in his famous 1911 essay 'The Ant-Colony as an Organism,' brought the concept explicitly into sociobiology. 'The ant-colony is an organism,' he wrote, 'and not merely the analogue of the person.' The colony, Wheeler pointed out, has several diagnostic qualities of this status: (1) it behaves as a unit. (2) It shows some idiosyncrasies in behavior, size, and structure, some of which are peculiar to the species and others of which distinguish individual colonies belonging to the same species. (3) It undergoes a cycle of growth and reproduction that is clearly adaptive. (4) It is differentiated into "germ plasm" (queens and males) and 'soma' (workers)" (Hölldobler and Wilson, *The Superorganism*, 10).

70. Hölldobler and Wilson, *The Superorganism*, 85, Figure 5.1.

71. Peter Miller, "Swarm Theory," *National Geographic* 22, no. 1 (2007): 127–42. As Sakata and Katayama put it in their article on ant colony defense systems, "A colony of social insects, consisting of a large number of individuals, shows highly context-specific and well-organized behavior, similar to a sophisticated organism. . . . Within each colony, each individual gathers only a small part of the information necessary for decision-making, and makes only a limited response. Sophisticated behavior of an organism often consists of responses of many subunits

(e.g., organs and cells). A colony of social insects is an excellent model to observe the mechanism of information processing and decision-making through interactions among subunits with limited skills" (Hiroshi Sakata and Noboru Katayama, "Ant defence system: A mechanism organizing individual responses into efficient collective behavior," *Ecological Research* 16, no. 3 [2001]: 395). For a simple account of such rule following, see Hölldobler and Wilson, *The Superorganism*, 65: "Her decision rules can be stated as follows: (1) Not enough nectar collectors in the field? If yes, and if you also have immediate knowledge of a producing flower patch, perform the waggle dance. (2) Is the flower patch rich or the weather fine or the day early or does the colony need substantially more food? Perform the dance with appropriately greater vivacity and persistence. (3) Not enough active foragers to send into the field? Perform the shaking maneuver. (4) Not enough nectar processors in the hive to handle the nectar inflow? Perform the tremble dance. Hundreds of bees making such decisions more or less simultaneously yield the overall response of the superorganism."

72. Hölldobler and Wilson, *The Superorganism*, 7.

73. Hölldobler and Wilson, *The Superorganism*, 58–59.

74. Passino, Seeley, and Visscher give an excellent example of swarm cognition in their study of honeybee nest selection: "The swarm's distributed group memory is distinct from the internal neural-based memory of each individual bee. What is known by the swarm is actually *far more* than the sum of what is known by the individual bees, as the swarm's knowledge includes the information stored in the bees' brains *and the information coded in the locations of the bees and their actions.* No bee can know all the locations and activities for all other bees. But this information is coded at the swarm level and . . . is explicitly used in decision making" (Kevin M. Passino, Thomas D. Seeley, and P. Kirk Visscher, "Swarm Cognition in Honey Bees," *Behavioral Ecology and Sociobiology* 63, no. 3 [2008]: 407, authors' emphasis.

75. Cf. "The ants, bees, wasps, and termites are among the most socially advanced nonhuman organisms of which we have knowledge" (Hölldobler and Wilson, *The Superorganism*, xviii).

76. Hölldobler and Wilson, *The Superorganism*, 114.

77. Hölldobler and Wilson, *The Superorganism*, 53.

78. Hölldobler and Wilson, *The Superorganism*, 58.

79. Seeley, "The Honey Bee Colony," 549.

80. J. Scott Turner, *The Extended Organism: The Physiology of Animal-Built Structures* (Cambridge, MA: Harvard University Press, 2000), 2.

81. Turner, *The Extended Organism*, 2.

82. Hölldobler and Wilson, *The Superorganism*, 117. They continue: "Thus, while a brief surveillance of an insect colony may seem to disclose a confusing kaleidoscope of activity, longer periods of observation reveal that patterns are built from many quite individual minds linked by a high degree of organization. That amount of order is central to the colony's survival and reproduction" (119). "To

conclude that the central tendencies of role change with aging have a genetic basis is not to imply that it is rigidly determined. Instead, the ensemble of genes that program the sequence of role changes have, like all such hereditary units, a norm of reaction, the array of possible outcomes in physiology and behavior determined by the interaction of the genes and the particular environment in which the development occurs" (121).

83. Hölldobler and Wilson, *The Superorganism*, 55.

84. Hölldobler and Wilson, *The Superorganism*, 116. Though they would no doubt deny the connotation, the idea of a "central tendency" seems scarcely different than referring to final causality or a telos. As Turner argues in his chapter, there is real purpose in nature.

85. J. Scott Turner, "A Superorganism's Fuzzy Boundaries," *Natural History* 111, no. 6 (2002): 63.

86. See Turner, "Fuzzy Boundaries," 63: "The fungi are the major heavy breathers in the nest, consuming oxygen about five times faster than the termites do. Why, then, do termites work so hard to build an earthen lung if the fungi, Termitomyces, actually do the most to make the nest air stuffy? To be sure, the act is not altruistic, because the fungi, by breaking down the termites' food, are performing a critical function. In a sense, the termites are "paid" for their work. But the fungi may be gaining much more than simply having termites supply them with a steady diet of cellulose: Termitomyces, you see, have competitors."

87. Turner, "Fuzzy Boundaries," 63.

88. See Turner, "Fuzzy Boundaries," 65: "The flow of the wind pushes air through the porous soil on the windward side and sucks it out on the leeward side, allowing the nest atmosphere to mix with fresh air from the outside world. This in itself is not surprising; lots of animals build structures that do similar things. What is remarkable is the pattern of ventilation: an in-and-out movement very similar to the way air flows into and out of our own lungs. In fact, what most distinguishes the action of the two 'organs' is that the termites' is powered by the ebb and flow of wind instead of by the contractions of muscle."

89. Turner, "Fuzzy Boundaries," 66.

90. Turner, "Fuzzy Boundaries," 67. For his part, Whitehead is not even sure that we can define where the human organism begins and ends: "We think of ourselves as so intimately entwined in bodily life that a man is a complex unity—body and mind. But the body is part of the external world, continuous with it. In fact, it is just as much part of nature as anything else there—a river, or a mountain, or a cloud. Also, if we are fussily exact, we cannot define where a body begins and where external nature ends" (Whitehead, *Modes of Thought*, 21).

91. Turner, *The Extended Organism*, 2.

92. J. Scott Turner, *The Tinkerer's Accomplice: How Design Emerges from Life Itself* (Cambridge, MA: Harvard University Press, 2007), 1.

93. Turner, *The Tinkerer's Accomplice*, 13.

94. Turner, *The Tinkerer's Accomplice*, 218–19. Notice Turner's rejection of "thing" metaphysics in favor of a "process" language.

95. Turner, *Purpose and Desire*, 8–9.

96. Turner, *The Extended Organism*, 25.

97. James Lovelock, *The Vanishing Face of Gaia: A Final Warning* (New York: Basic Books, 2009), 179.

98. Richard Dawkins, *Extended Phenotype* (Oxford: Oxford University Press, 1982), 236.

99. Dawkins, *Extended Phenotype*, 236.

100. David M. Wilkinson, "Homeostatic Gaia: An Ecologist's Perspective on the Possibility of Regulation," in *Scientists Debate Gaia: A New Century*, ed. Stephen H. Schneider, James R. Miller, Eileen Crist, and Penelope J. Boston (Cambridge, MA: MIT Press, 2004), 71.

101. Wilkinson, "Homeostatic Gaia," 73.

Chapter 7

1. René Descartes, *Discourse on Method. The Philosophical Writings of Descartes*, vol. 1 (Cambridge: Cambridge University Press, 1985), 141, 59

2. Whitehead, *Process and Reality*, xiii, 167, 29. See also chapter two of this volume on value.

3. Leibniz is of course a notable exception to this, foreshadowing Whitehead's work in many respects. See Nicholas Rescher, *On Leibniz: Expanded Edition* (Pittsburgh: University of Pittsburgh Press, 2013), 304. Note that we are here setting aside the tradition of metaphysical idealism. For an excellent discussion of environmental ethics, metaphysics, and Whitehead's thought from an idealist perspective, see T. L. S. Sprigge, "Are There Intrinsic Values in Nature?" *Journal of Applied Philosophy* 4, no. 1 (1987): 21–28.

4. See chapter three of this volume for a discussion of the debate between Callicott and Rolston on subjective versus objective value.

5. Taylor, *Respect for Nature*; Rolston, *Environmental Ethics*.

6. For a more developed discussion of teleology from a Whiteheadian perspective, see Spyridon Koutroufinis, "Teleodynamics: A Neo-Naturalistic Conception of Organismic Teleology," in *Beyond Mechanism: Putting Life Back into Biology*, eds. Brian G. Henning and Adam Scarfe (Lantham: Lexington 2013), 309–44.

7. Charles Sanders Peirce, *The Essential Peirce*, vol. 1, edited by Nathan Houser and Christian Kloesel (Bloomington: Indiana University Press, 1992), 299.

8. See Peirce, *The Essential Peirce*, vol. 1, 299: "The state of things existing at any time, together with certain immutable laws, completely determine the sate of things at every other time (for a limitation to *future* time is indefensible). Thus, given the state of the universe in the original nebula, and given the laws of

mechanics, a sufficiently powerful mind could deduce from these data the precise form of every curlicue of every letter I am now writing."

9. Charles Sanders Peirce, "The First Rule of Logic," *The Essential Peirce*, vol. 2, Ed. (Bloomington: Indiana University Press, 1899).

10. Peirce, *The Essential Peirce*, vol. 1, 308.

11. Peirce, *The Essential Peirce*, vol. 1, 308. See also, vol. 1, 310: "I make use of chance chiefly to make room for a principle of generalisation, or tendency to form habits, which I hold has produced all regularities. The mechanical philosopher leaves the whole specification of the world utterly unaccounted for, which is pretty nearly as bad as to boldly attribute it to chance. I attribute it altogether to chance, it is true, but to chance in the form of a spontaneity which is to some degree regular."

12. Peirce, *The Essential Peirce*, vol. 1, 312. See also vol. 1, 331: "What we call dead matter is not completely dead, but is merely mind hide-bound with habits. It still retains the element of diversification; and in that diversification there is life."

13. See Peirce, *The Essential Peirce*, vol. 1, 310: "I make use of chance chiefly to make room for a principle of generalisation, or tendency to form habits, which I hold has produced all regularities. The mechanical philosopher leaves the whole specification of the world utterly unaccounted for, which is pretty nearly as bad as to boldly attribute it to chance. I attribute it altogether to chance, it is true, but to chance in the form of a spontaneity which is to some degree regular."

14. Peirce, *The Essential Peirce*, vol. 1, 331.

15. Peirce, *The Essential Peirce*, vol. 1, 331.

16. Peirce, *The Essential Peirce*, vol. 1, 331.

17. See Peirce, *The Essential Peirce*, vol. 1, 331: "But the word coordination implies somewhat more than this; it implies a teleological harmony in ideas, and in the case of personality this teleology is more than a mere purposive pursuit of a predeterminate end; it is a developmental teleology. This is personal character. A general idea, living and conscious now, it is already determinative of acts in the future to an extent to which it is not now conscious."

18. Aristotle is not perfectly uniform on this point, but he is fairly consistent in identifying the formal and final causes with each other. See, for instance, Aristotle, *Parts of Animals* 639b7–640a20; *Physics* 198a22–34, 198a36–198b9, 198b17–199a7, 199b10–18; Aristotle, *Generation of Animals* 715a4–6; and Aristotle, *Metaphysics* 1044a33–b1, 1050a5–16.

19. As discussed in chapter six of this volume, the physiological biologist J. Scott Turner suggests that this rejection of teleology has brought contemporary biology to a point of crisis. "In a nutshell, this is where the crisis of biology looms, because our prevailing modes of thinking about life—the triumphant confluence of mechanism, materialism, and atomism that has made the twentieth century a golden age for biology—do not deal well with the concept of agency: that ineffable striving of living things to *become* something. This was the real source of annoyance for that reviewer of *The Tinkerer's Accomplice*, because intentionality is, among other

things, the manifestation of living agency, as are purposefulness, desire, and striving. Philosophically fencing those things off, as much of the modern science of biology has done, has brought the science of life to the brink of its crisis" (Turner, *Purpose and Desire*, xv).

20. Peirce, *The Essential Peirce*, vol. 1, 331.

21. Peirce, *The Essential Peirce*, vol. 1, 359–60.

22. Peirce, *The Essential Peirce*, vol. 1, 352. It is worth quoting Empedocles at length on this point: "A twofold tale I shall tell: at one time they grew to be one alone out of many, at another again they grew apart to be many out of one. Double is the birth of mortal things and double their failing; for the one is brought to birth and destroyed by the coming together of all things, the other is nurtured and flies apart as they grow apart again. And these things never cease their continual interchange, now through Love all coming together into one, now again each carried apart by the hatred of Strife. So insofar as they have learned to grow one from many, and again as the one grows apart grow many, thus far do they come into being and have no stable life; but insofar as they never cease their continual interchange, thus far they exist always changeless in the cycle" (Empedocles Fragment 17, in Kirk, Raven, and Schofield, *The Presocratic Philosophers*, 287).

23. See Aristotle, *Metaphysics* 1072b1–3

24. Peirce, *The Essential Peirce*, vol. 1, 352.

25. Peirce, *The Essential Peirce*, vol. 1, 353.

26. Recall that it is precisely because Eros can move without itself being moved that Aristotle (and Thomas Aquinas) defines love as the ultimate way in which the unmoved mover is the final cause of all motion.

27. P Peirce, *The Essential Peirce*, vol. 1, 353.

28. Peirce, *The Essential Peirce*, vol. 1, 354.

29. Peirce, *The Essential Peirce*, vol. 1, 362. Peirce notes that tychasm is actually a species of agapasm. "This only shows that love cannot have a contrary, but must embrace what is most opposed to it, as a degenerate case of it, so tychasm is a kind of agapasm. Only, in the tychastic evolution progress is solely owing to the distribution of the napkin-hidden talent of the rejected servant among those not rejected, just as ruined gamesters leave their money on the table to make those not yet ruined so much the richer. In genuine agapasm, on the other hand, advance takes place by virtue of a positive sympathy among the created springing from the continuity of mind. This is the idea which tychasticism knows not how to manage" (362).

30. Peirce, *The Essential Peirce*, vol. 1, 364.

31. Peirce, *The Essential Peirce*, vol. 1, 369.

32. Peirce, *The Essential Peirce*, vol. 1, 354.

33. Rolston, *Environmental Ethics*, 175. This reference to Rolston is not inapt, given that he is also trying to recover teleology and because he adheres to the view that the universe itself is aimed at increasing complexity and diversity. See,

for instance, his discussion of the strong anthropic principle. See especially chapter six of his *Environmental Ethics*.

34. Whitehead, *Adventures of Ideas*.

35. Whitehead, *Process and Reality*, 24–25, 47, 69.

36. Whitehead, *Process and Reality*, 25, 27–29, 45, 47, 85–86, 222, 245.

37. Whitehead, *Process and Reality*, 222.

38. We are told in the preface of *Adventures of Ideas* that *Science and the Modern World*, *Process and Reality*, and *Adventures of Ideas* can all be read separately, but "they supplement each other's omissions or compressions" (vii). I would suggest that one of the omissions that *Adventures of Ideas* remedies is the discussion of beauty as the teleological aim of the universe. See *Adventures of Ideas*, 265: "The teleology of the Universe is directed to the production of Beauty. Thus any system of things which in any wide sense is beautiful is to that extent justified in its existence. It may however fail in another sense, by inhibiting more Beauty than it creates. Thus the system, though in a sense beautiful, is on the whole evil in that environment."

39. Whitehead, *Adventures of Ideas*, 66.

40. Whitehead, *Adventures of Ideas*, 25.

41. Whitehead, *Adventures of Ideas*, 148.

42. Whitehead, *Adventures of Ideas*, 207.

43. Whitehead, *Adventures of Ideas*, 207.

44. It is noteworthy that Whitehead concludes that Eros is not by itself sufficient to explain the creative urge of the universe. See Whitehead, *Adventures of Ideas*, 285: "Something is still lacking. It is difficult to state it in terms that are wide enough. It clings to our notion of the Platonic 'Harmony,' as a sort of atmosphere. It is somewhat at variance with the notion of the 'Eros.' . . . Apart from it, the pursuit of 'Truth, Beauty, Adventure, Art' can be ruthless, hard, cruel; and thus, as the history of the Italian Renaissance illustrates, lacking in some essential quality of civilization. The notions of 'tenderness' and of 'love' are too narrow, important though they be. We require the concept of some more general quality, from which 'tenderness' emerges as a specializations. We are in a way seeking for the notion of a Harmony of harmonies, which shall bind together the other four qualities, so as to exclude from our notion of civilization the restless egotism with which they have often in fact been pursued. 'Impersonality' is too dead a notion, and 'Tenderness' too narrow. I choose the term 'Peace' for that Harmony of Harmonies which calms destructive turbulence and completes civilization. Thus a society is to be termed civilized whose members participate in the five qualities—Truth, beauty, Adventure, Art, Peace."

45. Whitehead, *Adventures of Ideas*, 275.

46. Frederick Ferré, *Living and Value: Toward a Constructive Postmodern Ethics* (Albany: SUNY Press, 2001). See chapter four of this volume for an account of kalocentrism.

47. Whitehead, *Adventures of Ideas*, 265.

48. Aristotle, *Metaphysics*, XII, 1072a.

49. Indeed, in some passages of *Process and Reality*, Whitehead seems to recognize this himself. "There is, however, in the Galilean origin of Christianity yet another suggestion which does not fit very well with any of the three main strands of thought. It does not emphasize the ruling Caesar, or the ruthless moralist, or the unmoved mover. It dwells upon the tender elements in the world, which slowly and in quietness operate by love; and it finds purpose in the present immediacy of a kingdom not of this world. Love neither rules, nor is unmoved; also it is a little oblivious as to morals. It does not look to the future; for it finds its own reward in the immediate present" (343). The difference between the account of the consequent nature of God in *Process and Reality* and Platonic Eros in *Adventures of Ideas* is so stark that I am left wondering if Whitehead had begun to abandon his account of God entirely.

50. An anonymous reviewer rightly notes that an agapistic notion of teleology is potentially found in Whitehead's discussion of God in his earlier (1929) work *Process and Reality*, especially his discussion of the "consequent nature" of God as "the fellow-sufferer who understands" (351). It is likely that various accounts of the divine are potentially compatible with the position being here defended, though it is not clear that any reference to the divine is needed in order to provide an adequate metaphysical basis for environmental ethics, which is the primary focus of this project.

51. Carl R. Hausman, "Eros and Agape in Creative Evolution: A Peircean Insight," *Process Studies* 4, no. 1 (1974): 16.

52. Hausman, "Eros and Agape," 16.

53. Whitehead, *Process and Reality*, 222.

54. Hausman, "Eros and Agape," 15.

55. Hausman, "Eros and Agape," 17.

56. Peirce, *The Essential Peirce*, vol. 1, 314.

57. James, *Some Problems of Philosophy*, 155.

58. Whitehead, *Process and Reality*, 35.

59. James, *Some Problems of Philosophy*, 183n2.

60. Peirce, *The Essential Peirce*, vol. 1, 331.

61. McHenry and Shields write persuasively that Whitehead is indeed an important figure in the history of analytic philosophy. They quote Peter Simons as saying: " 'I agree wholeheartedly . . . that Whitehead *is* an analytic philosopher. The opposition between analytic and process philosophy is an historical artifact, due to accidents of the time. Analytic philosophy is now a broad church and has been for decades. Whitehead is anything but a positivist, but he is scientific. He is anything but a linguistic philosopher, but he cares passionately about logic and language. He is anything but a mere analyzer of concepts, but he values exactness of concept and their applications. He is in the same grand scientific metaphysical tradition as Russell and Quine, but he has a mind of his own.' (2003: 666)" (Leemon B. McHenry

and George W. Shields, "Analytical Critiques of Whitehead's Metaphysics," *Journal of the American Philosophical Association* 2, no. 3 [2016]: 500). See also Bogdan Rusu and Ronny Desmet, "Whitehead, Russell, and Moore: Three Analytic Philosophers," *Process Studies* 41, no. 2 (2012): 214–34.

62. These letters are expected to be published as part of the *Edinburgh Critical Edition of the Complete Works of Alfred North Whitehead*. See http://whiteheadresearch.org/research/critical-edition/.

63. Moore, *Principia Ethica*, 54.

64. Moore, *Principia Ethica*, 55.

65. Moore, *Principia Ethica*, 59.

66. Moore, *Principia Ethica*, 61.

67. Moore, *Principia Ethica*, 68. See also, 62: "Ethics aims at discovering what are those other properties belonging to all things which are good."

68. Moore, *Principia Ethica*, 175.

69. Moore, *Principia Ethica*, 62.

70. Moore, *Principia Ethica*, 164–65.

71. Moore, *Principia Ethica*, 91–92.

72. Moore, *Principia Ethica*, 93.

73. Moore, *Principia Ethica*, 93.

74. Moore, *Principia Ethica*, 161.

75. Moore, *Principia Ethica*, 161.

76. Moore, *Principia Ethica*, 163–64.

77. See Plato, *Republic*, book 7.

78. Moore, *Principia Ethica*, 169.

79. Moore, *Principia Ethica*, 166.

80. See Descartes, *Mediations on First Philosophy*, meditations one and two. See also Descartes, *Principles of Philosophy*.

81. Moore, *Principia Ethica*, 236.

82. Moore, *Principia Ethica*, 237.

83. Moore, *Principia Ethica*, 246.

84. Moore, *Principia Ethica*, 237.

85. David Hume, *A Treatise of Human Nature* (New York: Penguin, 1969), 523, emphases in original. See chapter 1 of Henning, *Ethics of Creativity*, for a more complete treatment of Hume in particular and modern axiology in general.

86. Moore, *Principia Ethica*, 238.

87. Whitehead, *Process and Reality*, 166: "The subjectivist principle is that the whole universe consists of elements disclosed in the analysis of the experiences of subjects. Process is the becoming of experience. It follows that the philosophy of organism entirely accepts the subjectivist bias of modern philosophy. It also accepts Hume's doctrine that nothing is to be received into the philosophical scheme which is not discoverable as an element in objective experience. This is the ontological principle."

88. René Descartes, *The Philosophical Writings of Descartes*, vol. 2, 210.

89. Whitehead, "Immortality," 687

90. See Whitehead, *Process and Reality*, 138: "In the philosophy of organism a subject-predicate proposition is considered as expressing a high abstraction." See also Whitehead, *Science and the Modern World*, 151: "The technical phrase 'subject-object' is a bad term for the fundamental situation disclosed in experience. It is really reminiscent of the Aristotelian 'subject-predicate.' It already presupposes the metaphysical doctrine of diverse subjects qualified by their private predicates. This is the doctrine of subjects with private worlds of experience. If this be granted, there is no escape from solipsism. The point is that the phrase 'subject-object' indicates a fundamental entity underlying the objects. Thus the 'objects,' as thus conceived, are merely the ghosts of Aristotelian predicates."

91. Whitehead, *Process and Reality*, 50.

92. Kerr makes a similar claim: "The naturalistic fallacy, expressed in its strongest form as falsifying all forms of ethical naturalism, presumes that all existential statements are empirical or contingent. Yet metaphysical inquiry, a major and long-standing branch of philosophical thought, rejects this common contemporary presumption or claim, and if the argument of this paper is true, environmental ethics should consider a metaphysical basis for environmental ethics. Such consideration would, at least, require formulating a metaphysical state of affairs upon which to base a definition of the good. In turn, the definition of the good would itself be 'metaphysical,' lacking in alternatives by the major premise of the naturalistic fallacy. In Frankena's terms, it would be good to use the term good to refer to a metaphysical state of affairs because this naturalistic definition of the good would not be chosen among alternatives, for any existential condition actual or possible is an illustration of the metaphysical state of affairs and never an alternative to it" (Andrew J. Kerr, "The Possibility of Metaphysics: Environmental Ethics and the Naturalistic Fallacy," *Environmental Ethics* 22 [2000]: 96–97).

Chapter 8

1. See the introduction to this volume.

2. J. Baird Callicott, "The Worldview Concept and Aldo Leopold's Project of 'World View' Remediation," *Journal for the Study of Religion, Nature and Culture* 5, no. 4 (2011): 516. He also refers to it as "worldview remediation" (510).

3. Andrew Light, "Environmental Pragmatism as Philosophy or Metaphilosophy?" in *Environmental Pragmatism*, ed. Andrew Light and Eric Katz (New York: Routledge, 1996), 325–38; Ben A. Minteer, "Intrinsic Value for Pragmatists?" *Environmental Ethics* 23, no. 1 (2001): 57–75; Bryan Norton, "Environmental Ethics and Weak Anthropocentrism," *Environmental Ethics* 6 (1984): 131–48; Bryan

Norton, *Toward Unity Among Environmentalists* (Oxford: Oxford University Press, 1991); Anthony Weston, "Beyond Intrinsic Value: Pragmatism in Environmental Ethics," *Environmental Ethics* 7 (1985): 321–39.

4. Andrew Light and Eric Katz, *Environmental Pragmatism* (New York: Routledge, 1996), 1.

5. Lars Samuelsson, "Environmental Pragmatism and Environmental Philosophy: A Bad Marriage," *Environmental Ethics* 32, no. 4 (2010): 405.

6. For instance, Norton wonders, "Could it be that the polarized thinking that paralyzes environmental policy today results from false alternatives forced upon us by the assumption, unquestioned by neoclassical economists and by most of their opponents among environmental ethicists alike, that whatever the units of environmental value turn out to be, there will be only one kind of them?" (Bryan Norton, "Integration or Reduction: Two Approaches to Environmental Values," in *Environmental Pragmatism*, ed. Andrew Light and Eric Katz [New York: Routledge, 1996], 106).

7. Light and Katz, *Environmental Pragmatism*, 2.

8. Robert Frodeman, "The Policy Turn in Environmental Ethics," *Environmental Ethics* 28 (2006): 3.

9. Frodeman, "The Policy Turn," 4.

10. Norton, "Integration," 131.

11. Norton, "Integration,"106.

12. Norton, "Integration,"106.

13. Bryan Norton, *Toward Unity Among Environmentalists* (Oxford: Oxford University Press, 1991).

14. Norton, "Integration," 108.

15. Norton, "Integration," 111.

16. Light and Katz, *Environmental Pragmatism*, 1–2.

17. V. Masson-Delmotte et al., eds., "Summary for Policymakers," in *Global Warming of 1.5°C. An IPCC Special Report on the Impacts of Global Warming of 1.5°C above Pre-Industrial Levels and Related Global Greenhouse Gas Emission Pathways, in the Context of Strengthening the Global Response to the Threat of Climate Change, Sustainable Development, and Efforts to Eradicate Poverty* (Geneva, Switzerland: World Meteorological Organization, 2018), https://www.ipcc.ch/sr15/chapter/spm/.

18. Light and Katz, *Environmental Pragmatism*, 1.

19. "Perhaps not inconsequentially, Douglas cited, in his las paragraph, Aldo Leopold's essay "The Land Ethic." Also subconsciously influencing Douglas's thinking might well have been his knowledge that Muir—the founder of the Sierra Club (the plaintiff in the Mineral King case)." J. Baird Callicott, "Should Endangered Species Have Standing? Toward Legal Rights for Listed Species," *Social Philosophy and Policy* 26, no. 2 (2009): 328.

20. Callicott, "Should Endangered Species Have Standing?"

21. J. Baird Callicott, "The Pragmatic Power and Promise of Theoretical Environmental Ethics: Forging a New Discourse," *Environmental Values* 11, no. 1 (2002): 4.

22. J. Baird Callicott, "Environmental Philosophy Is Environmental Activism: The Most Radical and Effective Kind," in *Environmental Ethics: What Really Matters, What Really Works*, ed. David Schmidtz and Elizabeth Willott (Oxford: Oxford University Press, 2012), 15.

23. Callicott, "Environmental Philosophy Is Environmental Activism," 16.

24. Mikael Stenmark, "The Relevance of Environmental Ethical Theories for Policy Making," *Environmental Ethics* 24, no. 2 (2002): 140.

25. Stenmark, "The Relevance of Environmental Ethical Theories," 140.

26. Andrew Light has long been deeply involved in international climate policy negotiations, even serving in the Obama administration addressing climate policy. The degree to which he practices what he philosophically preaches (i.e., environmental pragmatism) is admirable in its consistency.

27. UN Secretary-General and World Commission on Environment and Development, "Report of the World Commission on Environment and Development," August 4, 1987, https://digitallibrary.un.org/record/139811, 27.

28. Paris Agreement (2015), Article 2, section 1(a), https://unfccc.int/sites/default/files/english_paris_agreement.pdf.

29. 350ppm was first cited by former NASA lead climate scientist James Hansen in a presentation called "Climate Tipping Points: The Threat to the Planet" to the American Geophysical Union, December 13, 2007.

30. Callicott, "Pragmatic Power and Promise," 14.

31. Callicott, "Pragmatic Power and Promise," 15.

32. Norton, "Integration," 131.

33. Norton, "Integration," 131.

34. As Weston puts it: "One charge of anthropocentrism should not detain us. Pragmatism is a form of subjectivism—it makes valuing an activity of subjects, possibly only of human subjects—but subjectivism is not necessarily anthropocentric. Even if only human beings value in this sense, it does not follow that only human beings *have* value; it does not follow that human beings must be the sole or final objects of valuation. Subjectivism does not imply, so to say, subject-*centrism*: our actual values can be much more complex and world-directed" (Weston, "Beyond Intrinsic Value," 321–22).

35. Mark Michael contends that Norton's version of environmental pragmatism is ultimately relativistic and, as a result, is unable to avoid "reprehensible implications" (Mark Michael, "Environmental Pragmatism, Community Values, and the Problem of Reprehensible Implications," *Environmental Ethics* 38, no. 3 [2016]: 349). Michael notes that Norton's position is grounded thoroughly in the work of Peirce and Dewey and that, therefore, if Norton is an exemplar of pragmatist thinking, then pragmatism is also guilty of leading to reprehensible implications. "From

here on, the focus of this paper is Norton's proposal for avoiding simplistic relativism—my criticisms are directed specifically at that proposal. But it is worth noting that Norton argues extensively throughout *Sustainability* that his view is grounded in the views of classical pragmatists such as Peirce and Dewey. . . . I accept that claim and so take Norton's view as paradigmatic of environmental pragmatism. If that is right, then any critique of Norton's solution to the problem of reprehensible implications will also count as a critique of environmental pragmatism generally, unless some alternative solution to that problem within that tradition is offered. I have no argument to show that there *cannot* be some other kind of solution that is consistent with pragmatism generally" (Michael, "Environmental Pragmatism," 349n9).

36. Frodeman, "Policy Turn," 3.

37. Frodeman, "Policy Turn," 3.

38. Samuelsson, "Environmental Pragmatism," 408–9.

39. Samuelsson, "Environmental Pragmatism," 408.

40. Samuelsson, "Environmental Pragmatism," 414.

41. Samuelsson, "Environmental Pragmatism," 410.

42. See Samuelsson, "Environmental Pragmatism," 411: "Astrophysics in general could probably also do more to contribute to solving environmental problems, as could psychologists and linguists—they all possess critical talents. It is not necessarily the case that environmental philosophers are best suited to attend to the practical matters highlighted by environmental pragmatists. Actually, much of what Light says about these matters suggest that they are not."

43. There are forms of pragmatism that are not themselves related to the classical American philosophers. In this chapter I am for convenience using "classical American pragmatism," "classical American philosophy," and "American pragmatism" interchangeably.

44. See William James, *The Meaning of Truth*, 1914, http://archive.org/details/in.ernet.dli.2015.201748; and William James, *Essays In Radical Empiricism*, 1912, http://archive.org/details/in.ernet.dli.2015.188766.

45. Again, see chapter one of this volume for a complete defense of this claim.

46. See Henning, *Ethics of Creativity*, especially chapter 1.

47. See, for instance, chapter seven of this volume on teleology for an account of Peirce's rejection of necessitarianism.

48. For many of the classical American philosophers, these positions seem to be an expression of the deep influence of their reading of Hegel and Schelling.

49. Whitehead, *Process and Reality*, xii.

50. Indeed, I was happy to coedit a collection of essays exploring the relationship between Whitehead's philosophy of organism and the classical American pragmatists. Brian G. Henning, William Myers, and Joseph John, eds., *Thinking with Whitehead and the American Pragmatists: Experience and Reality* (New York: Lexington, 2015).

51. Whitehead, *Modes of Thought*, 174.

52. Charles S. Peirce, *Collected Papers of Charles Sanders Peirce*, ed. Charles Hartshorne and Paul Weiss, vols. 5–6 (Cambridge, MA: Belknap Press of Harvard University Press, 1978), 5.414.

53. J. Baird Callicott et al., "Was Aldo Leopold a Pragmatist? Rescuing Leopold from the Imagination of Bryan Norton," *Environmental Values* 18, no. 4 (2009): 462.

Chapter 9

1. Brian G. Henning, "Philosophy in the Age of Fascism: Reflection on the Presidential Addresses of the APA, 1931–1940," in *Historical Essays in 20th Century American Philosophy*, ed. John R. Shook, vol. 11 (Charlottesville, VA: RTH, 2015), 69–95.

2. The addresses of the APA are published in *American Philosophical Association Presidential Addresses*, 11 vols., gen. ed. Richard Hull (Charlottesville, VA: Philosophy Documentation Center, 2015). For a list of past presidents and their addresses, see "APA Divisional Presidents and Addresses—The American Philosophical Association," accessed May 4, 2022, https://www.apaonline.org/page/presidents.

3. As I note in my "Philosophy in the Age of Fascism," 88: "Although from our twenty-first century vantage point, the eventual victory of the Allies might seem to have been inevitable, in the closing years of the 1930s, Japan had invaded and committed terrible atrocities in China, and Hitler and Mussolini were on the march across Europe. Eventual victory was not so certain then, and the existential threat to democracy was palpable in many of the addresses delivered during this period."

4. J. A. Leighton, "History as the Struggle for Social Values," 539–40.

5. See especially the addresses by James H. Tufts (Pacific Division President 1934–1935), "The Institution as an Agency of Stability and Readjustment in Ethics"; E. T. Mitchell (Western Division President 1935–1936), "Social Ideals and the Law"; J. A. Leighton (Western Division President 1937–1938), "History as the Struggle for Social Values"; Glen R. Morrow (Western Division President 1939–1940), "Plato and the Rule of Law"; and Edward O. Sisson (Pacific Division President 1939–1940), "Human Nature and the Present Crisis." Note that the Western Division has since been renamed the Central Division.

6. The extinction crisis, which predates the climate crisis, is of equal concern and has causes broader than just greenhouse-gas emission, such as anthropogenic habitat fragmentation and appropriate, spread of invasive species, and water pollution. See Eileen Crist, *Abundant Earth*; and Elizabeth Kolbert, *The Sixth Extinction* (New York: Henry Holt, 2014).

7. Gardiner's work on climate change as a "perfect moral storm" is very helpful here: Stephen M. Gardiner, "A Perfect Moral Storm: Climate Change, Intergenerational Ethics, and the Problem of Corruption," in *Climate Ethics: Essential Readings*, ed. Stephen M. Gardiner et al. (Oxford: Oxford University Press, 2010),

87–98. See also Dale Jamieson, "Ethics, Public Policy, and Global Warming," *Science, Technology, Human Values* 17 (1992): 149. "There are three important dimensions along which global environmental problems such as those involved with climate change vary from the paradigm: Apparently innocent acts can have devastating consequences, causes and harms may be diffuse, and causes and harms may be remote in space and time."

8. A keyword search of the terms "climate change" and "global warming" in the fifty-four presidential addresses from 2003 to 2021 reveals very little engagement with the climate crisis, with only six fleeting references: Nicholas Smith, "Modesty: A Contextual Account" (2007–2008 Pacific Division presidential address); Linda Martín Alcoff, "Philosophy's Civil Wars" (2012–2013 Eastern APA presidential address); Elizabeth Anderson, "Moral Bias and Corrective Practices: A Pragmatist Perspective" (2014–2015 Central APA presidential address); Nancy Frasher, "Is Capitalism *Necessarily* Racist?" (2018 Eastern APA presidential address); Jennifer Nagel, "Epistemic Territory" (2019 Central APA presidential address); and Christina Mercer, "Empowering Philosophy" (2020 Eastern APA presidential address). The extinction crisis receives even less attention, with a keyword search of the term "extinction" revealing no references.

9. Stephen M. Gardiner, "Ethics and Global Climate Change" *Ethics* 114 (April 2004): 555.

10. The inactivity of the APA is in contrast to, for instance, the American Academy of Religion (AAR). Much of the 2014 annual meeting of the AAR was dedicated to the topic of climate change, including a session with former president Jimmy Carter on "The Role of Religion in Mediating Conflicts and Imagining Futures: The Cases of Climate Change and Equality for Women" and plenary panels with, among others, 350.org founder Bill McKibben and the then-chair of the Intergovernmental Panel on Climate Change (IPCC), Rajendra K. Pachauri. More to the point, Linda Zoloth's presidential address was dedicated to the topic "Interrupting Your Life: An Ethics for the Coming Storm."

11. I find Karen J. Warren's definition of a conceptual framework to be helpful here: "A *conceptual framework* is a set of basic beliefs, values, attitudes, and assumptions which shape and reflect how one views oneself and one's world. A conceptual framework functions as a socially constructed *lens* through which one perceives reality. It is affected and shaped by such factors as sex-gender, race/ethnicity, class, age, affectional orientation, marital status, religion, nationality, colonial influences, and culture" (Warren, *Ecofeminist Philosophy*, 46). For the purposes of this essay "narrative," "worldview," "story," and "conceptual framework" will largely be used interchangeably.

12. The term "Anthropocene" was popularized by Paul Crutzen and Eugene Stoermer in 2000. See the 2019 report of the Anthropocene Working Group of the IUGS Subcommission on Quaternary Stratigraphy, http://quaternary.stratigraphy.org/working-groups/anthropocene/. On the question, "Should the Anthropocene be

treated as a formal chrono-stratigraphic unit defined by a GSSP [or Global Stratotype Section and Point]?" 88 percent voted in favor. However, the larger issue as to whether to consider the Anthropocene a formally defined geological unit within the Geological Time Scale has not yet been decided. Thus, geologically, for now we still live within the Meghalayan Age of the Holocene Epoch. However, the Anthropocene Working Group is in the process of considering a proposal to formalize the Anthropocene.

13. John Houghton, the founding cochair of the Intergovernmental Panel on Climate Change, notes that natural variations in the Earth's orbit (called Milankovich cycles, after the Serbian mathematician who discovered them) would eventually usher in a new glacial period and end the temperate Holocene. "It so happens that we are currently in a period of relatively small solar radiation variations and the best projections for the long term are of a longer than normal interglacial period leading to the beginning of a new ice age perhaps in 50 000 years' time" (John Houghton, *Global Climate Change: The Complete Briefing* [Cambridge: Cambridge University Press, 2009], 87).

14. "Welcome to the Anthropocene," *The Economist*, May 26, 2011, http://www.economist.com/node/18744401.

15. Eileen Crist, "On the Poverty of Our Nomenclature," *Environmental Humanities* 3 (2013): 129.

16. Crist, "Nomenclature," 129–30.

17. See Crist, *Abundant Earth*, 45: "Flagging the interchangeability of "human supremacy" and "anthropocentrism" is not simply a semantic clarification, but intended to highlight a substantive point reiterated through this work: anthropocentrism does not in the least serve human interests—anymore than white supremacy has ever served the ostensible interests of the putative Caucasian race. All forms of supremacy entrench violence as a way of life, which, beyond the obvious grave harms it inflicts on the denigrated, profoundly disgraces the perpetrators themselves."

18. Crist, *Abundant Earth*, 2–3.

19. Crist, "Nomenclature," 133.

20. See Crist, "Nomenclature," 131: "For the Anthropocene discourse our purposeful effects must be rationalized and sustainably managed, our inadvertent, negative effects need to be technically mitigated—but the historical legacy of human dominion is not up for scrutiny, let alone abolition."

21. See chapter eight of this volume on environmental pragmatism. For more on this, see chapters 3 and 4 of Brian G. Henning, *Riders in the Storm: Ethics in an Age of Climate Change* (Winona, MN: Anselm Academic, 2015).

22. Jamieson, "Ethics, Public Policy," 142.

23. Jamieson, "Ethics, Public Policy," 146.

24. Jamieson, "Ethics, Public Policy," 147. See also chapter two of this volume on moral ideals.

25. Crist, "Nomnenclature," 141. See also, 131: "The Anthropocene discourse delivers a Promethean self-portrait: a genius if unruly species, distinguishing itself from the background of merely-living life, rising so as to earn itself a separate name (anthropos, meaning 'man,' and always implying 'not-animal'), and whose unstoppable and in many ways glorious history . . . has yielded an 'I' on a par with Nature's own tremendous forces."

26. Crist, "Nomnenclature," 131. See also Ned Hettinger, "Valuing Naturalness in the 'Anthropocene': Now More than Ever," in *Keeping the Wild* (Washington, DC: Island Press, Center for Resource Economics, 2014), 179: "In conclusion, I see the recent focus on the age of man as the latest embodiment of human hubris. It manifests a culpable failure to appreciate the profound role nonhuman nature continues to play on Earth and an arrogant overvaluation of human's role and authority. It not only ignores an absolutely crucial value in a proper respect for nature but leads us astray in environmental policy. It will have us downplaying the importance of nature preservation, restoration, and rewilding and also have us promoting ecosystem invention and geoengineering. Further by promoting the idea that we live on an already domesticated planet, it risks the result that monetary and public support for conservation will seem futile and dry up. We should not get comfortable with the Anthropocene, as some have suggested, but rather fight it. Such comfort is not the virtue of reconciliation but the vice of capitulation."

27. In order of descending length of duration, the units of geochronology are Eon, Era, Period, Epoch, Age, and Chron.

28. In my *Riders in the Storm*, written with an undergraduate audience in mind, I develop many of these themes more extensively, including a discussion of the shortcomings of the sustainability and stewardship narratives and the need for Berry's richer alternative.

29. Berry, *Evening*, 60.

30. See, for instance, "Asteroid Mining May Be a Reality by 2025," Mike Wall, Space.com, August 11, 2015, http://www.space.com/30213-asteroid-mining-planetary-resources-2025.html.

31. "Second Blumberg Dialogue on Astrobiology May 27–28," Library of Congress, accessed May 4, 2022, https://www.loc.gov/item/prn-15-082/astrobiology-and-history-philosophy-of-science/2015-05-08/.

32. Berry, *Evening Thoughts*, 83. See also Berry, *Great Work*, 4: "In reality there is a single integral community of the Earth that includes all its component members whether human or other than human. In this community every being has its own role to fulfill, its own dignity, its inner spontaneity. Every being has its own voice. Every being declares itself to the entire universe. Every being enters into communion with other beings. This capacity for relatedness, for presence to other beings, for spontaneity in action, is a capacity possessed by every mode of being through the entire universe."

33. Leopold, *Sand County Almanac*, 202–3.

34. Leopold, *Sand County Almanac*, 204.

35. Leopold, *Sand County Almanac*, 203.

36. Berry, *Great Work*, 48.

37. Berry, *Great Work*, 48.

38. It is noteworthy in this context that in his recent Papal Encyclical, *Laudato Si'*, Pope Francis gives a central role to the notion of "integral ecology": "An integral ecology is also made up of simple daily gestures which break with the logic of violence, exploitation and selfishness. In the end, a world of exacerbated consumption is at the same time a world which mistreats life in all its forms" (166). See Brian G. Henning, "Stewardship and the Roots of the Ecological Crisis: Reflections on Laudato Si'," in *For Our Common Home: Process-Relational Responses to Laudato Si'*, ed. John B. Cobb Jr. and Ignacio Castuera (Anoka, MN: Process Century, 2015), 40–51.

39. Crist, "Nomenclature," 144.

40. Crist, "Nomenclature," 143.

41. Leopold, *Sand County Almanac*, 224. See chapter four of this volume for more on Leopold and the role of beauty in environmental ethics.

42. See Berry, *Great Work*, 7–8: "Our own special role, which we will hand on to our children, is that of managing the arduous transition from the terminal Cenozoic to the emerging Ecozoic Era, the period when humans will be present to the planet as participating members of the comprehensive Earth community. This is our Great Work and the work of our children."

43. Berry, *Great Work*, 3; Berry, *Evening Thoughts*, 97.

44. Berry, *Evening Thoughts*, 38. See also Berry, *Great Work*, x–xi: "That future can exist only when we understand the universe as composed of subjects to be communed with, not as objects to be exploited. Intimacy with the planet in its wonder and beauty and the full depth of its meaning is what enables an integral human relationship with the planet to function. It is the only possibility for humans to attain their true flourishing while honoring the other modes of earthly being." See also Berry, *Evening Thoughts*, 18 and 96. For a discussion of the metaphysics behind the overcoming of the subject-object bifurcation, see the introduction and chapter six of this volume.

45. For more on this, see Brian G. Henning and Adam C. Scarfe, eds., *Beyond Mechanism: Putting Life Back into Biology* (Lanham, MD: Lexington, 2013).

46. Though there was nothing systematic about Berry's work, he did at times explicitly embrace a form of pansubjectivism: "Indeed, since the universe is a singular reality, consciousness must, from its beginning, be a dimension of reality, even a dimension of the primordial atom that carries within itself the total destiny of the universe" (Berry, *Evening Thoughts*, 65). However, like much of Berry's work, such passages are better taken as suggestive than systematic. See also Berry, *Evening Thoughts*, 23: "Throughout its vast extent in space and its long sequence of transfor-

mations in time, the universe constitutes a single multiform sequential celebratory event. Every being in the universe is intimately present to, and is influencing, every other being in the universe."

47. Berry, *Great Work*, 105.

48. Berry, *Great Work*, 159.

49. Not only do philosophers need to become more engaged in addressing climate change, but there needs to be the inclusion of more diverse philosophical voices as well. For instance, despite more than forty years of scholarly work developing biocentric and ecocentric approaches to environmental ethics, very few of the edited collections on climate ethics include such perspectives. For instance, the 2010 Oxford volume *Climate Ethics: Essential Readings*, edited by Stephen M. Gardiner, Simon Caney, Dale Jamieson, and Henry Shue, seems to include no biocentric or ecocentric approaches. On the other hand, Cambridge's *The Ethics of Global Climate Change*, edited by Denis G. Arnold, does include an essay by Clare Palmer called "Does Nature Natter? The Place of the Nonhuman in the Ethics of Climate Change." A notable exception is Brian G. Henning and Zach Walsh, *Climate Change Ethics and the Non-Human World* (New York: Routledge, 2020).

Bibliography

"A Very Brief History of the Origins of Environmental Ethics for the Novice." March 14, 2011, https://www.cep.unt.edu/novice.html.

Alexander, Samuel. *Space, Time, and Deity*. Vol. 2. New York: Macmillan, 1920.

Aristotle. *The Complete Works of Aristotle*. Princeton, NJ: Princeton University Press, 1984.

Armstrong, Susan. "Whitehead's Metaphysical System as a Foundation for Environmental Ethics." *Environmental Ethics* 8 (1986): 241–57.

Armstrong, Susan, and Richard G. Botzler. *Environmental Ethics: Divergence and Convergence*. 3rd ed. New York: McGraw-Hill, 2004.

Arnold, Denis Gordon, ed. *The Ethics of Global Climate Change*. Cambridge: Cambridge University Press, 2011.

Belaief, Lynne. *Toward a Whiteheadian Ethics*. Lanham, MD: University Press of America, 1984.

———. "Whitehead and Private-Interest Theories." *Ethics* 76 (1996): 277–86.

Bernstein, Richard J. "Metaphysics, Critique, and Utopia." *The Review of Metaphysics* 42, no. 2 (1988): 255–73.

Berry, Thomas. *Evening Thoughts: Reflections on Earth as a Sacred Community*. Berkeley, CA: Counterpoint, 2015.

———. *The Great Work: Our Way into the Future*. New York: Broadway, 2000.

Blackstone, William T., ed. *Philosophy and Environmental Crisis*. Athens: University of Georgia Press, 1974.

Bracken, Joseph A. *Society and Spirit: A Trinitarian Cosmology*. London: Associated University Presses, 1991.

Brightman, Edgar Sheffield. "An Empirical Approach to God." *The American Philosophical Association Centennial Series*, January 1, 2013, 411–28. https://doi.org/10.5840/apapa2013644.

Callicott, J. Baird. "Animal Liberation: A Triangular Affair." *Environmental Ethics* 2 (1980): 311–38.

———. *Beyond the Land Ethic: More Essays in Environmental Ethics*. Albany: SUNY Press, 1999.

———. "Environmental Philosophy Is Environmental Activism: The Most Radical and Effective Kind." In *Environmental Ethics: What Really Matters What Really Works*, edited by David Schmidtz and Elizabeth Willott, 11–17. Oxford: Oxford University Press, 2012.

———. *In Defense of the Land Ethic: Essays in Environmental Philosophy.* Albany: SUNY Press, 1989.

———. "Intrinsic Value, Quantum Theory, and Environmental Ethics." *Environmental Ethics* 7, no. 3 (August 1, 1985): 257–75. https://doi.org/10.5840/enviroethics19857334.

———. "Non-Anthropocentric Value Theory and Environmental Ethics." *American Philosophical Quarterly* 21, no. 4 (1984): 299–309.

———. "The Pragmatic Power and Promise of Theoretical Environmental Ethics: Forging a New Discourse." *Environmental Values* 11, no. 1 (2002): 3–25.

———. "Should Endangered Species Have Standing? Toward Legal Rights for Listed Species: J. Baird Callicott and William Grove-Fanning." *Social Philosophy and Policy* 26, no. 2 (2009): 317–52.

———. "The Worldview Concept and Aldo Leopold's Project of 'World View' Remediation." *Journal for the Study of Religion, Nature and Culture* 5, no. 4 (2011): 510–28. https://doi.org/10.1558/jsrnc.v5i4.510.

Callicott, J. Baird, William Grove-Fanning, Jennifer Rowland, Daniel Baskind, Robert Heath French, and Kerry Walker. "Was Aldo Leopold a Pragmatist? Rescuing Leopold From the Imagination of Bryan Norton." *Environmental Values* 18, no. 4 (2009): 453–86.

Clarke, W. Norris. "God and the Community of Existents: Whitehead and St. Thomas." *International Philosophical Quarterly* 158 (2000): 256–88.

———. *The One and the Many: A Contemporary Thomistic Metaphysics.* Notre Dame: Notre Dame University Press, 2001.

Cobb, John B., Jr. "Christian Existence in a World of Limits." *Environmental Ethics* 1, Journal Article (1979): 149–58.

———. *Is It Too Late? A Theology of Ecology.* Milwaukee: Bruce, 1972.

———. "Palmer on Whitehead: A Critical Evaluation." *Process Studies* 33 (2004): 4–23.

———. "Protestant Theology and Deep Ecology." In *Deep Ecology and World Religions*, edited by David Landhis Bamhill and Roger S. Gottlieb, 213–28. Albany: SUNY Press, 2001.

Couzin, Iain. "Collective Minds." *Nature* 445, no. 15 (2007): 715–16.

Crist, Eileen. *Abundant Earth: Toward an Ecological Civilization.* Chicago: University of Chicago Press, 2019.

———. "On the Poverty of Our Nomenclature." *Environmental Humanities* 3 (2013): 129–47.

Dalai Lama. *Ethics for the New Millennium.* New York: Riverhead, 1999.

Dawkins, Richard. *The Extended Phenotype*. Oxford: Oxford University Press, 1982.

Deckers, Jan. "Should Whiteheadians Be Vegetarians? A Critical Analysis of the Thoughts of Hartshorne and Dombrowski." *Journal of Animal Ethics* 1, no. 2 (2011): 195–209. https://doi.org/10.5406/janimalethics.1.2.0195.

Descartes, René. *Meditations on First Philosophy*. Translated by Donald A. Cress. Indianapolis: Hackett, 1993 [1641].

———. *The Philosophical Writings of Descartes*. Vol. 1. Cambridge: Cambridge University Press, 1985.

———. *The Philosophical Writings of Descartes*. Vol. 2. Cambridge: Cambridge University Press, 1985.

———. *The Philosophical Writings of Descartes*. Vol. 3. Cambridge: Cambridge University Press, 1991.

Devall, Bill, and George Sessions. *Deep Ecology: Living as If Nature Mattered*. Salt Lake City: Gibbs Smith, 1985.

Dombrowski, Daniel A. *Divine Beauty: The Aesthetics of Charles Hartshorne*. Nashville: Vanderbilt University Press, 2004.

———. *Hartshorne and the Metaphysics of Animal Rights*. Albany: SUNY Press, 1988.

———. *The Philosophy of Vegetarianism*. Amherst: University of Massachusetts Press, 1983.

———. "The Replaceability Argument." *Process Studies* 30 (2001): 22–35.

Donaldson, Brianne, ed. *Beyond the Bifurcation of Nature: A Common World for Animals and the Environment*. Cambridge: Cambridge Scholars Press, 2015.

———. *Creaturely Cosmologies: Why Metaphysics Matters for Animal and Planetary Liberation*. Lanham, MD: Lexington, 2015.

Donaldson, Brianne, and Christopher Carter, eds. *The Future of Meat Without Animals*. London: Rowman & Littlefield, 2016.

Edwards, Rem B. *An Axiological Process Ethics*. Claremont, CA: Process Century Press, 2014.

Felt, James W. "Whitehead's Misconception of 'Substance' in Aristotle." *Process Studies* 14 (1985): 224–36.

Ferré, Frederick. *Being and Value: Toward a Constructive Postmodern Metaphysics*. Albany: SUNY Press, 1996.

———. *Living and Value: Toward a Constructive Postmodern Ethics*. Albany: SUNY Press, 2001.

Francis, Pope. *Laudato Si': On Care for Our Common Home*. Vatican, 2015, https://www.vatican.va/content/francesco/en/encyclicals/documents/papa-francesco_20150524_enciclica-laudato-si.html.

Freeland, Cynthia. "Nourishing Speculation: A Feminist Reading of Aristotelian Science." In *Engendering Origins: Critical Feminist Readings in Plato and Aristotle*, edited by Bat-Ami Bar On, 145–46. Albany: SUNY Press, 1993.

Gardiner, Stephen M. "A Perfect Moral Storm: Climate Change, Intergenerational Ethics, and the Problem of Corruption." In *Climate Ethics: Essential Readings*, edited by Stephen M. Gardiner, Simon Caney, Dale Jamieson, and Henry Shue, 87–98. Oxford: Oxford University Press, 2010.

———. "Ethics and Global Climate Change." *Ethics* 114, no. 3 (2004): 555–600.

Gardiner, Stephen M., Simon Caney, Dale Jamieson, and Henry Shue, eds. *Climate Ethics: Essential Readings*. Oxford: Oxford University Press, 2010.

Gier, Nicholas F. "Whitehead, Confucius, and the Aesthetics of Virtue." *Asian Philosophy* 14 (2004): 171–90.

Goodpaster, Kenneth. "On Being Morally Considerable." *The Journal of Philosophy* 22 (1978): 308–25.

Green, Edward. "A Note on Two Conceptions of Aesthetic Realism." *British Journal of Aesthetics* 45, no. 4 (2005): 238–40.

———. " 'It Don't Mean a Thing If It Ain't Got That Grundgestalt!'—Ellington a Motivic Perspective." *Jazz Perspectives* 2, no. 2 (2008): 215–49.

Griffin, David Ray. *Whitehead's Radically Different Postmodern Philosophy: An Argument for Its Contemporary Relevance*. Albany: SUNY Press, 2007.

Gunter, Pete A. Y. "Whitehead's Contributions to Ecological Thought: Some Unrealized Possibilities." *Interchange* (2000): 211–23.

Hacker, P. M. S. "On Strawson's Rehabilitation of Metaphysics." In *Strawson and Kant*, edited by Hans-Johann Glock, 43–65. Oxford: Oxford University Press, 2003.

Hargrove, Eugene. *Foundations of Environmental Ethics*. Hoboken: Prentice Hall, 1989.

———. "The Historical Foundations of American Environmental Attitudes." *Environmental Ethics* 1 (1979): 209–40.

Hartshorne, Charles. "The Aesthetics of Birdsong." *The Journal of Aesthetics and Art Criticism* 26 (1968): 311–15.

———. "The Aesthetic Matrix of Value." In *Creative Synthesis and Philosophic Method*, 302–22. LaSalle, IL: Open Court, 1970.

———. "Beyond Enlightened Self-Interest: A Metaphysics of Ethics." *Ethics* 84 (1974): 210–16.

———. "The Kinds and Levels of Aesthetic Value." In *The Zero Fallacy and Other Essays in Neoclassical Philosophy*, edited by Mohammad Valady, 203–14. Chicago: Open Court, 1997.

———. "The Rights of the Subhuman World." *Environmental Ethics* 1, no. 1 (1979): 49–60.

Haught, John F. *God After Darwin: A Theology of Evolution*. 2nd ed. Boulder, CO: Westview Press, 2008.

Henning, Brian G. "A. N. Whitehead's Influence on Martin Luther King Jr." Whitehead Research Project, accessed January 7, 2023, http://whiteheadresearch. org/2022/01/17/a-n-whiteheads-influence-on-martin-luther-king-jr/.

———. *The Ethics of Creativity: Beauty, Morality, and Nature in a Processive Cosmos*. Pittsburgh: University of Pittsburgh Press, 2005.

———. "On the Possibility of a Whiteheadian Aesthetics of Morals." *Process Studies* 31 (2002): 97–114.

———. "Philosophy in the Age of Fascism: Reflection on the Presidential Addresses of the APA, 1931–1940." In *Historical Essays in 20th Century American Philosophy*, vol. 11, edited by John R. Shook, 69–95. Charlottesville, VA: Richard T. Hull, 2015. https://doi.org/10.5840/apapa20159.

———. *Riders in the Storm: Ethics in an Age of Climate Change*. Winona, MN: Anselm Academic, 2015.

———. "Saving Whitehead's Universe of Value: An 'Ecstatic' Challenge to the Classical Interpretation." *International Philosophical Quarterly* 45, no. 4 (2005): 447–65.

———. "Standing in Livestock's 'Long Shadow': The Ethics of Eating Meat on a Small Planet." *Ethics & the Environment* 16, no. 2 (2011): 63–93.

———. "Stewardship and the Roots of the Ecological Crisis: Reflections on Laudato Si'." In *For Our Common Home: Process-Relational Responses to Laudato Si'*, edited by John B. Cobb Jr. and Ignacio Castuera. Anoka, MN: Process Century Press, 2015.

Henning, Brian G., Mary Kate Birge, Rodica Stoicoiu, and Ryan Taylor. "From Exception to Exemplification: Understanding the Debate Over Darwin." In *Genesis, Evolution, and the Search for a Reasoned Faith*, 73–98. Winona, MN: Anselm Academic, 2011.

Henning, Brian G., and David Kovacs, eds. *Being in America: Sixty Years of the Metaphysical Society*. Amsterdam: Rodopi, 2014.

Henning, Brian G., William T. Myers, and Joseph David John, eds. *Thinking with Whitehead and the American Pragmatists: Experience and Reality*. Lanham, MD: Lexington, 2015.

Henning, Brian G., and Joseph Petek. *Whitehead at Harvard, 1924–1925*. Edinburgh: Edinburgh University Press, 2019.

Henning, Brian G., and Adam C. Scarfe, eds. *Beyond Mechanism: Putting Life Back into Biology*. Lanham, MD: Lexington, 2013.

Henning, Brian G., and Zack Walsh, eds. *Climate Change Ethics and the Non-Human World*. London: Routledge, 2020.

Hettinger, Ned. "Valuing Naturalness in the 'Anthropocene': Now More than Ever." In *Keeping the Wild*, 174–79. Washington, DC: Island Press, Center for Resource Economics, 2014. https://doi.org/10.5822/978-1-61091-559-5_15.

Hewson, Chris M., Mark Miller, Alison Johnston, Greg J. Conway, Richard Saunders, John H. Marchant, and Robert J. Fuller. "Estimating National Population Sizes: Methodological Challenges and Applications Illustrated in the Common Nightingale, a Declining Songbird in the UK." *Journal of Applied Ecology* 55, no. 4 (2018): 2008–18. https://doi.org/10.1111/1365-2664.13120.

Hölldobler, Bert, and E. O. Wilson. *The Superorganism: The Beauty, Elegance, and Strangeness of Insect Societies*. New York: Norton, 2009.

Houghton, John. *Global Climate Change: The Complete Briefing.* 4th ed. Cambridge: Cambridge University Press, 2009.

Howard, Christine, Philip A. Stephens, James W. Pearce-Higgins, Richard D. Gregory, Stuart H.M. Butchart, and Stephen G. Willis. "Disentangling the Relative Roles of Climate and Land Cover Change in Driving the Long-Term Population Trends of European Migratory Birds." *Diversity and Distributions* 26, no. 11 (2020): 1442–55. https://doi.org/10.1111/ddi.13144.

Hull, Richard T., and American Philosophical Association, eds. *Presidential Addresses of the American Philosophical Association 1931–1940.* Dordrecht: Kluwer Academic, 2001.

Hume, David. *A Treatise of Human Nature.* New York: Penguin, 1969.

———. *Enquiry Concerning Human Understanding.* Cambridge: Hackett, 1993.

Inwagen, Peter van, and Meghan Sullivan. "Metaphysics." Stanford Encyclopedia of Philosophy Archive, September 10, 2007, substantive revision October 31, 2014, accessed March 31, 2023. https://plato.stanford.edu/archives/win2014/entries/metaphysics/.

James, William. *A Pluralistic Universe.* In *William James' Writings 1902–1910.* New York: Library of America, 1987.

———. *Essays In Radical Empiricism.* New York: Longmans, Green, 1912. http://archive.org/details/in.ernet.dli.2015.188766.

———. *The Meaning of Truth.* New York: Longmans, Green, 1914. http://archive.org/details/in.ernet.dli.2015.201748.

———. "The Moral Philosopher and the Moral Life." In *The Will to Believe and Other Essays in Popular Philosophy*, 184–215. New York: Dover, 1956.

———. *Principles of Psychology.* New York: Dover, 1890.

———. *Some Problems of Philosophy: A Beginning of an Introduction to Philosophy.* New York: Longmans, Green, 1911.

Jamieson, Dale. "Ethics, Public Policy, and Global Warming." *Science, Technology, Human Values* 17 (1992): 139–53.

Jones, Judith. *Intensity: An Essay in Whiteheadian Ontology.* Nashville: Vanderbilt University Press, 1998.

Kann, Christoph. "Renewing Speculation. The Systematic Aim of Whitehead's Philosophic Cosmology." In *Beyond Metaphysics?: Explorations in Alfred North Whitehead's Late Thought*, edited by Roland Faber, Brian G. Henning, and Clinton Combs, 27–44. Amsterdam: Rodopi, 2010.

Kant, Immanuel. *Groundwork of the Metaphysics of Morals.* New York: Harper Torchbooks, 1964.

Kerr, Andrew J. "The Possibility of Metaphysics: Environmental Ethics and the Naturalistic Fallacy." *Environmental Ethics* 22 (2000): 85–100.

Kimmerer, Robin Wall. *Braiding Sweetgrass: Indigenous Wisdom, Scientific Knowledge, and the Teachings of Plants.* London: Penguin, 2020.

King, Jr., Martin Luther. *I Have a Dream: Writings and Speeches That Changed the World*. Edited by James M. Washington. San Francisco: Harper Collins, 1986.

Kirk, G. S., J. E. Raven, and M. Schofield. *The Presocratic Philosophers: A Critical History with a Selection of Texts*. 2nd edition. Cambridge: Cambridge University Press, 1984.

Kolbert, Elizabeth. *The Sixth Extinction: An Unnatural History*. New York: Henry Holt, 2014.

Koutroufinis, Spyridon. "Teleodynamics: A Neo-Naturalistic Conception of Organismic Teleology." In *Beyond Mechanism: Putting Life Back Into Biology*, edited by Brian G. Henning and Adam C. Scarfe, 309–44. Lanham, MD: Lexington, 2013.

Lachs, John. "Good Enough." *Journal of Speculative Philosophy* 23, no. 1 (2009): 1–7.

Lango, John W. "Does Whitehead's Metaphysics Contain an Ethics?" *Transactions of the Charles S. Peirce Society* 37 (2001): 515–36.

Latour, Bruno. *Facing Gaia. Eight Lectures on the New Climatic Regime*. Translated by Catherine Porter. Cambridge: Polity, 2017.

Leighton, J. A. "History as the Struggle for Social Values." In *Presidential Addresses of the American Philosophical Association 1931–1940*, edited by Richard T. Hull, 511–42. Dordrecht: Kluwer Academic, 2001.

Leopold, Aldo. *A Sand County Almanac; And Sketches Here and There*. Oxford: Oxford University Press, 1949.

Light, Andrew. "Contemporary Environmental Ethics from Metaethics to Public Philosophy." *Metaphilosophy* 33, no. 4 (2002): 426–49.

———. "Environmental Pragmatism as Philosophy or Metaphilosophy?" In *Environmental Pragmatism*, edited by Andrew Light and Eric Katz, 325–38. New York: Routledge, 1996.

Light, Andrew, and Eric Katz. *Environmental Pragmatism*. New York: Routledge, 1996.

Locke, John. *Second Treatise of Government*. Indianapolis: Hackett, 1690.

Lovelock, James. *The Vanishing Face of Gaia: A Final Warning*. New York: Basic Books, 2009.

Manley, David. "Introduction: A Guided Tour of Metametaphysics." In *Metametaphysics: New Essays on the Foundations of Ontology*, edited by David Chalmers, David Manley, and Ryan Wasserman, 1–37. Oxford: Oxford University Press, 2009.

Masson-Delmotte, V., P. Zhai, H.-O. Pörtner, D. Roberts, J. Skea, PR. Shukla, A. Pirani, et al., eds. "Summary for Policymakers." In *Global Warming of 1.5°C. An IPCC Special Report on the Impacts of Global Warming of 1.5°C above Pre-Industrial Levels and Related Global Greenhouse Gas Emission Pathways, in the Context of Strengthening the Global Response to the Threat of Climate Change, Sustainable Development, and Efforts to Eradicate Poverty*. Geneva, Switzerland: World Meteorological Organization, 2018. https://www.ipcc.ch/sr15/chapter/spm/.

McHenry, Leemon B. *The Event Universe: The Revisionary Metaphysics of Alfred North Whitehead*. Edinburgh: Edinburgh University Press, 2015. https://doi.org/10.3366/edinburgh/9781474400343.001.0001.

McHenry, Leemon B., and George W. Shields. "Analytical Critiques of Whitehead's Metaphysics." *Journal of the American Philosophical Association* 2, no. 3 (2016): 483–503. https://doi.org/10.1017/apa.2016.21.

McMullin, Ernan. "Two Faces of Science." *The Review of Metaphysics* 27, no. 4 (1974): 655–76.

McShane, Katie. "Why Environmental Ethics Shouldn't Give Up on Intrinsic Value." *Environmental Ethics* 29, no. 1 (2007): 43–61.

Michael, Mark. "Environmental Pragmatism, Community Values, and the Problem of Reprehensible Implications." *Environmental Ethics* 38, no. 3 (2016): 347–66. https://doi.org/10.5840/enviroethics201638329.

Miller, Peter. "Swarm Theory." *National Geographic* 22, no. 1 (2007): 127–42.

Minteer, Ben A. "Intrinsic Value for Pragmatists?" *Environmental Ethics* 23, no. 1 (2001): 57–75.

Mitchell, E. T. "Social Ideals and the Law." In *Presidential Addresses of the American Philosophical Association 1931–1940*, edited by Richard T. Hull, 387–404. Dordrecht: Kluwer Academic, 2001.

Moore, G. E. *Principia Ethica*. Revised ed. Cambridge: Cambridge University Press, 1993.

Morito, Bruce. "Intrinsic Value: A Modern Albatross for the Ecological Approach." *Environmental Values* 12, no. 3 (2003): 317–36.

Morrow, Glen R. "Plato and the Rule of Law." In *Presidential Addresses of the American Philosophical Association 1931–1940*, edited by Richard T. Hull. Dordrecht: Kluwer Academic, 2001.

Muraca, Barbara. "Relational Values: A Whiteheadian Alternative for Environmental Philosophy and Global Environmental Justice." *Balkan Journal of Philosophy* VIII, no. 1 (2016): 19–38.

Nagel, Thomas. *Mind and Cosmos: Why the Materialist Neo-Darwinian Conception of Nature Is Almost Certainly False*. New York: Oxford University Press, 2012.

Norton, Bryan. "Environmental Ethics and Weak Anthropocentrism." *Environmental Ethics* 6 (1984): 131–48.

———. "Integration or Reduction: Two Approaches to Environmental Values." In *Environmental Pragmatism*, edited by Andrew Light and Eric Katz, 105–38. New York: Routledge, 1996.

———. *Toward Unity Among Environmentalists*. Oxford: Oxford University Press, 1991.

———. "Why I Am Not a Nonanthropocentrist: Callicott and the Failure of Monistic Inherentism." *Environmental Ethics* 17, no. 4 (1995): 341–58.

O'Neill, John. "The Varieties of Intrinsic Value." *The Monist* 75 (1992): 119–37.

Palmer, Clare. *Environmental Ethics and Process Thinking*. Oxford: Clarendon Press, 1998.

———. "Response to Cobb and Menta." *Process Studies* 33, no. 1 (2004): 46–70.

Partridge, Brian L. "The Structure and Function of Fish Schools." *Scientific American* 246, no. 6 (1982): 114–23.

Passino, Kevin M., Thomas D. Seeley, and P. Kirk Visscher. "Swarm Cognition in Honey Bees." *Behavioral Ecology and Sociobiology* 63, no. 3 (2008): 401–14.

Peirce, Charles Sanders. *Collected Papers of Charles Sanders Peirce*. Edited by Charles Hartshorne and Paul Weiss. Vols. 5–6. Cambridge, MA: Belknap Press, 1978.

———. *The Essential Peirce*. Vol. 1. Bloomington: Indiana University Press, 1992.

———. *The Essential Peirce: Selected Philosophical Writings*. 2 vols. Indianapolis: Indiana University Press, 1992.

Plumwood, Val. *Feminism and the Mastery of Nature*. London: Routledge, 1993.

Popper, Karl. *The Logic of Scientific Discovery*. London: Hutchinson, 1959.

Poser, Hans. "Whitehead's Cosmology as Revisable Metaphysics." In *Whitehead's Metaphysics of Creativity*, edited by Friedrich Rapp and Reiner Wiehl, 94–114. Albany: SUNY Press, 1990.

Mike Wall. "Asteroid Mining May Be a Reality by 2025." Space.com, August 11, 2015, https://www.space.com/30213-asteroid-mining-planetary-resources-2025.html.

Randall, John Herman. "Metaphysics and Language." *The Review of Metaphysics* 20, no. 4 (1967): 591–601.

Regan, Tom. *The Case For Animal Rights*. Berkeley: University of California Press, 1983.

Rescher, Nicholas. *On Leibniz: Expanded Edition*. Pittsburgh: University of Pittsburgh Press, 2013.

Rodman, John. "Four Forms of Ecological Consciousness Reconsidered." In *Deep Ecology for the 21st Century: Readings on the Philosophy and Practice of the New Environmentalism*, edited by George Sessions, 121–30. Boston: Shambhala, 1995.

Rolston, Holmes III. "Are Values in Nature Subjective or Objective?" *Environmental Ethics* 4 (1982): 125–51.

———. "Caring for Nature: From Fact to Value, From Respect to Reverence." *Zygon* 39, no. 2 (2004): 277–302.

———. "Ecology: A Primer for Christian Ethics." *Journal of Catholic Social Thought* 4, no. 2 (2007): 293–312.

———. *Environmental Ethics: Duties to and Values in the Natural World*. Philadelphia: Temple University Press, 1988.

———. "F/Actual Knowing: Putting Facts and Values in Place." *Ethics & the Environment* 10, no. 2 (2005): 137–74.

———. "Is There an Environmental Ethic?" *Ethics* 18, no. 2 (1975): 93–109.

———. "The Land Ethic at the Turn of the Millennium." *Biodiversity and Conservation* 9 (2000): 1045–58.

———. "Perpetual Perishing, Perpetual Renewal." *The Northern Review* 28 (2008): 111–23.

———. *Three Big Bangs: Matter-Energy, Life, Mind*. New York: Columbia University Press, 2010.

———. "Value in Nature and the Nature of Value." In *Philosophy and the Natural Environment*, edited by Robin Attfield and Andrew Belsey, 13–30. Cambridge: Cambridge University Press, 1994.

Ross, Don, James Ladyman, and David Spurrett. "In Defence of Scientism." In *Every Thing Must Go*, edited by James Ladyman and Don Ross, 1–65. Oxford: Oxford University Press, 2007. https://doi.org/10.1093/acprof: oso/9780199276196.003.0001.

Rusu, Bogdan, and Ronny Desmet. "Whitehead, Russell, and Moore: Three Analytic Philosophers." *Process Studies* 41, no. 2 (2012): 214–34.

Sakata, Hiroshi, and Noboru Katayama. "Ant Defence System: A Mechanism Organizing Individual Responses into Efficient Collective Behavior." *Ecological Research* 16, no. 3 (2001): 395–403.

Samuelsson, Lars. "Environmental Pragmatism and Environmental Philosophy: A Bad Marriage." *Environmental Ethics* 32, no. 4 (2010): 405–16.

Schilpp, Paul Arthur. "Whitehead's Moral Philosophy." In *The Philosophy of Alfred North Whitehead*, edited by Paul Arthur Schilpp, 2nd ed., 561–618. LaSalle, IL: Open Court, 1951.

Library of Congress. "Second Blumberg Dialogue on Astrobiology May 27–28." Accessed January 8, 2023. https://www.loc.gov/item/prn-15-082/ astrobiology-and-history-philosophy-of-science/2015 05-08/.

Secretary-General, UN, and World Commission on Environment and Development. "Report of the World Commission on Environment and Development." United Nations, August 4, 1987, https://digitallibrary.un.org/record/139811.

Seeley, Thomas D. "The Honey Bee Colony as a Superorganism." *American Scientist* 77, no. 6 (1989): 546–53.

Sherburne, Donald. *A Whiteheadian Aesthetic*. New Haven: Yale University Press, 1961.

Siegel, Eli. *Aesthetic Realism: Three Instances*. New York: The Terrain Gallery & Definition Press, 1961.

———. "The Aesthetic Center." *Definition* 10 (1962).

———. "Ugliness & Beauty in Oneness." *The Right of Aesthetic Realism to Be Known*, no. 1691 (May 2, 2007). https://aestheticrealism.net/tro/ ugliness-beauty-appreciation/.

Sisson, Edward O. "Human Nature and the Present Crisis." In *Presidential Addresses of the American Philosophical Association 1931–1940*, edited by Richard T. Hull. Dordrecht: Kluwer Academic, 2001.

Smith, Andrew F. *A Critique of the Moral Defense of Vegetarianism.* New York: Palgrave Macmillan, 2016. https://doi.org/10.1057/9781137554895.

Sölch, Dennis. "Wheeler and Whitehead: Process Biology and Process Philosophy in the Early Twentieth Century." *Journal of the History of Ideas* 77, no. 3 (2016): 489–507.

Sprigge, T. L. S. "Are There Intrinsic Values in Nature?" *Journal of Applied Philosophy* 4, no. 1 (1987): 21–28.

Stenmark, Mikael. "The Relevance of Environmental Ethical Theories for Policy Making." *Environmental Ethics* 24, no. 2 (2002): 135–48. https://doi.org/10.5840/enviroethics200224227.

Strawson, Galen, and Anthony Freeman, eds. *Consciousness and Its Place in Nature: Does Physicalism Entail Panpsychism?* Exeter, UK: Imprint Academic, 2006.

Swimme, Brian, and Thomas Berry. *The Universe Story: From the Primordial Flaring Forth to the Ecozoic Era—A Celebration of the Unfolding of the Cosmos.* New York: HarperOne, 1992.

Taylor, Paul W. *Respect for Nature: A Theory of Environmental Ethics.* Princeton: Princeton University Press, 1986.

"The Paris Agreement." United Nations, 2015. https://unfccc.int/files/essential_background/convention/application/pdf/english_paris_agreement.pdf.

Tufts, James H. "The Institution as an Agency of Stability and Readjustment in Ethics." In *Presidential Addresses of the American Philosophical Association 1931–1940,* edited by Richard T. Hull. Dordrecht: Kluwer Academic, 2001.

Turner, J. Scott. "A Superorganism's Fuzzy Boundaries." *Natural History* 111, no. 6 (2002): 63.

———. *The Extended Organism: The Physiology of Animal-Built Structures.* Cambridge, MA: Harvard University Press, 2000.

———. *The Tinkerer's Accomplice: How Design Emerges from Life Itself.* Cambridge, MA: Harvard University Press, 2007.

———. *Purpose and Desire: What Makes Something "Alive" and Why Modern Darwinism Has Failed to Explain It.* New York: HarperOne, 2017.

Varner, Gary. *In Nature's Interests?: Interests, Animal Rights, and Environmental Ethics.* Oxford: Oxford University Press, 1998.

Warren, Karen J. *Ecofeminist Philosophy: A Western Perspective on What It Is and Why It Matters.* New York: Roman & Littlefield, 2000.

Weston, Anthony. "Beyond Intrinsic Value: Pragmatism in Environmental Ethics." *Environmental Ethics* 7 (1985): 321–39.

White, Jr., Lynn. "The Historical Roots of Our Ecologic Crisis." *Science* 155 (1967): 1203–7.

Whitehead, Alfred North. *Adventures of Ideas.* New York: Free Press, 1933.

———. *The Aims of Education and Other Essays.* New York: Free Press, 1929.

———. "Alfred North Whitehead to Henry S. Leonard." January 10, 1936. Washington, DC: Manuscript Division, The Library of Congress.

———. *The Concept of Nature*. Cambridge: Cambridge University Press, 1920.

———. *Essays in Science and Philosophy*. New York: Philosophical Library, 1947.

———. "First Lecture." In *Whitehead at Harvard, 1924–1925*, edited by Brian G. Henning and Joseph Petek, 41–55. Edinburgh: Edinburgh University Press, 2020.

———. *The Function of Reason*. Princeton: Princeton University Press, 1929.

———. *The Harvard Lectures of Alfred North Whitehead, 1924–1925: Philosophical Presuppositions of Science*. Edited by Paul A. Bogaard and Jason Bell. Edinburgh: Edinburgh University Press, 2017.

———. "Immortality." In *The Philosophy of Alfred North Whitehead*, edited by Paul Arthur Schilpp, 2nd ed., 682–700. LaSalle, IL: Open Court, 1951.

———. *Modes of Thought*. New York: Free Press, 1938.

———. "Objects and Subjects." *Proceedings and Addresses of the American Philosophical Association* 5 (April 2022): 130–46.

———. *Process and Reality*. Corrected ed. New York: Free Press, 1978.

———. *Science and the Modern World*. New York: Free Press, 1925.

Wild, John. "The New Empiricism and Human Time." *The Review of Metaphysics* 7, no. 4 (1954): 537–57.

Wilkinson, David M. "Homeostatic Gaia: An Ecologist's Perspective on the Possibility of Regulation." In *Scientists Debate Gaia: A New Century*, edited by Stephen H. Schneider et al., 71–76. Cambridge, MA: MIT Press, 2004.

Index

Note: Page numbers in *italics* indicate illustrations.

acacia trees, 124
"actual entities/occasions," 11–12, 216n43
actuality, 125; time and, 176; value and, 40, 51–52, 111–112
Adams, Carol, 126
Addams, Jane, 198
aesthetic circle, *99*, 99–100, 236n40
aesthetic realism, 100–102
aesthetics, 19, 91, 95–96, 106, 109. *See also* beauty
agape, 165–166, 168–170, 254n29
Aldo Leopold Foundation, 5
Alexander, Samuel, 88–89, 234nn82–83
Amazon rainforest, 77, 191
American Academy of Religion (AAR), 263n10
American Philosophical Association (APA), 203–205, 263n10
Amsterdam Declaration (2001), 159
anacasm, 166
analytic philosophy, 27–29, 198; Moore on, 173–174; Simons on, 256n61
animal rights, 65, 234n14
animism, 127, 132, 136

"anthroparchy," 18, 117–122, 133; definition of, 109–110
Anthropocene, 203–212, 263n12
anthropocentrism, 50–51; axiological, 63–65, 184; Crist on, 264n17; of deep ecologists, 238n4; of Descartes, 21; forms of, 63–65, 104; intergenerational, 184, 190–192; Leopold on, 93; of process philosophy, 106–107; Rolston on, 118; "sentiocentrism" versus, 59–60
anthropomorphism, 242n74
anti-philosophical projects, 195–198
ants, 147–148, 151–155, *153*
Aquinas, Thomas, 28–29, 35, 221n22; on Eros, 254n26; Scholasticism of, 23, 161; on substance, 139–141, 146
Aristotle, 28, 34–35, 180; *Categories*, 216n40; on chain of being, 86, 105–106, 110–111, 115–116; on Eros, 165, 254n26; on golden mean, 98–99, *99*; on individuality, 80; on nature, 110; on *psuchê*, 80, 110, 180; Scholasticism and, 23, 161; on slavery, 111; on subject-predicate logic, 136; on substance, 139–142,

Milton Keynes UK
Ingram Content Group UK Ltd.
UKHW011124050624
443649UK00006B/528